The Italian Renaissance produced a new type of stage comedy, experimental and even revolutionary in its time, by copying and updating the dramatic formats of Plautus and Terence from ancient Rome. The influence of these innovations on European drama – Shakespeare, Jonson, Molière, Lope de Vega – is a well-known fact in outline, but the Italian plays themselves are unfamiliar to English-speaking readers and theatregoers. They were written and performed for private audiences, and show a surprising variety of tone, from sober moralism to scurrilous farce. Authors range from the well-known and respectable Ariosto and Machiavelli through the anarchic Aretino to the barely accessible genius of Ruzante – and some plays, not the least successful, had collective authorship.

This book gives an account of how the new dramatic experiment was born and grew, moving from closed courtly audiences to a wider public. By concentrating on the order in which things happened, it underlines the novelty of almost everything that was produced. By highlighting performing qualities, rather than literary ones, it is able to show how improvised *commedia dell'arte* depended to a surprising degree on these relatively respectable antecedents. Scripted and improvised comedy are treated as part of the same phenomenon – and in this way a crucial phase in the development of European theatre is explored for the first time.

SCRIPTS AND SCENARIOS

SCRIPTS AND SCENARIOS

The performance of comedy in Renaissance Italy

RICHARD ANDREWS

Professor of Italian,
University of Leeds

CAMBRIDGE
UNIVERSITY PRESS

Published by the Press Syndicate of the University of Cambridge
The Pitt Building, Trumpington Street, Cambridge CB2 1RP
40 West 20th Street, New York, NY 10011-4211, USA
10 Stamford Road, Oakleigh, Victoria 3166, Australia

© Cambridge University Press 1993

First published 1993

Printed in Great Britain at the University Press, Cambridge

A catalogue record for this book is available from the British Library

Library of Congress cataloging in publication data
Andrews, Richard, Professor of Italian.
Scripts and scenarios: the performance of comedy in Renaissance
Italy / Richard Andrews.
p.   cm.
Includes bibliographical references.
ISBN 0 521 35357 2
1. Italian drama – To 1700 – History and criticism.
2. Italian drama (Comedy) – History and criticism.
3. Theater – Italy – History – 16th century. 1. Title.
PQ4149.A48   1993
852'.05230903 – dc20   92-23446   CIP

ISBN 0 521 35357 2 hardback

CE

For Bimandy

Molte cose stanno ben nella penna che nella scena starebbon male.

(Lots of things work well on the page which on the stage would work badly.)

Ruzante

Nothing with kings, nothing with crowns –
Bring on the lovers, liars and clowns.

Stephen Sondheim

Contents

Preface

Theatre historians recognize in general terms that it was the Italians, in the early sixteenth century, who took the first steps towards a modern European concept of theatre – paradoxically, by reviving models which were sometimes two thousand years old. But the plays which were produced in the process – initially almost always in the form of comedy – are relatively neglected outside Italy. In English they tend to be treated either dismissively, or with emphasis on their sources rather than their qualities as an innovative, if sometimes immature, form of theatre. This can leave behind a misleading picture, both of scripted 'erudite' comedy as such, and of the extent to which *commedia dell'arte* (better known, and more romantically approved of) actually depended on *commedia erudita* for its raw material and its very existence. One of the aims of the present study is to give a simple account of this whole seminal process, taking things as much as possible in their chronological order. In the writing, it emerged that the story was too long for one book. This one can claim to cover with reasonable thoroughness the period from 1500 to the 1550s, a decade which it is convenient to treat as a watershed. *Commedia dell'arte* had probably begun by then to take on a separate identity; and other cultural changes were in process which can be seen as concluding what can usefully be called the 'Renaissance' in Italy. Hence I can justify the use in the sub-title of the term 'Renaissance', rather than the 'sixteenth century' which had originally been proposed.

However, as well as retelling facts which are already known at least to Italian scholars and readers (and for which I am heavily indebted to Italian secondary sources), I have tried in this book to emphasize aspects of the story, and of the plays, which have previously been explored in less detail or in no detail at all. Italian critics have been used to treating Renaissance drama as literature,

xi

and are skilled in analysing its literary qualities. In addition, more recently, they have produced impressive large-scale accounts of Renaissance theatre in general as a cultural, social and even semiotic phenomenon. What has been infrequent so far, in studies of *commedia erudita*, has been the close theatrical analysis of individual plays. There has been little attempt to look closely at dramaturgical techniques; or at how such comedies might have functioned, scene by scene, in the face of a live audience. The standpoint, in other words, has been that of a reader: rarely that of a spectator, and almost never that of a theatre practitioner. In missing these lines of inquiry, Italian scholars have also tended to underestimate how the early writers of Humanist comedy were working entirely without any supporting tradition of performance in their new genre, and how almost every aspect of their dramaturgy was an experimental shot in the dark. Admittedly, that statement applies to methods of composition more than to the choice of plot material. Italy at this time possessed a substantial common stock of fictional and narrative *topoi*, which were used indiscriminately in texts for reading and in texts for performance. This should not blind us, though, to the fact that dramatic artefacts differ substantially from literary ones in their compositional technique. The 'early modern' dramatists of sixteenth-century Italy were rather like people attempting to produce a brand new style of three-dimensional sculpture, basing themselves mainly on two-dimensional paintings.

Throughout this book, therefore, I have tried systematically to foreground those aspects of dramatic texts which are *not* shared by a work of fiction intended just for reading; and to bear in mind, within the limits of my admittedly amateur experience, the practical aspects of turning a script into performance. Such an approach can be one-sided in its turn: it means airily waving away a number of legitimate lines of inquiry, especially in relation to authors who have an established literary personality and who wrote also in non-dramatic genres. If Ariosto, Machiavelli, Aretino and Bruno have been treated superficially in this volume, I apologize to their ghosts – but they have suffered only a temporary snub in the cause of treating theatrical texts as theatre, and of giving the 'text–audience' relationship priority (for once) over the 'author–text' one which has traditionally been addressed. If there are any unifying themes in this book, they will be found in the attention paid to the techniques of composing comic dialogue for the stage, on the level of the individual scene; and in my speculations on the particular comic experience offered to contemporary audiences, first by *commedia erudita* and then by *commedia dell'arte*. Both of these contribute to a study of what Italians might call the 'constituent elements' of the European comic stage, in a period when those elements were being created, sometimes rather tentatively, for the first time. They are presented here primarily as part of a continuing collective process, by which modern comedy was built – and only secondarily as discrete achievements by individual talents.

This book in its turn also comes from efforts which were not purely solitary, and some acknowledgements must be recorded. With the working conditions currently prevalent in British universities, the volume might never have been completed without a grant from the Leverhulme Trust, which liberated me for the whole of the academic year 1990–1. As well as my deep gratitude for this, I must express thanks to friends who have read portions of the text and given perceptive advice – most notably Professor Peter Brand, Ann and Michael Caesar, Christopher Cairns, Maria Rees, and my close colleague Brian Richardson. Sarah Stanton of Cambridge University Press has exercised some necessary control, but also shown a notable amount of tolerance. My wife and children are in these pages somewhere – partly because they too have commented on bits of the text and helped with the index, but mostly because they are part of the way I think. The dedicatees know, I hope, how important they are in everything. If I have been foolish enough to ignore the contributions, explicit and implicit, of any of these people, then the fault and the errors are mine.

I must also claim responsibility for all translations in this volume which are not otherwise attributed.

Introduction: Italy in the sixteenth century

There was of course no political state called Italy in 1500. From the time of Petrarch, in the fourteenth century, a small educated class had made claims for an 'Italian' cultural identity with a Roman heritage superior to that of the 'barbarians' beyond the Alps. But such common ground as did exist between communities in Italy was balanced by an equal amount of diversity: from one city to another Italians spoke different vernaculars, obeyed different governments, and were far more used to viewing each other with mistrust and hostility than to pursuing aspirations to any kind of unity. The southern half of the peninsula in particular, a monarchy with a landowning aristocracy and an increasingly backward economy, had very little in common with the urban trade-based civilization of the north and centre. Even those who spoke eloquently of Italian values made no proposals for an Italian state – there had never been such a thing, and in the middle ages it was impossible to imagine one.

In popular cultural history the term 'Renaissance' is often linked with concepts of liberation from repressive 'medieval' structures (mental, cultural, religious, political). That there were profound changes in this period is beyond question; however, a close look at what was happening to Italian states and society between 1450 and 1600 offers little support for an image of shackles being cast off. Collective committee government characteristic of the city commune was giving way to control by monarchs and princes. Economically too the power was being concentrated at the centre, so the cultural patronage of competitive groups within society was yielding to that of the ruler, court or state. The pace and details of such changes varied in different centres, but the history of Italian Renaissance comedy has to be seen always in a context of decreasing enterprise and increasing constraint. On the largest scale, one can

1

hardly characterize as 'liberating' the two most obvious trends in
sixteenth-century Italy: conquest by foreign powers, and the
increasing autocracy of a reformed Church.

It was in the 1490s that two successive French kings brought
invading armies into Italy, testing their opportunistic claims to the
Kingdom of Naples and the Duchy of Milan. (The earliest comedies
which will be discussed in these pages appear in the next decade,
1500–10.) From then on, for fifty years or more, the peninsula was a
rich prize for predators, and a symbolic battlefield on which larger
European powers disputed their primacy. These powers soon
resolved into two: the Kingdom of France (notably under François
I, reigned 1515–47), and the formidable accumulation of dominions
which had fallen dynastically into the Habsburg hands of Charles V,
Holy Roman Emperor (1519–56), King of Spain (from 1506), ruler
of Burgundy and of Austria. By legal precedents dating from
Charlemagne, the Empire included all of Italy, except Venice,
north of the Papal State; and in the south the Aragonese or Spanish
had ruled Sicily since 1416 and Naples indirectly since 1435. It was
in fact the Empire and Spain which finally triumphed, and at the
end of the century most of Italy was part of the international
Catholic hegemony created by the Habsburgs. Part of that hegemony involved a greater religious control over art and culture,
imposed by Church decree and by an altered climate of opinion.

The Italian Wars, and the shifts of political alliances and prejudices which accompanied them, sometimes provide a background
to comic plots and texts. A very brief outline will indicate, if nothing
else, certain key dates which may be cultural as well as political
watersheds.

In 1469 (accession to effective power in Florence of Lorenzo de'
Medici, 'il Magnifico'), there were five Italian states seen as major
powers within the peninsula. The Duchy of Milan and the Kingdom
of Naples were monarchic and centralized. The Papal State was a
kind of federation in which certain centres, notably Urbino, had
their own character, and where the city of Rome itself was only
slowly becoming a centre of economic and artistic activity. Florence
was a republic in theory, but its committee procedures were manipulated by the Medici family, who were princes in all but name.
Venice continued stable under its peculiar but successful structures
– a republic, but with an elected constitutional monarch in its Doge;
a state administered exclusively by its aristocracy, but retaining full

Map 1   *Italy in 1492* (death of Lorenzo il Magnifico).
Only Venice, Genova, Florence, Siena and Lucca were republics. All the other
states were kingdoms, lordships, or under some other form of 'monarchical' rule.
Only Sicily and Sardinia were under direct foreign rule; though the kings of Naples
were a cadet branch of the Aragonese royal family, and Spanish (or, more strictly,
Catalan) culture predominated.

Map 2   *Italy in 1559* (Treaty of Cateau-Cambrésis).
Only Venice, Genova and Lucca were nominally republics, and Genova owed its
existence to French protection, and later to Spanish/Imperial protection. Shaded
areas belonged to the Austro-Spanish Habsburg Empire set up by Charles V.
Dotted areas were to some extent Habsburg protectorates.

popular support. Of these major centres, Venice, Florence and Rome were to play significant parts in the development of the new comedy, though the role of Florence was less pioneering than the city had been earlier in art, architecture and neoplatonic philosophy. Equally important, and more innovative, in theatrical history were some of the smaller centres: the twin Duchy of Ferrara and Modena ruled by the Este family, Mantua ruled by the Gonzaga, and the obstinately resistant Tuscan republic of Siena. Precisely because these states were small and threatened, they sought to enhance their image and prestige by cultural statements, and in Ferrara and Siena in particular such statements employed the medium of theatre.

The first French invasion of 1494 had led directly to the expulsion of the Medici from Florence. For nearly twenty years, until 1512, that city turned its back on its unofficial princes and tried to fight its corner as a genuine republic, while Italian states in general were juggling with the competing forces of France, Spain, Austria and the Swiss. Milan lost its ducal family and its independence in 1500, and from then on changed hands with bewildering frequency. The exiled Medici established a power network outside their native city, and with two Medici Popes in Rome (Leo X 1513–21, Clement VII 1523–34), Florence was obliged to accept their dominance and become a junior partner in an axis between the two cities. It was under Clement VII, however, that in 1527 Spanish and Imperial troops sacked Rome with great brutality, gave Italians a crisis of confidence from which they never really recovered, and persuaded the Papacy that its future role was one of partnership, not rivalry, with Imperial and Catholic Spain and Austria. Florence's republican illusions were crushed (after a three-year rebellion) by the creation of a Medici duke under Habsburg protection, and from 1530 the city, like most other centres, had a princely court offering artistic patronage and control. At a second stage, in 1557, Florence swallowed Siena (as it had been trying to do for centuries) with Imperial help, creating a new Grand Duchy of Tuscany. In 1597 the direct Este line died out, and Ferrara (but not Modena) reverted to the Papal State where Popes had always thought it belonged. Venice alone retained its autonomy, identity and constitution into the seventeenth century and beyond.

The chief significance of these changes for theatre history is that the organization of performed spectacle varied according to whether there was a central court or a more loosely structured republic, and whether a city was autonomous or subject to another. By 1600 the major Italian centres were once more Naples, Florence, Milan, Rome and Venice; but only the last two of these could claim to have maintained the political identity of 1469, and the ideological character of Rome had changed beyond recognition. Naples (from 1503) and Milan (from 1535) were ruled directly by Spain. Florence was no longer a city republic but the ducal capital of Tuscany, dependent first on the Habsburgs and later on France. Smaller centres of culture were provided by Mantua (especially active in music), Modena, and the brand new Duchy of Parma. Ferrara and Siena had been absorbed.

Throughout all this, there was one social and cultural constant which had distinguished northern and central Italy from the rest of Europe since at least the thirteenth century. All notions of culture, progress and civilization in Italy were city-based, and were felt always to have been so. 'The City' was not a new social and ideological problem for Italians, as it was in England in the time of Jonson, but an environment taken absolutely for granted. Republican or princely, bourgeois or aristocratic, these were thoroughly urban societies – one of the many reasons why they took over so easily the theatrical plots and models of the ancient cities of Athens and Rome.

LANGUAGE AND DIALECTS

The break-up of the Roman Empire had left behind innumerable varieties of colloquial Latin speech: in an age of poor communications every region, indeed every village, spoke a slightly different Latin-based vernacular. The emergence of national languages – French, Spanish, Portuguese, Italian – was a political or a cultural process, or both, by which the dialect of one region in particular was given over-riding status (Castilian, in Spain; the speech of the region round Paris, in France). In the sixteenth century this process had at least begun in the emerging national states beyond the Alps; but in Italy, with no national state, the position was more complex.

Two hundred years previously, three major writers had produced widely diffused masterpieces all in the Florentine dialect: the *Divina Commedia* of Dante (1265–1321), the lyric poems of Petrarch (1304–74), and the prose works, in particular the *Decameron*, of

Boccaccio (1313–75). Florentine was a dialect which was central not just geographically but also linguistically, with the advantage of having lost or distorted fewer sounds from the Latin roots, so the educated and literate found it more accessible whatever their own mother tongue. After Petrarch and Boccaccio, there was a period during which Latin was preferred for most serious written communication. The sixteenth century, with which the present book deals, is characterized by a drive to make *fourteenth*-century Florentine, as found in the three 'canonical' writers, the basis of a literary language which would be accepted throughout the peninsula for written cultural communication. There was rather less attempt (because it was harder, and more controversial) to identify this same Florentine 'Italian' as a medium of *spoken* communication for the educated and courtly upper classes, who met and mingled across state boundaries.

The policy of turning back to fourteenth-century Florentine as a literary model was begun by the Venetian Pietro Bembo (1470–1547) and continued later in the century mainly by Florentines (who could claim a spurious cultural leadership from the fact that it was their own dialect, albeit in an older version, which was being favoured). It was probably the only practical linguistic solution in a politically divided peninsula, but it remained nevertheless artificial. The mother tongue of the vast majority of Italians was different from Florentine – as different, say, as Spanish was, and indeed Spanish was probably no more difficult to understand. Literary 'Italian' (often referred to as 'Tuscan' at this time) was something which had to be deliberately learned.

This presented relatively few problems for texts intended to be read: those who could read at all were a minority, and were usually prepared to make the necessary efforts to understand. For theatre the difficulties were potentially more serious, if one accepted at all (as some writers probably did not) that stage language should bear some relation to living speech. All popular theatre, including that with serious religious content, had previously been written in a local vernacular for local consumption. The 'regular' comedy based on Latin models, which is the subject of this book, was initially offered to a very restricted audience and could afford to use (and in fact to promote) literary 'Tuscan' for the educated spectator. But comedy thrives on the down-to-earth, on realism, on robust caricature of authentic behaviour and language. Audiences, especially less sophisticated ones, like to be appealed to by constant reference to who and what they are, which includes acknowledging the way they speak. Sooner or later, in one way or another, the existence of a multiple range of spoken vernaculars was going to have to be recognized on the comic stage. The rather tortuous way in which this necessity was faced in Italy forms one of the strands or episodes of the story told in this book.

CHAPTER I

Precedents

SOME DEFINITIONS

This book deals with performed 'regular' comedy in Italy, principally between 1500 and about 1555. In defining the boundaries of our topic, we shall mostly be accepting sixteenth-century definitions of what constituted 'comedy', definitions which depended in their turn on what it was thought *comedia* had meant in classical Latin. In the medieval period the term had been used in ways which did not necessarily imply either theatrical performance or the intention of provoking laughter. In the Renaissance, however, the Latin word *comedia* was applied to a genre of theatrical writing. It was defined in ways which usually did not list laughter as an essential component, but in practice most Renaissance comedies were also meant to be funny. In discussing them, therefore, we shall be unable to avoid using the words 'comic' and 'comedy' with the primary meaning which they possess in modern English conversation: they will apply to an artefact or performance intended to make people laugh. Words such as 'satire' or 'farce', when used at all, will be seen as sub-species of the category 'comedy', or *comedia* in Latin, not as contrasting categories. (The Italian word *commedia*, on its own, will be avoided in these pages: it is confusingly used by many English-speaking scholars as a synonym for *commedia dell'arte*, an important but specialized phenomenon which will be discussed in Chapter 5.)

In describing comedy as 'regular', a term actually used at the time, we mean that it conformed or at least alluded to formats derived from the Roman comedies of Plautus and Terence. In the period we are discussing, many other sources and styles were also progressively introduced; but a continuous tradition can always be traced back to dramatists who were consciously reviving and imitating the Roman models. Initially the use of such models was programmatic, even revolutionary; and the discussion of any phenomenon which appears or claims to be new has to be introduced by some allusion to what has gone before. In our case, this means things which preceded and influenced 'regular' comedy, but equally the practices which it chose to reject. This chapter will discuss both the continuity and the discontinuity between 'medieval' and 'Renaissance' drama in Italy, in terms of content and structure.

Before even doing that, however, we must also say something about the 'comic', in the modern sense of the 'laughable', in both the life and the art of the period leading up to 1500. It is intended in these opening pages to offer some orienting observations on laughter, particularly as it functioned in the medieval Italian culture which preceded and therefore introduced 'regular comedy'.

USES OF COMEDY

There are great pitfalls in the way of any attempt to relate the physical act of laughing to a single emotional attitude or judgement. No matter what theorists tell us is, or should be, the essence of laughter, some aspect of people's real behaviour will soon provide an awkward exception, and every proposition can be countered by its opposite. The unthinking assumptions which people hold on the subject can be quite contradictory, as an anecdotal example shows. During the early 1980s, two separate complaints were made to the BBC, in the form of letters to the *Radio Times*, about different TV programmes both of which happened to deal with the Second World War.[1] One was on the long-running series *Dad's Army*, which had been about a motley group of Home Guard volunteers who displayed comic inefficiency in a succession of increasingly fanciful situations. The complainant said, more or less, that it was disgraceful to offer such a demeaning picture of what in reality had been a serious and dedicated body of men. A second correspondent objected to *Private Schultz*, a six-week drama serial in black comedy vein in which an amoral con-man survived the period of the Third Reich in Germany. The complaint this time was that the Nazis were too horrifying to be laughed at. Thus the first correspondent was expressing the theory that laughter always attacks and degrades its object; whereas the second writer was stating that it always implies indulgence and that by laughing at a crime we are in some sense forgiving it. These two theories may not be utterly unreconcilable, but there is certainly opposition or tension between them. A unitary view of how laughter functions, if based on one of the two approaches only, would risk ignoring the essential insights provided by the other.

An easier premise would be that laughter, like weeping, is a physical reaction which the human organism uses for more than one purpose – it covers a range of feelings and attitudes not all of which will be involved in every laugh, and some of which can seem incompatible with each other when analysed verbally from outside. Laughter, as opposed to smiling, is first provoked in young infants (in my experience at least) by a playful assault on their bodies carried out by someone they trust. The swooping hand or head ought to be a message of danger, which induces tension; but the child has learned, even before learning to talk, that this danger is in jest not in earnest, so the tension is dissolved in giggles rather than in screams of fear. Later on, though, children can laugh out of sheer unmixed delight, with no tension or discrepancy to resolve at all. They can also laugh at silly mistakes in life or in fictional stories, because they feel superior to them (even if the mistakes are their own): this can develop into aggressive group derision of an individual who is failing to conform. However, it also becomes possible to laugh in approval, rather than in rejection, as one appreciates the cleverness of a an invention or piece of wordplay; and this, by verbal logic at least, is the very opposite emotional pole from derision. In adulthood, although all these motives are available singly or in combination, an individual temperament may make one type of laughter more characteristic than others. Some of us are more prone, and others less prone, to derisive or scornful laughter, and the same is true of laughter at inventive nonsense or whimsy.

As with individuals, so with societies or cultures. There is a wide range of alternative cultural uses for laughter, implying to some extent different definitions of what is funny and what is not, of which kinds of laughter are acceptable and which are taboo. For example, in the Anglo-Saxon cultures of the twentieth century, the notion that you are a 'good sport' if you can accept or foster a joke against yourself is extended to people of power and dignity, so that in the right circumstances a political leader can actually win approval by doing something undignified or by gracefully acknowledging satirical attack. British politicians of all parties have sometimes performed snippets of pantomime, caricaturing themselves, on television at Christmas time. Margaret and Denis Thatcher, as Prime Minister of Great Britain and her spouse, felt obliged to attend a performance in London of the aggressive dramatic satire *Anyone for Denis?* to show (or pretend) that they could take it in good part. In 1982 it was reported that Mrs Nancy Reagan, wife of the American President, performed a rewritten version of the song *Second-Hand Rose* for journalists at a White House party: she was sending herself up after criticisms about the extravagance of her wardrobe. There may have been two alternative and incompatible reasons, on the night, for laughing at her performance; but in the USA it was not unreasonable to assume that by responding in such a way, and deliberately making a fool of herself, she might defuse the criticisms and do herself good rather than harm. Such an assumption would be viewed with utter perplexity by many of the world's other cultures, including those of Mediterranean Europe, where the understanding is that any mockery of a person in power is bound to be materially subversive of that person's authority. If this view is shared by subjects or citizens as well as by rulers, then by definition it becomes true as far as that society is concerned. In Italy in 1963 the appointment as Prime Minister of a certain Giovanni Leone took place in a week when Italian TV had proposed to transmit an undoubtedly harmless farce entitled *Un leone nel mio letto* ('A Lion in my Bed'). The play was banned at the last minute, not for its content, but because of the word *leone* in its title.[2] A sufficient number of influential people, and certainly the new Prime Minister himself, felt that even the casual association of his surname with a mildly titillating romp (it would have been very mild, in 1963) would undermine his authority. As a young Anglo-Saxon I found this view comically diverting in its turn. But there were some aspects of the Italian sense of humour, as expressed in jokes, stories and performed comedy, which I found uncomfortably aggressive and therefore not funny; and the same problem often appears among British students reading and discussing Italian comic literature (for example, some stories by Boccaccio). Without trying to be moralistic about it, one has simply to observe that a British cultural formation gives less permission to laugh at misfortune or suffering – certainly in ordinary life, and in many cases also in fiction.

All this preamble points to a set of principles, or at least of caveats, for the present study of Italian Renaissance comedy. As we examine performed comic fiction produced by a culture now long past, it will be borne in mind that people can laugh for different and even incompatible reasons; and that what one person or society finds funny another may find repugnant. It is better not to start with a limiting *a priori* definition of how comedy functions, from which a large amount of material is then excluded. In principle any litera- ture or drama which once succeeded in making somebody laugh is comic – even if it seems to have little in common with other material which is also comic, and even if we are repelled by the idea that it was regarded as funny. (These are the traps which theorists fall into: Bergson excludes or ignores anything which jars with his neat attractive theory, and Meredith averts his eyes from humour unacceptable to cultivated society.[3]) The category 'comic' is to be defined historically and socially, more than intellectually or aesthet- ically, and it will include manifestations which now seem tedious or offensive. The historical approach will in turn dictate its own limitations and exclusions, because we shall find that sixteenth- century Italy came to impose its own conventions about the style and the subject matter of comedy on stage.

The modes of laughter used by any given culture in its comic fiction will not coincide absolutely with the uses made of it in ordinary social life. Fiction exists in order to be an alternative to fact, as well as to reflect it. Nevertheless, there is bound to be some relationship between laughter in a society, whether spontaneous or ritualized, and the spirit and structure of its comic artefacts.[4] One of the main uses made of laughter in pre-modern Europe was to single out and humiliate the deviant and even the criminal. The chief purpose of the stocks and the pillory was to make the delinquent feel foolish and suffer shame: the general public seized on the chance to feel superior (more virtuous, or cleverer at not getting caught), and any passing torments inflicted on the convict were both a social duty and a hilarious pleasure. It is quite possible that similar mirth was felt at the sight of more serious punishments – public whippings, maimings, and even capital executions.[5] Whether we like it or not, the human species is capable of responding to such spectacles with laughter. It is not so long in British educational history since school- boys regularly enjoyed the sight of one of their number being ritually beaten, and such an event often formed the climax to a

merry tale in what we significantly refer to as a children's comic.
The writer and journalist Penelope Mortimer once tackled a Saudi
Arabian lawyer on the physical mutilations which figure as punishments in strict Islamic law, and discovered that 'amputation seemed
to him not only just, but hilariously funny'.[6] 'Ha ha!' laughs the
schoolboy in the comic strip, 'serves you right!'

In some societies therefore it is a mistake to suppose, along with
the *Radio Times* correspondent who objected to *Private Schultz*, that
laughing at a miscreant must imply indulgence or forgiveness.
Medieval Italy did not suppose this, and the fact is reflected in its
literature. Dante's *Divine Comedy* (completed by 1321) is not in
essence a comic poem, in our terms: the poet took the Latin word
comedia in quite a different sense,[7] as indicating a mixture of linguistic and stylistic registers. However, some of the sinners in the *Inferno*
are punished for all eternity with the vicious humour, even sarcasm,
which we also associate with those scenes in medieval mystery plays
where the devils are let loose on the wicked. In Cantos xxi–xxii this
parallel is explicit as the 'barrators' or corrupt politicians are teased,
abused and contested with, in and around their river of boiling
pitch, by a troop of devils whose brutish vulgarity is surely meant to
be laughed at, just as it would be in an equivalent dramatized scene.
In such a construct the moral inferiority of the sinners is emphasized, for the reader or spectator, by the fact that God has put them
at the mercy of such degraded creatures; and the devils themselves
can be laughed at in the same contemptuous spirit, as enemies of
God who have been deservedly defeated and confined in Hell to
perform a despicable task. This rather complex moral strategy of
having villains punished by other villains is particularly exploitable
in drama, though in the Renaissance we may find it used more often
in English than Italian theatre.[8] In other cantos of the *Inferno*, even
some of the most serious and intense, sinners are punished directly
by God in ways which are scornful, ironic, humiliating and therefore
potentially funny. Seducers and pimps are flogged round in proces-
sion, as they might have been in Dante's Florence, and the poet
enjoys their lively response to the whip (*Inf.* xviii, vv. 37–9); flat-
terers are immersed in dung, with features comically obscured
(xviii, 116–17); and simoniacs are plonked head downwards in holes
with flames playing on the soles of their feet (xix, *passim*). Our last
view of Satan himself is the undignified sight of his huge goat's legs
waving in the air (*Inf.* xxxiv, v. 90): his genitals are the centre of the

universe's gravity, and the pilgrims Dante and Virgil have to climb down his top half and then up again towards his feet. All these figures deserve their fate, as is made fiercely clear by Dante's poetry, but the fact that they look ludicrous and the spectator laughs is part of their punishment. 'Not only just, but hilariously funny.' In this kind of writing, the firm opposition proposed by Ernst Curtius[9] between the categories of 'jest' and 'earnest' is questionable, and might well lead to a misreading of a text.

Humiliating punishments were not always formal and judicial. In many communities, people who offended against unwritten proprieties rather than the written law were subjected by the majority, or by a self-appointed section of it, to ordeals which made them look ridiculous and which had something of a theatrical element. We all know the function of the ducking stool as a punishment for obstreperous women. In a Charivari, clamorous demonstrations could be held outside the victim's house, and he (or she, or they) could be paraded round in effigy or in person, comically dressed and mounted backwards on an ass. The objects of this disapproval might be adulterers or cuckolds, but also (according to Enid Welsford) 'those who married widows, or were beaten by their wives, or beat their wives in the month of May'.[10] 'Laughter in the villages', says Keith Thomas, 'was a crude form of moral censorship.'[11] Readers of Thomas Hardy will know that a Wessex Charivari, or skimmington-ride, provides a turning point in the plot of *The Mayor of Casterbridge*. Those who plan it look forward to a splendidly entertaining time: ''Tis the funniest thing under the sun ... A good laugh warms my heart more than a cordial.'[12] This heart-warming piece of enjoyment breaks the heart of one of its victims, who dies not long afterwards.

The justification for these japes is that certain people, by deviancy or misbehaviour or simple inferiority, put themselves beyond sympathy, and that the rest of us are entitled to have a good laugh at their expense. We should beware of imagining that we are entirely removed from such an attitude, since it is a guiding principle in a number of literary and dramatic texts which we still enjoy. In Shakespeare we may now feel uncomfortable when it is applied to Shylock and to Katherina the Shrew, but we are less sensitive and more prepared to join in the fun when the butt of the joke is a Malvolio or a Parolles. Most of Molière's protagonists put themselves sufficiently in the wrong for us to accept the tricks played on

them. Contemporary TV sitcoms make victims and scapegoats of
chosen characters, as punishment for the illiberal or obstructive
attitudes which they are made to display. Having said that, one
must also acknowledge that there are some 'comic' passages in
medieval Italian literature at which most modern readers will fail to
laugh. Franco Sacchetti, in his *Trecentonovelle* of the late fourteenth
century, tells with great cheerfulness how the jester Dolcibene
tricked some Jews into adorning themselves with excrement (no.
xxiv: the trick is utterly implausible, but we are intended to enjoy
it), and then how the same Dolcibene merrily organized the judicial
castration of a priest (no. xxv). Categories of people ridiculed in
such literature regularly included the ignorant, the ugly, the slow off
the mark, or simply the losers in any given contest; and they were
also likely to include the lower classes by definition, and women
equally by definition.

All these uses of laughter in society and in art are aggressive, and
indeed often repressive. At the level of the group they reinforce the
moral or social norm, and single out those who deviate as worthy
objects of derision. On an individual level they are an exercise in
self-consolation and the relief of anxiety: 'Isn't it splendid that
he/she is so ludicrous and I am so acceptable? How exhilarating to
know that this is happening to that person, and not to me!' Taken
alone, these examples reinforce what eventually became the central
perception of most Renaissance theorizing about humour, culminating in the formulation of Hobbes, which has been rather weakly
paraphrased as 'laughter is a sudden glory felt at the sight of an
inferior'.[13] And however one-sided this observation may be, it is true
for some of the time in all cultures – can anyone claim *never* to have
laughed at a piece of speech or behaviour because it is different,
unfamiliar, incorrect and therefore absurd?

So far we have been providing material for a classic intellectual or
moral view of laughter. We laugh at what we reject, and we reject
the laughable because of some discrepancy from what is rational and
proper. Even if the error is not a harmful one, and even if we wish no
harm to its perpetrator, we still scorn it and dissociate it from
ourselves. The village idiot who dives into the pool after the
reflected moon, the half-educated person whose speech is full of
malapropisms, are no threat to the fabric of society; but we perceive
their error and laugh at their discomfiture, just as in the case of more
seriously 'deserved' humiliation or punishment.

However, this pattern does not manage to cover every case. It may be true that ninety per cent of what makes human beings laugh involves some discrepancy from a perceived correctness or normality (though the phenomenon is slippery enough to contain another ten per cent which evades even that definition). But for much of the time, or with much of our minds, the absurdity which makes us laugh may not be rejected at all, weird or inappropriate or immoral as it may be. Sometimes we want to embrace or accept what is deviant, either as a holiday from ordinary constraints or to help subvert them. The Italian comedies which are the object of this study were, to start with, performed mainly at carnival time. Carnival was a deep-rooted institution to which everyone could instinctively respond, even though they found it difficult to explain.

In live society, carnival can take many shapes from the ritualized to the anarchic. Its essence was that people were allowed to do, or got others to act out for them, things which were normally taboo. In its most formalized manifestations, social roles and hierarchies were reversed so that the king in his court had to obey a Lord of Misrule, and a choirboy or subdeacon took the place of the bishop for a day. Normal ceremonies and rituals, even the most sacred, could be systematically parodied, as in the burlesque investiture of buffoon knights at Ferrara in 1490,[14] or the masses performed in French cathedrals at Epiphany with pudding and sausages and the braying of an ass.[15] Authorities were sometimes in two minds about this momentary anarchy, especially in the ecclesiastical sphere. Frequently, though, such occasions were tolerated as a necessary letting off of steam, in the knowledge that they were limited as to time (perhaps only one day), and as to how anarchic they were allowed to become ('not more than three buckets of water at most must be poured over the *Precentor Stultorum* (Fools' Choirmaster) at Vespers'[16]). Wine-barrels break, it was solemnly explained, if their bung-holes are not occasionally opened to let in the air – 'and the clergy, being nothing but old wine-casks badly put together, would certainly burst if the wine of wisdom were allowed to boil by continued devotion to Divine Service'.[17] More secular forms of Saturnalia, especially at court, needed less theoretical backing and flourished unchecked in their season. It is as if a sane but confused instinct recognized that all social institutions, even sacred ones, are at bottom only an arbitrary code, and that it is salutary once in a while to turn that code inside out. Carnival revellers were perhaps acting out a deconstruction of the text of society. Certainly, whereas before we have been examining uses of laughter which reinforce the daily code by attacking those who break it, in carnival the Fool stops being an object of contempt and becomes a hero, so that his subversions and absurdities are attractive and even offered as possessing a paradoxical wisdom. In the same mood and context, approval can be extended to the rogue and the trickster, and respectable citizens can admit into their minds the fun involved in humiliating an enemy, disrupting a ceremony, cheating a sucker, or going to bed with someone else's spouse.

The most important comic structures in Italian literature before 1500 revolve round this competitive type of story, where some characters get the better of others in order to achieve satisfaction – and more often than not the satisfaction is one of which normal society disapproves. Such narratives are central to the short story or *novella* tradition, presided over in Italy by Boccaccio's *Decameron*. Since its appearance around 1350, this masterly collection had been known and enjoyed by practically every Italian with the leisure to read or be read to, and as a source for Italian Renaissance comedy it is no less important than Plautus and Terence. It is not exclusively a comic volume, but those stories which are comic almost always narrate a contest in which there are winners and losers. The losers qualify as such by stupidity, inadequacy, or sometimes (but not often) immorality: the winners triumph through intelligence, energy, singleness of purpose and intensity of desire. Adultery, as is well known, is a frequent motivation in the *Decameron*. Most of the time a wife and her lover combine to outwit the husband, and the story leaves them to enjoy their illicit pleasure with the cuckold left in ignorance or resignation. Occasionally the wife herself, as prey, is tricked into bed by false identity or expectations, as in Day III, story 6. But there are some contests in Boccaccio for other prizes too: Day VIII, story 10 recounts a trick and counter-trick over goods and money; and in VI, 10 the cheeky Friar Cipolla gulls a whole community into venerating a false relic. The single famous recurrent character, Calandrino, is the butt of a series of jokes by his friends aimed chiefly at showing up his monumental credulity (VIII, 3 and 6; IX, 5), and only one of these stories relates to sex. Only once, in Day IV, story 2, is an adulterer regarded with such disfavour as to be tricked in his turn into exposure and punishment (in the form of an improvised Charivari). The others live happily ever after in their irregular liaisons, often blessed by their narrator with some such formula as: 'acting with prudence, they frequently again took pleasure from their love. God grant that we may take pleasure in ours' (III, 6).

Such apparent collusion with crime may suggest a link between the polished stories of the *Decameron* and the wilder phenomenon of carnival. In a substantial number of Boccaccio's stories the reader is invited to take the side of a rogue or rogues who pursue the claims of selfish desire without regard either to the social code or to the claims of a competitor. As with carnival itself, there are two possible explanations of what is going on. Carnival, and stories of immoral trickery, present alternative sets of rules to the ones which apply to most of the people most of the time. If the alternative is taken as a serious proposal, then real social or ideological subversion can be involved. The demoting of the bishop in favour of the choirboy, the ritual abuse of the king by his fool or by the Lord of Misrule, can be turned into vehicles for a philosophy of levelling or inversion which aims at changing the system – or which preaches how the splendours and indignities of the flesh which we all share are more significant than the outward forms which divide us. By this account, as has indeed often been argued,[18] the *Decameron* contains a calculated plea in favour of Nature and the demands of the flesh as against Reason and the social code. But carnival itself is more often seen as a deliberate structured holiday from reality – an alternative explored and played with for a day, 'temporary liberation from the prevailing truth and from the established order'.[19] In that analysis it becomes proper this time to follow Curtius, and make 'jest' the opposite of 'earnest', as was not appropriate with laughter used as a social and moral sanction.

In relation to the *Decameron* and similar collections of *novelle*, and then eventually in relation to Renaissance comedy, we have always to ask whether the jest was in any way in earnest or not. Boccaccio's leisured company of young men and maidens are making use of pleasurable fictions in order to insulate their minds against the infecting reality of the Black Death of 1348 – and these narrators resemble the actual readership of the *Decameron*, of whom indeed they are projected images, more closely than do any of the participants in the tales told. They may laugh exultantly at the triumph of Love Eternal over the despicable cuckold, and they may pray for God to grant them similar pleasure, but their creator and controller Boccaccio insists that they never in fact followed suit. At the end of each day's story-telling they are made to listen to a courtly song, dance a civilized dance, and then retire with propriety each to his or her own bedchamber. What they give assent to in artistic fiction is not necessarily what they are prepared to do themselves.

In any case, the model of carnival cannot be offered without reservation as an explanation of the *Decameron* or of any other comic artefact from the Middle Ages or Renaissance. Carnival, as Bakhtin argues, makes no distinctions but programmatically reduces (or raises) everyone to the same level, trickster along with tricked, spectator along with actor:

It is, first of all, a festive laughter. Therefore it is not an individual reaction to some isolated 'comic' event. Carnival laughter is the laughter of all the people. Second, it is universal in scope: it is directed at all and everyone, including the carnival's participants. The entire world is seen in its droll aspect, in its gay relativity. Third, this laughter is ambivalent: it is gay, triumphant, and at the same time mocking, deriding. It asserts and denies, it buries and revives.[20]

In a tale of the *Decameron*, the reader or listener sets aside certain inhibitions so as to identify with the entertaining rogue or the determined lovers. But an equal part of the entertainment is provided by the 'deserved' discomfiture of their victims. The victim Calandrino, to whom we feel superior, is more memorable and vivid than the characters who humiliate him on our behalf. Scornful laughter co-exists in this narrative structure along with festive liberating laughter – not merged in ambivalence, as Bakhtin describes, but rather directed separately at different participants in the story. Social hierarchies may sometimes be undermined, but a pecking order based on talent, energy and attractiveness is the very marrow of the narrative and its appeal. Even more importantly, Bakhtin rightly excludes from carnival, in its pure form at least, the finished comic artefact which forces a separation between the spectator (or reader or listener or consumer) and the object or event which entertains. The structure of the *Decameron*, with its fictional narrators telling and enjoying fictional tales, emphasizes rather than reduces such separation. It is hard to believe that the reader, identifying with three youths and seven maidens gently secure in their villa gardens on the Tuscan hills, is impelled to feel any carnivalesque fraternity with Andreuccio da Perugia climbing sodden and filthy out of his well (ii, 5), or with Peronella being humped from behind as she bends over her barrel (vii, 2). When we come to the earliest manifestations of Italian Renaissance comedy, the same reservations will apply. The new genre of secular comic theatre was not, initially at least, intended to provoke 'the laughter of all the people', nor to sink social differences in a feeling of common humanity. It was staged by and for a courtly educated élite, who were more attracted by the pecking order involving winners and losers.

One of the 'carnival' events mounted regularly in Ferrara around 1500 was the Palio di San Giorgio, St George's Trophy.[21] A strange mixture of competitors ran through the streets to a winning post – young bloods and grooms on thoroughbred horses, boys on donkeys, and some lower categories of person on foot. These last might include menial servants, prostitutes (dressed indecently so they exposed themselves as they ran) and Jews (possibly made to run naked).[22] It was obvious from the start who would win: the upper class, the golden youths or their representatives on their expensive horses. It was equally obvious who was going to lose, ritually, and be derided in the process. The court which organized and enjoyed this spectacle, sanctifying an oppressive hierarchy through the use of laughter, was the same court which launched the revival of secular comic theatre on Roman models. If comedy, in these circumstances, was going to be able to impose its anarchic, subversive or healing potential, it was going to have to compete with the vested interest, shared equally by noble courtiers and by humanist playwrights, in affirming and enjoying their own superiority. Ludovico Ariosto, not the most aggressive of humourists, accepts this prevailing mood in his first prologue to *La Lena* of 1528, which seems to take for granted that the audience prefer to enjoy themselves at other people's expense. In tripping *endecasillabi sdruccioli*, he offers his own play to the audience's mercy, or to its scorn:

> Whether it's good or terrible
> Will make no odds – we'll still find cause to laugh at it;
> Because, if wit is lacking in the dramatist,
> Then he exposes his pretentious arrogance,
> And we can entertain ourselves by mocking him.[23]

PATTERNS OF PERFORMANCE

Italian scholars usually begin the history of Italian vernacular drama by examining compositions which seem to belong to the realm of lyric poetry. This is partly because of the way in which religious drama developed (as did ancient Greek drama) out of chorally performed lyric. The *laude* of central Italy in the thirteenth century were devotional poems sung and perhaps danced by religious confraternities. It is sometimes possible to distinguish between a *lauda lirica* and a *lauda drammatica*, but the difference is blurred more often than not by the evangelical nature of the content: whether we call it song or drama, it needs to be performed, so that the confraternity can exemplify and preach to others its revivalist fervour. It is thus only a short step from an expository hymn to a dramatized debate (between Soul and Body, Riches and Poverty), or to a biblical dialogue (between the Madonna and Christ crucified, as in the masterly *Donna di paradiso* by Jacopone da Todi[24]). It is usual to see a continuous line of development from such lyrics to the *sacre rappresentazioni* which are the Italian equivalents of mystery, miracle and morality plays. The largest corpus of these comes from fifteenth-century Florence: most of them are attributable to a named author, and their tradition continued independently into the sixteenth century and beyond.

Secular theatre too, to judge by surviving texts, seems to begin with compositions in lyric verse metre. The activities of professional entertainers or *giullari*, now being so brilliantly reinterpreted by Dario Fo, were built around set-piece verse texts for one or at the most two performers. Usually, one imagines, no texts survive, and it is probable that most of these professionals were illiterate, learning and composing by ear like archaic Greek bards, or like their equivalents who still perform in modern Turkey. Their repertoire of narrative as opposed to dramatic material led eventually in Italy to the Renaissance epic. On the dramatic side there are just enough surviving texts to show how a *giullare* might display his virtuosity in elaborate patter songs (*frottole*), boasts (*vanti*), satirical verses, and dramatized debates or quarrels (*contrasti*) in which the single performer may well have shown off his range of voices and mimic gestures by taking both sides of the argument. Even if the text itself indicated monologue rather than dialogue, there was inevitably an element of role-playing. In relation to the early thirteenth-century boasting exercise by Ruggieri Apugliese, Emilio Faccioli has justly remarked[25] that a distance is carefully maintained between Ruggieri the performer and composer and Ruggieri the grotesque character in the text, and that the audience is thus involved in a triangular relationship. (Such a triangle is always constructed, over a period of time, by any good comic performer: we laugh at Charlie the tramp, and at the same time appreciate the skill of Mr Chaplin.) The important point for the present study (and here we dissent perhaps from Dario Fo) is that *giullari* did not perform exclusively for 'the people': more of the texts which have actually survived are likely to have been for the consumption of princes or wealthy men, in whose circles the texts might more often have been recorded in writing.

Medieval court entertainments were often much more elaborate than verses performed by a *giullare* or court jester. Pageants and spectacles mounted for big occasions could involve a lot of story-line and very few words (as in a siege of the Castle of Love), a lot of words and very little story (a debate between Celibacy and Marriage, or a speech of welcome to a guest of honour), or few words and no story but a lot of imagery (as in a procession of allegorical floats, or a tournament). Altogether, in court circles and perhaps elsewhere too, it seems likely that the commonest relationship between audience, text and performer before 1500 was not the one which we now regard as most straightforward. The 'modern' one was in fact re-proposed by the humanists in the sixteenth century. Modern theatre, for all its post-naturalist experimentation, still commonly takes as its starting-point the notion of actors submerging their own personalities in stage 'characters' in order to act out a 'story', expecting that the prime question in the audience's mind will be 'what happens next?' in the plot. (And this format is now deeply rooted in most spectators by the more common example of cinema and television drama.) By contrast, medieval entertainments probably started from the presuppositions of modern vaudeville or pantomime – the 'story' was intermittent, if there was one at all, and the performers faced their public more openly, holding attention by means of an ambiguous merger between their own everyday personalities (often familiar to most of those present) and the role adopted for the occasion. By 1500 Italian courtiers understood how to respond to a comedian or Master of Ceremonies who talked at them head on; and they were used to *contrasti* performed for an audience, with the flow of verbal invective or argument providing the substance of the drama. They were probably less used to having to follow a complicated intrigue acted out on stage; and also unaccustomed to the convention whereby characters in a story pretend to be totally self-absorbed, and act as if the audience were not there. The need for a Master of Ceremonies or *giullare* figure, and a tendency to prefer rhetoric to complex action, both leave their mark for better and for worse on the scripts of Italian Renaissance plays.

The new comedy which the humanists introduced into Italy, and which went on to influence most of Europe, was in the eyes of its authors an overdue revival of intellectually respectable forms of theatre. It recreated the way things had been done in ancient Greece and Rome, and by humanist definition the ancients knew best. Although the new texts were not at first accompanied by much formulated theory – that was to come later – one senses from the start a polemical attitude in writers who were in effect accomplishing a theatrical revolution, hoping to transform the assumptions held by their audience as to what constituted acceptable patterns of performed art for the upper classes. Previous forms of theatre and spectacle were invalid, and to be ignored: this included all kinds of popular drama, naturally, but also some more 'literary' types of spectacle which up to then had been produced for the community or the court. Whereas in France, Spain and England there was later a more organic development, whereby many of the procedures and codes of medieval drama mingled richly with the new classical models, in Italy the humanists had at least the intention of rejecting all recent formats, so as to start with a clean sheet. There is in fact in Italy less continuity than elsewhere between medieval and Renaissance drama. However, we cannot entirely ignore earlier performing structures. On the one hand, old habits and tastes always die harder than revolutionary polemicists care to admit, and the revolutionaries themselves are not immune from them. On the other hand, the very novelty and attractiveness of the Classical modes of drama has to be explained partly by their contrast with what had existed before.

The new dramaturgy was based on that of Roman comedy, texts of which had been revived or rediscovered during the fifteenth century and made steadily more familiar to the sons of the rich by their use in the humanist educational syllabus. The plays of Plautus came from fragmented sources, and twelve of them had been rediscovered only in 1429. The six comedies of Terence, which had a

longer tradition of pedagogical use, had been handed down in
unitary form, and in 1435 they were put together with the newly
discovered essays and commentaries of 'Donatus' from late antiquity
(now known to be the work of two authors, Donatus and Evanthius).[26] It was from 'Donatus' that teachers and pupils would have
acquired some notion of the theoretical principles which lay behind
Roman comedy, though the texts themselves were a clear enough
example and contrasted in many ways with medieval theatre. The
most simple formal contrast, and one which quickly became a
symbolic badge of humanist intent, was the division of a play into
five acts. All the surviving texts of Plautus and Terence (and of
tragedies by Seneca) had been transmitted in this form. Ironically,
Classical scholars will now claim that Roman comedy had no such
structure, that it was imposed on the Latin texts in late antiquity to
make them look more similar to the Greek New Comedies which
preceded them. The humanists knew nothing of this, and accepted
the texts as they found them. The five-act structure was so axiomatic
that it becomes the simplest criterion by which we can decide
whether a comedy composed before 1520 has ambitions to belong to
the new humanist 'regular' comedy (dubbed by modern critics as
commedia erudita).[27]

In the long run, the importance of the ancient models for Europe,
and not just for Italy, was to provide a model of theatre as an
activity in its own right, with what we now call 'artistic' status. A
play, like a book, was to become something experienced for itself
rather than as a subordinated expression of a social or religious
occasion. The way was being opened to the circulation of playtexts
as cultural products; to theatre performances divorced from fixed
public or private festivals, and eventually offered to paying customers; and to the construction of buildings dedicated to theatre activity
and to nothing else. Of these three outcomes, only the first was
achieved in Italy in the early decades after 1500, but with hindsight
it is easy to see where the wind was already blowing. In the meantime there was a real and sudden revolution within the play scripts
themselves: the Roman comedies suggested a number of concrete
ways in which a dramatic text could achieve a new kind of internal
autonomy, one which theorists would eventually hail as more
'rational'.

We can perhaps identify three main characteristics of the earlier
dramatic modes as institutions against which the revolution raised

its barricades. Firstly, medieval drama, whether religious or courtly, had been imprecise and fluctuating as to where its enacted events were taking place – Jerusalem and Saragossa in the same play;[28] on a classical mountain, but at the same time here in *this* hall, for the benefit of *this* named guest.[29] Secondly, use was regularly made of a dramatic language which was more than mimetic – biblical and morality characters carried a weight of liturgical or symbolic meaning, and the actors in court entertainment played fantasy figures or personifications whose function was also symbolic. In both cases fictional characters acted as encoded signifiers, and spectators understood that they had to seek the signified in their own world rather than in the one created by the drama. The third characteristic was a consequence of the first two: within a dramatic script the audience's presence was acknowledged implicitly, and often explicitly – a mystery play had an overt function for its spectators, to bolster their faith or make them mend their ways, and a court pageant was part of a social occasion in which actors and watchers were ultimately indistinguishable.

The scripts of Roman comedies, on all these three points and others besides, offered a contrast which must have been self-explanatory, even without their example being supported by theoretical precepts or a performing tradition. Firstly, all of them were set in a single place for the duration of the story. In the great majority of cases this was a public street or square in a named town, showing the front doors of a number of houses inhabited by people in the story. 'Unity of place' was not so much argued as learned by example: it was simply a fact, rather than a stated precept, that in Plautus and Terence the scene did not change.[30] In revivals and imitations it was thus possible to establish the implicit claim that the stage represented, or was, an autonomous fictional space with an enclosed internal logic, rather than a shifting magical platform half in the audience's world and half out of it.

The human figures who moved about this space would also appear to have increased autonomy to humanist-trained audiences, because they operated mimetically rather than symbolically. Revived classical concepts of *decorum*, and the supporting model of Theophrastus' *Characters* (319 BC), recommended a systematic matching of gesture, speech, behaviour and emotion to broad categories of person in society. In this system, characters on stage had to mimic as closely as possible the observable speech and behaviour (rather than the inherent moral or poetic significance) of such social and psychological types. Inner thought and motivation had to emerge from realistic emotional outburst, rather than through the authorially heightened language of poetry. The referential nature of drama (and its didactic value, which was still recognized) came from its reflecting a consensus view of what was typical, a view based on the exterior observation of behaviour. We may now see this kind of *dramatis persona* as an alternative encoding of reality, simply using a different language from the medieval one. Around 1500, however, this was less clear, and the contrast with past practice was sharp. It must have seemed that instead of alluding verbally and symbolically to a world which existed off stage, Roman drama was attempting to drag that world on to the stage in recognizable form, and to become a convincing slice of reality in its own right. The new humanist drama therefore set itself the same targets. (This, at least, would be the impression given by the written scripts. The effect may have been interfered with by acting and performing styles which we cannot now reconstruct.)

Roman models thus offered, by comparison with medieval ones, self-contained dramatic worlds with their own inner logic, and dramaturgy which tended to concentrate on an external depiction of humanity. To speak metaphorically, the drama tended towards the physical rather than the spiritual. To extend metaphor into analogy, we might propose that humanist playwrights were re-capturing laws of dramatic perspective and proportion, and finding that the soul might be portrayed through an accurate delineation of the body – as had been recommended and achieved by the radically altered techniques of painting and sculpture which triumphed in Italy during the fifteenth century. In both cases 'imitation of Nature' and 'imitation of the ancients' were seen as equivalent concepts, axiomatically to be pursued. It is no surprise therefore that the illusionistic perspective set, created with painting methods already well established, attached itself from the start to productions of new-style comedy in Italian, giving the courtiers a comforting sense of modernity and reinforcing by visual means the separateness of the stage from the auditorium. The logic of all these tendencies was a 'fourth wall' approach to drama: the audience had no place in the world of the characters, and should not be acknowledged by them. Dramatic writing now operated not by directing overt mes-sages at the spectators, nor by engaging them in dialogue, but by

allowing them to overhear a series of events without the participants' knowledge. 'Donatus', writing on Terence, had made the
point explicit: 'he never makes an actor speak to the public or
outside the play' – and this incorrect practice is described as 'a fault
which is very common in Plautus'.[31] It is common indeed, if fault it
be, and on this point the strict logic of the new dramatic mode gave
way regularly to the practical demands of comedy as well as to
deeply ingrained social and dramatic habits. It is hard to perform
comedy, and impossible to deliver a comic monologue, without
addressing the audience or winking at them for some of the time.
The fact that Plautus allowed this to happen and Terence did not
coincides, frankly, with the fact that Plautus is funnier than
Terence. Italian humanist writers wanted in theory to keep direct
address for the Prologue and the *plaudite*, but if they had any instinct
for comic theatre they usually followed Plautus in the end. They
were encouraged in the same direction by the courtly occasions for
which they usually wrote, because both patron and public expected
to be drawn into their entertainment and included in the festivities,
and were used to being harangued or teased by the *giullare* rather
than pushed to the margins of the action and turned into eaves-
droppers. In this sense, then, comic scripts remained less totally
self-contained than strict logic would seem to demand. Nevertheless,
the weight of the other changes was enough to give the impression
that dramaturgy and theatre itself were breaking with the immme-
diate past and starting afresh using an older model which paradoxically gave an impression of greater modernity.

Other important inheritances from the ancients concerned the
content of the comedies: the plot structures, stock characters, and
the very use of the word *comedia* to define a particular type of play.
Scholars were instructed by Cicero and Horace, as well as by
'Donatus', that stories suitable for comedy involved the urban
middle class and their slaves, and that the events enacted should be
entirely private in their scope, concerning only the participants and
their families. It was tragedy which dealt with the highest social
class, rulers and aristocrats from whom better behaviour was
expected and whose rise and fall had public implications. Such
social segregation was foreign to medieval drama, and different
classes and styles went on mingling on the Renaissance stage in
England and Spain. In the early years in Italy, with noble audiences, it would give the comfortable experience of laughing at one's

social inferiors, though the composition of the public shifted with time. Curiously, however, laughter as such was rarely offered as a defining ingredient of *comedia*. Histories of the genre in the Renaissance, all derived from notions in 'Donatus', implied that comedies directed critical barbs at some target in contemporary life, and we have seen that this process could traditionally call forth scornful laughter. However, the best known succinct definition of comedy, said by Donatus to come from Cicero, concentrated on dramatic mimesis rather than on the 'comic' in our modern sense: 'Comedy is an imitation of life, a mirror of manners, and an image of truth.'[32]

To us it may seem odd that those who sought images of truth were happy to copy the stereotyped plots and characters of Roman comedy straight on to their own contemporary stages. The copying was in fact often meticulous, especially in the early years, and it embraced a variety of plot devices which we now see as conventional rather than truthful. The patterns are still well known to us, because they were used in European theatre until 1800 at least, and are still recycled from time to time. Roman comedy relied on highly implausible intrigue, on cross purposes, on deceit, disguise, and fortuitously mistaken identity. It invited its audience to connive at trickery or immorality for a while, in the confidence that normality would be restored in a predictable dénouement. Even the range of tricks and intrigues was limited by the range of standard characters: the foolish old man in love, the miserly puritanical father, the helpless young lovers, the wily slave, the parasite, the braggart soldier and the pimp. It was all right for a slave to cheat his master out of money, on stage, because the young master wanted to purchase a slave girl from a pimp, and we know that in the theatre we must be indulgent to a lover. It was all right for a young man to have married the companion of a prostitute in secret, without his father's consent, because the girl was decent and virtuous, and would obviously turn out to be a free-born citizen, long-lost daughter of the man next door. While waiting for the expected happy ending, the audience could at leisure be made to laugh, reflect, moralize, or indeed all three.

How could these conventional distortions of ancient social patterns reappear on stage in the sixteenth century and claim to be images of truth? Certain adjustments were in fact made rather rapidly, most of all in the details of sexual intrigue, but an enormous amount survived the transplant, took root and grew. It seems that the structures, inhibitions, prejudices and proprieties of urban Italian society in the Renaissance were remarkably similar to those of urban antiquity. Many of the Roman stereotypes still struck familiar chords. Tensions between father and son, between master and servant, between patron and parasitical client,[33] were still of the same kind; and where taboos and constraints are similar, the jokes can be similar too. It is observed increasingly often by cultural historians how the Italian ruling class in the Renaissance called up images of celebrated Greeks and Romans in order to find reflections of themselves, prestigious justifications for their own life style and values.[34] There was a considerable dose of fantasy involved here, but perhaps an equal amount of genuinely common ground. The dynamics of Mediterranean culture seem to have changed little: they had produced two similar societies at different points in history, aided by parallel stages of development in terms of affluence and technology. More than anything else, perhaps, there was the fact that both ancient and Renaissance cultures were structured around the city, and saw the countryside as subordinate or peripheral. Habits, prejudices, and patterns of human contact – which is to say all the models which must underlie any form of mimetic drama – were shaped by the dynamics of an urban, rather than rural, community.

Speculations apart, it must be recorded that the revolution operated by humanist-trained playwrights did eventually work in performance and had a lasting effect. We must now turn to a narrative of the process by which the new dramatic language was first proposed and then established as the norm.

CHAPTER 2

The first 'regular' comedies

REVIVALS OF ROMAN COMEDY

The most natural public for Roman comedy in the original was to be found in an academic environment, among those who taught and studied the texts as part of the humanist educational package. It is likely therefore that there were many university performances of the plays, including unrecorded ones as well as those which we know about. University theatre was in any case an extensive phenomenon in the fifteenth century. As well as revivals, it involved the composition of original works in Latin: 'humanist comedy'[1] which often had very little in common with the Roman models, to the extent of failing to observe any unity of place or time, ignoring the five-act structure, and dealing with subjects far from the family-based intrigues of Plautus and Terence.

The dramaturgy of original humanist comedy can be interesting and even effective, but the whole phenomenon was too esoteric to influence court or public theatre in the vernacular. (It might at most have left its mark on two eccentric and slightly mysterious comedies of the sixteenth century: Agostino degli Pennacchi's *La Perugina*, published in 1526,[2] and the more celebrated anonymous *La Veniexiana* currently dated at 1536.[3]) Student revivals of Roman comedy were eventually of more importance. They helped to disseminate the view that acting on stage, in strictly all-male casts, could be a good training in public speaking and deportment (both essential features of humanist education) and thus might not be ruled out as a pastime for young gentlemen. As long as the plays were left in Latin, however, there was little chance of their being offered to a more general audience, even among the upper classes.

Little chance, that is, except in papal Rome, where there was a large audience of international clerics who used Latin fluently and comfortably among themselves. Here there is evidence that Roman comedy could be offered, perhaps by students in the first instance, as something more approaching court entertainment. This tradition culminated in a major cultural event in 1513. A production of Plautus' *Poenulus* formed part of a massive spectacular celebration, involving an attempt to reconstruct a proper Roman theatre on the Capitoline Hill.[4] The occasion of all this pomp and expenditure was political propaganda. Giovanni de' Medici, of the family of exiled Florentine rulers, had just become Pope Leo X: he arranged the festival to mark the conferment of spurious titles of 'Roman citizen' on two of his nephews, who were then to be given the more concrete task of re-establishing Medici dominance in Florence. The visual, musical and balletic spectacle was exactly to the taste of the glittering spectators – satisfying enough to let them tolerate a dramatic text which at best they only half understood.

The Capitoline celebrations constitute a kind of portent for theatre historians. They were offered to an audience at once captive and privileged, keen to celebrate its own participation in a structure of power, deeply sensitive to display and expense and to the messages broadcast by lavishness, but fairly indifferent to the words and story being performed on stage. We see here an emblem of what dramatists and actors would have to contend with throughout the century – a massive resistant background against which both their successes and their failures must be measured.

The record of performances of Plautus and Terence in Rome, Florence and elsewhere between 1482 and 1513 is confused and probably incomplete.[5] But a leading role was taken by the court of Ferrara, ruled by the Este dynasty and specifically by Duke Ercole I from 1471 to 1505. Twenty-two separate productions of Plautus and Terence are recorded during his reign in Ferrara itself, starting in 1486, and others in the Duchy of Mantua, where his daughter Isabella was Marchioness. The plays were done in Italian translations, mostly commissioned for the purpose. Not many translations have survived, but those which remain help to explain why these revivals were received by the courtiers with dutiful tolerance rather than enthusiasm. The Roman originals had been in verse: Italian versions therefore appeared either in *terza rima* (groups of three lines rhyming ABA BCB CDC ... etc., as in Dante's *Divina Commedia*) or in eight-line stanzas of *ottava rima*. There is nothing incurably un-dramatic about either form, but in practice they led to extreme turgidity: in *terza rima* versions which have survived, the translators have felt obliged never to give any interlocutor less than the full three lines for every speech.[6] Plautus' quick-fire dialogue, sometimes giving only a word or two to each speaker, becomes immensely heavy and drawn out with this level of padding, and it is not very surprising to read that Isabella d'Este found a performance of the *Bacchides* in 1502 'longa et fastidiosa' (long and wearisome), or that when she and other courtiers wrote to their friends about these entertainments they devoted their descriptive energy to the trap-pings and interludes of the performance and hardly ever mentioned the play.[7]

This was because the abandonment of the Latin tongue was not the only concession made to the unscholarly weakness of the audi-ence. At the end of each act the play was suspended in favour of an interlude or *intermezzo*, which offered the sort of undemanding variety spectacle which the courtiers had always been used to, and which related to the festive occasion, or to nothing in particular, rather than to the plot of the comedy. At the very least there would be a dance number, often a *moresco* (morris dance), and sometimes it would be a full-scale pageant or procession with allegorical verses or other allusions to the event. Humanist learning was reflected in a different sense in these spectacles, by an increasing use of Classical mythology as a standard symbolic or allusive language.

Letters from courtiers describing these dramatic evenings enthuse in great detail over the lavishness of the decoration, scenery and costumes, and the inventiveness or symbolic charm of the *intermezzi*. For them, it often seems, the success of the party was determined by the amount of money which had been spent. It is significant that while the actors and director (if there was one) of the comedies were all gentlemen amateurs, the scene-painters, costume designers, choreographers and musicians were all professional. The money was spent where the audience felt it mattered.

About the physical staging of these performances there is little direct evidence, and still some controversy. Referring to some con-temporary frescoes, scholars[8] now suggest that from 1502 at the latest it was customary to construct a row of solid wooden house fronts across the back of the stage, to represent the line of a city street such as most of the comedies demanded as their setting. The stage in front of this scenery seems to have been wide but not very deep, enabling characters to be well separated at opposite ends for scenes where one was being overheard by another, or where they were operating as ignorant of each other's presence. Around this acting space there was likely to be a great deal of festive but irrelevant decoration, relating to the carnival or other event being celebrated. This would continue round the whole hall or courtyard which had been adapted as temporary theatre. Seating arrangements would be various and makeshift, involving always some prominent place for patron and guests of honour, a certain amount of tiered seating (usually with rigorous segregation of male and female spectators), and often standing-room in the middle where the less fortunate would be tightly and uncomfortably crammed.[9] The extent to which the acting area was framed by any sort of rudimentary proscenium is not always clear; but we do know of occasions when the front of the stage platform was a mock-up of battlemented city walls, over which the spectators had the illusion of peering as they spied on the doings of the characters in their autonomous urban world.

The logical tendency of what still ranked as antiquarian revivals of ancient Roman material would have been to attempt also a reconstruction of the shape of a Roman theatre, with tiers of seats in a semicircle around a stage with a permanent architectural background. Scholars were working on the evidence which might lead to this, but in the event their researches were pre-empted by developments which contemporaries found more exciting. The time was ripe for revivals to be replaced by modern creations in the same vein – and, by an unusually satisfying historical coincidence, the first full-scale modern dramatic text was accompanied by the first example of truly modern scenography.

FIRST STEPS IN THE VERNACULAR: FERRARA

The Este family had worked hard to impose Roman comedy on its courtiers, sugaring the pill with the more familiar entertainment modes of the interludes, and relying on the snob value already attached to all things 'ancient' after a couple of generations of humanist education for the upper classes. Surviving evidence tends to suggest, however, that the plays themselves were not yet of enormous interest to their captive audience. We cannot tell how much of this was due to cautious or clumsy acting styles. We know nothing at all about how rehearsals and performances were conducted, nothing about levels of realism or stylization aimed at, and nothing about the physical appearance of actors in costume. It is not even possible to say firmly whether at this stage they wore masks (in imitation of what was known about ancient Roman habits), or not: there are occasional uses of the word *maschera* in prologues,[10] but the meaning of this word at the time is not precise enough for us to say whether it refers to facial masks as such or simply to notions of 'costume' and 'disguise'. We do not know therefore what combination of novelty and tradition the courtiers were having to absorb on this level – but we are left with the poor quality of the translations, and the clear testimony from letters and documents that more interest (or at least more comprehension) was felt for the visual and spectacular sides of the occasion than for the drama as such.

It is easy to imagine, though, that the select group of courtiers who got involved in performing the plays would build up their own private enthusiasm for the enterprise, and perhaps begin to see how the experience could be made more palatable. It was Ludovico Ariosto (1474–1532), future author of the chivalric masterpiece *Orlando furioso*, who saw the opportunities inherent in composing new plays in Italian, in an identical mode to that of Roman comedy, with greater stylistic adhesion than had been shown by the translators to the pace and rhythms of the Roman originals.

In strict chronological order, though, Ariosto was not the first person to attempt this. In 1503, in neighbouring Mantua, an anonymous scholar (indeed possibly a gifted schoolboy, but his identity is now irrecoverable) had produced a brief five-act comedy in prose entitled *Formicone*, which was performed by his comrades in the flourishing humanist school of Francesco Vigilio.[11] The author called himself Publio Philippo Mantovano. The performance was arranged for the Marchioness Isabella d'Este, who took a close interest in the school's activities and was already establishing herself as an intelligent patroness of artistic, scholarly and literary activity. *Formicone* enacts a story taken from Book IX of Apuleius' *Golden Ass*, in which a young man just manages to escape punishment and disaster, having arranged a night of love with the concubine of a very jealous elderly merchant. Formicone himself is the merchant's slave, who gets bribed and blackmailed into helping the deception. The play is brief by later standards (and by modern standards), but economically written, with a good eye both for pantomime caricature and for the kind of inconsequential delays which can add comic spice to a scene. Perhaps its most important lesson for Ariosto, though, if he took note of it, was the fact that it is written in prose, and is thus able to model itself both on the rapidity of Plautus and on the sharp colloquial verbal style which had already established itself in the Italian prose *novella*. Although there was still a strong feeling that verse was 'normal' for the theatre, it seemed that prose was a better guarantee of liveliness in performance when enacting this new kind of story where fast intrigue, together with plentiful quick-fire jokes, were ultimately more important than poetic or rhetorical elaboration. There may be a case for stating that in these early years a distinction was made between two versions of a play script – a more workaday (prose?) one for actual performance, and a more respectable literary (verse?) one for publication and private reading.[12] Isabella d'Este, whose impatience with the laborious verse translations has already been noted, is known to have preferred prose even for reading purposes,[13] and her preference may well have been influential on 'Publio Philippo' and subsequently on Ariosto.

Ariosto's first original comedy, *La cassaria*[14] ('The Play of the Strongbox', using a linguistic formula common in Plautine titles) was produced in the Ferrarese court for the carnival of 1508 – the Duke by this time being Isabella's brother Alfonso I. In neighbouring Mantua, Isabella was regularly informed by the courtier Bernardino Prosperi about events and celebrations back home, and his account of this seminal occasion is worth quoting at some length:

On Monday night the Cardinal had one [a comedy] performed which was composed by Messer Ludovico Ariosto of his household, translated into the form of a *barzeleta* or *frottola*, which from start to finish was as elegant and pleasing as any I ever saw done, and was greatly commended. The story was a very good one about two men in love with two courtesans who had been brought by a pimp to Taranto, and it was filled with many devices and deceits, surprising twists and fine moralities, not half of which can be found in Terence's plays . . . The best part of all these plays and festivals has been the scenery in which they have been performed, which was by one master Peregrino [Pellegrino da Udine], a painter employed by his Lordship – there is a road and a perspective of a town with houses, churches, belfries and gardens. A person cannot tire of looking at it, for the variety of things depicted there, all cleverly contrived and well planned, and I think that it will not be wasted but they will keep it to use on other occasions.[15]

The significance of these remarks is multiple. Prosperi (in my view) simply made a mistake about the verbal form of Ariosto's comedy. He expected it to be in verse, because plays always were – not being able to detect a regular metre, he assumed it must be the irregular *frottola* format with lines of varied length which the *giullari* so often used in their virtuoso patter.[16] But his enthusiasms are ultimately more important than his mistakes. To start with, this is the first time that so much has been said about a play itself, rather than its trappings, and it tells us that from the start Ariosto's text made more impression than any translation had done previously. At the same time we must observe that in a passage not quoted here Prosperi continued to pay due attention to the *intermezzi*, which included a dance of supposedly drunken cooks, girded with pots and pans and beating time with wooden spoons. The visual trappings, moreover, are important to us as well as to Prosperi, because he seems to be describing the first appearance of a scenic backcloth painted in full perspective, which was eventually canonized as standard practice for productions of classical-style comedy by Sebastiano Serlio in his *Secondo Libro di Perspettiva* of 1545. In Serlio's definitive version, the backcloth in the centre had practicable houses as wings on either side. Ariosto's play, like most of the genre, requires entrances and exits through front doors, as well as along the street.

The skills involved in perspective painting were not new in 1508: they had been current for a good seventy years. There are many Italian paintings from the fifteenth century in which scenes full of drama are portrayed in an urban street painted in perspective. To our eyes now, these already look like a stage set with characters in front of it. But the excitement of the Ferrarese audience seems to show that perspective had not, to their knowledge, actually been used on stage before. A humanist archaeologist would never have thought of it, since it played no part in ancient Roman theatres. It was clearly the initiative of a professional painter, of Pellegrino da Udine himself, a logical experiment with existing techniques which was bound to be tried sooner or later. There is, however, a twofold coincidence. On the one hand, the first perspective set coincides neatly with the first full-length original *comedia* in Italian. More importantly, perspective illusion as such coincides with and even

reinforces everything which was innovatory about the new dramatic mode – its setting in a street outside houses, its unchanging
fictional time and place, its whole status as 'overheard' drama with
a well-defined dramatic space of its own. Perspective was an
up-to-date visual resource which harmonized with ancient comic
forms, but lifted them out of their status as museum pieces because it
was an achievement of the Renaissance period itself. It must have
been crucial in persuading the courtiers that this might after all be a
theatrical form of and for their own time; and Prosperi's prediction
that it would be 'used on other occasions' was perceptively
accurate.

In terms of plot, *La cassaria* does not stray very far from Plautine
models. The version which was published is set, not in Taranto as
Prosperi remembered, but in the Greek town of Metellino (perhaps
intended as the contemporary Italian colony in the Levant, rather
than the Mytilene of antiquity[17]), as Plautine comedy was normally
set in Athens. Two young men wish to buy two slave-girls from a
pimp, so as to have them as their own concubines rather than let
them be forced into indiscriminate prostitution – a conventional use
of Roman social patterns which was much less plausible in the
sixteenth century. Their slaves or servants launch a number of
crooked devices to extract money from the pimp himself or from the
young men's fathers, and after a series of cliff-hanging deceptions
and disguises all ends in triumph for the lovers and forgiveness for
the slaves.

In this play, then, the plot lagged behind the scenery in terms of
recognizable relevance to the contemporary world. But Ariosto
perhaps observed the success of his designer and understood its
implications. The following year, 1509, he came up with a second
comedy, *I suppositi* ('The Substitutes'), which was eventually translated into English as *The Supposes* by George Gascoigne and furnished the sub-plot of Shakespeare's *Taming of the Shrew*.[18] The most
obvious step forward, as was duly noted by Prosperi in another letter
to Isabella, was that it was placed in a modern setting, in contemporary Ferrara itself. This being so, the anachronistic aspects of
Plautus and Terence had to go: there could be no more pimps with
virgin slave girls to sell. In *I suppositi* the hero is a travelling student
of good family who falls in love with a respectable Ferrarese girl. In
order to get into her house he exchanges identities with his own
servant, gets employed by the girl's father, and seduces her after

revealing his true identity. All this happens before the play starts. The single day's action of the comedy includes making a stranger impersonate the young man's father, the immediate arrival (as in Shakespeare) of the real father, and a series of frenetic crises involving also a foolish old lawyer and a parasite. In the end, the young man's identity, respectability and cash supply are established, and so he is permitted to regularize his liaison and marry the girl. There were, of course various musical *intermezzi*, culminating in a ballet scene in which Vulcan and his Cyclops mimed beating out arrow heads in their forge, walloping with hammers and shaking the bells on their legs in time to the music.

The plot of *I suppositi* is still full of Classical borrowings: the identity swaps recall Plautus' *Captivi* and Terence's *Eunuchus*. But the main story of illicit seduction being regularized by marriage has something about it of the medieval *novella*, and thus represents a pattern of sexual intrigue far more familiar to a courtly audience.[19] In only his second attempt Ariosto had brought Classical *comedia* up to date, providing a story with Boccaccian overtones which first exalts the anarchic demands of the flesh and then reconciles them to the restraints of society. In addition, placing the action in the audience's home town allowed for a number of topical and even mildly satirical references, not only to the courtiers themselves (in the Prologue) but to general conditions of travel and the arrogance of minor public officials. In private theatre, where most of the spectators know most of the actors personally, such references are always greeted with particular delight (as nowadays in a show put on by and for a small community or club); and the evocation of shared knowledge is probably a more important aim than real satire. And there is one other characteristic moment which underlines how much the audience valued a sense of cosy continuity. In Act II, Scene 2, in a superfluous throwaway comment, an unnamed servant is made to ask: 'Do you want me to pretend to be dumb, like I did that other time?' The 'other time' was last year's production of *La cassaria* for the same audience, when the actor concerned must have played the part of Trappola – a character who, in Act IV, Scene 7 of that first play, did indeed act the mute in a desperate attempt to get out of trouble. The 'dumb scene' must have tickled the audience's fancy enough for Ariosto to want to remind them of it – another useful indication that his very first script had achieved genuine theatrical success.

ARIOSTO'S DRAMATURGY

Ariosto eventually redrafted both *La cassaria* and *I suppositi* into verse, in editions which were printed after his death (in 1546 and 1551 respectively). His later comedies, starting with the first version of *Il negromante* drafted in 1520, are also in his rather unusual metre of unrhymed *endecasillabi sdruccioli*. (This is an Italian equivalent of English blank verse, but with the oddity that the lines all end with the dactylic rhythm – *préndere, útile, medésimo* – which takes some effort to sustain in Italian.) He seems in the end to have been determined about this choice, and to have believed that he was getting as close as was possible to the metres of Roman comedy. It may even be the case that the prose drafts of the first two plays were meant for actors only, and never intended to be published. In that case it would be ironic that these perhaps grudging prose versions established a norm for the overwhelming majority of subsequent Italian comedies in the 'erudite' vein; and that Gascoigne's 1566 translation of *I suppositi* performed a similar function by introducing prose on to the English stage for the first time. (*I suppositi* also found three French translators between 1545 and 1594;[20] and was the first 'new' Italian comedy known to have been performed in Spain – at Vallalodid in 1548.[21])

The need for prose, to reproduce the rapid flexible dialogue of the Roman models, arose from the relatively fluid nature of native Italian verse. An attempt to split it into more than two pieces is liable to leave it with no audible metric identity at all. An awareness of this fact may have lain behind the turgid caution of the fifteenth-century translators. The use of prose eliminated the problem at once; and the only inhibition against it was the desire to make the published text of a *commedia erudita* look as much as possible like one of the new printed texts of Terence, in order to establish its humanist (and therefore essentially literary) credentials. Eventually Ariosto was to attack the problem in his verse comedies, take more risks in dividing lines between several speakers, and perhaps hope (with a certain justice) that the unusual cadence of the *sdrucciolo* ending would influence the verse as a whole into being more emphatically rhythmic. Even his best efforts, however, show that it was hard work, and the resulting texts have to sacrifice comic colloquialism without achieving anything much like poetry in compensation. In the two earliest comedies, on the other hand, working without any previous models except the half-transformed Roman ones in his head (and perhaps Publio Philippo's relatively sketchy *Formicone*), he managed remarkably often to produce workmanlike comic dialogue for the stage.

As a first example, let us consider an early scene of *La cassaria*, where Ariosto has to tackle the common problem of explaining a fairly complicated intrigue to the audience without losing the comic pace. Erofilo is the nervous, wimpish young master, who wants to acquire his mistress from the villainous pimp but has no idea how to go about it; Caridoro is his young friend, in an identical position; Volpino ('Foxy') is the crafty servant who provides the traditional motor to drive the plot.

VOLPINO: ... Now listen what I want us to do. I've just come across a great friend of mine, a servant of the Sultan's Mamelukes, who's come here to Metellino to do a job for his master. He's never been here before, and I don't think there's a soul who knows him. I spent a lot of time with him in Cairo, about a year ago when I went there with your father and we stayed more than two months; and he's due to leave town at dawn tomorrow.

EROFILO: What's this friend of yours got to do with us?

VOLPINO: I'll tell you now, listen. I want to dress this fellow up as a merchant: I'll get some of your father's clothes. He's got an impressive look about him, and on top of that I'll fit him out so that no one will doubt, looking at him, that he's in business on a big scale.

EROFILO: Go on.

VOLPINO: So this bloke, dressed up like that, will go and see the pimp, and have that chest you've got hold of brought along, and leave it with the pimp as security.

EROFILO: Security?

VOLPINO: So he can take charge of the girl.

EROFILO: And where does he leave this security?

VOLPINO: With the pimp.

EROFILO: With the pimp?

VOLPINO: Until he gets the payment for your Eulalia.

EROFILO: You really mean leave it with the pimp?

VOLPINO: The chest, yes: and he gets given the female, and he brings her to you.

EROFILO: Well, I get the point, but I don't like it ...

VOLPINO: Then I want us all to go ...

EROFILO: I've heard enough of this. Are you really saying I should leave goods of that value in the hands of a pimp who'll just skip off with it?

VOLPINO: I've thought of all that – listen.

EROFILO: There's nothing to listen to. It's too risky.

VOLPINO: It's not, if you'll listen a moment. We'll easily be able ...

EROFILO: Easily be able to what?

VOLPINO: If you won't listen, then it's your loss. I'm crazy to waste my time.

CARIDORO: Let him finish.

EROFILO: Go on, then ...

VOLPINO: I'm damned if I'm going to bother ...

CARIDORO: Don't go, Volpino, he'll listen. Come on now, give him a chance.

EROFILO: All right. What is it that you're proposing?

VOLPINO: What's that? 'What is it that I'm proposing?' You've been begging, pleading and pestering me, night and day, to find a way for you to get hold of this girl. I've come up with a hundred ways, and you don't like any of them: one's too difficult, another's too dangerous, this one's too complicated, that one's too obvious. You're not making sense: you will and you won't, you want it and you don't know what it is. Look, Erofilo, believe me, you can't bring off anything worth while without effort and without risk. Do you think that if you just beg and plead and moan enough, the pimp will hand her over?

EROFILO: But I still think it's idiotic to take such a big risk with such a valuable property. You know as well as I do, that chest is stuffed full of rolled gold, you'd be lucky to buy it for two thousand ducats. And it's not ours, it belongs to Aristandro, my father's looking after it for him. This isn't a pair of shears to fleece the pimp, it's a way of fleecing us.

(*La cassaria* (prose), Act I, Scene 1)

Volpino then goes on to explain the second component of his stratagem – which involves accusing the pimp Lucrano of having stolen the trunk, and denying that it was ever left there voluntarily.

Ariosto shows here a well-developed instinct for composing dialogue which will work in performance, however uninteresting the words may be when read off the page. To a reader, Erofilo's repetitive interruptions may seem lacking in literary point, and even irritating. On stage, however, there is comic value in the scene because the behaviour of any stage character who displays increasing panic is funny in itself, and because insistent repetition of any phrase at all ('with the pimp ...') can raise a laugh almost independently of its content. Volpino's frustration at not being allowed to continue is then comic in its turn, and his longer speech towards the end of the extract becomes a stage event, an outburst to relieve tension, and no longer the sententious piece of writing which it would appear in prose narrative. In the mean time an important function has been performed for the audience. Erofilo's horror at the idea of handing over valuable property to a manifest villain, his appalled repetition of the point because he cannot believe it, has given the audience time to understand the first stage of Volpino's plan, and to digest it before he moves on to describe the rest. To spectators who had never (literally, never) had to absorb and remember a brand-new intrigue of this sort in performance conditions, such calculated help on the dramatist's part was essential: more necessary than it would become later on, when comic plots had become commonplaces and the tricks enacted fell into patterns which were by that time largely predictable.

In other cases such repetition, or the technique of spelling things out for the audience, can seem overdone, and can betray the tentative nature of these early scripts. Ariosto in 1509 was still an apprentice, who saw the basic value of repetitive inconsequence in stage farce, but lacked the experience and repertoire which would have helped him to create variations on a theme and allow scenes to take flight.

In a published script which hoped to resemble texts of Plautus and Terence, there seems to have been an unwritten law that stage directions are never included. (Medieval play texts are full of practical instructions in Latin, a fact which may have contributed to their exclusion from a genre which consciously rejected such 'plebeian' models.) When physical action, especially violent action, takes place on stage, the dramatist may not always be sure how to deal with it in the purely verbal text for publication. In the next extract from *La cassaria*, the character Trappola (Volpino's friend from Cairo, in the scene quoted above) has got hold of the girl Eulalia by deceit, and is bringing her through the streets at night to the young hero Erofilo. A gang of servants from Erofilo's house have not been informed of this plot, and do not know that Trappola is on their young master's side. They thus decide to ruin the whole plan by taking Eulalia away on their own initiative. We can guess, but are not told, that Trappola's first speech below is an aside to the audience, and the next two by Morione and Gianda are spoken out of Trappola's hearing:

TRAPPOLA: I'm still not sure whether to carry on alone, at this time of night. I didn't think that stupid fool was going to leave me in the lurch.
MORIONE: You lot hold him off with your fists and feet, and Corbachio and I will make off with the girl.

GIANDA: Come on then. Cut the cackle.

TRAPPOLA: Oh dear! What's this gang coming up behind?

GIANDA: Stop there, merchant.

TRAPPOLA: What do you want?

GIANDA: What's this piece of goods? [*i.e the girl Eulalia*]

TRAPPOLA: Stop poking your nose in. Am I supposed to pay duty on her?

GIANDA: I bet you never declared her to the customs. Where's your chitty?

TRAPPOLA: What chitty? You don't pay duty on this sort of merchandise.

GIANDA: You pay duty on everything.

TRAPPOLA: You pay tax when you make a profit. On this sort of thing you make a loss.

GIANDA: How right you are: 'cos you're about to lose her. We've caught you in the act of smuggling. Let her go.

CORBACHIO: Eulalia, come on, we'll go and find your Erofilo . . .

GIANDA: Let her go, or else I'll . . .

TRAPPOLA: Is this the way you treat foreign guests? Attack them?

GIANDA: If you don't shut up, I'll have your eyes out.

TRAPPOLA: You scum, if you think you're going to . . . Help, help!

GIANDA: Split his skull! Rip his tongue out!

TRAPPOLA: You filthy hooligans! Are you stealing my woman?

GIANDA: Let's take our leave. He can yell his head off.

TRAPPOLA: What the hell shall I do? I'll have to follow, if they kill me for it, and see where they're taking her.

GIANDA: If you don't get back there, I'll smash your ugly face into more little bits than a pane of glass. If you want to lay a complaint, come to the customs house tomorrow.

TRAPPOLA: I'm in a real mess: they've taken the woman, shoved me in the mud, torn my clothes and punched my face in. (*La cassaria* (prose), Act III, Scene 5)

The verbal accompaniments to violence ('Split his skull . . .') can presumably even at this early stage be taken as an indication to actors that they can do a certain amount of improvisation. There are, however, a number of lines in the text which performance should make redundant: 'What's this gang coming up behind?'; 'Attack them?'; 'Are you stealing my woman?'; and then Trappola's rather pedantic description of what has just happened to him, which the audience ought to be able to see for themselves. There is a certain direct imitation of Roman texts here, but it still leaves unanswered questions. Were acting and performance so tentative or stylized that a verbal commentary was really needed, to make sure the spectators understood what they had just seen? Was there some formal requirement, in the traditional etiquette of stage performance, that actions should be ritually confirmed and sealed by words? (We are dealing, after all, with a society in which the coupling of actions and statements before witnesses had an immense formal and legal part to play, in establishing what was officially true and what was not.) Or are such insertions dictated principally by literary rather than dramatic ambitions, the author having one eye from the very start on the eventual printing of the play, on establishing it in a new canon of artistic products which would embrace Latin and vernacular texts alike?

There is another type of writing which raises questions about the relationship between words and action – the kind of leisurely verbal commentary on society, morals or behaviour which neither explains nor advances the plot. It is most often conveyed either by direct monologue, or by longish set speeches from one character who is prompted or supported by another. In *I suppositi*, for example, Filogono is first seen arriving in Ferrara after a long journey; he exchanges banalities with an anonymous Ferrarese, apparently met on arrival

FILOGONO: I came as far as Ancona with some gentlemen from my own city, who had vowed a pilgrimage to Loreto; and from there to Ravenna in a boat, which was also carrying pilgrims but was not exactly comfortable. But coming from Ravenna to here, upstream against the current, was more unpleasant than the whole of the rest of the journey.

FERRARESE: And the lodgings are bad there, too.

FILOGONO: Terrible. But that's nothing compared with the trouble one gets from the pestering customs officials who operate along that route. I don't know how many times they opened a trunk I had with me in the boat, and that bag there, and emptied out everything inside, and tossed it all around. And they wanted to look inside my pouch, and even inside my clothes! Sometimes I was afraid they would flay me alive, to see if I had dutiable goods under my skin.

FERRARESE: I have heard how outrageous they can be.

FILOGONO: Well, it's absolutely true. But I'm not surprised, because anyone who wants to do a job like that is bound to be an evil-minded swine.

FERRARESE: All this past unpleasantness will just accentuate your happiness when you can relax with your son beside you. ... Why did you send him here?

FILOGONO: When he was at home, he was hot-headed and fidgety like most young men, he kept company I didn't approve of, and there wasn't a day when he didn't do something which upset me. So, not realizing

how sorry I would be later, I encouraged him to come and study in
whatever city he thought best; and so he came up here ... (*I suppositi*
(prose), Act iv, Scene 3)

A conventional mode of criticism might see this passage as filling
out the 'character' of Filogono, as well as containing at least the
potential for what Prosperi in his letter had referred to as 'fine
moralities' and what the Jacobeans would identify as *sententiae*.
However, it is doubtful whether rounded individual 'character', in a
more modern sense, was ever an aim of Italian Renaissance comedy.
Filogono's family sentiments are more likely to have interested the
1509 audience (however little they may interest us), not because
they are particular to him, but because they are common to all. His
detailing of travel arrangements which the spectators all knew very
well would be of interest precisely because they all knew them. His
sour comments on customs officials would be welcomed, not for their
novelty, but because they had been voiced or felt so often before by
those present in the hall; and the spectators would be more struck by
the simple identification of the experience than by any serious
attempt at criticism or satire. In our present culture, bombarded
incessantly as we are by clichéd verbal messages, we have to make an
effort to imagine the pleasure that could once be felt at hearing
someone give public expression, in unexciting but accurate words,
to opinions or sentiments already commonly shared. If you have
never before heard the banalities of your life represented or discussed on stage, the experience can be surprisingly satisfying.

There are implications here for the theatrical language being
used, for the relationship between the *fabula* and the spectator.
Filogono's position as a fictional father in a fictional story is almost
secondary, at this moment in the drama, to his role as spokesman for
the audience in generalizing about their lives. The drama itself,
therefore, does not remain within the self-contained 'overheard'
parameters of the new Classical mode – it is more mixed than the
purist perhaps wishes or bargains for. There is, indeed, a story being
enacted in its own terms on stage, in a fictional Ferrara which holds
the mirror up to real Ferrara: this constitutes the new Classical form
of drama, or of theatre, to which an audience in 1509 was still trying
to adapt. But for this audience, the fact of being addressed discur-
sively by one actor/character at a time is also a theatrical experience, and one which they relate to more instinctively. The *giullare*, in
this case a rather sober bourgeois *giullare*, turns his head and looks

across the footlights, saying: 'This is the way I see things – how about you?' By some modern criteria this is unsatisfactory – it threatens to be a harangue rather than an enactment, rhetoric rather than drama. But in the sixteenth century, rhetoric was precisely the kind of drama which was best understood. All scripted Italian comedies of the period will contain it in some measure. It contributed perhaps to the literary respectability of the published text; but that does not mean that audiences of the time found it, by their standards, untheatrical.

ROME AND FLORENCE

Ariosto's first two comedies were rushed into print, somewhat prematurely in his own view,[22] in anonymous editions which for convenience we date around 1510. The court of the Este dukes then went through a period of political, military and financial crisis, under increasing pressure from the fierce Pope Julius II who wanted to reabsorb Ferrara into the Papal State. There was no surplus energy for theatrical ventures for another decade or more. Ariosto's next comedy was drafted by 1520 (*Il negromante*, first version), but the new Medici Pope to whom it was offered did not get round to mounting it, and a revised version was finally produced back in Ferrara in 1528.

The period between 1508 (formation of the League of Cambrai) and 1527 (Sack of Rome) in fact included the toughest and most chaotic phases of the Italian Wars, with the destructive presence in the peninsula of French, Swiss, German and Spanish troops in various confrontations and alliances. There was no reduction in artistic activity and patronage: many of the great masterpieces of High Renaissance visual and literary art were commissioned, produced or conceived in this period. But these were durable monuments contributing to cultural politics: many states and communities, Ferrara perhaps more than most, found it harder to organize ephemeral spectacles of such an avowedly experimental nature as *commedia erudita* still seemed to be. Landmarks in the history of the genre remain rather sparse in the first quarter of the sixteenth century. Those which did emerge continued to have the heightened importance and influence of isolated pioneers, and two of them are usually credited with quality well above average.

The Duchy of Urbino was one of many semi-autonomous

territories within the State of the Church. Its court is the seed-bed and the model for Castiglione's great dialogue on social and political manners, *The Book of the Courtier*. Three separate plays were put on in Urbino in 1513, to celebrate a short-lived peace treaty. There was a schoolboy offering, of which the text has not survived but which sounds as if it was based impeccably on Roman models. The other two texts were both published soon afterwards, and are available in modern editions: Nicola Grasso's *Eutychia*,[23] and the *Calandra*[24] (in many subsequent editions, *Calandria*) of the courtier Bernardo Dovizi (1470–1520), known to all as 'Bibbiena', after his home town in the Tuscan Appenines.

Eutychia has a rather clumsy plot which, it has since been suggested, was aimed at the local audience rather than at the cosmopolitan visitors from Rome. Most readers would agree that it fails to get off the ground, but it does contain significant innovations: the use of real contemporary history to create the family separations which underlie so many conventional Roman plots; an attempt to make physical doubles the occasion of a sub-plot; a greater emphasis on the large-scale vagaries of Fortune, as opposed to the mechanical chance occurrences which interfere with trickery; and the rather cautious concession of greater dramatic interest to the female characters, still in the form of monologues rather than dramatic action or initiative. The young eponymous heroine is even allowed a fairly spirited confrontation with an impertinent boy servant.

Bibbiena's *Calandra* also uses contemporary history as an excuse for its split family intrigue, also gives weight and autonomy to its female characters, and makes the physical similarity between twins the main pretext for its comedy. Its plot is no more realistic than that of *Eutychia*, but Bibbiena (a well-known practical joker, as well as a tireless politician) had the knack of picking on the kind of implausibility which transforms into an acceptable theatrical game. Whereas Nicola Grasso's inventions are psychologically inept, Bibbiena's characters are driven by wildly exaggerated but perfectly simple urges; where Grasso's stage events are heavy and uninteresting, Bibbiena's cheerfully explode the constraints of physical or social realism, but are firmly disciplined as pieces of stage ritual. The result is an anarchic fantasy of sex and one-upmanship which was found irresistible, and the play was revived and reprinted more often than any other in the genre – twenty-six separate editions between 1521 and 1600. (Machiavelli's *Mandragola*, which will be discussed shortly, boasts fifteen printings in the sixteenth century.)

By writing a comedy of identical twins, Bibbiena might just have been imitating Plautus' *Menaechmi* – a comedy which was to become a popular source of pedestrian imitations later in the century,[25] exploiting as it does one of the simplest pleasures of stage comedy: the gleeful superiority of an audience which knows more about what is going on than the characters on stage do, and can thus enjoy their errors and confusion. Bibbiena, however, added a crucial twist by giving his twins different sexes. In a society of rigid gender roles, this provided the potent hilarity which arises from breaking taboos, as well as an increased opportunity for sheer bawdry. In *Calandra*, Santilla has disguised herself as a boy to escape the worst attentions of the Turks, who scattered her family with the capture of Modone in 1500. She has since been adopted, in her new identity as 'Lidio', by a respectable Roman family, and is increasingly embarrassed and threatened by proposals that she should marry their daughter. (No member of her host family ever appears on stage – she and her servant companions conduct their business entirely in the street.) Her twin brother, the real Lidio, is also in Rome, conducting a steamy adulterous affair with the bourgeois wife Fulvia, whom he visits conveniently disguised as a girl and calling himself 'Santilla'. The complications, arising from the fact that neither twin knows that the other is occupying the same stage, are milked by Bibbiena to the utmost, playing in particular on the lustful appetite of Fulvia, and her frustrated terror when she finds herself visited by a real girl, as opposed to a boy in girl's clothes. (She has been employing a phoney magician, thinks that his spell has worked all too well, and pleads with him to 'restore the knife to her sheath'.) Fulvia's husband Calandro, an archetypal credulous booby, has meanwhile fallen in lust with the false 'Santilla', and a number of scenes are devoted to getting as much fun as possible out of him and his ludicrous capacity for being deceived. The chief architect of the japes and games is Fessenio, allegedly servant in the household of Calandro and Fulvia, but really Lidio's man planted there for the purpose.[26] The plot strands are thus multifarious and unfocussed; but when Fulvia is threatened with being exposed to her brothers as an adulterer, she is saved by a quick substitution, the twins having meanwhile finally identified each other. The triumphant solution of this manufactured crisis is the concealment of the adultery, the establishment of Calandro in the audience's eyes as a rubber-stamped cuckold – and, rather briefly and cynically, the marriage of Santilla to Fulvia's son and of Lidio to the daughter of Santilla's previous hosts. Neither of these spouses of convenience ever appear on stage.

The twin emphases of *Calandra* are on a rather mechanical sexual hedonism, and on the merciless exploitation of Calandro as the world's biggest sucker.[27] Both elements would recall Boccaccio's *Decameron*, in a social world where that book was a comic and narrative commonplace. Bibbiena quite deliberately played up the similarity: his gullible Calandro is a version of Boccaccio's Calandrino (*cf.* Chapter 1 above, pp. 18–20), and there is a calculated tendency in the longer speeches to lift whole sentences from the *Decameron*'s more memorable paragraphs, opting thus for a verbal style which was literary and mannered even in 1350, rather than for the contemporary speech of 1513. (In shorter exchanges, where there is no room for Boccaccio's rhythms to be deployed, the tempo is much sharper and the tone more colloquial.) Bibbiena is being open and almost polemical in this strategy of imitation.[28] To fellow dramatists he is pointing out that Boccaccio is an important source of comic material, perhaps felt to be more contemporary than Plautus and Terence. To his immediate audience he is showing that the new mode of comic theatre is not as bewildering or difficult as they thought: the familiar verbal rhythms will reassure them that this is simply a Boccaccio-style intrigue which they can watch performed on stage, rather than have read to them.

A comedy which ends in the triumph of adultery, and therefore in the victory of immorality over social norms, could perhaps be justified by the spirit of carnival, and perhaps also by the established literary models of Boccaccio and other *novella* literature. It had, we would say, to belong clearly in the realm of fiction rather than fact – if, that is, it was going to draw merry laughter from an audience which included patriarchal males, all ultra-sensitive to the shame which could come upon them from misbehaviour among their own womenfolk. Such tolerance reveals a level of sophisticated confidence which was not in fact destined to last, and later in the century such plots found much less favour. Even in these first two decades there were those who recognized that the relationship between carnival humour and social morality was not simple. Castiglione's *Book of the Courtier*, a dialogue imagined as taking place in 1507, has Bibbiena himself as the courtier entrusted with explaining the roles of verbal humour and of practical jokes in upper-class social intercourse (Book II, chapters 45–95). Late in this discussion, stories from Boccaccio appear as examples alongside real tricks played by or on Bibbiena. To crown a complicated argument about what is acceptable and what is not (in real life or in literature? by now it is not clear, and both may be intended), a contrast is made between two Boccaccio stories. In Day III, Novella 6, a man named Ricciardo Minutolo tricks a virtuous wife into committing adultery with him, deceiving her into thinking she is lying with her husband. In Day VII, Novella 7, a much more typical story, we have a certain Beatrice duping her husband into becoming a cuckold, and getting him soundly beaten into the bargain. Bibbiena is made by Castiglione to draw a distinction: the first story is unacceptable, and the second one more tolerable, 'for Ricciardo, by means of a trick, violated the woman and made her do of herself something she had no wish to do, whereas Beatrice tricked her husband in order to do of her own free will something she wished' (trans. George Bull). It is useful to note that this moral distinction was perceptible around 1510, because it lies at the heart of our own possible reactions to the next major comedy in chronological sequence.

In republican and individualistic Florence, there was no princely court in which to experiment with avant-garde humanist theatre, particularly before the Medici restoration of 1512–13. Florentine drama early in the century tended to be cautious about *commedia erudita*, and a number of texts survive[29] which, while sometimes in five acts and with classical overtones, still retain more moralistic symbolism than secular mimicry, perhaps showing a reluctance to abandon this city's very craftsmanlike achievements in religious drama (*sacre rappresentazioni*). Lorenzo di Filippo Strozzi (1482–1549) wrote three five-act comedies in blank verse which are without doubt secular and 'erudite', and two of which have been tentatively dated 1506 (on very thin evidence) and 1518.[30] But information about any performances is scarce, and none of the three ever got into print. There is some uncertainty also about the date of *La mandragola* ('The Mandrake')[31] of Niccolò Machiavelli (1469–1527), now usually given also as 1518. But we do know that it was performed (perhaps more than once) in a private house,[32] for what amounted to a literary and social club – an audience which may well have had no women in it at all. It was printed three times in the 1520s, and innumerable times thereafter to the present day; and it has become by far the best known and most translated of all the comedies written in sixteenth-century Italy. Whether it really

typifies *commedia erudita* is debatable: it might be easier to argue that
its content and dramaturgy are exceptional, in both their qualities
and their possible defects.[33]

The play's first exceptional quality is its sheer single-mindedness.
It deals with the successful attempt of young Callimaco, aided by
the parasite Ligurio and a corrupt friar, to get into bed with
Lucrezia, wife of a foolish old lawyer named Nicia who vies in
archetypal credulity with Bibbiena's Calandro. Nicia is persuaded
(taking Callimaco for a medical man) that his and Lucrezia's failure
to have a child can be cured by an infusion of mandrake root.
However, the potion is said to have an unfortunate side-effect: it is
likely to kill the first man who has relations with the woman after she
has drunk it. The solution would seem to be to pick up a passing
vagabond (Callimaco again, of course), force him into bed with
Lucrezia for a night, and then abandon him to his own devices. The
predictably Boccaccian outcome is that Lucrezia quietly accepts
'Doctor' Callimaco as protector and friend of the family for the
foreseeable future, with her husband's excited consent. This intrigue
is pursued by Machiavelli with swift, practical economy. Most
unusually for classical comedy, Fortune (or coincidence) does not
once intervene to threaten or frustrate the plan, which therefore
appears as a text-book example of successful human ingenuity.
Equally untypically, there are hardly any minor characters, no
sub-plots, no leisurely passages of rhetoric or humour, no padding or
one-line 'jokes' (except for a brief scene in Act III between the friar
and one of his female parishioners, which may have a topical value
now lost to us). The only relative indulgences are some monologues,
which can be seen as relating strictly to the intrigue itself, or to
characters' motivation, or to a general picture of social and religious
corruption.

Can the word 'corruption' seriously be applied to this kind of
carnival romp, to the wish-fulfilling fantasy whereby the flesh
triumphs (but on stage, in fiction only) over a puppet husband who
exists only to be a victim? In relation to most *Decameron* stories, or to
Calandra, the term would seem unsuitably pompous; but with *La
mandragola* we are not so sure. The whole surface dynamic of the
action seems indeed to invite us to glory in the victory of the astute
over the foolish – it is a dynamic which in 1518 could not yet call
upon a theatrical tradition, but which the established model of the
novella seems to make automatic, irresistible. Callimaco, Ligurio and

Fra Timoteo may not be estimable characters, but Nicia always stands out below them in his callous or obtuse willingness to murder a stranger in order to procreate an heir. Fra Timoteo shows himself willing to procure an abortion (that is, to commit murder, according to Church doctrine) as well as to arrange adulteries; and his casuistry in persuading Lucrezia to sin (Act III, Scene 11) is a violence done to theology and morality. However, we have already proposed (Chapter 1) that earlier societies were capable of laughing in contempt, and that religious drama sanctified a pattern whereby a sinner may be punished by a devil, both being the object of derision. So we may be invited to laugh at practically everyone on stage, in a spirit of moralistic rejection. Alternatively, the dramatist and his audience may have decided to prefer the delights of the flesh to the claims of religion, and to push carnival to the level of near blasphemy: the final ritual of the play is not a marriage but an outrageous 'churching' ceremony, in which Lucrezia is purified in advance for the birth of the child conceived (we assume) in adultery.[34] On this second interpretation the comedy may be disturbingly strong for some stomachs, but would still present its outcome as a victory for sexual and sensual instinct – to be approved in this case, rather than condemned.

The question is whether the heroine herself sees things that way; and to that question the script as it stands does not give a clear answer. Lucrezia only appears in three scenes. In Roman comedy, young heroines, especially respectable ones, were kept off stage by social propriety; and Italian humanist drama showed similar inhibitions at first, perhaps also influenced by lack of confidence that such parts could be properly played by male actors. (We have seen that the two Urbino plays were the earliest to break this mould.) Machiavelli's Lucrezia starts with a longish speech to her mother, making it clear that both adultery and murder are repugnant to her. She then has seven short speeches of virtuous bewilderment in Act III, faced with the grotesque persuasions of Fra Timoteo. She emerges in Act v after her overnight conversion, and has eight even briefer speeches which show that her submissiveness to her husband has gone, but tell us little else about her feelings. The only thing we are sure of is that she started by wanting to be chaste, and in no way colluded with Callimaco, and so what has been practised on her is effectively rape. The story is subject, in fact, to the same objections as were made in *The Book of the Courtier* to *Decameron* III, 6. This

Lucretia, unlike the exemplary Roman one well known from Livy, accepts her rape and succumbs – but in what spirit? Callimaco, recounting what happened in Act v, Scene 4, naturally thinks that he has initiated her into unimagined sexual pleasure. But he does not actually quote her as saying so. The only words which he quotes from her, behind her back, are as follows:

> Since your cunning, my husband's stupidity, my mother's simple-mindedness and my confessor's villainy have led me to do what I would never have done on my own, then I must take it as a decree of Heaven that things must be this way, and I am not so bold as to refuse what Heaven wants me to accept. Therefore I take you for my lord, master and guide: I want you to be my father, my protector, and all the good I possess [*ogni mio bene*]; and what my husband wanted for one night, I want him to have for ever …

Between these words and her brusque utterances at the end, there is no textual way of deciding whether Lucrezia is indeed joyfully liberated into sensuality. There are other ways of interpreting her transformation in the final scene, in which the one thing which *is* clear is that she has stopped being supine and started ordering her husband about. She could be grimly resigned and revengeful; or adopting a personality imposed by events, and by what she regards as authority. All we can say is that if we are expected to rejoice with her, Machiavelli has been inefficient about making the fact clear on paper. (It could, of course, have been transparently obvious in production.) It seems more likely that the violence done to her chastity is recognized as evil, in the eyes of real society. This does not necessarily involve Machiavelli and his possibly all-male audience in any pro-feminist sympathy for her as an individual character. An unsympathetic but not implausible reading of the play would have her represented, through contemptuous masculine eyes, as female and therefore infinitely malleable. The corruption of her innocence would in this reading still be deplorable – but because of its attack on patriarchal property and honour values, rather than because Lucrezia personally may find it hateful. At all events, the word 'corruption' can have a case made for it, and the comedy thus contains a tension between its surface structure of carnival hedonism and some more serious, sour-tasting implications about contemporary society. This ambiguity, this greater density, may justify the superior status conferred on the work by critics over the years. One is inclined to suspect as well, though, that it has been interpreted over-subtly at times, and had too much read into it, just because it was written by a major political thinker and star of the Italian Renaissance.

In addition to a straight translation of Terence's *Andria*,[35] Machiavelli produced one other comedy, *Clizia*,[36] which was first printed in 1537, ten years after its author's death. It was performed in the house of the Falconetti family in Florence on 13 January 1525, to welcome Jacopo di Filippo home from exile. It is not clear whether such private performances could ever afford expensive *intermezzi*; but we know that the scenery was designed by a prestigious artist, Bastiano da Sangallo, and that madrigals were composed by the Fleming Philippe Verdelot to be sung, probably between the acts, by a female singer much in vogue, Barbara Raffacani Salutati. As a female who exhibited herself in public, 'Barbara Fiorentina' had a *demi-mondaine* status in society. The fifty-six-year-old Machiavelli was known to be besotted with her. This gives a personal twist to the plot of *Clizia*, which otherwise would appear as a reworking of Plautus' *Casina*. It concerns a middle-aged gentleman, Nicomaco (NICColò MAChiavelli?): he is determined to possess a young orphan girl who is a ward of his family, and he therefore intends cynically to marry her to the servant Pirro who has agreed to concede conjugal rights to his master. But Nicomaco is rival to his own son Cleandro, who wants to marry Clizia; and his resourceful wife Sofronia is determined to nip the whole family scandal in the bud. She achieves this by 'marrying' Pirro to a boy servant in disguise. Nicomaco's attempt to usurp the wedding night is thus so humiliating that he comes to his senses, and family order is restored. However, Sofronia has not acted in the name of her son's youthful passion – she intended the fatherless girl to make a respectable but modest marriage to the bailiff (*fattore*) of the family farm. It is only when, in traditional fashion, the girl's lost father turns up to establish her acceptable parentage that Cleandro is allowed to have her. Sofronia has acted implacably in the name of conventional family values – honour and property once again. Clizia, whose personal destiny is at stake, never once appears on stage. Whether or not the play has dramatic merit, it is an informative and unambiguous social document. It deals mercilessly with a type of deviant who was always regarded with contempt – the man of mature years who allows his patriarchal dignity to be disturbed by sexual passion. The fact that Machiavelli was turning these guns on himself, with his mistress taking part in the performance, must have made for a fascinating social and theatrical event in Palazzo Falconetti, in 1525.

The year of Machiavelli's last comedy was the year of Pietro Aretino's first – *La cortigiana*, presented in Rome. We can see Aretino as the beginning of something new, and he belongs to a new chapter; as do the original experiments of Angelo Beolco ('Ruzante') in Venice and Padua, starting around 1521. Otherwise, the tally of *commedia erudita* which reached print before the Sack of Rome only needs to have added to it two anonymous pieces of dubious competence and no known theatrical history: *Floriana* (in verse) and *Aristippia* (in prose). There were also a few comedies which were never published: the two by Lorenzo Strozzi already alluded to (*Commedia in versi*, and *La Pisana*), and an untitled comedy which has since been called *Il geloso*, also in verse, transcribed as early as 1520 in Venice and tentatively attributed to a Francesco Serleone.[37]

THE COMIC TEXT: BIBBIENA AND MACHIAVELLI

Comedies are composed to instruct and to entertain their audience. It is very instructive for anyone, especially for young people, to be shown the avarice of an old man, the frenzy of a lover, the deceits of a servant, the gluttony of a parasite, the wretchedness of a poor man, the ambition of a rich one, the flatteries of a prostitute, and the faithlessness of men at large: and comedies are full of examples of all these things, all of which can be shown on stage with perfect propriety. But in order to entertain people, one has to make them laugh, which cannot be done by keeping one's speeches solemn and decorous; because the words that make people laugh have to be either silly or insulting or amorous. It is necessary therefore to represent silly, slanderous, or love-sick characters; and therefore comedies which are full of these three qualities are full of laughter, whereas those which do not have them will not manage to provoke any laughs at all.

Since our author, therefore, does indeed want to entertain his audience and make them laugh from time to time, and since he has introduced no idiots into this play and given up insulting people, he has been obliged to have recourse to people in love, and to the situations which love intrigues can produce. If, in dealing with these matters, something not quite decent should appear, it will be said in such a way that the ladies can hear it without blushing.

This piece of comic theory comes from the Prologue to Machiavelli's *Clizia*. In the forefront of the dramatist's mind may have been the problem of presenting to a mixed audience a description of the abortive wedding night between Nicomaco and the boy

Siro. He is led to express a general view of comedy as moral instruction, which assumes that what we laugh at always falls below
acceptable standards of behaviour – words 'either silly or insulting
or amorous' ('o sciocche, o ingiuriose, o amorose'). It is a 'punitive'
theory of laughter, such as we discussed in Chapter 1. In the
absence, as yet, of any contemporary theoretical canon, Machiavelli
must have formulated it spontaneously – influenced no doubt by
Classical theory and practice, but also responding to the existing
social instincts of himself and his audience.[38] *Clizia* itself is a text
dedicated to bringing the deviant back into line by means of
mockery: the audience could sympathize unashamedly with the
trickster Sofronia, because her trick was played in a good cause. In
La mandragola the position is more complex and problematic; but it is
equally true that the laughter inspired, sour as it may be, arises from
the discrepancy between enacted behaviour and moral or intellectual norms. Nicia is picked on because he is both immoral and
stupid: our problem of interpretation arises because we are not sure
whether spectators who side against him with Callimaco and Fra
Timoteo are doing so in the name of morality or of sexual hedonism.

In the case of Bibbiena's *Calandra*, most readers will be in no
doubt that the pleasure principle rules. Calandro, like Nicia, is on
stage to give the audience the delight of feeling superior, of deriding
him in the full sense of the word. The tricks played on him have no
claim to reimpose morality – quite the reverse. To take the side of
Fessenio, Lidio and the charlatan Ruffo is to give ourselves a
carnival holiday from normal restraints. But if in this respect
Machiavelli and Bibbiena seem to be pulling in opposite directions,
they have in common the use of derision as the basic source of
laughter. The energy put into mocking the losers outweighs any
attempt to make the winners attractive. Even young lovers, traditional objects of sympathy in a more romantic mode of comedy, are
treated either satirically or with minimal attention. Readers of
English drama will perhaps have in mind, as points of reference for
Renaissance comedy, *Twelfth Night* and *As You Like It*. In early
commedia erudita they will find Sir Toby and Malvolio, Audrey and
Sir Oliver Martext, caricatured versions of Orsino and Olivia, – but
no Viola, no Orlando and Rosalind. Those who appreciate Jonson
as opposed to Shakespeare will find themselves more at home; and
indeed a case could be made for paralleling the ambiguous strategies
of *La mandragola* with those of *Volpone*.

When it comes to the methods by which characters are derided on stage, there is again a marked separation between the two authors, a difference of approach which was to be of some significance for the future development of the genre. Let us consider an early scene from *Calandra*, between the servant Fessenio and his idiotic master. They are discussing a 'Santilla' who, as Fessenio and the audience know, is really Lidio disguised as a girl.

FESSENIO (*alone*): Now I see that gods have a sense of humour, just like mortal men. Here is the god of Love, who usually entraps only noble and courteous hearts; and now he has entered into that bleating ninny Calandro, and refuses to budge. Cupid must have time on his hands if he is willing to penetrate such an utter baboon. I suppose he wants Calandro to stick out amongst real lovers like a cart-horse among the thoroughbreds. And look whose hands he's made him fall into – mine! Talk about a lamb to the slaughter!

CALANDRO (*entering*): O, Fessenio, Fessenio!

FESSENIO: Who's that calling? Oh it's you, boss.

CALANDRO: Have you seen Santilla?

FESSENIO: I have.

CALANDRO: What do you think of her?

FESSENIO: You've got good taste. I can't imagine a more exquisite apparatus – she must be the daintiest dish that never existed. You must do everything possible to get her.

CALANDRO: I'll have her, even if it means going naked and barefoot.

FESSENIO (*aside to audience*): Eloquent words, worthy of a true lover.

CALANDRO: If I ever get my hands on her, I'll eat her whole.

FESSENIO: Eat her? Oh, ha ha ha, Calandro, have pity on her! Wild beasts eat other beasts – men don't eat women. It's true you can drink women, but you can't eat them.

CALANDRO: What? You drink them?

FESSENIO: You drink them, that's right.

CALANDRO: How do you do that?

FESSENIO: Don't you know?

CALANDRO: Not at all.

FESSENIO: Oh dear! Such a splendid potent fellow, and he doesn't know how to drink women!

CALANDRO: Can't you teach me? Please?

FESSENIO: I'll tell you, then. When you kiss her, don't you suck?

CALANDRO: Yes.

FESSENIO: And when you drink something, don't you suck that too?

CALANDRO: Yes.

FESSENIO: Well then! Whenever you're kissing a woman, and you suck, you're drinking her up.

CALANDRO: I suppose that's right. It must be right ...! (*Calandra*, Act I, Scene 7)

This is one of a number of scenes in which Fessenio, in leisurely dialogue, gets Calandro to believe any fantasy which comes into his head, and winks at the audience as he displays the man's credulity. Later, in order to get him transported in a box to 'Santilla''s house, he sells him stories about being able to dismantle his own body, or die and come to life at will; and he commits ludicrous physical assaults on his master, to test each theory. The structure is that of a simple variety double-act, between the clever and the stupid partner (*il furbo* and *il fesso*, in modern Italian terminology – Fessenio's name now seems inappropriate). The stupid character is steadily and implacably put down – there is none of the modern tendency (as Nino Borsellino has remarked[39]) to allow the fool to gain a paradoxical victory over the wise man. The *furbo* is totally in charge of proceedings, both within the fiction and outside it – because he is not only a fictional character but also a *giullare*, openly orchestrating the scene for the audience's benefit and even adding over-anxious asides in case they miss the point. The result is that the whole exercise is overtly theatrical, more an independent sketch than a phase in a narrative.

Machiavelli's Nicia is exposed more subtly, and more within the confines of the enacted plot. In Act I, Scene 2, he is simply allowed by Ligurio to chatter on and demonstrate his foolishness, with only the gentlest of prompts and mocking asides. Afterwards his position as a victim emerges more through action than through talk. In Act III, Scene 4 he is persuaded to pretend to be deaf, and is thus at a helpless disadvantage in the negotiations between Ligurio and Fra Timoteo: he has to listen to promises of large sums of money without daring to protest. The plot to capture the anonymous vagabond (Callimaco) has him in disguise and looking foolish, and his prurient enthusiasm for the business of putting a stranger in bed with his wife is devastating enough not to need extra theatrical emphasis. Machiavelli gives his audience the illusion, in proper humanist style, of overhearing a stupid man behaving stupidly in a real situation. Similarly Nicomaco, in *Clizia*, only becomes funny when his unsuitable amorous passion emerges in a natural situation (chiefly in Act IV, Scene 2), and when he recounts the story of his humiliation at the hands of Siro (in Act V, Scene 2). The latter scene is 'unrealistic' in the sense that Nicomaco makes too good a story of the disaster – one cannot quite imagine a man weeping with shame on the one hand, and squeezing the utmost narrative effect out of the shameful details on the other. The dramatist's desire to get a response from his audience has taken over at this point. But in general one detects in Machiavelli a great determination to stick to the rules of Classical comedy, and to tell his story via statements and actions which are mimetic of ordinary social life. The intrigue of *Clizia* is covered comfortably in Acts I, IV and V. But Acts II and III are not filled with disconnected theatrical jokes and routines. Machiavelli gives us instead a series of diplomatic skirmishes between the members of this seriously divided household, exploring on stage the different ways in which people try to persuade, evade and deceive one another. His audience may well have been fascinated by this attempt to drama- tize and typify the casual verbal fencing matches of their own ordinary lives. For Machiavelli, comedy was indeed 'an imitation of life, a mirror of manners', and this emphasis (more Terentian than Plautine) continued as a tradition in a number of subsequent comedies through the century – particularly, but not exclusively, in Florence. Not all his imitators managed the job with Machiavelli's own penetration and economy: Francesco Landi's *Il commodo*,[40] for example (performed for the Medici dukes in 1539), contains quanti- ties of unrelieved bourgeois chatter which may have held the atten- tion of its first audience, but which a modern reader finds entirely without entertainment value.

Bibbiena, on the other hand, represents an alternative view of what respectable courtiers wanted to watch. The main plot of *Calandra*, like that of *Clizia*, takes up much less than a full five acts. But Bibbiena's 'padding' consists of the whole sub-plot devoted to making a fool of Calandro, with all its attendant gags and routines. (This on the assumption that the 'main' intrigue, solved by the final dénouement, is the ultimate fate of the twins Lidio and Santilla.) In addition, Bibbiena is more inclined than Machiavelli to write scenes with a self-contained structure: formal debates, as between Lidio and his tutor in Act I, Scene 2; the numerous conversations in which Fessenio makes fun of Calandro; and the two very ritualized scenes (III, 23 and V, 1) in which the twins are both on stage together and a third character hovers and dithers at some length between them. The following scene, for example, is a brief exercise in bawdry in its own right, not remotely necessary to any strand of the plot. Fessenio is knocking at the door: Samia is inside, and has just told us that she is seizing the chance to enjoy herself with her lover.

FESSENIO: (*Knocks.*) Are you deaf in there? Hey! (*Knocks again.*) Open up! Hey! (*Knocks.*) Can't you hear?

SAMIA (*inside*): Who's knocking?
FESSENIO: It's only Fessenio. Open up, Samia.
SAMIA: Wait a minute.
FESSENIO: Why don't you open?
SAMIA: I've got to get the key into the lock.
FESSENIO: Hurry up, then.
SAMIA: I can't find the hole.
FESSENIO: Come out here.
SAMIA: Ooh! Ooooh! Ah! I can't, yet.
FESSENIO: Why not?
SAMIA: The hole's stuffed up.
FESSENIO: Blow into it, then.
SAMIA: I'm doing better than that.
FESSENIO: What?
SAMIA: I'm wiggling it about as hard as I can.
FESSENIO: What's the delay?
SAMIA: Ooooh! Ooooh! Oooooh! Praise be to the broom-handle, Fessenio,
    I've done all the necessary, and the lock is oily now, so it will open
    more easily.
FESSENIO: Open up, then.
SAMIA: That's it. Can't you hear me pulling the key out? (*Calandra*, Act III,
    Scene 10)

This scene is so self-contained that it could be used in any play; and
the same situation is in fact exploited, just as explicitly but without
the double-entendres, in Act III, Scene 10 of Alessandro Piccolomini's *L'amor costante*, first produced in Siena in 1536.

In *Calandra*, therefore we have signs of an entertainment pieced
together with the help of prefabricated structures; and such a
procedure (Plautine rather than Terentian, but endemic to comic
theatre in general) was going to be an alternative influence during
the coming century, rivalling the more sophisticated narrative and
mimetic drama which literary humanists probably preferred.
Machiavelli was a scholar, as well as a student of practical politics:
in drama he appreciated qualities which could also be associated
with non-dramatic fiction – 'literary' qualities, to use a slightly
dangerous shorthand term. Bibbiena, essentially a courtier and
politician, was more prepared to deploy 'theatrical' structures
which had immediate appeal in performance, but may inspire less
interest in a meditative reader.

Where 'literary' and 'dramatic' methods could be seen to merge,
especially in the age of humanism, was in the art of rhetoric: the
skills deployed are mainly verbal, but the aim is to persuade, move

or otherwise affect a group of listeners. The very core of humanist education (and the reason why the ruling classes embraced it so willingly) was the image of the orator, the man who by means of eloquence could bend other people to his will. In the new drama, characters could be given the opportunity to display their rhetorical skills on one another, in a good or bad cause. The most obvious example covered so far is Fra Timoteo twisting theology to persuade Lucrezia in *La mandragola*; though the simultaneous presence of Lucrezia's mother Sostrata, assaulting her daughter with arguments of a more practical type, makes this extraordinary scene fully 'dramatic' by anyone's standards. We could also draw attention to some of the dialogues in *Clizia* between members of the family who are adversaries, and the formal debate between Lidio and his tutor in *Calandra* I, 2. More congenial still, however, was the relationship created between a single actor/character and his audience, in a monologue or a set speech which is a near-monologue. The established habits of *giullare* entertainment would make courtly spectators feel very much at home with such speeches, and there would be no objection to their being fairly prolonged. In the early comedies so far discussed, monologues develop a variety of modes and purposes. They can have a practical function, as when a character active in the intrigue explains to the audience what he wants to do next, perhaps with an abundance of military metaphor based on models in Plautus. They can digress from the story to offer moral or satirical reflections, in which case they are subject to the analysis already proposed in relation to Act IV, Scene 3 of Ariosto's *Suppositi*. They can also be used for character exploration, but this is as yet more rare and does not always involve playing for sympathy. Callimaco's monologue at the start of Act IV of *La mandragola* seems to be a display of excess emotion, intended to arouse derision at the exaggerations of a typical young lover.[41] The successive monologues in *Calandra* of the sexually furious Fulvia and the more cynical Samia (Act III, Scenes 5–8) operate in the same area, though they also tease the audience more openly about the pursuit of carnival gratification in the teeth of social restraint. Only in the two Urbino plays are monologues used in the name of pathos, to invite the audience to sympathize with a character's difficulties. The real Santilla in *Calandra*, and Grasso's eponymous Eutychia, are both given the chance to inveigh against the injustices of Fortune[42] and the disadvantages of being a woman. In both cases we feel we are reading a rhetorical exercise, a series of commonplace images and *topoi* redeployed for the occasion. Once again we should observe that the dramatists saw their task as to generalize, to pinpoint precisely what might be felt and said by all languishing heroines, rather than to make them and their language startlingly individual. It is also true, though, that the speeches concerned have little influence on the overall tone of the plays. Eutychia is given her set speech, but appears very little thereafter. Santilla has more chances to lament her position, but is easily distracted into playing tricks on Fulvia and generally getting into mischief. When it comes to psychology, early Classical comedy prefers behaviourism to introspective analysis.

CHAPTER 3

The second quarter-century, outside Venice

DEMARCATIONS

Composition of 'regular' comedies (in five acts, with an urban setting and secular 'mimetic' content) had been sparse, then, in the pioneering period before the Sack of Rome. Statistics are approximate, because they depend on which criteria are adopted for the effective public appearance of a play – but a generous assessment produces only ten such comedies which eventually reached a printer (accepting that some were published *after* 1527),[1] and another four which were left in manuscript only,[2] at least until modern times. Between 1528 and 1555, Classical-style comedies total over a hundred, even excluding some shorter pieces in less than five acts, which on other grounds still seem to belong to the genre. (By 1600, the tally for the whole century is over 250.[3])

The early 1550s seem to constitute a watershed, at least in the recognition accorded to the comic playscript by printers. It must be assumed that they were responding to a demand perceived in their customers, and that comic drama had 'arrived' as a legitimate form of cultural production. Printing of comedies was very sparse in the 1530s and early 1540s. From 1545 the number of published scripts increased; and then suddenly production became systematic, with a backlog of texts performed in previous decades emerging from the presses in what we would now call retrospective editions. In 1550 the comic production to date of the Florentine Giovan Maria Cecchi was celebrated in a single collected volume printed in Venice by Giovanni Giolito – all the more significant in that Cecchi was still in full flow, with thirty more years of dramaturgy ahead of him. Two posthumous initiatives were launched, also in Venice, in 1551: Gabriele Giolito attempted a series of definitive revised versions, in single volumes, of Ariosto's comedies; and Stefano De Alessi issued, again in single volumes, most of the comedies of Angelo Beolco ('Ruzante') (which, with one exception,[4] had never previously been printed). Ariosto had died in 1533, and Beolco in 1542: both authors were to have their plays collected later in the century in single-volume anthologies.[5] Even more significant was the enterprise of Girolamo Ruscelli, who in 1554 began to produce his own choice of the best vernacular Italian comedies, in the volume entitled *Delle commedie elette nuovamente raccolte insieme, con le corettioni & annotationi di G. Ruscelli* ('Chosen comedies newly collected together, with corrections and annotations by G. Ruscelli'). It was intended to be Volume 1 of a series, and it contained Bibbiena's *Calandra*, Machiavelli's *Mandragola*, and three Sienese plays which will be discussed in this chapter: *Gli ingannati*, *L'amor costante*, and *Alessandro*. If comedies could be reissued in edited form, with textual emendations and annotations, then the genre had reached the status of 'literature' from which the best examples could be selected and presented as approved canonical models. Parallel things were occurring during the same period in respect of literary texts by other Italian authors, from the 'classic' fourteenth-century Petrarch and Boccaccio to Ariosto and other contemporary writers. This assimilation of dramatic texts to other serious works of literature was probably what the humanist authors had been aiming for all along. From their point of view it confirmed that 'regular' comedy was superior to earlier (medieval) modes and styles of composition for performance: for the modern scholar it marks an important contrast with the way in which English Renaissance drama emerged from the practical world of artisan professional theatre.[6]

In surveying this second stage of development in *commedia erudita*, various strategies could be adopted. There is the choice between a strictly chronological approach on the one hand, and on the other hand a separate assessment of what happened in each major centre of performance – given that each state or city did have a character and autonomy of its own, which in many cases its theatre aimed quite deliberately to assert. A chronological approach can be revealing, and is less often attempted; but there will emerge some special practical reasons why comic theatre in the Republic of Venice will have to be considered separately. The present chapter, therefore,

will deal with the most important events and texts outside the
Venetian Republic. The one figure of importance who (characteristically for him) cannot be so easily pinned down is Pietro Aretino,
who starts his career in this chapter and closes it in the next.

Pietro Aretino (1492–1556) was the son of a shoemaker in Arezzo,
too humble by birth even to have a proper surname – he was known
simply by his town of origin.[7] His education was elementary, and he
claimed at a late age still to be incapable of reading a Latin text.
Nevertheless he ended his life as an established member of the
otherwise aristocratic cultural élite of the Italian peninsula. He
achieved this entirely by the use of his pen, in a career which is often
compared to that of a modern-day journalist.[8] The comparison is
not always flattering. It is generally agreed that a major part of his
technique was to deploy such devastating, and sometimes scurrilous,
verbal aggression that princely and even royal patrons recognized
the necessity of keeping him on their side, or at least not on the side
of their current adversary. (The alternative response was assassi-
nation, which was tried more than once without success.) By the end
of his life he had published works ranging from religious treatises to
outright pornography: they included one stage tragedy, and five
comedies of which two will be discussed in this chapter.[9]

In the early part of his life, Aretino – like many of his social betters
such as Ariosto, Machiavelli, Castiglione and Bibbiena – had to seek
career and identity by dependence on a patron, in what was becoming a deeply hierarchical society. He was thus, in a loose sense, a
'courtier', and found himself expressing in writing – again like his
social betters – his own critical response to the frustrations of
'courtly' dependence and subordinacy.

He was in Rome, most of the time, between 1516 and 1526, under
the Medici Popes Leo X and Clement VII – first of all in the
household of the Sienese banker Agostino Chigi, and thereafter in
functions which are less clear to his biographers but which seem to
relate directly or indirectly to papal patronage. The 'court' of Rome
in this period was pluralistic and chaotic, with a large number of
conflicting power bases. At all levels there was a fierce struggle
for wealth, influence, security and protection, with 'masters' and
'servants' at all levels exploiting one another. Or at least that is the

picture which seems to lie behind the astonishing comedy *La corti-giana*, which Aretino first drafted in 1525, and which by lucky chance has survived in this first version in a single manuscript in Florence.[10] The title could mean 'The Courtesan', but is more likely to mean 'The Courtiers' Play' (along the lines of some Plautine titles, and the more recent *Cassaria* and *Calandra*): it could well involve a sarcastic dig at Castiglione's idealistic *Libro del Cortegiano* ('Book of the Courtier'), drafts of which were circulating in manu-script even though it was not published until 1528. *La cortigiana*, as we shall see, was completely rewritten for publication in 1534, by which time Aretino was settled permanently in Venice.

Aretino always adopted a combative attitude to the platitudes of official literary culture, whether these were stylized Petrarchan language (which he mocks in the prologue to *La cortigiana*) or ancient Classical models. It was an opposition based on considerable knowledge, however acquired, rather than ignorance. In 1525 he seems to have had a clear idea of what were taken to be the 'rules', as yet unformulated in print, of erudite comedy;[11] and we can assume that both his adherence to and his divergence from conventional patterns were conscious and deliberate.

La cortigiana is written in five acts and in prose; and it embraces the mimetic mode of Roman comedy – except perhaps in its ten-dency to break down barriers between actors and spectators, about which more will shortly be said. Its plot is less conventional, having nothing to do with families or marriages, not much to do with adultery until Act v, but everything to do with the particular form of dramatic contest or confrontation provided by the *beffa*, or practical joke. It has two quite separate main plots, which in the first version Aretino hardly even pretends to link together: there are two sets of characters co-existing alternately on the streets of a theatrical Rome, two plays being enacted simultaneously on one stage. On the one hand there is Messer Maco from Siena, a character so breath-takingly stupid as to enter the realm of pure cardboard fantasy, way beyond the schematic level even of Bibbiena's Calandro. He has come to Rome, presumably with plenty of money, to become a courtier – however he has no idea of what a courtier is (or a cardinal or a duke or a pope, for that matter), but is drifting in the mental world of a six-year-old for whom words have a life of their own and can be made to mean anything. He is snapped up by a painter called Maestro Andrea, who puts him through brutal physical ordeals (on the pretext that he has to be melted down by steam and remoulded into a new 'courtly' identity),[12] and plays other subsidiary tricks which lead to Maco's being chased through the streets dressed as a porter, and then driven in his shirt from the house of the courtesan Camilla Pisana. The second plot concerns Parabolano from Naples, who has recently acquired the status of a lord and thus has a string of dependants around him, of descending social rank. One of these is the Greek Rosso, who is fed up with his master's arrogance, and with his own lowly status of having to eat in the servants' kitchen (the *tinello*, which he describes at revolting length in a bravura passage, Act v, Scene 15). Parabolano is languishing with fashionable love for a noble lady, who has the suitably Petrarchan name of Laura. Rosso takes advantage of this, butters his master up (thus demoting the faithful but over-honest courtier Valerio from their master's favour), and arranges with the old bawd Aloigia to place Parabolano in a darkened room with a very plebeian baker's wife called Togna.

Despite an element of mechanical surreality (for a modern reader, it is hard not to imagine the two victims as characters in a cartoon film), these two stories could both carry a charge of satire against the Roman rat-race – against the pointless attraction of the court for an outsider like Messer Maco, against the blind arrogance and injustice with which Parabolano reacts to his arrival at the top of the ladder. In the more considered rewrite of 1534, this satire is accentuated: by then Aretino had left Rome, and could survey the place with a retrospective detachment which actually made his attack on it more forceful. In 1525, however, he was still in the thick of the very scene he was trying to describe, and its frenetic energy is part of him and of the comedy as well as being an external target. The one judgement on which all critics agree in relation to this first version, whatever different emphases they may then pursue, is its air of white-hot immediacy – the text's remarkable ability to convey, even through its many obscurities, a sense that its action springs directly from the life which its audience lives from day to day, and indeed that the distinction between stage and auditorium is very blurred. The two main tricksters of the play, Rosso and Maestro Andrea, are both documented as historically existing – Maestro Andrea was actually killed by Spaniards in the Sack of 1527. Numerous other figures referred to and not seen are also real, including well-known whores such as Camilla Pisana. The text, in fact, often becomes unmanageable for the modern reader because it is so thick with ephemeral allusions which could only make sense to its chosen audience, and because of its brilliant, nervy, elusive reflection of topical street jargon, which makes its language unlike that of any other Italian dramatist (and sets problems for a translator which are often strictly insoluble).

The play's dedication to the robust practical joke is itself a reflection of the documented tastes and activities of the Roman 'court' – it is noteworthy that Rosso's scheme is motivated by vague resentment rather than profit, and Maestro Andrea is driven by pure love of the game. When Parabolano finds out what has been done to him, he consoles himself with several similar japes which have previously made him laugh at others' expense, all seemingly taken from reality. Altogether, the play constantly gives the impression of overflowing into, or being an overflow from, the crowded street which it represents – a situation summed up by the courtier character Valerio, as he speaks the *plaudite* to the audience at the end:

VALERIO: ... Well, gang, if this story has been a long one, I'll remind you that here in Rome everything tends to drag on a bit; and if you didn't like it, that's fine by me, because I didn't ask you to come in the first place. Anyway, if you wait there until next year, you'll hear an even sillier story. But if you can't wait that long, I'll see you all at Ponte Sisto. (*La cortigiana* (1525), Act v, Scene 22)

Ponte Sisto was the area where the whores and other low life were to be found – if the spectators went there, they would find in reality more of what they had just seen enacted on stage. And the fact that we say this with such conviction is all the more notable, in that we are not sure in what circumstances or for whom the play was meant to be performed, nor whether the performance actually took place.

Aretino may have picked up some of the broader principles of Classical comedy, and he had certainly read or seen the comedies of his immediate Italian predecessors, but he was not able to read Plautus or Terence in the original. His detailed writing is thus less influenced by the Roman models, and more by existing native stage formats: the witty conversations and monologues of both popular and courtly *giullari*, and the comic routines of illiterate street theatre.[13] Both these influences make for a static structure, with a majority of scenes centring on talk rather than action: the worst physical humiliations of both Maco and Parabolano take place off stage, the pursuit of both plots is conducted in a leisurely manner, and time is constantly taken off for gossip, wit, bravura speeches, moralizing, and the occasional self-contained practical joke against figures introduced solely to be victims. There is a tendency for characters simply to talk, in monologue or dialogue, in the presence of the audience, and also to take the audience explicitly into their confidence, even with direct second-person address,[14] thus breaking the classical prohibition of 'Donatus' (see Chapter 1, pp. 27–8). However, most of what we might call the set-piece numbers take the form of a one-sided dialogue in which one character deploys most of the verbal invention and the other acts as support. (There is, for example, a scene in which Rosso expands for no particular reason on the pleasures of the tavern, with a fellow-servant as his feed man.) The play's presentation of the Roman underworld, its all-important local colour, also comes from dialogue which is in strict terms irrelevant. Here is our first meeting with Aloigia, who as well as being a bawd and go-between has been trained up by her 'mistress' in even less savoury skills:

ROSSO: Where are you off to in such a frenzy?
ALOIGIA: All over the place, trying to cope.
ROSSO: Why should you need to? It's you who run Rome.
ALOIGIA: Maybe, but I'm all taken up with my mistress's troubles.
ROSSO: What's the matter? Isn't she well?
ALOIGIA: She won't be well soon, she's been put on the Honours List: they're burning her tomorrow. Does that seem right to you?
ROSSO: Not right or just. What the hell's she being burnt for? She didn't crucify Christ.
ALOIGIA: She didn't do a thing.
ROSSO: Are they burning people now for doing nothing? It's criminal, the way they go on these days. Rome is going to the dogs, mark my words.
ALOIGIA: She drowned a little nipper for her lady friend, just out of softness of heart.
ROSSO: Is that all?
ALOIGIA: She put a spell on her cousin, as a favour to a pal.
ROSSO: That's just being polite.
ALOIGIA: She gave some poison to Georgina's husband, because he was a rotten swine.
ROSSO: His Worship can't take a joke.
                              [. . .]
ALOIGIA: Absolutely everyone used to consult her: butchers and vendors, at the market, at the docks, at the fair, at the baths, at the barber's,

at the customs house, in the tavern; law officers, cooks, messengers, priests, soldiers. She was like a female Solomon.

ROSSO: All this hanging and burning, there won't be a decent man or woman left alive. (*La cortigiana* (1525), Act II, Scene 6)

The repetitive structure, whereby Aloigia lists a series of crimes, one by one, and Rosso responds with variants on a single comment, is likely to be a format from street theatre, and we shall be examining it further in Chapters 4 and 5. In the meantime we should note Aretino's tendency to fill the stage, and his spectators' minds, with his words and what they evoke: our attention in the above passage is focussed off stage, on a character who is created entirely by words and whom we never see.

One way of responding to this tendency (and it is the core of the very subtle thesis of Giulio Ferroni, 1977) is to see a desire in Aretino that his words should take over the whole spectacle, and that the audience should ultimately relate more to the author himself, directly, than to the characters who are his puppets. In the first *Cortigiana* there are some conversations involving a courtier named Flaminio, one of Parabolano's household but not involved in the plot. These are the most overtly 'satirical' passages of the comedy, working off spleen against the indignities of courtly servitude, and they are so separate from the rest as to represent quite transparently the voice of the author.

FLAMINIO: Certainly, if our masters wanted to, they would smash the evil destiny of the people who serve them. Like the Archbishop of Ravenna did the other day, Ancona's nephew: he'd promised a benefice to that fine man Messer Ubaldino, and when it didn't work out he borrowed a thousand crowns at interest, and just gave them to him, so that Fortune should not have her way.

VALERIO: But there's only one Archbishop of Ravenna, isn't there?

FLAMINIO: That's why I'm going to take my leave, so at least I can find a master who will look me in the face once a month, and perhaps when I address him won't answer as if I'm crazy and off my head, and won't reduce me to pawning my cloak and doublet so as not to starve ... I shall go to Mantua, where His Excellency the Marquis Federico doesn't deny bread to anyone; and I'll stay there until our new Pope [Clement VII] has sorted out the affairs of the world, not just of Italy. I'm sure His Holiness will reward talent again, as his cousin Leo did before him.

VALERIO: Let's talk about it again soon: if you'll do things my way, you'll be all right. Flatter the master, and when he's in his bedroom with a

woman, or a boy, tell everyone he's saying his prayers – they all want
people to bow down before their good deeds and bad deeds alike.
You're too loose with your tongue, and you go your own way ... (*La
cortigiana* (1525), Act III, Scene 7)

The invitation to identify Flaminio with Pietro Aretino comes not
just from the comment that he is 'too loose with his tongue' – he had
in fact built great notoriety with his scurrilous satirical verses, or
pasquinades – but in the statement of intent to move to Mantua,
which is just what Aretino did shortly afterwards. Passages like this
are laden with comments reflecting the author's detailed antagon-
isms, friendships and careerist hopes: a complimentary reference
may be a return for favours given or a bait for future patronage;
while an attack, or the threat of one, might involve revenge or
blackmail. Aretino's dramatic writing accentuates from the start the
impression, common to all private or coterie theatre, that as well as
the *fabula* being narrated on stage there is quite a different drama, or
dialogue, taking place in coded messages from the author – a drama
which, for an audience fully in the know, may be more absorbing
than the story ostensibly enacted. This of course makes Aretino's
plays date very quickly – Act III, Scene 7, for example, had to be
completely rewritten for the 1534 printing, to contain a quite
different (and much longer) sequence of references to new friends
and patrons, centring on the intention of Flaminio to go to Venice
rather than Mantua.[15]

The published version of the comedy is in fact a thorough rewrite,
with hardly a line remaining exactly as in the original, though the
plot is unaltered and many jokes and expressions are retained in a
slightly different guise. A really detailed study of the changes and
their rationale remains still to be undertaken, though Paul Larivaille has given us a pertinent summary with well chosen
examples.[16] Aretino's desire simply to update the play from 1525 is
beyond dispute, and it reflects equally his wish to portray his own
new position and his need to acknowledge developments in Rome –
there are references to the Sack, even though Maestro Andrea
remains a protagonist. The satirical and adulatory passages are both
more considered and more extensive, aiming at broader targets – the
1534 version is about a fifth longer than that of 1525.[17] Larivaille
also speaks of a desire to 'improve the work on the literary and
theatrical level' (p. 127): there is more attempt to link the two main
plots together, and to involve all the chief characters in the

dénouement; and a number of scenes have arguably been given a more satisfactory rhythm, from 'an entirely verbal and gratuitous buffoon dimension' to 'a more *committed* comedy, aimed firmly at caricaturing the [Roman] setting' (pp. 125–6; Larivaille's emphasis). We can go along with this, at least until a really exhaustive comparison appears; but for the sake of our present study, another observation needs to be added.

Aretino's improvements, as Larivaille says, may be both literary and theatrical, but the introduction of any literary aims at all is significant in itself. The very fragility and elusiveness of some of the 1525 script may stem from its never having been conceived as a text for a reader – some of the apparent gaps and uncertainties would be filled in production with visual elements of costume, action and gesture already clear in the author's mind. Its quality of immediacy springs from its having been conceived exclusively for a single occasion and a single audience. When it came to recasting the whole play for a general readership, Aretino seems to have moved at least some of the way towards observing the criteria felt to be necessary for a 'regular' comedy in print. Two facts, at least, point in this direction. In the first place, the dramatist has systematically eliminated, the second time round, every verbal formulation which expresses or implies a direct communication from actor/character to audience: he has imposed the 'Donatus' prohibition in 1534 where he ignored it in 1525.[18] Secondly, one type of alteration which recurs in the 1534 version is to make characters spell out in dialogue things which an audience would be able to see – a tendency of 'Classical' dramaturgy which we discussed in Chapter 2 (pp. 44–5) in relation to *La cassaria*, iii, 5. With space at a premium, let us take a very brief example from Act ii, Scene 2 of *La cortigiana* (both versions). Messer Maco has been undergoing instruction off stage in how to be a courtier, and now Maestro Andrea presents him in ridiculous clothes to show off his new mannerisms. In the second version, the significant additions will be given in italics.

1525 version:
M. ANDREA: That outfit really suits you: you're a real paladin!
MESSER MACO: You're making me laugh, you are.
M. ANDREA: You've really remembered everything I've taught you, I hope?
MESSER MACO: I can do them all.
M. ANDREA: Do a Duke.

MESSER MACO: Like this ... like this ... this way. Hell, I've fallen over.
M. ANDREA: Get up again, you booby!
MESSER MACO: Make me two eyeholes in the cloak, in the robe, 'cos I can't manage to do a Duke in the dark.

1534 version:
M. ANDREA: That outfit suits you like a paladin.
MESSER MACO: You're making me laugh, you are.
M. ANDREA: Does Your Lordship remember everything that I've taught you?
MESSER MACO: I can do them all, I can.
M. ANDREA: Have a go at being a Duke, the way every hooligan does to make out he's a Cardinal in disguise.
MESSER MACO: Like this, *with my robe over my face?*
M. ANDREA: Yes sir.
MESSER MACO: Hell, I've fallen over, *I couldn't do a Duke in the dark.*
M. ANDREA: Stand up, you lovely little coughdrop.
MESSER MACO: Get me two eyeholes made in the cloak, if you want me to do a Duke. I almost had to say my prayers to stand up again.

The addition of 'with my robe over my face', and the shifting of the line about 'doing a Duke in the dark' both give us some help (though perhaps not enough, nowadays) in visualizing what is going on, and show the dramatist relating to a reader of the text as well as to a possible spectator. (This version of the play was in fact performed, in Bologna in 1537.) The same considerations, along with those already indicated by Larivaille, may underly a great deal of the rewriting, even of the set-piece speeches which felt somewhat literary even in the first draft. Aretino's *Cortigiana*, in its two versions, might well be a precious indication of how a dramatist at this time could apply different criteria to a performance text and to a text for printing. But it is a unique case, in terms of surviving evidence; which leaves us unable to say whether in this respect it is representative or an absolute freak.

There is in fact every reason to suppose that Aretino's second comedy, *Il marescalco* ('The Stablemaster'),[19] went through exactly the same phases of development – the crucial difference is that we do not possess an early manuscript version. The play is firmly bound to the court of Mantua, where Aretino spent some months in 1526 with the Marquis Federico Gonzaga. It must have been conceived and drafted at that time, but the first printing was in 1533. Christopher Cairns has fully demonstrated how the long list of flattering comments in Act v, Scene 3 is oriented towards the circle of friends and patrons whom the author was cultivating during his early years in Venice – in other words, the text has been updated in the same way as the 1534 *Cortigiana*. Whether the rewriting was extensive in other ways, we shall never know.

Il marescalco is an even more eccentric comedy than *La cortigiana*, probably just as closely tied to a particular audience in a particular place as was the first play in 1525. Its story, such as it is, could conceivably be true, and many of its apparently supernumerary characters may have been living members of the Mantuan court. We cannot now tell if some of the various courtiers, officials ('Messer Phebus'), servants and tradesmen were figures offering the chance for a harmless piece of mimicry, or whether indeed the individuals concerned played themselves on stage. That this is not an implausible suggestion is shown by the gap in the action left between Act II, Scenes 4 and 5, where the court fool 'Ser Polo' is given space to mock the Stablemaster in an improvised scene of his own devising.[20] Aretino thus continues to be cavalier about the rules of Classical literary comedy, and he adapts himself without fuss to the demands of other formats – in this case, a loose court entertainment, making use of a performer who happened to be available and who would do his own number in his own way.

The comedy tells of the Marquis's court Stablemaster, whose preferences are firmly homosexual, but who is informed by his prince that, as a signal personal honour, he is going to be given a rich young wife. As we are told in the prologue (and as the intended audience would know anyway, if it was a true story), the whole thing is a practical joke – the 'wedding' will take place, but the bride will be a page boy dressed up. This duly happens on stage towards the end of Act v: the Stablemaster was informed that he must marry in the first scene of the play. Between these two simple stages of a very simple joke, nothing actually happens at all. The play is taken up with the Stablemaster's range of despairing moods in response to a proposal which he finds abhorrent, and with the reaction of a string of other characters to his reaction. He is variously teased, mocked, cajoled, argued with and agreed with in his antipathy to marriage, and the play consists of a loosely connected series of conversations, monologues, *contrasti* and the occasional self-contained *beffa* (as when two page boys tie some fire-crackers to the gown of a Pedant). It is more of a revue or pantomime than a dramatic narrative. Some scenes take on the character of a formal debate on the subject of marriage. In Act I, Scene 6 the Stable-master's old Nurse paints an idealized picture of domestic bliss; in II, 5 a courtier named Ambrogio gives a dismal satirical view, refuting the Nurse's points one by one; in IV, 5 another courtier, Messer Jacopo, speaks in favour of marriage and more especially of parent-hood. There is something here of a humanist debate, with thesis, antithesis and synthesis, but it comes across more as an enter-tainment to pass the time than as a serious inquiry. Many other scenes are set pieces or bravura items with their own independent appeal: these include the long list of complimentary references in V, 3, which has the thin pretext of finding exalted models of virtue and talent for the Stablemaster's son (or daughter) to emulate – if he has a child, if he gets married. There are also gratuitous pieces of self-publicity: in III, 6 a jeweller is told that 'necklaces should be like the one the King of France sent as a present to Pietro Aretino in Venice, and which weighs eight pounds' (trans. George Bull, p. 153).

Some of the individual characters come to life on the page, while others are left to the mimicry or fantasy of the performer. The Stablemaster's own household – his Nurse, and the irrepressible boy servant Giannicco – are well developed and memorable. Consider-able space is given to the Pedant – possibly the first caricature on stage[21] of what was to become increasingly popular as a theatrical figure of fun. An educated audience would seize gleefully on the mockery of their own boring tutors or schoolmasters; and Aretino, with the chip of his limited education on his shoulder, would take particular delight in his own verbal skill as he mingled bad Latin, good Latin, Latinized Italian, and endless superfluous scholarly references.[22]

At the centre of all stands the Stablemaster himself, protagonist of the play but impotent, protesting against his status as a puppet in the hands of the all-powerful Marquis whom it is impossible, or fatal, to resist. (The Marquis does not appear on stage, of course – he was meant to be in the equivalent of the royal box, and Aretino can no more afford to mock him or trifle with him than the Stablemaster can.) The spectators can laugh at the protagonist's rages, his dis-tress, his desperate arguments, because they know in advance that the whole thing is a joke.[23] There is nevertheless an uneasily con-cealed cutting edge to the play, relating to the genuine impotence of real courtiers and subjects in the face of absolute rulers, and the play has a quota of satirical comments on court life which give it something in common with *La cortigiana*. It avoids danger, in the face of the very court which it attacks, by withdrawing into a game of theatrical mirrors. The Stablemaster's despairing antics are the object of amusement to the other characters, who treat him as a performance of which they are spectators. He tries to react, in v, 3, by taking the part of a derisive spectator to the Pedant's interminable list of contemporary worthies whom his son might imitate. However, none of the characters realize that they are all playing out a spectacle for the amusement of the invisible Marquis off stage; because they have not been let in on the joke, any more than its chief victim has, and they do not know that the marriage is a fiction. Meanwhile the whole play, including its off-stage Marquis, both mirrors and entertains the real Marquis and his real court.

In 1527 Aretino found himself a permanent home in Venice, an oligarchic but genuinely collective republican state where there were no absolute rulers, where he could spread his dependence among a multitude of patrons and supporters and thus build a niche that was free from them all. When he returned to writing comedies in the 1540s, as we shall see later, he was able to drop his obsession with courtly servitude, and operate in a very different theatrical context. His first two plays, meanwhile, had been eccentric, both in their loose non-Classical formats and in his drive to bring everything under his own personality, his own vision, his own polemical allusions, his own unmistakable verbal style. His early theatre bears witness to some of the concealed tensions, which probably affected other dramatists too, between the demands of the performing occasion and those of a dramatic literature intended for posterity.

ARIOSTO'S VERSE COMEDIES

Ariosto's insistence on writing his later comedies in verse has already been mentioned (p. 40 above). His motives are generally understood to relate equally to a programmatic imitation of Roman models, and to his temperamental preference for artistic control. Verse was a guarantee that a work of art existed on its own plane, and was not confused with documentary reality: at the same time, the kind of verse chosen, he thought, should reflect as closely as possible the rhythms of ordinary speech without surrendering to them.[24] Ariosto believed that his chosen verse line, with its dactylic ending, achieved this aim, as the iambic trimeter had done in Roman comedy. The mixed responses which have greeted this choice down the years have, in the end, simply reflected the extent to which readers have agreed or disagreed with his judgement. The Marquis of Mantua, like his mother Isabella d'Este before him, preferred prose – to the extent of disappointedly returning to the author the verse texts of all four completed comedies, in March 1532, as unsuitable for his purposes.[25] Nevertheless, Ariosto's subsequent comedies, including the verse rewrite of *La cassaria*, found sufficient support in Ferrara itself to be performed, and in some cases revived more than once, on various court occasions. And modern critics, whether or not they are convinced by the choice of the *endecasillabo sdrucciolo*, continue to take these compositions seriously. Their author took an active interest throughout his life in the practicalities of mounting stage performances.[26] His later plays can be seen as a series of experiments, creating different kinds of encounter between, on one side, a theatrical experience governed by pre-existing models, and on the other side a desire to relate such experience to real issues and real behaviour.[27]

The first one we shall examine is usually left until last in anthologies, because it was never finished – but I am not alone in feeling that in ideal terms it seems to represent the next stage of thought after the prose *Suppositi* of 1509.[28] Ariosto's provisional title was *I studenti* ('The Students'), and drafting may have begun as early as 1518.[29] It never got further than Act IV, Scene 3: it was completed in two alternative versions, with different titles, after Ariosto's death in 1533, by his younger brother and by his son.[30]

What *I suppositi* and *I studenti* have in common is a plot centred on false identities, and a pattern whereby a first attempt at deception brings a series of further deceptions in its wake in order to fend off discovery. This chain reaction of disguise, leading to a situation where half the characters seem to be passing themselves off as someone else (and at the same time confusing and distressing allies whom they do not want to deceive at all), constitutes the play's main source of fun. Young Eurialo welcomes his fugitive orphaned lover Ippolita into his house. He pretends she is someone else, not to deceive his moralistic father, who is absent, but to trick his overloyal servant Pistone who would report everything to the father. The person most heavily involved in all the deceits is respectable old Bonifazio, who lets rooms to students and is the landlord of the second young hero Claudio. Bonifazio, with no family ties or personal involvement, decides to support the cause of young love for altruistic reasons, and eventually has to play a false role for one set of characters while retaining his true identity for another set.[31]

There is a relative absence in *I studenti* of comic 'games' and tricks on stage; and also of characters who by their personal energy, or their caricatured nature, push the entertainment along by being funny in their own right. The writing, on the page, thus seems rather sober, and critics have been quick to detect 'serious' elements of characterization and moral commentary. One must not underestimate, however, the extent to which laughter would spring from the exasperated tangle of the plot mechanism – an audience can find it amusing if characters are forced progressively to pile deceit upon deceit, just to sustain a plan which started as being simple. In this area, the performing experience could be very different from that of reading the script. The same is true of what some have seen as potentially 'pathetic' moments, where the audience might take a character's predicament seriously. At one point, young Claudio becomes convinced that he has been betrayed by his best friend. We know that the young lady closeted in Eurialo's house is in fact Ippolita, Eurialo's own lover; but the identity he has chosen to publish for his guest is that of Flamminia, the girl with whom Claudio is in love (and who never appears on stage). Foolishly, Eurialo does not let his friend into the secret: Claudio, on garbled information, naturally gets the wrong idea, and reacts accordingly in a miserable speech delivered to Bonifazio. Like Othello losing Desdemona, he feels that his occupation (as a law student) is gone:

CLAUDIO:
                    ... I'll bid farewell to Padua,
  Bologna, all those towns with universities
  Have seen the last of me. Set texts and comment'ries
  Are finished. I'll take Balduses and Bartolos
  And all those books, and rip them and set fire to them.
  Damn being born at all! It would be better if
  The rotten midwife, straight after delivery,
  Had drowned me and so saved me all this misery.
                                        (*Exit*)
BONIFAZIO:
  He's really desperate! The poor young gentleman,
  He's just like all those others who allow themselves
  To fall into the hands of Love, the murderer,
  And let him steal their brains, their richest property ...
  (*I studenti*, Act II, Scene 5)

Claudio is indeed desperate, and it is also true that the image of Love as a murderer echoes an expression from one of the tensest moments of Ariosto's *Orlando furioso*.[32] However, Bonifazio elsewhere thinks young men in love deserve conspiratorial support, rather than moral harangue (IV, 1); and the language of Claudio's speech, with its 'rotten midwife' ('puttana balia'), seems sufficiently over the top to invite amusement rather than pity – rather like Callimaco's monologue in *La mandragola*, IV, 1. What is more, since the audience knows that Claudio is not really betrayed at all, the general tone and expectations of comedy are likely to make them laugh, rather than cry, as with any other misunderstanding enacted in the play. We should also note that Bonifazio's musings are interrupted by the arrival of his female servant, Stanna, with a brace of pigeons: she invites her master to 'feel them', and gets a predictable mammary-oriented response. If there was any seriousness in the treatment of Claudio's distress, it is dispelled very quickly. Even the most civilized comedy is based on an element of callousness.

An attempt to visualize *I studenti* as theatre, then, can attribute to the play more comic verve than it is sometimes given credit for. Nevertheless, Ariosto left it unfinished. In his other two new comedies, he made progress in extending his theatrical technique, and in giving his plays some satirical bite which (unlike that of Aretino) is expressed within the fiction, rather than by an intrusive authorial voice.

We may not have either of these plays in quite the form which their author would have chosen. In all his writings Ariosto was a slow worker, prone to numerous second and third thoughts which do tend to be improvements on the first draft. He never managed, as he did with his poetic masterpiece, to oversee any printing of his later comedies. An early draft of *Il negromante* ('The Magician') was rushed to Pope Leo X in 1520, before it was really ready, and then not performed. For some reason it was this version which was chosen for most of the posthumous printings of the play – as many as six competing editions in 1535, and three more thereafter. It was not until Giolito's retrospective editions in 1551 that readers were able to peruse the vastly improved second version,[33] which was certainly performed in Ferrara in the late 1520s, though the canonical date of 1528 has now been called into question.[34] We have also to be cautious about the performing dates of *La Lena*, usually listed as 1528 and 1529, with a further revival in 1532. We do know that an early version was two scenes shorter than what we now have.[35] There are also signs that the surviving text was picked up in a somewhat provisional state (perhaps a draft which *precedes* a full prompt copy), with uncertainties and possibly lacunae in the fourth and fifth acts.[36] *La Lena*, like *Il negromante*, was posthumously printed several times from 1535 on; and it was reedited for Giolito in 1551.

In its second perfected version, *Il negromante* is a workmanlike piece with a greater charge of comic aggression than is found in Ariosto's previous plays. The love intrigues which are the pretext for its action are derivative (from medieval *novella*, as much as Roman comedy) and somewhat tortuous. Young Cintio, adopted son of Massimo, is secretly married to Lavinia, adopted daughter of his neighbour Fazio.[37] Massimo, unaware of this, has married him a second time to a girl named Emilia – so in order to maintain his faith to Lavinia, Cintio is feigning impotence with Emilia, and causing great concern. Emilia is also the object of the attentions of another young man, Camillo, who is foolish (and callous) enough to attempt trickery and even violence to possess her. Ariosto is still unwilling to bring his young girls on to the stage, so their situations have no emotional interest, and they remain the more or less emblematic focus of contrasting goals and desires among the menfolk – little more than pretexts for the action. What the play is really about is the efforts of all concerned to make use of a fake magician to gain their ends. Massimo wants his son-in-law cured of impotence; Cintio therefore has to try and suborn the conjuror to his own side, in self-defence; and Camillo is persuaded into a ludicrous plan whereby he will be smuggled into Emilia's bedroom in a trunk. The play, like *La cassaria*, thus revolves round intrigue, counter-intrigue, and the usual doses of disastrous coincidence to upset everyone's schemes. Equally conventionally, reconciliation is reached by the discovery (told in a long narrative in the style of Molière's *L'Avare*) that Lavinia is Massimo's long-lost daughter, so Massimo is happy to marry her to his adopted son. The difference from the earlier play lies in the prominence given to a single villain – Master Iachelino, the 'Astrologer'. The assault mounted by Ariosto against this trickster and his dupes can only imply that they represent a real target of satire (which can hardly be said of the entirely Plautine pimp of *La cassaria*). Like Aretino, though with less overt rhetorical flourish, and staying firmly within the bounds of 'overheard' Classical drama, Ariosto has built his comedy round a polemical theme.

There is evidence from his other writings that he found magical pretences and the occult particularly irritating, and he must have put his Astrologer on stage in the same spirit as that in which Molière caricatured doctors in the following century. Like Molière, he uses the common sense of a lower-class figure to undermine the gullibility of his 'betters' – Cintio's servant Temolo is the only character who is totally sceptical about the Astrologer's miraculous powers. The audience knows clearly that Temolo is right: so the existence of a polemic, and the central role played in the plot by the Astrologer's trickery, give these passages the character of satire which we were less willing to attribute to the earlier plays.

The Astrologer himself, we are told in passing, is a converted Spanish Jew – a sad reminder of prejudices which even the liberal Ariosto would have shared. He is also a firmly theatrical figure, with a personality still based on the cheerfully open villainy of a Plautine *leno*, or pimp. He and his servant Nibbio ('Kite'), as is often the case with villains on stage, strike a closer relationship with the audience than do their virtuous opponents. Their intention is to get large sums of money from their victims, and then leave town – in particular, while the idiotic Camillo is locked overnight in his trunk, his house is to be stripped bare. The Astrologer has a long speech categorizing different kinds of sucker as animal species, to be milked, fleeced or butchered as appropriate. Nibbio has two direct speeches to the audience, *giullare*-style, in a play which otherwise has few genuine monologues. At the beginning of Act II he tells us all about his master, to introduce him before his delayed first entrance. In the last scene of all, when their various schemes have failed and they are on the run, he decides that instead of bringing their belongings from the inn to the boat he will just scarper with them. The trickster is betrayed by another trickster, the sinner is punished by a devil, Volpone has the tables turned on him by Mosca. But just previously, in a more effective scene, the 'good' servant Temolo has gulled the Astrologer into lending him his cloak. With it swathed round his own shoulders, and with the villain standing there shorn of his impressive trappings, Temolo remarks: 'Now the Astrologer / Is me, not you.' This theatrical use of objects as well as words to convey the message is unusual in *commedia erudita*.[38]

The dramaturgy of *Il negromante* focusses in the middle of the play around the spectacle of the Astrologer deceiving his victims with elaborate nonsense and lies – a certain anticipation of Jonson's *Alchemist*. There is a scene with Cintio (III, 1), one with Massimo (III,

4) and two with Camillo (II, 3 and III, 3), who is given ample space to display his own gullibility and fatuous passion (in the reading of a love letter allegedly from Emilia, but actually composed by the Astrologer).[39] What has less often been remarked is how, in these scenes and others, Ariosto seems to be experimenting with structures in which characters act or speak simultaneously but independently, giving the audience a double focus. In all four of the 'gulling' scenes just mentioned, Nibbio is sent into a corner to offer a string of sarcastic asides on what his master is really up to, so the audience has to switch back and forth between him and the other two characters on stage. In the first version of the play this device is used just once, the first time,[40] as though its function was only informative, ensuring that the audience understands that deception is being practised. In the second version it becomes programmatic and is used every time, as if Ariosto has seen it as a theatrical experience with a validity of its own.[41] Then there are further variants on this 'split screen' approach to drama: they often seem to foreshadow operatic ensemble, though it is too early to talk seriously in such terms. For a part of Act v, Scene 2, we have a dialogue on one side of the stage alternating with an independent monologue on the other; and in IV, 4 and v, 4 there are similar separations, for some of the time, between characters. On two occasions (IV, 5 and v, 3) Ariosto tries the rather creaky device, fairly common in Plautus, where a character bursts on stage with news which he delivers in an agitated monologue, to no one in particular: other characters on stage overhear the information, rather than having it told to them direct.

Il negromante is set in contemporary Cremona,[42] not very far from Ferrara but far enough to be detached and neutral. This was a choice which became common in *commedia erudita*. It discouraged an audience from seeking any reference in the plot to real people and families in their own community, and therefore helped them to see the play as an artistic generalization. We have already seen, though, that dramatists could alternatively choose to set an action in the audience's home town, either to exploit a number of harmless homely references to local life (as in *I suppositi*), or else to reinforce a more unmistakable satire against local phenomena (as in Aretino, and perhaps Machiavelli). Ariosto's last complete comedy, *La Lena*, seems to belong to this latter category, though his satirical targets are more selective and his style more controlled than those of Aretino.

In *La Lena*, even more than in *Il negromante*, the ostensible plot involving love and marriage is only a pretext for the things which take up real stage time and the audience's attention. Flavio, son of Ilario, is in love with his neighbour Licinia, daughter of Fazio; and he enlists the help of Lena, who is employed as the girl's tutor and chaperone, to allow an illicit indoor meeting and seduction. Lena, like the Plautine *leno* or pimp whom her name recalls, is adamant that she will only do this for hard cash in hand. Flavio and his servant Corbolo have great difficulty in procuring the money, so the eventual coupling is delayed until Act v by a build-up of obstacles and cliff-hanging confusion. Put that way, the story sounds just like Plautus, with the single disturbing variant that the *leno* figure is a woman, and one abusing a position of trust. But the emphases of the play are nothing like those of the Plautine prose *Cassaria*. At the end, when the seduction is quickly discovered, both fathers agree readily to the marriage of Flavio and Licinia, so one wonders just what was the obstacle which Flavio had to overcome. However, the dramatist does not devote much attention to the hero and heroine as such. Not only does Licinia never appear on stage, but we do not see Flavio again either, after he has set things in motion in Act i. He spends the rest of the play concealed, comfortably or uncomfortably, in either Lena's house or Licinia's – or, for a part of Act iv, in a barrel moving between the two, which is stopped on stage and disputed over at some length while the audience enjoys the thought of our hero huddled inside it not daring to move. The arguments over the barrel have been created by a *tour de force* of theatrical plotting involving minor characters, all drawn from the banalities of Ferrarese city life: the friend who owns the barrel, the creditor and the bailiffs who want to claim it in lieu of debt, the surveyor and his assistant who happen to be going about quite separate business at the same time. The accumulation of absurd cross purposes over Scenes 2–7 of Act iv is all the more enjoyable because it has a weird plausibility about it, and in terms of stage entertainment it is one of the high points of the comedy. It is rooted in its turn on Ariosto's wish to make his play allude regularly to aspects of Ferrarese administration and justice which are corrupt or mismanaged – a stance which in other plays (and sometimes here too) is conveyed just in digressive speeches, but which in *La Lena* he manages to bring into the main intrigue. The law officers ('Sbirri') in Act iv are loutish uncontrollable characters, who end up trying to walk off with the surveyor's cloak in the absence of other pickings. Elsewhere the targets of satire are members of the Duke's own household: his gamekeepers are selling off the pheasants which they are supposed to guard (II, 3), and his grooms are ready to join Corbolo in a scheme to blackmail some smugglers and share out their loot (v, 1). The atmosphere in the Ferrarese court must have been quite relaxed in the late 1520s if Ariosto could get away with attacking people whose authority came from the Duke himself, even if they are low-grade officials taking the law into their own hands. A point is admittedly made of absolving the Prince from collusion with his employees. When the surveyor Torbido protests against his cloak being confiscated, the Sbirri try to pull rank on him: 'Is this the way to treat His Lordship's officers?' Torbido's loyal monarchist response is 'The Duke does not keep thieves among his servitors.' No doubt someone had to say this, at some point in the play, so that the decencies were observed; but it is interesting that Ariosto could claim the licence of an aristocratic jester, within the four walls of a court where his ultimate allegiance was known to be beyond question. What might rank as sedition in public can be taken as loyal criticism in private.

La Lena, then, is a Ferrarese play expressing a critical view of Ferrara. This part of its content was likely to seem more important to its audience than the mechanical love intrigue which drives it on the surface; but Ariosto, unlike Aretino, expresses his satire within the terms of the enacted *fabula*, rather than haranguing from outside it. The play also has things to show about moral behaviour in its central characters; and these include a relationship which is unique in *commedia erudita*, and has no source in previous fictional structures.

From the very beginning, the behaviour of Lena herself, in being prepared to sell off the virginity which she is supposed to be guarding, leaves a bad taste in the mouth – and the parallel with the Duke's gamekeepers could well be deliberate. Corbolo, whose master is to profit by the treachery, is sufficiently moved to comment on it in the very first scene. Young Flavio himself is too self-centred to care much about her motives: 'Whether she's right or wrong, why should I fuss myself? / She's doing me a favour, I'm obliged to her', showing thus a whiff of the entirely pragmatic relationships of alliance and patronage on which Italian society was based at that time (and, some would say, still is to this day). But the more thoughtful Corbolo has already introduced us to the motives for the betrayal: Fazio, Licinia's father, has for a long time been Lena's lover and patron, she is fed up with not being properly rewarded,

and means both to get paid from another source and revenge herself
into the bargain. (Once again, as in Machiavelli's plays, the fate of a
young girl is seen primarily in terms of the honour or dishonour of
her male relations.) Fazio, then, like so many affluent males in
reality at that time, feels entitled to keep a female as sexual drudge,
and is meaner than most at paying for the facility. What is more,
Lena has a weak and complaisant husband, aptly named Pacifico,[43]
who goes along with his wife's infidelities for the very meagre
reward, constantly under threat, of a rent-free house from Fazio.
The latter appears in a very bad light – selfish, exploitative, and
miserly enough (as well as foolish enough) to entrust his daughter's
education to a guardian he knows to be unchaste. To crown it all, a
misunderstanding arrives whereby Fazio thinks that young Flavio
has been in bed with Lena – he reaches the depths of degradation,
by the standards of the time, by succumbing to a fit of jealousy over
the undeserving woman. Not only can he not pay his dues, he
cannot even control his emotions. At the end of the play he sends a
rather sheepish message to Lena, while she is quarrelling with
Pacifico, to say that things will continue to be as before, despite
previous threats to evict her – this amounts to such a shattering of
decorum for a family patriarch that Ariosto could not bring himself
to have Fazio deliver the necessary speech himself, entrusting it
instead to a female servant. The unsavoury psychological triangle,
Fazio–Lena–Pacifico, provides the note on which the comedy ends.
This is all the more significant dramaturgically in that very little of
the detailed intrigue depends on it. It is a set of relationships
investigated for its own sake in what almost approaches psychological drama, however distorted in the name of satirical derision.

In the story enacted, Lena has of course been shamefully treated,
and it is tempting nowadays to approach the play from a feminist
angle, as has also been done in modern revivals of Marston's *Dutch
Courtesan*. We must recognize, however, that though such a reaction
to the play is our privilege, it is also an anachronism. Lena is easily
visualized by a modern reader as a role for a forceful actress who,
while not concealing her whoredom and avarice, might also establish her human point of view. In the 1520s the role would have been
played by a man in drag – and, regretfully, we must assume that it
would have been an unmerciful caricature of derided 'sluttish'
female behaviour. Ariosto contributed a great deal of sophisticated
thought to the development of 'regular' comedy in Italy, and he

pointed the way in particular to the incorporation of satire in the genre without disturbing its essential dramatic language. But he did not manage to break up the misogynistic patterns of his Roman models, and made no attempt to explore female experience in stage terms, so as to give it equal validity with male experience. For first steps in that direction, we have to look to Siena, and to a new type of performing organization.

THE CONGRESS OF BOLOGNA: TUSCANY

After Aretino's *Marescalco* and Ariosto's *Lena,* but before the next comedies which we must examine, there occurred a political event of some significance. In the winter of 1529–30, Pope Clement VII and the Emperor Charles V met in Bologna to formalize the outcome of the war in which Imperial forces had defeated a League of Italian states (including the Papacy) and France. The Pope was in no position to do much bargaining, after the disastrous Sack of Rome in 1527. The Emperor, as victor, effectively imposed his own decisions on Italy: he was determined to reaffirm the status of Holy Roman Emperor, theoretically over the whole of Europe. To underline the new alliance between supreme spiritual and temporal powers he made the Pope crown him in February 1530, first with the ancient iron crown of Lombardy and then with the gold crown of the Empire. A few days earlier, on 4 February, the combined courts and ambassadors at this summit conference had been treated to a theatrical entertainment: a brand new comedy entitled *I tre tiranni* ('The Three Tyrants') composed in blank verse by Agostino Ricchi of Lucca, currently a medical student in Bologna and destined to become a papal physician much later under Julius III.

The 'three tyrants' of the play are not a dangerous political accusation, but a reference to the tyrannical power over men of three universal forces: Love, Fortune and Gold. The comedy thus has lingering elements of morality play about it, though these come out more in the occasional generalizing speech than in any dramatic abstractions. More predictably, there is a scene at the start of Act v when long speeches are made in praise of Emperor, Pope and other suitable dignitaries. In deference to Charles, part of this is done in Spanish, on the thin pretext that one character has been on a pilgrimage to Compostela and come back incognito, disguised as a Spaniard. This diversification of language was a portent for the

future: so, perhaps, was the incorporation of encomiastic material
into the text, rather than the use of *intermezzi* as in Urbino in 1513.
Otherwise, the comedy sank without trace, due to clumsy plotting,
confused handling of time scale, and uncertain characterization.[44] It
was printed in a single Venetian edition of 1533. The occasion was
symbolically important, however, in that a comedy which was more
or less in the new 'regular' classical style had been judged an
appropriate offering to the rulers of Europe. It was a significant
boost for what, among respectable writers, was still very much a
minority genre.

The decrees of the Congress of Bologna had a material effect on
most Italian states – not least Ariosto's Ferrara, which staved off a
papal threat by having backed the winning Imperial side. The
impact was especially far-reaching in Tuscany. Clement VII was of
the Medici family, and had continued the Florence–Rome political
axis set up by his cousin and predecessor Leo X in 1513. Florence
had been steadily absorbing its Tuscan neighbour states for two
centuries, but to its south the Republic of Siena remained obstinately independent. With Medici rule squeezing it from north and
south, this little state had been under great pressure, as well as split
by its own political factions. Unable to survive without a big brother
to protect them, the Sienese had to choose between a French or an
Imperial alliance, and if possible they chose whichever great power
was currently opposed to the Medici Popes. In 1526, in the War of
Camollia, they had successfully beaten back from their city gate an
attack sponsored by the Pope, the Florentines, and (as was usually
the case in such stories) a contingent of Sienese exiles hoping to get
back home and banish their opponents instead. The city could not
expect to go on resisting without support, but on the other hand its
Imperial allegiance was having unpleasant side-effects: 'friendly'
Spanish troops wreaked havoc in the territory, and the Emperor
meddled increasingly in internal Sienese politics. The troops themselves were no joke, though jokes were made about them in
comedies.

The Florentines were also divided, and at the mercy of larger
forces. When the Sack of 1527 rendered Clement VII suddenly
powerless, the anti-Medici party seized control and made one final
attempt to resurrect a true Republic of Florence. It lasted just three
years, and was brought to an end, after a siege, by the Emperor at
the Congress of Bologna. Strangely, Charles put the Medici back in

charge. The Medici Pope had been making war against him, but in future the two powers needed to be reconciled and work together. Moreover, the Emperor was a monarch to his bones, and believed in the rule of hereditary princes. To get rid of the republican nonsense once and for all, Alessandro de' Medici was installed in 1530 as head of state, and created Duke of Florence in 1532, thus formalizing and making definitive the position of a family which had dominated the city, with intervals, for a hundred years. This left large ducal Florence looming in Tuscany over small republican Siena, from 1530 until the mid 1550s. Within Florence it inaugurated a period in which the new dynasty was establishing its ascendancy and credentials, using theatre and spectacle, among other things, for that purpose.

These events form a background, and sometimes even an explanation, for the stage comedies which emerged in the 1530s first in Siena and then in Florence.

SIENA AND ITS ACADEMY

Even before the rise of 'regular' comedy based on antique models, Siena had been a city known for its theatrical activity and expertise. Groups of middle-class artisans created a genre of peasant farce – that is, a partly aggressive and partly indulgent mockery by a city population of a despised rural class and way of life. In the early 1530s such interests were formalized in the creation of the Congrega dei Rozzi ('Roughnecks' Society'), who pledged themselves to the pursuit of a homely vein of literary and dramatic composition, carefully distancing themselves from upper-class humanist culture and even banning from membership anyone with a knowledge of Latin. Interesting though they are, the Rozzi cannot be brought within the compass of the present study. Even more interesting, but still regretfully to be passed over, is the generation of so-called 'Pre-Rozzi', covering the first three decades of the century before the foundation of the Congrega.[45] The Pre-Rozzi include figures such as Mariano Maniscalco, and Niccolò Campani known as 'Strascino': the latter was known as a performer as well as dramatist, and attracted Aretino's attention during time spent in Rome. These writers produced a broader range of 'mixed' compositions, sometimes using the five-act structure but with no unity of place or time. Some of the subject-matter was rustic and farcical, but other plays were more serious or more mixed, dealing with stories which have roots in folk tale, medieval and Hellenistic romance, morality play and *novella*. There are stories of kings and queens, princes and princesses, family dissensions and jealousies which lead to exiles and journeys far from home, spread over long periods of fictional time. In subject-matter, if not in style, they have a resemblance to the relaxed and varied modes of early Elizabethan drama – one thinks of Peele's *Old Wives' Tale* – and perhaps show how Italian theatre might have developed if the humanists had not been so determined to force it exclusively into Roman models. This is all the more true in that such plays were performed in academic circles as well as in the middle range of society: the recently rediscovered *Parthenio*, by Giovanni Pollio Lappoli ('Pollastrino') of Arezzo, who was a tutor of Pietro Aretino, clearly belongs to the 'Pre-Rozzi' genre and was performed for the academic body of Siena University in 1516.[46]

The main plot of *Parthenio* concerns the stubbornly faithful efforts of a young wife to be reunited with her princely husband, who is separated from her and thinks she is dead: at a certain point she takes service with him in male disguise. The theme of the constant suffering wife is a recurrent one in romance and folk tale, the lady often having to contend with a false accusation of unchastity which she has to disprove. It is listed by Leo Salingar (*Shakespeare and the Traditions of Comedy*, 1974, pp. 39–59) as a recurrent inherited motif in English Renaissance drama, including Shakespearian comedy. Both English and Italian writers would have found it in well-known tales from the *Decameron*: Day III, story 9, of Giletta di Narbona, which eventually led to *All's Well That Ends Well*; and Day II, story 9, of a falsely accused wife who is an ancestor of Imogen in *Cymbeline*, and who serves her husband in male disguise as does the heroine of *Parthenio*. Students of English drama are so accustomed to such material in essentially comic plots that it needs to be stressed that neither this motif nor romance themes in general have appeared in any comedy we have discussed so far. It was the Sienese who brought into 'regular' comedy the figure of the faithful and yet enterprising heroine; and they may have acquired a taste for it via the non-'regular' compositions of people such as Lappoli and Mariano Maniscalco, as well as directly via Boccaccio. We have seen how the only previous attempts to make an audience consider the predicament of a heroine came in the two Urbino plays of 1513; and of these only Bibbiena's *Calandra* gave the heroine any initiative, again making use of the freedom bestowed by male disguise. In that case the motivation was sheer survival, with an element of gratuitous mischief, and did not involve any exaltation of what Renaissance society saw as the prime virtue to be sought by the female sex – constancy, *fede*, unswerving loyalty to a sexual and emotional bond or contract previously established with a chosen male.

The representation of this idea in fiction had always led to a greater examination of the emotional plight of a woman protagonist, and on that level at least it meant taking female characters more seriously. If faith had to be maintained against the odds, it also led to women playing a more active part in the fiction – taking initiative, or at least being stubborn, in circumstances which could range from the moderately plausible to the wildly fantastic. Interest in such stories can be associated, among other things, with aristocratic courtly society, where leisured women could be more prominent in social exchanges and emotional games. It may be no coincidence that the two plays we have just referred to were produced in Urbino, the seed-bed for Castiglione's literary model of a Renaissance court, in which he tries within the limits of what was possible to give women a serious and indispensable role.

The context in which erudite comedy was launched in Siena was that of a kind of imitation court, in a community which had no princely centre and where the aristocrats had to organize themselves deliberately into societies which would project their class dominance in terms of social behaviour patterns and cultural production. The generic title of 'Academy' was chosen, and it was to have a long future in Italy and Europe in a range of different contexts. Because the life of Sienese politics and government was too chaotic, controversial and fraught with tension, it was made clear that the institutions set up were non-political, at least in theory, and concerned only with a combination of pleasure and high culture. (In practice, politics were unavoidable, and emerged in playscripts as well as in other activities.[47]) An early Accademia Senese ('Sienese Academy') was succeeded around 1525 by the Accademia degli Intronati.[48]

The word *intronato* has nothing to do with 'enthroned' (which would be *intronizzato*). It means 'deafened' by clangour – and in the local vernacular, by extension, it came to mean vague, thick-headed and slow in the uptake. We might translate the name as 'The Academy of the Deaf and Daft'. The founding articles explained that the academicians had been 'intronati' by the constant noise of war and upheaval, and were thus retiring, cutting themselves off from politics, and dedicating themselves to culture and enjoyment. There was an elaborately self-deprecating game being played here, and members took on academic pseudonyms which sometimes had the same tone, such as 'Il Bizzarro' ('Bizarre'), 'Lo Sfacciato' ('Cheeky'), amd 'Il Dappoco' ('Worthless'). There was an elaborate formal constitution with over-playful rules, such as often seems to develop in fundamentally all-male associations; but in fact the Intronati involved their womenfolk extensively in their social and cultural functions, making them (in a rather archaic courtly fashion) both the inspiration and the arbiters of their production and activity. This emerges very clearly in the context surrounding their first successful venture into 'regular' comedy[49] – an occasion and a text which turned out to be a decisive landmark in the development of the genre.

On the night of Epiphany 1532 ('1531' Sienese style, since their years were numbered from March[50]), the Academy staged a kind of pageant or masque of a kind common enough as court entertainment. It was addressed to the ladies in the audience, those to whom the academicians claimed to have devoted their passions and literary talents in vain. Despairing of sympathy and encouragement, they explained, they now proposed to renounce love entirely and pursue intellectual achievement on their own with no more courtly dedications. Each member of the Academy in turn, thirty men in all, stepped up to a pagan altar and burned upon it some symbol of his former attachment – a tear-soaked handkerchief, a lock of hair, a portrait – reciting some verses composed for the occasion. They were renouncing the service of Venus in favour of Minerva. The ashes of their tokens were scattered, and a final recitation reproached the ladies for their ingratitude, hinting that it might not be too late for them to change their minds.

This charade was obviously light-hearted, and probably the device of presenting a comedy to the same ladies as an apology and peace-offering had been planned all along.[51] All the early editions of the play print the text of the Epiphany pageant first, and the volumes are entitled *Il sacrificio degli Intronati*. The title of the comedy itself was *Gli ingannati* ('The Deceived'): it was presented as the collective work of the Academy, and its authorship remains the subject of speculation.[52] Despite this, it was one of the most appreciated and widely diffused of Italian Renaissance comedies. In Italy itself it was revived as far afield as Naples (in 1545), printed twenty times between 1537 and 1611, and closely imitated in a number of later comedies and scenarios. It was translated into French by Charles Etienne, as *Les Abusez*, in 1543 – the earliest foreign translation of any Italian play. A shorter Spanish reworking, *Los Engañados* by Lope de Rueda, is dated between 1539 and 1558. It penetrated England as early as 1547, in a Latin version, and influenced a number of fictional and dramatic compositions, culminating (in the view of posterity) in Shakespeare's *Twelfth Night*, which takes over its central amorous intrigue between two misdirected lovers and a pair of twins.[53]

In 1532 the comedy was ostensibly being offered entirely to the ladies in the audience, to make amends for the 'insult' offered at Epiphany. A long teasing Prologue, as well as developing sexual innuendo suitable for the last night of carnival, ends by stating the comedy's tongue-in-cheek message:

There are two lessons above all to be learned from this story: how much depends on chance and luck, in matters of love; and the value, in such affairs, of long patience aided by good advice. This will all be demonstrated to you by two shrewd young girls; and if you can profit by their example, then you ought to be grateful to us. As for the men, if they get no pleasure out of what we have to offer, they can still thank us for giving them at least four hours at a stretch in which to feast their eyes on your celestial beauties. (*Gli ingannati*, Prologue)

(This last sexist remark may refer to a seating arrangement, known to have been used later in Florence, where the men were on the floor of the hall and the women on raked seats at each side almost acting as a secondary spectacle.)

The most important 'shrewd young girl' in the play, the equivalent of Shakespeare's Viola, is called Lelia. She is a young Modenese of good family, stubbornly in love with Flamminio, and now aware that he is directing his attentions unsuccessfully to a certain Isabella (who thus becomes the equivalent of Shakespeare's Olivia). Lelia escapes in boy's clothes from the convent where she was staying (with the help of a conniving aunt who is a nun) and takes service with her fickle 'Orsino'. She carries messages to Isabella, who duly falls in love with her; and the situation is unscrambled by the arrival of Lelia's twin brother Fabrizio ('Sebastian' in Shakespeare), who was thought to have perished in the Sack of Rome five years before. Isabella marries Fabrizio, and Flamminio is reconverted to marrying Lelia, moved by her constancy and the revival of his earlier love.

This summary spells out the core of similarity to *Twelfth Night*: the differences are more significant for characterizing Italian Classical comedy. The action takes place in the city of Modena, in the year of performance 1532. Flamminio is a free agent, like Shakespeare's prince Orsino; but all the other three have to contend with the normal restrictions of family life – they are not cast via shipwreck into a fantasy Illyria for a private voyage of self-discovery. Lelia is not only in the care of her father Virginio, but about to be married off for financial reasons to an older man: in her boy's disguise she is circulating in her home town, trying to avoid recognition by those who know her. Her prospective fiancé, Gherardo, gleefully carica-tured as an old man unsuitably in love, is also father of Isabella ('Olivia'). Isabella herself, cooped up indoors and only released on to the stage in two scenes, is glimpsed as sexually frustrated and uncontrollable; and whereas in *Twelfth Night* Viola pities Olivia's amorous gender mistake and tries to draw back, Lelia exploits Isabella's passion for her, to ensure that Isabella remains cold to Flamminio. (She thus combines elements of the suffering heroine or 'rejected bride' of folklore with the mischievous trickster of other types of tale, a blend foreshadowed by Bibbiena's Santilla in *Calan-dra*.) Fabrizio arrives out of the blue, as does Shakespeare's Sebas-tian, but quickly gets involved with his family even before he recognizes them. His father Virginio, having got wind of what his daughter is up to, spots Fabrizio in the street and mistakes him for Lelia in disguise. Fabrizio is thus locked into a bedroom with Isabella for safe keeping, nature takes its carnival course, and in fact both marriages are preceded by timely fornications, which ensure that the old fathers' previous plans have to be abandoned. The happy ending is the result of both male misjudgement and female astuteness – at the end, when Lelia's energy has faltered, the initia-tive is taken over by her nurse Clemenzia, who manipulates Flam-minio carefully into a mood of reconciliation by telling him Lelia's story in the right way.

The plot of *Gli ingannati* is made more varied by a number of supporting characters – Clemenzia herself, various servants, Fabri-zio's tutor, innkeepers, and a Spanish soldier. The cast list thus adds up to an apparent seventeen, with every role clearly characterized and offering some meat for a performer: on this level the play is eminently revivable for a modern cast, as experience has recently shown.[54] A contest between Giglio ('Lily') the Spaniard and the maidservant Pasquella forms a separate little play in its own right, over just three separated scenes. Their immediate function was clearly to vent Sienese resentment over the occupying Spanish troops; and Giglio is a gross caricature of misplaced arrogance and stupidity, humbled in cartoon fashion by a series of tricks played by a woman. He is made to speak Spanish throughout, and is thus the first example of what was to be a theatrical cliché – a Braggart Soldier perhaps partly suggested by Plautus, but even more by sad contemporary reality, and made more ludicrous by an accent or language which distances him from the spectators. Giglio's scenes can be excised from the play without affecting the rest, and were in fact cut in Etienne's translation. Their apparent literary irrelevance is misleading, though, since they contribute considerably in performance to the play's range of comic variety. The other cliché character, Fabrizio's fussy homosexual tutor Messer Piero, is integrated more into the main plot. (As Pedant, he foreshadows the Dottore of *commedia dell'arte*, in the same way as Giglio is a prototype of the Capitano.)

There is one more major point to be made about *Gli ingannati* if we are to convey the play's full character. All the internal evidence suggests that the two twins were intended to be played by the same actor (presumably a boy): they never appear together, not even in a final family reunion such as one would expect in a normal dénouement.[55] This increases enormously the amount of theatrical innovation already contained in the comedy, and radically affects the response of an audience to the heroine Lelia. Her situation is the main focus of attention during the first two acts, and the mixture of pathos and entertainment is about even. By the end of Act II, she has retreated in despair to her nurse's house, having heard Flamminio (not knowing whom he is addressing) swear to hate his former love Lelia for ever more; and then Flamminio has discovered that his 'page boy' was dallying with Isabella, and is out to take violent revenge. There is a build-up of tension here which is at least semi-serious, and the audience takes the heroine's predicament as its main object of concern. At the start of Act III this mood is exploded by the appearance of the same actor in the role of Lelia's twin brother. From that point on, the game of theatrical virtuosity must surely take precedence over any elements of heroic pathos (which are nevertheless reintroduced in Act v). There is significance in this first attempt at 'doubling' physically identical roles, a device which has a long history thereafter in European farce, via Goldoni down to Feydeau and Dario Fo. There is equal significance in the fact that a play is allowed to be dominated by *any* device which is purely theatrical, rather than rooted in the verbal, conceptual or psychological sides of the script. The special contribution of the Intronati to Italian Renaissance theatre was in their attempt (which was theorized by their leading figure, Alessandro Piccolomini) to offer an integrated spectacle in which words, scenery, music, dance and performance were all equally important.[56] It was an approach which drew its cultural respectability from the Latin works on oratory so dear to humanist scholars – especially Book VI of Quintilian's *Institutio Oratoria*, which turned an apparently verbal art into one also involving performing skills.

Gli ingannati remains especially successful as a theatre text because its authors managed to write it so well in detail. Its language flows smoothly and achieves an easy colloquial feel, without losing contact with the literary *lingua franca* which educated people in other parts of Italy had some chance of understanding. In its stage narrative, mockery, jokes and games it manages to tread a middle way between approaches which in earlier chapters we had to analyse as alternative extremes. This is particularly true in a scene towards the end of Act I, which is devoted to making fun of Gherardo the old man in love, and thus invites comparison with techniques used by Bibbiena and Machiavelli. Gherardo is having to deal with the ill-concealed irony of both his own manservant Spela and the nurse Clemenzia: this means that he can be teased and exposed for the audience's benefit (as in *Calandra*), but with a greater degree of autonomous realism on the surface (as in Machiavelli), since each of his tormentors, within the fiction, is playing games for the benefit of the other. (Spela's name comes from *spelare*, to pluck or depilate: his name needs translating, because jokes are made about it.)

CLEMENZIA (*aside*): Oh what a fine Prince Charming for a tender young bride! So help me, I'd sooner throttle her than let her be given to that stale, mouldy, dribbling, putrid, snotty piece of decrepitude. I must get a few laughs out of him, at least. (*To Gherardo*): A very good morning to you, Gherardo, sir! You look as fresh as a cherub this morning.

GHERARDO: And a fistful of good mornings to you, my dear, and a handful of ducats into the bargain.

'PLUCK' (SPELA): I'm the one that needs those.

GHERARDO: Oh Pluck, how happy I would be if I were this good lady here!

'PLUCK' (SPELA): You mean you wish you'd had the pleasure of all those husbands, instead of just one wife? Or is there some other reason?

CLEMENZIA: What do you mean, you, Pluck? I'll have you plucked and shaved before I've finished with you. 'All those husbands', indeed! Feeling jealous? Wishing you'd been one of them?

'PLUCK' (SPELA): My God, yes – that really would have been a privilege.

GHERARDO: Quiet, you ape! That's not what I meant at all.

'PLUCK' (SPELA): What did you mean, then?

GHERARDO: Because if I'd been Clemenzia, I could have hugged and kissed my little Lelia over and over again – sweet Lelia, sugar and gold, milk and roses . . .

'PLUCK' (SPELA): Ugh! Uuugh! Here, guv'nor, we'd better go home. Quick!

GHERARDO: Why?

'PLUCK' (SPELA): You're sickening for something, you're feverish. It won't do you any good to stay out in this cold air. (*Gli ingannati*, Act I Scene 4)

The game of pretending that Gherardo is ill is strung out for a while longer; and then Clemenzia takes her turn:

CLEMENZIA: . . . why have you been spinning things out for a whole year before you come to terms? Let Lelia know, one way or the other.

GHERARDO: What? Does Lelia think that's my fault? Doesn't she know that I've been pestering her father every day, and there's nothing I'd like better in the world than to marry her right here and now? May I be carried out of that house feet first if it isn't true.

CLEMENZIA: Well, may God grant your wish. I'll tell her everything you've said. But do you know what? She'd like to see you going round a bit differently – not like the way you do now, like an old ram.

GHERARDO: Old ram? I've not had the chance to touch her.

CLEMENZIA: No, it's not that. It's the way you go about muffled up in those skins all the time.

'PLUCK' (SPELA): What's he supposed to do, then? Have himself flayed? Or run around the town stark naked? I don't know what things are coming to. (*ibid.*)

In this scene, the performers' eyes are implicitly on the audience, but the structure is not as overt and clumsy as it was when Bibbiena's Fessenio was displaying Calandro. It also gives a good idea of the frequency of casual verbal jokes inserted throughout this play to keep the public laughing – the Intronati recognized better than any of their predecessors except perhaps Aretino how a cheerful comic atmosphere needs to be maintained by a stream of one-liners. These are most essential of all in one-to-one confrontations rooted in the tradition of the *contrasto*, such as the scenes between Pasquella and the Spaniard Giglio (II, 3; IV, 6; V, 4), and the vigorous verbal punch-up (IV, I) between the Pedant and the derisive gluttonous servant Stragualcia ('Squint'). But they are also fairly plentiful in scenes which carry the narrative forward, including the central 'eavesdropping' scene in Act II, an extract of which must be quoted because it develops Ariosto's 'split screen' technique to the limit and underlines the enormous tonal difference between *Gli ingannati* and *Twelfth Night*. Lelia has been carrying messages from Flamminio to Isabella (as Shakespeare's Viola does from Orsino to Olivia); Isabella is besotted with the 'boy' messenger, rather than the messages, and is reluctant to let 'him' go. The two are observed on the doorstep by two servants: Scatizza ('Stoke') is a neutral bystander, but Crivello ('Sifter') has been supplanted in Flamminio's favour by the 'boy' Lelia and is delighted to catch him betraying the boss. Isabella's rampant approaches provide the servants with much entertainment, and the separate pairs of characters both amuse the audience; but once again the script gives no overt indications, and the reader has to work out who is audible to whom. Even the kisses (indicated below) have to be deduced from the dialogue.

ISABELLA: Step inside the door a moment.
SCATIZZA: They're off!
ISABELLA: You're very shy.
LELIA: Someone will see us.
[*Isabella kisses 'Fabio'*]
CRIVELLO: Hey, hey, hey! How about one for me, now?
SCATIZZA: I told you he'd kiss her.
CRIVELLO: And I'm telling you that I'd rather have seen that kiss, with you as witness, than earn a hundred crowns.
SCATIZZA: I saw it, all right. I wish I'd felt it too.
CRIVELLO: Now what is the boss going to do when he finds out?
SCATIZZA: Bloody hell! You're not going to tell him?
ISABELLA: Forgive me. You're too handsome, and I love you too much, so I've done what I shouldn't, and perhaps now you'll despise me. But God knows I couldn't hold back any longer.
LELIA: You need not explain yourself to me, my lady; I know how it is with me too, and how much I have been led to do by too much love.
ISABELLA: What have you done?
LELIA: What? Oh ... I have deceived my master, and it is not right.

ISABELLA: To hell with your master!

CRIVELLO: And that's what you get for trusting a tart! It serves him right. No wonder the snooty little fop was trying to persuade him to give her up.

SCATIZZA: The Lord helps those who help themselves – and he's helping himself with a vengeance. They're all the same, these women, when you get down to it.

LELIA: It's late, and I have to find my master. God be with you.

ISABELLA: Wait. [*Another kiss.*]

CRIVELLO: Wheeee! And one for luck! You wait, my pretty boy, it won't taste so nice in an hour or two!

SCATIZZA: Jesus Christ, I've grown an extra leg!

LELIA: Lock the door now. Good-bye.

ISABELLA: Do what you like with me!

LELIA: I'm all yours. [*Isabella goes in.*] I don't know what I'm going to do. On the one hand I'm having the time of my life, bamboozling that silly wench into thinking I'm a man; on the other hand, I'm getting into a mess, and I don't know how to get out of it. She's got as far as kissing now, and she'll try to go further when she gets the chance; and that will expose my weak point, and the whole trick will fall apart ... (*Gli ingannati*, Act II Scene 6; stage directions not in the original)

We must note that, because of previous inhibitions about showing young female characters, this is the first staged love scene in Italian 'regular' comedy, and it is loaded with more than its share of complexity. Even a simple wooing would have to contend with the fact that both parts were being played by male actors: here we have two boys playing two girls, one of whom (in the fiction) thinks the other is a boy – a heady plunge into sexual ambivalence, all the more potent in that both boys would have been personally known to the audience. Subsequently in the fifth act the play provides us, again for the first time, with an on-stage happy ending, an encounter and more legitimate pairing between Lelia and Flamminio.

Lelia, involved in all these scenes, seems to be poised between the audience's pity and derision. She is faithful, and given her chance to deploy her emotions in soliloquies (especially II, 7); but at the same time she is making a fool of herself and of others, and her transsexual disguise evokes the carnival atmosphere to which the play ultimately belongs. Other comedies had been written for carnival, but this one makes a particular point of the fact, even with some discreet symbolism. Act III, Scene 2 contrasts two competing hostelries in Modena, the Looking Glass and the Fool. The Pedant reminds us of the exemplary image of the 'Mirror of Prudence', and so the argument about who belongs in which tavern becomes a separation of the foolish from the wise. For a reader who misses the symbolic overtones (or for a modern director who chooses to play them down), the episode still has theatrical effectiveness: the competition for custom between the two innkeepers comes across as a kind of 'genre' scene which puts an everyday banal street transaction on to the stage.[57] Here, the tendency of earlier Sienese theatre to evoke plebeian life in drama may be relevant. It is less likely to have been inspired by imitation of Plautus and Terence, who rarely indulge in local colour; in earlier Italian 'regular' comedy both Aretino and Ariosto had tried it, but with less sense of relaxation and more dependence on an over-riding intrigue.

At the end of the play everyone, not excluding the Pedant himself, seems to have ended up under the sign of the Fool, and Stragualcia in the final speech invites the audience (the Academy of the Deaf and Daft) to come and join them there for the concluding feast. Not least among the attractive traits in *Gli ingannati* is the fact that its mockery is good-humoured, rueful and all-embracing. Only the detested Spaniard is firmly humiliated and defeated on stage: all the other 'gulls', even the ridiculous Gherardo, are let down gently in the end. The intrusion of romance and even a touch of allegory into strict humanist formulae has produced a play which is varied, enjoyable and heart-warming without renouncing any of the major virtues of the Classical dramatic language.

In some ways *Gli ingannati* represents a momentary balance between extremes. Subsequent plays from the Intronati Academy were just as important and influential in their own time, but for the modern reader they contain various perplexing elements which would make an attempt to revive them more problematic.

An early enthusiastic member of the Academy was Alessandro Piccolomini (1508–79), who gave himself the pseudonym of 'Lo Stordito' ('Dazed', or 'Absent-Minded'). He was a collateral descendant of the fifteenth-century Pope Pius II, and like his forbear he entered the Church, eventually becoming Coadjutor to the Archbishop of Siena, and himself titular Archbishop of Patras in Greece. He was a considerable scholar and polymath, producing works of moral philosophy and astronomy, and commentaries on Aristotle's *Rhetoric* and *Poetics*. He was also a constant anchoring presence for the Intronati throughout their troubled history of dissolutions and revivals, before and after the collapse of the Sienese republic. By the end of his life he had in effect become its ideological guru; and it is probable that a great deal of the Intronati house style, in other fields as well as in drama, is attributable to his presiding influence.[58]

Piccolomini's letters and commentaries are a major source for our understanding of the Intronati's dramatic practice, as Daniele Seragnoli (1980) has shown. It is from the commentaries, for example, that we learn of their dislike of *intermezzi*, especially when unrelated to the plot of the play, a view which firmly separates Sienese theatre from Ferrarese and Florentine. We also get an impression of theatre as a genuinely collaborative enterprise, with different experts taking charge respectively of plot structure, characterization, dialogue and language, and of the various aspects of staging from acting style through to dance, music and scenography. Perhaps there was no single author for any Intronati play. The later comedy *La pellegrina* (see Chapters 6–7) is a case in point.[59] The next two published Sienese comedies after *Gli ingannati* – entitled *L'amor costante* ('Constant love'), and *Alessandro* – are both attributed to Piccolomini; but perhaps the time has come to wonder whether they too are collective efforts.

L'amor costante has a plot aimed at justifying its title. The heroine, known to all as Lucrezia, eloped some time previously from Spain and married in secret, but was immediately separated from her husband by pirates. She has ended up in the house of a gentleman in Pisa, as his adopted daughter or ward, and has made him swear never to speak to her of marriage. Her guardian, Guglielmo, does not know that this is due to fidelity to an existing husband. Lucrezia's Spanish family has in fact been dispersed by ill fortune, and no one on stage realizes that Guglielmo is her real father, or that young Giannino who is trying to court her is her brother. (In this play, most of the main characters are using false names.) Meanwhile her husband has found her, and has taken service with Guglielmo to observe and test her – he only reveals himself and plans a second elopement at the beginning of Act II. Giannino meanwhile is pursued by Margarita the doctor's daughter, whom he resists until he realizes that Lucrezia is his sister. The characters (twenty-eight in all) include numerous servants and hangers-on, a Spanish Captain, and a ludicrous Neapolitan cleric who professes poetry and Petrarchan love at an indecorously advanced age.

In her introduction to an edition of the play (1990), Nerida

Newbegin points out a substantial number of plot and character
similarities to the earlier Sienese comedy *Aurelia*, unpublished until
1981. The tendency of the Intronati to re-use material in this way
certainly needs to be registered: recycling of similar roles may
indicate a 'safe' casting policy, with actors repeating what they were
known to do well. Equally important is the fact that some of the
material has a very much older origin. Leo Salingar (1974) breaks
the plot of *L'amor costante* down into five standard motifs from
romance and folk-tale, in the light of the remarkable coincidence
that all five recur punctually in an early Elizabethan romance
drama called *Common Conditions*, dated 1576. The relationships and
misunderstandings are in that play applied to characters who 'travel
from Arabia to Phrygia, with an excursion to quell an ogre on the
Isle of Marofus' (p. 35), and Salingar characterizes the story as
'complicated' and as a 'farrago suggest[ing] the influence of some
hellenistic romance'. Without wanting to be too ironic – after all,
some Shakespeare plots are almost as implausible – we should take
the point that the story of *L'amor costante* is an extravagant one, and
sits uneasily in sixteenth-century Pisa. One essential motif, common
to both plays, is that when Guglielmo discovers his daughter and
son-in-law (still unrecognized) about to elope, he locks them up and
makes them drink poison, after first allowing them to confess to a
friar – high-handed behaviour which seems to belong more to a king
or feudal lord in a legendary castle than to an urban Renaissance
gentleman, Spanish or not. (The 'poison' turns out to be harmless,
Margarita's father having prudently supplied a placebo.) For a
modern reader or spectator, there is something difficult to take in
the fact that even after this behaviour Guglielmo (now revealed as
Pedrantonio) is included in the emotional family reunion and happy
ending. What kind of sympathy can be bestowed on a character who
has to exclaim with feeling: 'Wretched old man! Unhappy Pedrantonio! What cruel fate has made me, in the space of a single day,
first find my daughter and then kill her?' (*L'amor costante*, Act v,
Scene 4)?

The whole extreme situation is an excuse for a programmed
celebration of female constancy: Guglielmo/Pedrantonio is reacting
here to the revelations of his daughter, who has come on to the stage
(for the first and last time in the play) to set the record straight,
believing herself to be at the point of death:

GUGLIELMO: If all this is true, then there was never a lady more chaste than you, nor a love more constant. But I don't believe you.

LUCREZIA: I beg of you, Guglielmo, if ever you loved me as a daughter, do me the grace before I die to believe me, because it is true. And the only reason I have told you was in order not to leave this unjustified stain in your memory of me; and also, if you have the chance, so that you may testify in my home country, and before my uncle, to my innocence and chastity . . . (*L'amor costante*, Act v, Scene 4)

Later, the servant Agnoletta, who has not up to now seemed distinguished for her celibacy, draws the other heroine Margarita into this approved circle of 'constancy' in a summarizing monologue:

AGNOLETTA: How pleased you are going to be, Margarita, when you hear such good news! Now you will gather the fruit of so much firmness and perseverance; now you will put an end to the miserable life you have led until today; now your sighs and tears will convert to sweet embraces; now your constant love will be an example to the whole world. Ladies, learn from her to be constant in your thoughts, and to have no fear of the outcome. You lovers, learn not to give way in your troubles, and to endure your sufferings until prosperous times come . . . (*L'amor costante*, Act v, Scene 9)

This element of direct moralizing from character to audience is new, and a first sign of the moral unease which was soon to hit Italian culture about the function of fictitious stories in general and comedy in particular. In fact most of the plot intrigues of this play foreshadow the style of Giovambattista Della Porta, who composed comedies in the 1590s.

L'amor costante was intended to be staged before Charles V, Holy Roman Emperor and King of Spain, during his visit to Siena in 1536, though the performance seems to have been cancelled through financial and organizational uncertainty. (The episode nevertheless confirms the way in which the Intronati Academy were allowed to represent the ruling class of Siena, for ceremonial and cultural purposes.) The comedy contains a number of overt adaptations to the occasion: a prologue in both Spanish and Italian, the Captain who speaks Spanish throughout (but is less of a grotesque caricature than Giglio in *Gli ingannati*), and a number of encomiastic passages particularly relating to Charles's recent crusading expedition to Tunis. Piccolomini's next play, *Alessandro*, is believed to have been performed in 1543 or 1544: it was printed in 1545 and reprinted thirteen times to 1611, thus having a very similar fortune to the previous comedy. It continues the tendency to run a romantic story alongside more scurrilous episodes, and to culminate in an affecting reunion between long-separated lovers. In this case the young couple, scattered by a political upheaval in Sicily seven years before (the setting is Pisa again, in about 1540), have both been roaming around in transsexual disguises. The pretended youth 'Fortunio' (really Lucrezia) is bewildered by the passion she feels for the apparent girl 'Lampridia' (really her childhood sweetheart Aloisio); so, for the audience, the romantic emotions have a titillating element as we toy with an appearance of lesbian love ('I'm not the first woman to love another woman' – Act II, Scene 1).[60] Using her 'masculine' initiative, 'Fortunio' gets into her beloved's bedroom, with predictable results. Interleaved with this story, there are two others. Young Cornelio makes a straight attempt to win the consent of Lucilla, daughter of old Costanzo. (Cornelio's sceptical but supportive friend Alessandro, for some reason, gives his name to the comedy.) Costanzo meanwhile has a senile passion for Brigida, wife of the braggart Captain Malagigi: he is persuaded by scheming servants to enter her house disguised as a tinker, and is beaten out unrecognized by the returned husband. This plot motif of trickery by forced disguise was regularly used to humiliate Pantalone, in later scenarios of the *commedia dell'arte*: it is not clear whether its first appearance on stage is in *Alessandro* or in one of several Venetian scripts which we cannot date with precision. In similar vein, the Captain has his obligatory scene of military posturing followed by cowardly rout.

Piccolomini's two plays, in the large-scale relationships and plot units which they explore, share numerous features with *Gli ingannati* and with the unpublished *I prigioni* and *Aurelia*. However, in many smaller-scale aspects of their writing the two plays are quite dissimilar. If they had remained anonymous like the other Intronati comedies, we might have seen a family likeness at the plot level, but concluded that the detailed scripting was by different hands. *Alessandro* sticks more closely to Classical precept in keeping its characters and events apart from the audience as 'overheard' drama: there are no winks across the footlights, even in soliloquy. The language is more monochrome, with no excursions into vernacular, dialect, or foreign speech. (The use of such linguistic variants, for reasons of verisimilitude, is a question on which Piccolomini himself is known to have been hesitant.[61]) *L'amor costante*, on the other hand, uses Spanish, Neapolitan dialect and even pidgin German, and is a text much more open to its audience and to the occasion for which it was intended. The breaking of dramatic illusion is made a regular source of laughter, in the more Plautine tradition rejected by Terence and 'Donatus'. Sguazza the parasite opens Act I, Scene 6 by asking the lady spectators if Guglielmo has come out of his house yet, in the style of modern English pantomime. Earlier, in I, 3, the servant Panzana tries to contain his laughter in front of all the 'foreigners', indicating that he means the audience: the response of Ligdonio is: 'Don't worry about them. Laugh away. They are in Siena, and we are in Pisa.' In addition, in this play as in the earlier unpublished *I prigioni*, dramatic action at certain key points is turned into ballet. Not only is the play concluded with two dances in the style of a court masque; but an armed conflict, with four partisans on each side, is expressed in a danced sword and buckler fight in IV, 11, followed in V, 1 by another danced encounter with long swords (*spadoni*) presided over by the Spanish Captain as Master at Arms. Of the dancers concerned, six are extras in roles created just for this purpose, but the other two are the young hero Giannino and his servant Vergilio who have substantial acting parts as well. No doubt some of these features can be related to the play's intended audience of an Emperor and traditional courtiers, but the general difference from *Alessandro*, in terms of dramaturgical style, is difficult to overlook. On the basis of our information about the later *Pellegrina*, we might guess that Piccolomini was more responsible for choosing characters, scene outlines and plot structure than for the detailed writing of both plays. (He might, of course, have written a greater proportion of one than of the other.)

There is clear evidence that Piccolomini was interested in drama as a set of identifiable units (or 'theatergrams', to employ the useful concept of Louise Clubb[62]) of character, dialogue and plot. In a dedicatory letter of 1561, attached to a book which has no obvious connection with theatre, he speaks to a friend and patron of a long-standing project which has fallen by the wayside:

First of all I had listed and described most of the types of person who can be, or normally are, represented in comedies, according to those distinctions which are usually found for various reasons in the ordinary life of men: that is to say, according to blood relationships, like fathers, sons, brothers, nephews and such like; according to diversity of fortune, such as rich and poor, servants and masters; of age, such as old, young and

children; of profession, such as lawyers, doctors, soldiers, pedants, parasites, whores, bawds, merchants, and so on; of emotional state, such as
angry, amorous, fearful, bold, confident, desperate, and so on; of habit of
mind, such as miserly, prodigal, just, prudent, foolish, jealous, fickle,
boastful, arrogant, cowardly, and other such; and in this way I was making
a survey of all those types of character and background [*di persone e di vita*]
which can represent in comedies the ordinary life of men. Now, to each one
of these characters I had planned to attach first of all sets of monologue
scenes, which although all different from one another would all be adjusted
to the decorum and quality of the people represented. And then, linking
and coupling these characters in various ways, as it were father with son,
master with servant, servant with servant, lover with beloved, bawd with
victim [*ruffiano con arruffianato*] ... I had planned to create various scenes for
each of these couples, having an eye always to verisimilitude ... so that they
could be applied to many different stories, with just small additions and
omissions ....[63]

He claimed to have composed three hundred such speeches and
scenes, out of an intended total of five hundred, before the manuscript was stolen or lost. Whether that is literally true, or whether
there were other reasons for shelving the project, remains a problem
for Piccolomini's biographers; we must also pass over, fascinating
though it is, the extent to which the exercise was one in anthro-
pology or moral philosophy as well as in theatrical method. For our
present purposes, at least two points must be noted. The first is the
extent to which the subjects and characters 'who can be, or normally
are, represented in comedies' ('che possano o sogliano rappresen-
tarsi ne le comedie') was already, by the 1560s, severely circums-
cribed by tradition and existing models. There is no mention in
Piccolomini's list (to give a by no means exhaustive set of examples)
of any aspect of country life, or of religious life, or of commerce, or of
education; and the relationships conceived are limited largely to
what we would call domestic encounter. The implications even of
this limited project, secondly, are large and to some extent puzzling
in their historical context. The idea of building up a theatrical
repertoire of stock characters and stock situations, which could then
be adapted to every new plot as chess pieces are manipulated in each
new game, is very close to what was going to be done, from the
middle of the century onwards, by professional theatre companies
working (as I shall suggest in Chapter 5) from a basis of illiteracy.
Commedia dell'arte scenarios are full of constantly recycled situations
and dialogues of exactly the kind which Piccolomini envisaged; and

professional improvising actors built up collections of speeches and expressions suitable to whichever character or mask they normally played. Piccolomini, however, was not a professional artisan but an aristocratic scholar, concerned with psychological and moral categories, verisimilitude and *decorum* (in the Latin sense of stylistic and behavioural plausibility, for which see Chapter 6). It is difficult to believe that there was no relationship between the scholarly and the practical versions of the same method – but just exactly where and how the interchange occurred, and who was borrowing ideas from whom, has (I think) still to be determined.

Under Piccolomini's tutelage, but operating as a team, the Intronati produced just three published plays, and yet made a major impact on Italian comic dramaturgy to 1555; and in fact considerable continuity was maintained even after the collapse of the Sienese state and its submission to Medici rule. The major source of laughter, for them as for their predecessors in other centres, was mockery of disliked or deviant behaviour, with the tortured Sienese political situation suggesting some topical targets for antagonism whenever the performing occasion allowed them to get away with it. (In fact they established as one of their norms a strict historical placing of every story in relation to a memorable past event.) They showed a taste as well, though, for more relaxed verbal wit and theatrical games, working hard at the atmosphere of good humour which was intended to prevail at their academic and social gatherings. More significantly still, they allowed into their comedies a wider range of theatrical experience than is covered by laughter as such. Drawing perhaps on morality plays as well as medieval *novelle*, they allowed their audiences to explore feelings of sympathy, genuine though not necessarily uncritical, for the predicament and emotions of selected characters. These characters were usually young, and they included females as well as males. Their intention of developing the character of an admirable and attractive heroine – which led later on to the motif which Louise Clubb has characterized as 'Woman as Wonder',[64] and had lasting effects also on drama in other countries – was however hampered by lingering technical problems. The full characterization on stage of young virtuous women was inhibited by the fact that such parts were still played by male actors.[65] (We know that the same inhibitions were not felt by Tudor and Stuart dramatists; but they were dealing with full-time professional apprentices, not gentlemanly youths dragooned into acting just once or twice in their lives.) They were also inhibited by the verisimilitude which was increasingly seen as a main characteristic of comedy. In the society which the plays sought to depict, young girls of good family had little control over their own lives, and were rarely to be seen in the public street except on chaperoned ceremonial occasions (though, as we shall see from a Florentine comment, they may have been relatively less constrained in Siena than elsewhere). The healthy development of female stage characters which we take for granted in European comedy of the seventeenth and eighteenth centuries was dependent to a great degree on a very simple change in staging conventions – the permission to shift the scene of dramatic action from the street or square to indoors. Until that happened, the sympathetic heroines of the Intronati either made few appearances on stage, or were forced into plots which put them in male disguise.

FLORENTINE COMEDIES

During the first three unstable decades of the sixteenth century, the surviving contribution of Florence to the new 'regular' comedy was limited to Machiavelli's two plays and one translation, plus the three unpublished verse comedies of Lorenzo di Filippo Strozzi. Under the freshly established ducal régime, the genre became fully institutionalized, a little later than in Siena. Thereafter, between 1536 and 1555, in contrast to the half-dozen plays produced by the Intronati, we can record the emergence of no fewer than twenty-six Florentine comedies, plus two by Angelo Firenzuola which were performed in neighbouring Prato. Of these twenty-eight, thirteen were by a single author, Giovan Maria Cecchi.[66] Our treatment of comedy in Florence must thus of necessity be a broader survey than has so far been adopted: we shall aim to generalize more and identify larger trends and categories. This approach is aided by the fact that, if we judge by their printing history, no single Florentine play had the impact of *Gli ingannati*, *L'amor costante* or *Alessandro*; and we shall be arguing that the influence of the Florentine tradition was more cumulative, and less dependent on single key texts.

Histories of theatre performance in Florence (Zorzi, 1977; Mamone, 1981) have concentrated on the organization of cultural spectacle by the Medici court, and on the ways in which theatre and other pageantry were made to serve and express the autocratic structures of the new régime. The plays themselves and their dramaturgy have tended to get pushed into the background; but it is arguable that for many people that was what happened at the time. Even before 1500, Florentine theatrical expertise had reached a high level of accomplishment in visual display and stage mechanics: the experience had been gained both in secular public processions and displays, and in elaborately evocative religious drama.[67] The new ducal court, after 1530, continued to make its celebrations as lavish as possible, and Florentine comedies were often swamped, as the early Ferrarese ones had been, by enormously expensive *intermezzi* which often bore no relation to the play. As in earlier Ferrara, it often seems that the five acts of narrative were seen by many spectators as the real 'intervals' between the song, dance and allegorical spectacle which they had actually come to see. However, on one bizarre occasion which cannot be precisely dated, Machiavelli's *Mandragola* and Cecchi's *L'assiuolo* were performed in the same hall on stages at opposite ends: Act I of one play was followed by Act I of the other, and so on, alternating so that each comedy provided the interludes for the other.[68] All the examples of comedies which were printed together with texts and descriptions of their *intermezzi* come from Florence; though as often as not the interludes were written up separately, as an act of cultural propaganda, by a suitably chosen literary courtier.

Entertainments were mounted in a number of suitable spaces, from large private houses to halls owned by guilds or confraternities, but wherever a Medici notable was a guest of honour we can assume that the princely family was also sponsoring and directing the proceedings. The extent to which high culture was made into a state monopoly is symbolized by one policy decision in particular. The Accademia degli Umidi ('Academy of the Damp') was formed in 1540 by a group of literary enthusiasts in a spontaneous attempt to put Florence once again at the centre of Italian cultural activity. Such resemblance as it had to the Sienese Intronati diminished sharply when it lost its autonomy – by 1542 the organization had been effectively hijacked for the state by Duke Cosimo. The rechristened Accademia Fiorentina became an arm of government, perhaps the Western world's first Ministry of Culture: its officers received stipends from the state, and its Consul combined his office with that of Rector of Florence University.

All these facts, which are common ground among historians, tend to emphasize the courtly, and thus aristocratic, contribution to the new style of comedy. The picture has to be completed by another element, however. The groups which performed theatrical compositions, including *commedia erudita*, in sixteenth-century Florence frequently included a more bourgeois (though still affluent and cultured) section of the citizenry. They developed out of the religious and neighbourhood confraternities which had performed so many *sacre rappresentazioni* in the previous century, and they continued to perform less 'regular' types of drama alongside the new style. They were still amateurs, as were Ariosto's courtly actors and the Intronati, but they represented a broader social base even when they performed for the princely family in a court context.[69] Being less sophisticated than courtiers, and perhaps being also more attached to previous theatrical habits, these bourgeois performers may have contributed to the fact that Florentine comedy is often more cautious and conservative, both culturally and morally. Some of the dramatists concerned, though not all, also came from the rich merchant, professional and artisan classes rather than the gentry.

The first 'regular' comedy under the new régime was typical of what was to follow in many ways, but untypical and inauspicious in others. On 13 June 1536, the comedy *Aridosia* was presented in conjunction with the wedding of Alessandro de' Medici, first Duke of Florence, to Margaret of Austria (an inevitably dutiful link with the dominant Habsburg dynasty). The scenery was designed by the prestigious Bastiano da Sangallo, nicknamed 'Aristotle', and involved a Roman triumphal arch, some detailed architectural relief work, and a new way of placing the musicians. Clearly the scenery was aiming to be a *tour de force* in its own right, and was much more splendid than the bourgeois setting of the play would require – as had been the case, among other examples, for the staging of Bibbiena's *Calandra* at Urbino back in 1513. Although this was a full-scale court celebration, there was as yet no obvious venue for it in the territory either of the old commune or of the new princely family, so a hall was borrowed from the Weavers' Company (Compagnia dei Tessitori) next door to the house of Ottaviano de' Medici. The scenic innovations were so radical as to require permanent building alterations, for which the Duke presumably paid. The mention of musicians makes it certain that there were interludes of song between each act, if not also full-scale pageants of tableau and dance. Who the performers were is not certain – the Weavers themselves could conceivably have acted the play, but there was undoubtedly also a contribution from the court, if only in the provision of professional musicians, designers, stage craftsmen, and perhaps costumiers.[70]

So far we have described those aspects of the occasion which set the tone of Medici-sponsored comedy in years to come; and the play itself, as we shall shortly see, can also be regarded as standard. The unusual feature was that the author was a Medici himself, young Lorenzo di Pierfrancesco, usually called Lorenzino, a distant relative of the Duke and a member of the court. What made the occasion an unfortunate precedent for future festivities was that in the following year, 1537, Lorenzino assassinated Duke Alessandro, ostensibly in an attempt to reestablish a Florentine republic.[71] (He fled to Venice, and was killed in return in 1548.) It must be fairly rare in theatre history for a dramatist subsequently to murder his guest of honour – as opposed, perhaps, to the other way around. At all events, there was no chance of a return to republican ways. The outcome was that in Cosimo I de' Medici, Florence (and eventually the whole of Tuscany) got itself a ruler of implacably firm, if also paternalistic, capabilities, in exchange for one who was both inefficient and capricious.

Aridosia is the play of the character Aridosio, and this 'arid' figure is an old miser, whose meanness is the major obstacle to the marriages of his two sons and one daughter. The happy endings are eventually procured via Plautine plots and intrigues from young men and servants combined, involving the manipulation of sums of money which can eventually serve as dowry. Old fathers in Roman comedy are often miserly, but a survey of Florentine comedy in this period reveals a concentration on themes of avarice and dowries which has not been seen before, and which may well represent the preoccupations (or, indeed, the moral unease) of an affluent city which had long prided itself on its business shrewdness and eye for profit.[72] *Aridosia* thus seems to touch a genuinely raw nerve in Florentine society, as well as being the first of many links in the long chain between Plautus's *Aulularia* and Molière's *L'Avare*.

In relation to Florentine comedy, Roman sources cannot simply be mentioned generically in passing, as was possible in relation to Ariosto and Bibbiena. Florentine dramatists tended to produce comedies which were 'erudite' in a much fuller sense. Following current practices of literary imitation (and the model of Machiavelli's *Clizia*) they based whole plots and scenes openly on

Plautine and Terentian sources, with careful additions and sub-
tractions which would blend the material into a recognizable contemporary Tuscan setting. (The scene of the action is most often in
Florence itself, or in Pisa.) Routine critical descriptions of Italian
humanist comedy have tended to dismiss the whole genre as a mere
rewriting of Plautus and Terence into the vernacular. The present
study has hoped to show that this is an inaccurate picture overall,
but for Florence in the second quarter-century it comes close to
being the truth. Perhaps it is no coincidence that it was in the year of
Aridosia, 1536, that a version of Aristotle's *Poetics* was first printed. It
is easy to envisage this giving rise to more public discussions of the
'rules' of Classical theatre, and to more dogmatic assertions about
the need to imitate antique masters. (We shall see that in Venice,
from 1540 onwards, Lodovico Dolce often pursued the same
approach to constructing a play, and that earlier even the great
Ruzante was not immune from it.)

There are distinctions to be made here about degrees and types of
'imitation'. Ariosto's *Cassaria* is not based on a single Plautine source
– indeed Angela Casella, who edited the play for Ariosto/Segre
(1974), had to make a meticulous list of small correspondences
which take in a large part of the Plautine canon, in order to
document what for most readers is no more than an instinctive
feeling. The situation with many Florentine comedies is quite different – one can often read whole acts or scenes with a single Plautus or
Terence comedy in the other hand, and note a close correspondence,
speech by speech, between the two texts. In one or two cases we may
be reading a straight translation, as is the case with Firenzuola's *I
Lucidi* (*c.* 1542) from Plautus' *Menaechmi*. But the degree of exact
dependence on a Roman model may vary. Benedetto Varchi's *La
suocera* ('The Mother-in-Law', composed 1546) is a translation (or
nearly) of Terence's *Hecyra*, but interleaved with an auxiliary plot of
the author's own invention which leads to two more marriages
between young couples: Varchi believed firmly in the virtues of
Terence, but recognized that his audience would by now prefer a
plot structure of more complexity. Giovan Battista Gelli's *La sporta*
('The Basket', 1543) is a careful reworking of Plautus' *Aulularia* – a
central miser figure again, hiding his hoard of gold in a basket rather
than a pot – with well-judged adaptation to the contemporary
Florentine context, and the addition of some extra characters for
local colour. A similar description would apply, in general terms

and with greater or lesser amounts of extra material, to Donato Giannotti's *Il vecchio amoroso* ('The Old Man in Love', 1536) and Cecchi's *La stiava* ('The Slave-Girl', 1546), both based on Plautus' *Mercator*; and to Cecchi's *La dote* ('The Dowry', 1544) and *I dissimili* ('The Incompatibles', 1550), based respectively on Plautus' *Tri-nummus* and Terence's *Adelphoe*. The central device of Plautus' *Mostellaria*, where people are put in fear of ghosts and an apparently haunted house, is used in more than one play, sometimes alongside a plot taken from elsewhere; and it foreshadows a long repetitive tendency in *commedia dell'arte* scenarios for characters to dash round the stage in foolish terror of 'spiriti'. In fact Lorenzino's *Aridosia*, with which we started, is a more subtle *contaminatio* (to use the term applied to Plautus and Terence themselves, in relation to their Greek predecessors) of *Aulularia, Adelphoe*, and the haunted house scene from *Mostellaria*. But even in this play whole scenes and speeches can be set alongside their obvious Roman originals.

If they stuck so closely to the Roman plots, these playwrights had constantly to deal with potential anachronisms, of the sort which Ariosto had left behind very quickly in his transition from *Cassaria* to *Suppositi*. The tendency in the Latin sources for young girls, the object of young men's desires, to have the status of slave or prostitute was always likely to push the story to the edge of implausibility. Slavery, and the status of a ransomable hostage, were both conditions which did exist in Renaissance Italy, but they were extreme situations which could rapidly seem overplayed; while relations with prostitutes were not likely to arouse an audience's sympathy. Florentine dramatists were thus wary of a 'happy ending' which consisted of the young hero taking possession of a concubine. If their Roman original was of that type, they might intervene and push the outcome in the direction of marriage, by discovering the girl's respectable relationship to a long-lost father, who would either arrive late on the scene or be present already in another function. This is done in *Aridosia, Il vecchio amoroso*, and *La stiava*; and also in Francesco d'Ambra's *Il furto* ('The Theft', 1544), which otherwise is less dependent on Roman sources. The device is itself traceable to Terence's *Andria* and *Eunuchus*, and no doubt beyond them to Greek New Comedy. It led to newly complicated backgrounds for some characters, with narrative explanations of how families had been separated by war or pirates, usually placed in a real historical context. This tendency would seem to assimilate the Florentine plays to those of the Sienese Intronati, based as we have seen on romance and *novella*. The difference in tone, however, is sharp. The Sienese plays make an attempt to dramatize the subjective effect on their characters, including the female ones, of the stressful vagaries of Fortune: for Florentine dramatists, the novellistic background simply provides a mechanical solution to an otherwise inextricable tangle of intrigue. Moreover, being so heavily under the influence of Roman dramatic models, the Florentines remain incapable of releasing their young female characters into any kind of dramatic autonomy: none of the plays we have mentioned allows a heroine on to the stage for long, and all of them contain at least one girl who is central to the plot but never seen by the audience at all. This may be due partly to imitation of models, but perhaps also to a greater strictness of conduct in Florence as opposed to other cities, including Siena. In Varchi's *La suocera*, the hero has a soliloquy of conventional complaint about the pangs of unsuccessful love, and comments: 'If only this were known to the person who is causing it! More power to Siena, in this respect ['Bene aggia Siena in questa parte']; if ladies are true ladies, they are not less virtuous for being more free, just less simple-minded' (*La suocera*, Act II, Scene 5).

While thus appearing hamstrung in any attempt to deploy young respectable females, Florentine playwrights still seem aware of the need to make some of their characters sympathetic and psychologically interesting. In Terence, more often than in Plautus, they would find precedents for the exposition on stage of personality types and moral issues – as, for example, in the debate in *Adelphoe* between two approaches to bringing up children, which is represented also as a clash in temperament between the brothers Micio and Demea. Lorenzino de' Medici took over this whole situation in *Aridosia* (his brothers are Marcantonio and the miserly Aridosio himself), and gave a sympathetic portrait of young Erminio's sensitivity to the contrasting claims of his pregnant mistress (whom we never see) and his generous adoptive father Marcantonio: Erminio's monologues of dilemma stand out sharply from the rather mechanical intrigues of some other scenes. In other plays too, young men are shown as people with problems and feelings, in contrast to the colourless or indeed callous natures which they still had in Ariosto. And if young heroines could not be developed, other female roles could, to some extent. The strong matronly figure of Sofronia, in Machiavelli's *Clizia*, probably reminded Giovan Battista Gelli that married women and widows could have some influence in contemporary families, and in *La sporta* he multiplied the character of Eunomia from his Plautine source *Aulularia* into three separate widows, each intervening on the plot in different ways. At the lower social level, in addition to caricatured crones such as the nurse or the bawd, we see emerging the vivacious, enterprising younger female servant, who was to be such a staple of European comedy in the following two centuries. The *fantesca* or *servetta* was also appearing in Sienese comedy, but in Florence we see her in Cecchi's *L'assiuolo* ('The Horned Owl', 1549) and Grazzini's *La gelosia* ('Jealousy', 1550).

It may be no coincidence, though, that these two last named plays are not based on Roman comedy so much as on the Boccaccian *novella*. In these decades, Boccaccio was emerging as a 'classic' alongside ancient writers. Dramatists of the time were as aware as modern critics are of the amount which the *Decameron* had contributed to the creation of 'regular' comedy, and in Florence they also had local pride in a masterpiece written by a compatriot. Cutting across the often cautious moralistic tone of so much comedy written in Florence there is an alternative streak whereby intrigue, trickery (*beffa*) and even adultery can be celebrated for their own sake. The Florentine character was, after all, legendary for its sharp-tongued mockery. Adultery plays, along the lines established by *Calandra* and *Mandragola*, were never in the majority among humanist comedies; but some were still written, and in Florence they could claim the patriotic justification of being literary exercises in imitation and celebration of a great classic which had brought prestige to the city. Grazzini's *Gelosia* is centred on *beffa*, but not on adultery: an old man is tricked out of his designs on a young girl, so that her young suitor can marry her instead. The amoral peak of this genre, however, is now reckoned to be Cecchi's *L'assiuolo*, the one which was performed turn and turn about with *La mandragola*. This is an elegant and heartless tale of symmetrical trickery, elaborating on a device first found in *Decameron* III, 6. Two young students end up triumphantly in beds where they have no business to be; while an old husband is left not only soundly cuckolded, but locked all night in a cold courtyard, miserably imitating the call of the horned owl which he thought was to be his password to an illicit night of love. The two young married women who participate in all this and reap their sexual reward are allowed some appearances on stage, and one even has a traditional *malmaritata* soliloquy on the tedium of a young wife with an old husband. But we are not allowed to see the widow with whom the old man hoped to enjoy himself, because although she too participates in the conspiracy she ends up with her virtue fully preserved.

The influence of the written *novella* may account for some of the detailed ways in which these playwrights adapted their Roman models, particularly where the source was Plautus rather than Terence. The *novella* provided a model of coherent narrative, and Terence offered one of smooth mimetic dialogue, whereas Plautus breaks down more often into a series of virtuoso theatrical 'numbers' for one or two performers. Florentine authors appreciated the value of verbal fireworks in comedy, but they preferred a scene or conversation not to become too stylized and self-contained – in the terms proposed in our Chapter 2, they tended to follow the 'literary' model of Machiavelli (and Ariosto) rather than the 'theatrical' model of Bibbiena (and Aretino). The best text to work on, in order to demonstrate this, is probably Gelli's *La sporta* – as well as being openly based on a single Plautine source (the *Aulularia*), it was approved sufficiently to be printed eleven times before 1605, the highest number of editions achieved among comedies from Florence.

Gelli learned from Plautus that there can be some virtue in starting a comedy with a scene of agitation and noise, to wake the audience up – most Italian plays produced before this one had tended to begin rather soberly, with a lot of narrative and exposition. So after his Prologue, we have the miser Ghirigoro ('Euclio' in Plautus) driving the wretched old female servant Brigida ('Staphyla') out into the street without explanation:

GHIRIGORO: Get out, get out, Brigida! Out, I say, do you hear me? Look at the way she moves – you'd think I was talking to someone else.

BRIGIDA: Oh Lord, what is it now? You're yelling as if you've gone berserk.

GHIRIGORO: And you've gone to the dogs. Hark at her answering back. I'm telling you to get out of that door.

BRIGIDA: And where am I supposed to go?

GHIRIGORO: Out of the house, here, into the street.

BRIGIDA: What for?

GHIRIGORO: You'll see. Do I have to give reasons to you for what I want? And she still won't unstick herself from that doorway.

BRIGIDA: All right, here I am, I'm out.

GHIRIGORO: (God, look at her, she's in a trance, she squints at you and rolls her eyes like an ostrich.) What do you think you're looking at?

She's still not moving. She looks just like a goose. Are you going to get
out of the way, or do I have to clout you on the head good and proper?

BRIGIDA: God knows what this is all about. What do you want me to do?

GHIRIGORO: Go further over there, and look away in that direction: and
don't look round until I call you, or else I'll break your skull.

BRIGIDA: All right, I've turned round. If that's all I've got to do, let's get
on with it. (I'd rather go and live in a you-know-what than have to
run round after this crazy old fool.)

GHIRIGORO: (What's she muttering to herself, the crook? God, what a
degenerate! I'll poke her eyes out, she's not going to see what I'm up
to . . .) (*La sporta*, Act I, Scene I[73])

A comparison with the equivalent opening scene of *Aulularia* (lines
40–59, after Plautus' Prologue spoken by the Household God) will
show that this is very close indeed, without being a direct translation. Another example of how close the two plays can be is in the
long scene between Euclio and Megadorus (lines 180–267), which in
La sporta becomes Act III, Scene I between Ghirigoro and Lapo – in
both cases a marriage is proposed, rather laboriously and with
interruptions, between the miser's daughter and the second old
man. But it is equally instructive to note what Gelli has chosen to
leave out of his original: for example, the desperate soliloquy of the
miser when he finds that his money has been stolen (*Aulularia* lines
713–26, the source for Harpagon's famous monologue in Molière's
L'Avare); and the banter between the cooks (lines 280–326) containing a series of music-hall gags about Euclio's extreme avarice ('He's
so mean that he saves his nail clippings . . .' etc.). Both these scenes
have good performing potential: one has to deduce that for Gelli
they actually contained too much 'performance', and went beyond
what he saw as the bounds of properly mimetic dialogue. This
avoidance of anything too overtly theatrical is a characteristic of
most Florentine playwrights at this time. It means that their scripts
offer fewer casual 'jokes' or one-liners compared with their Sienese
counterparts, a lack of verbal liveliness which many of them try to
compensate by the use of a consciously Florentine colloquial turn of
phrase, with proverbs and expressions which are graphic and familiar enough to raise a laugh of recognition in the audience. They
thus hoped to provide an enriched model of approved literary
'Tuscan', and at the same time to have the local appeal which
elsewhere would be obtained by writing in dialect.

There are two playwrights of whom brief separate mention should
be made, simply because they were so prolific. The 'regular'

comedies of Giovan Maria Cecchi (1518–87) do not stand out from
other Florentine works already discussed, but there are as many as
twenty-five of them (including three 'farces' in three acts)[74] out of
his total of fifty dramatic compositions of all kinds. Only ten were
published during the sixteenth century, leaving problems of dating
for some of those left in manuscript, but the best efforts of scholars
give Cecchi a career stretching from 1544 until his death in 1587.[75]
Douglas Radcliff-Umstead, in his study of 1986, divides the
comedies into those based more on Roman sources and those based
more on *novella* material. We have already mentioned those which
were composed before 1555, including the much appreciated Boccaccian *L'assiuolo*.

Even after Radcliff-Umstead's very welcome monograph, a good
deal remains to be discovered about Cecchi's place in Florentine
dramatic activity, and much of it would cast welcome light on the
nature and range of that activity itself. Cecchi seems to have written
principally for the bourgeois confraternities rather than for the
court, and to have stood on the social ladder a rung or two lower
than those dramatists more often patronized by the Medici. Such
more modest ambitions perhaps explain why only half of his
comedies were published, and also why only half of his total production consists of comedies His other dramas were developments of
morality plays and *sacre rappresentazioni*, in which the new classical
formats were grafted as much as possible on to plays with a religious
or moral message – some of these being stories or parables from the
Bible, some containing abstractions as well as human characters,
and all involving some overt intervention from the Christian super-
natural world. There is an increase in such didactic plays, and a
decrease in secular comedies, as Cecchi's career moved on, and
perhaps we should not be too resistant to the simple explanations for
such a change: the increasing sobriety which comes with getting
older, and the more restrictive moral climate of the Counter-
Reformation which we shall be discussing in Chapter 6. But we
should also note that in writing both genres Cecchi was catering to
the real tastes of a regular audience – nobody can produce as many
as fifty plays if people do not want to see them. The taste for 'regular'
comedy, even if mixed with other more traditional tastes, was
extending down into the middle ranges of Florentine society, so the
genre was no longer an exclusive preserve of the court and aristocracy.

Another aspect of Cecchi's writing which places him in a more conservative category is his eventual predilection for verse over prose in comedy. Six of his five-act comedies written in the 1540s were in prose, and anthologized in that version; but all except *L'assiuolo* and *I dissimili* were rewritten in verse for a subsequent 1585 anthology, and everything was in verse after 1550. (In secular comedy he used a simple blank hendecasyllable, without Ariosto's inconvenient *sdrucciolo* rhythm.) The debate about verse or prose was taken more seriously in Florence than elsewhere, and was conducted with constant reference to Classical precedent:[76] Florentine playwrights, and Cecchi in particular, swell considerably the modest proportion of Italian comedies which used verse in the sixteenth century.[77]

Anton Francesco Grazzini (1504–84) has eight surviving prose comedies (one, *Il frate*, in only three acts): six were published in a single-volume anthology in 1582, the author admitting that four of them had never been performed. *Il frate* ('The Friar') and *L'arzigogolo* ('The Quibble') were left unpublished until the eighteenth century; the performed plays were *Il frate* (1540), *La gelosia* (1550), and *La spiritata* ('The Bewitched Girl', 1560). Grazzini draws attention to himself in his prologues by questioning the dependence of modern comedy on ancient models, and suggesting that it is time to abandon a number of creaky devices which have no basis in contemporary life:

... out of all the comedies which have been performed in Florence, from the siege until now, every one has long-lost children in it, they all end in recognitions. And audiences have got so fed up with this, that when they hear in the Argument that girls and boys were lost in the capture of some city or in the sack of some castle, they realize they've heard it all before, and would gladly leave if they could do it without offence ... [These authors] should just translate, for Heaven's sake, if they haven't any imagination, rather than patch together and spoil other people's stuff and their own together: it's common sense and prudence to be able to adjust to the times ... So in this comedy there are no rediscoveries of lost children, because such things have never happened in our day, especially in Tuscany; and the same too with those pimps and merchants who trade in young girls and have women for sale. (*La gelosia*, Prologue (1551 edition))

('The siege' is the one of 1530 which brought the Republic finally to its end.) For a modern reader this sounds encouraging, and *La gelosia* itself, concentrating on the intrigues of a single night, does avoid all the pitfalls mentioned. However, critics from Sanesi onwards have remarked that Grazzini was more radical in theory than he often was in practice, and that 'rediscoveries' ('ritrovamenti') eventually find their way into his comedies too. Moreover, the fact that half his comedies were unperformed rather reduces Grazzini's significance for a theatre historian.

One has to take care not to denigrate Florentine comedy, or to discuss it with an over-obvious lack of enthusiasm. A number of modern preconceptions, not least the preference for originality, intrude on a fair historical judgement. The plays seem to possess little of the pioneering spirit which make some of their predecessors more exciting (and their faults more excusable); their careful avoidance of theatricality works to their detriment, in a genre which to us now has no hope of achieving much realism; and their laughter quotient is sometimes low – Benedetto Varchi, in his Prologue to *La suocera*, says that making people laugh is at best a secondary characteristic of comedy. Nevertheless, if we are to take the years around 1555 as a notional watershed, the contribution of Florence to a comic tradition cannot be ignored. The sheer quantity of plays produced tended to establish a kind of run-of-the-mill norm, for good or for ill; and the repetition of that norm fulfilled the all-important function of building theatrical genre expectations in a steadily wider audience. It is symptomatic that Grazzini could paint a brief picture of spectators saying, effectively, 'Here we go again, the same old stuff.' By 1555, as opposed to 1525, a public existed which understood what at the start of the century had been a revolutionary and possibly puzzling mode of theatre. Florence in particular (as well as Venice, which we are now about to discuss) may have been a place in which that public was middle class as well as aristocratic, thus aiding the process whereby a popular commercial form of theatre, *commedia dell'arte*, could confidently use story lines from *commedia erudita* as raw material. There grew up a steady repetition of plots which humiliated miserly fathers and old men in love, enjoyed the inventiveness and scurrility of servants, indulged but perhaps also mocked the self-absorbed passions and rhetoric of young lovers, and permutated a limited range of intrigue devices and deceits, centring most of all on mistaken or assumed identity. In its way, Florentine comedy was establishing a stock repertoire, just as Alessandro Piccolomini had wanted to do from Siena with his more academic project of sample characters and scenes – but Florence was doing it collectively, cumulatively, and in practice rather than in theory.

CHAPTER 4

The second quarter-century, Venice and Padua

SPECTACLE AND POLITICS IN VENICE

In the previous chapter, especially when dealing with Siena and Florence, some reference has been made to elements which might foreshadow the methods and content of *commedia dell'arte*, that unique form of popular professional theatre which created itself in considerable part out of the material which erudite 'regular' comedy had made available. However, if we have to search for a *principal* centre from which *commedia dell'arte* might have sprung, there would be no doubt among scholars that we must look to Venice. It is for this reason that the present study has chosen to approach Venice separately, breaking the more or less chronological pattern which has been followed so far, and starting the story over again in the 1520s.[1]

The features of *commedia dell'arte* which seem either unique to Venetian secular comedy, or else are more firmly established there than in other centres, can be listed here briefly as a preliminary orientation. The first point to make is the most banal and most convincing. The core of *arte* 'situation comedy' is generally recognized as being the confrontation between master and servant: the archetypal master is the Venetian Magnifico, later christened 'Pantalone'; the servant is Zani, who eventually gave rise to a multitude of other low-life masks including (by a more complex process) that of Arlecchino/Harlequin. Zani, and eventually also Arlecchino, speak the curious up-country dialect of the hills behind Bergamo – Pantalone naturally speaks his own Venetian. The region of Bergamo seems to have exported a lot of menial labour in the sixteenth

century, to various parts of Italy: there is a brief appearance of a
Bergamask or at least Lombard porter in Bibbiena's *Calandra*, set in
Rome. But Bergamo by now was part of the Republic of Venice, and
the city on the lagoon was the natural metropolis for the migrant
peasant from Val Brembana. In any case, Pantalone the master is
Venetian, and if this type of comedy has any root at all in a
rudimentary social realism, then the pairing of Pantalone and Zani
has to be set in Venice. Secondly, the convention that each character should speak its own distinct dialect is also rooted in Venetian
scripted models – we have seen other (Tuscan) examples of plays
with some linguistic variety, but it was in Venice that such an
approach was most characteristic. Thirdly, in the figures of
Ruzante, Calmo and Giancarli, the Venetian region produced the
first semi-professional playwrights who were also actors, and who
were each distinguished for their regular incarnation of a single
character or mask with a repeated repertoire. Linked to all this is a
more general point, harder to prove but left as a strong impression
by surviving evidence – that is, that Venetian performance organization was particularly open, compared with that in other centres,
to collaboration between upper-class amateurs and lower-class professionals. If this is true, then it would facilitate the process by which
relatively uneducated performers became acquainted with, and
took over, the material of *commedia erudita*.

When one speaks of 'Venice' in this period, one needs to define
one's terms. The Venetian Republic was a substantial territory
extending up into the Alps and across the Po valley nearly as far as
Milan.[2] For present purposes, however, we need not spread the net
so wide. The studies of Noemi Messora[3] have dealt separately with
how 'regular' comedy developed in Brescia, and how it failed to
develop in Verona, under the Venetian régime. It was on the lagoon
itself that the most individual theatre practices were born and
nourished; and the city of Padua, just thirty kilometres inland, has
to be included only because of the career of a single genius, Ruzante,
whose work was never very far from the attention of a Venetian
public.

The structures of the Venetian state and society were unique in
Italy and in Europe. There was a titular head, the Doge, elected
rather than hereditary; but he presided as constitutional monarch
over a republic which was run entirely by an officially recognized
group of noble families, all inscribed in the state's Golden Book.

Control was firm, it came from the top, but it was none the less collective, with individuals constantly changing one office for another. They thus succeeded remarkably well in reflecting the interests of a ruling class rather than a single person; and even more remarkably, patriotism and loyalty to the state seems to have been intense in all classes, even the disenfranchised. The most powerful families, when it came to the point, were prepared to subordinate the interests of their clan to those of the whole state, showing a solidarity which recognized a longer-term interest. It was this last fact, perhaps, which caused the admiration, mixed with irritation and perplexity, with which other Italians regarded the Venetian constitution: in no other city had family faction interests been suppressed by any means other than the enforced dominance of one dynasty over all the rest. (The rise of the Medici in Florence is a late example of this.)

Throughout the Renaissance and beyond, therefore, Venice was run by a strong centralized bureaucracy which yet had few of the characteristics of a princely court. Public entertainment and festivity always focussed on the celebration of Venice, but its organization was usually devolved to private groups, 'licensed' formally by the state for the occasion. By the sixteenth century, these groups included societies of young noblemen referred to collectively as Compagnie della Calza ('Companies of the Stocking', because they used coloured hose and garters as a distinctive heraldic uniform). There were many of these over the decades between 1450 and 1550: the system was that a group of noble friends from one generation would band together, adopt a name and a livery, and expect their Compagnia to flourish and then eventually to die with them. Typical names chosen were the Valorosi, the Eterni, the Cortesi, and the Fraterni.[4]

Venice made a relatively slow approach to 'regular' comedy. A longer period of original comedies in Latin was coupled with the lively maintenance of more local traditions of drama and spectacle: even Plautus and Terence in translation were not introduced to the city until 1507. Early performances took place in the private houses of interested nobles: when a Compagnia della Calza was involved, no doubt all the members subscribed to the expense, but quite early on there developed the practice of either distributing or selling tickets.[5] The response of the Venetian government, in December 1508, was formally to ban theatrical entertainment in the city; and it is a curious fact that the succeeding decades were punctuated by a series of such bans, obviously ineffective,[6] in what was to become the most theatre-oriented centre in Italy.

The local traditions just referred to were a complex mixture. Entertainments called *momarie* were mounted for public festivals, in which, in the words of Padoan, 'the religious theme was linked deliberately and inseparably to the celebration of the State, with the participation of the highest political authorities' (1982, p. 32). These were multiple spectacles, a blend of allegorical pageant, oratory, vaudeville and occasional drama, with an appeal ranging from the most intellectual to the most basic: they involved the collaborative participation of all classes, including professional buffoons and mountebanks (such as the Zuan Polo already mentioned in connection with Aretino's *Marescalco*). Similar shows were mounted on a smaller scale for private celebrations, such as weddings. Texts do not survive, but brief descriptions and records sometimes do.

In the years around 1500, the skills of buffoons and *giullari* were clearly much in demand, and one of those skills was the comic mimicry of non-Venetian accents and dialects, with the speech of Bergamo already established as a popular object of mockery. This led to a theatrical preoccupation (expressed in short dialogues and sketches, some of which have survived) with low-life characters generally. Comedies *alla bulesca* depicted in satirical and contemptuous light the *bulli*, or *bravi*, or professional thugs, who featured on the urban scene. On the mainland, where there was a proper rural community, the target of satire could be the peasants; and this subject matter became familiar to Venetians too. There are links in both style and substance (though not, of course, in language) between peasant sketches from the Veneto region and those being produced in Siena by the Congrega dei Rozzi. It seems to have been from Padua University that there came some texts known as *mariazi*, dramatic rituals of betrothal set in peasant villages. In these dramas, the crudity and awkwardness of peasant behaviour and language is taken to the limit, with extended double-entendres about the alleged freedom and brutishness of their sexual experience. Even in the early anonymous versions, a modern reader finds it difficult not to see a certain fascination, and even a concealed envy, on the part of the superior citizens who wrote and watched the plays. In depicting, and even impersonating, characters who seem to have none of the normal civilized constraints on their behaviour, Paduans and Venetians may on the one hand have been seeking the laughter of superior contempt, but there could also have been an element of carnival involved which they were less willing to acknowledge.

In 1508–9, the Venetian mainland state was suddenly attacked and nearly destroyed by the War of Cambrai, in which a huge coalition of Italian and larger foreign states ganged up against it. The alliance failed to hold together, and the peril passed; but Venetians had briefly seen, to their astonishment, that while the nobles in their subject cities were only too keen to collaborate with the invaders and shake off their yoke, the peasant class showed an obstinate and unexpected loyalty to the Lion of St Mark. In subsequent years, therefore, some stereotype views were shaken, and there was a new readiness to view the rural classes with tolerance and even some sympathy.

RUZANTE

Venetian gentlemen, even some who were not inscribed in the Golden Book, had come over the decades to know peasants better as tenants, since there had been a steady move in the fifteenth century towards the purchasing of country villas and estates. One particularly prominent and enterprising landlord was Alvise Cornaro (c. 1484–1566), who has been studied in his own right by economic historians. Cornaro shared the same surname (Cornèr or Corrèr in Venetian) as a leading noble family, but the Republic's lawyers had dismissed his claim to be included in the Golden Book. Excluded from the magic circle and from all political function, he camped on the Venetian doorstep in Padua like a rejected suitor trying to show his beloved what she is missing. He built up large estates by draining and reclaiming land near the lagoon, repopulated them with tenants, and increased their productivity. On the strength of the profits, he had some splendid houses built to his own design (some of which can still be visited), and set up a kind of private entourage or court which consciously promulgated a lifestyle based on Cornaro's personal ethic and medical régime.[7] He acquired a very respectable following of artists and writers, including one Angelo Beolco (c. 1495–1542), the illegitimate son of a senior academic at Padua University. Beolco acted for his patron in many capacities, including that of legal agent; but he has come down to posterity as a specialist in comic theatre and entertainment, under the name of the character whom he often played and made his own – 'Ruzante'.[8]

Beolco was a composer and performer of occasional entertainments, and it is likely that a considerable amount of what he wrote has not survived. A body of his work was published posthumously from 1551 onwards (see Chapter 3, p. 65); but his surviving production from before the Sack of Rome was left in manuscript until recent times: *La Pastoral* (now dated to 1521) and two versions of *La Betía* (1523 and 1525).[9] Neither play can qualify as 'regular' comedy in the classical mode; but Ruzante's career and contribution to the genre can only be discussed as a unity, and most critics would now see these two as belonging to the core of his individual achievement.[10]

La pastoral is a variegated entertainment in twenty-one scenes. It begins in the very stylized vein of classical pastoral imitation,[11] with Milesio the shepherd unsuccessfully wooing a nymph, and killing himself out of sentimental despair. His friend Mopso swoons with grief by his side. Into this atmosphere of high-flown preciosity stumbles Ruzante the peasant with his bird nets, and from then on the 'serious' characters and their literary language fight a losing battle with the subversive earthiness of broad rustic Paduan dialect, with a quack doctor speaking Bergamask thrown in for further confusion. The play resolves itself into a series of separate theatrical numbers, including a glorious repetitive confrontation between Ruzante and the Doctor in which the former plays linguistic havoc with the latter's medical jargon. Ruzante, who had spoken the first of two prologues (the second one being a 'serious' one in literary Italian), brings the proceedings to a close by leading a dance of actors and audience together. The whole composition is in verse, a very brief seven-syllable line with overtones of popular song.

La Betía, in its original longer version, uses the same metre, and stretches to more than five thousand lines in five leisurely acts. The core of its plot is the *mariazo*, already dramatized anonymously in the Padua region, in which a young peasant couple – after hesitation, dispute, and an abortive elopement – is formally betrothed by a person of suitable status in the village (here the innkeeper Taçío). Around this core of satirized ritual Beolco accumulated a somewhat bewildering series of set-piece scenes including a dialogue on platonic love parodying Pietro Bembo's *Asolani* (Act I); a ritual abduction; a fight on stage; a mock death; and a speech allegedly from Hell. Many of these were undoubtedly adapted versions of existing routines from mumming plays, street theatre and *giullare* patter monologues. But Ruzante also manages to develop a plot of rivalry, disagreement and betrayal which creates a drama of character and manners, transcending the limited scope of his anonymous models. The whole text is in rustic *Pavano* dialect, with no elements of literary 'Tuscan' at all. The play is now linked by theatre historians to a performance in Venice in the Ariani household in February 1525, mounted by a Compagnia della Calza called the Triumphanti; and its vulgarity did not go down well in respectable company.[12] Offence may have been caused not only by the language itself, but by one scene in Act II, where the peasant girl Betía lifts her skirts and shows her backside to her suitor as a gesture of derision. As a theatre practitioner Ruzante was effectively banished to the mainland for some time afterwards.

The character played by Beolco in *La Betía* bears the name 'Zilio', but is clearly the same figure in essence as the 'Ruzante' of the *Pastoral*, *Parlamento*, *Moscheta* and *Fiorina*, and the 'Mènego' of the *Dialogo facetissimo*. Beolco was adopting the expedient of many popular comedians in building on a figure which his audience had shown they would relate to, and simply developing it in a series of different (or sometimes very similar) situations. The continuity came from his exterior stage personality, rather than from a consistent inner psychology or social situation – and this makes 'Ruzante' a true mask (like Chaplin's tramp, who is not always a tramp), rather than a stock character. He was being 'professional' in playing to his strengths, and in basing his dramatic compositions on his stage practice and physical resources rather than on a more abstract literary or narrative conception. His public acknowledged him by remembering him more by his stage name than by the one under which he was christened.

The 'Ruzante' figure is basically a comic victim or underdog, and in this sense he seems to appeal to all the more aggressive instincts of a city audience eager to mock and humiliate the peasant. Zilio in *La Betía* is a wimpish, clumsy wooer who initially inspires Betía's contempt – he is urged on, mocked and exploited by the much more forceful figure of his friend Nale, who hopes to cuckold him (but finds the situation complicated by the appearance of his own wife Tamía). It is Nale who expresses, in a monologue in Act IV (vv. 117–60 of that act) the doctrine that God made suckers so that smart people can make fools of them, and it is thus our sacred duty to take the opportunity – an attitude which seems to sum up a great deal of Italian comic spirit in the early sixteenth century.

After 1525, Ruzante continued to create theatre for Cornaro's household, and seems sometimes to have been invited to neighbouring courts such as Ferrara, as dramatist or performer or both. He came into contact with Ariosto, and respected his expertise. All his compositions after *La Betía* are in prose, suggesting that he was persuaded by the example of what was happening in secular comedy in these other courts. Eventually he came to accept the five-act structure too, but continued to produce a number of much briefer occasional pieces for performance after dinner, without division into acts – he tended to call them *Dialoghi*. Three of them have survived, all dated by Giorgio Padoan to the year 1529. The first was performed in January, in Cornaro's hunting lodge, and appeared with the all-purpose title of *Dialogo facetissimo* ('Very Funny Dialogue'): it is a strictly occasional piece of great variety, mixing Paduan peasant characters and bullies with a symbolic forest magician (probably to be identified as Cornaro himself), and the offstage spirit of a recently dead friend. Cornaro's personal ethic, and the solidarity of his assembled household, are celebrated and gently mocked in the grim contemporary context of a disastrous famine.[13]

The other two pieces, which were published together just as 'Two Dialogues', are remarkable in the context of Italian Renaissance theatre. They are entitled *Parlamento de Ruzante che iera vegnú de campo* ('Conversation of Ruzante Returned from the Battlefield') and *Bilora* (possibly 'Weasel' in dialect, the name of the protagonist). Both contain a bleak subversive realism which in the *Parlamento* is wrapped in farce, and in *Bilora* is hardly veiled at all.

In the *Parlamento*, Ruzante is a peasant conscripted into the Venetian army, and returned from a campaign further west in the Po valley. He has dragged himself back to Venice, in utter misery and destitution. He has a monologue, and then an extended dialogue with his friend Menato, in which the unheroic details of soldierly behaviour are starkly and comically revealed. (Menato would be played by Beolco's colleague Marco Alvarotto, who was regularly given a more solid peasant part alongside the unstable Ruzante figure.) Ruzante has failed to capitalize on the war, and has spent most of his time on the march or in flight – he even had a reversible surcoat, so that in a rout he could mingle with the enemy troops instead of his own. He none the less tries to extract status from his experience, with a repeated 'If you'd been where I've been ...' phrase hard to translate well from the deliberately garbled dialect –

'S'a fossè stò là on' son stato io mi . . .' It then emerges that his wife
Gnua has come into town and is now living with a *bravo*, a member
of the strongarm urban underworld. When she appears, she is
unimpressed with Ruzante's derelict state, and not very inclined to
go back with him to live in rural poverty again. The *bravo* (a
non-speaking part) bursts in and beats Ruzante up; and the final
scene consists of our hero fantasizing (like Falstaff, among others)
about the dozens of men who have just set on him, and about the
violent deeds he could have performed had he realized that there
was only one of them. The end of the sketch is textually uncertain,
and may even have been left for Ruzante to improvise in response to
different performing occasions.

The *Parlamento* reveals a good deal about current economic and
miltary reality – it is one of the very few Italian Renaissance texts
which tell the truth about war, instead of turning it into heroic
rhetoric and symbolism. It is still cast in the tone of a rather crude
farce, though, and thus does not entirely break moulds already
established in Venetian theatre – it has enough of the knockabout
bulesca character to be familiar. *Bilora* goes several stages further,
and in terms of genre is entirely out on a limb. Bilora himself, a
tougher variant on 'Ruzante' rather than a simple repetition of the
mask, is a Paduan peasant come to Venice in search of his wife Dina,
who has been abducted by an elderly merchant called Andronico.
Bilora discusses the matter with his friend Pitaro (Alvarotto again);
and then with Dina who speaks from the merchant's window, and
who is torn between the unsavouriness of Andronico's embraces and
the attractions of a life of ease. We see Andronico himself, musing on
his desire to make up for what he lost in youth – and, in theatrical
terms, tracing the first outlines of the Pantalone mask, with his
upper-class Venetian dialect (quite distinct from Ruzante's *Pavano*)
and his old man's lust: he even has a Bergamask servant, Zane, who
only has one or two lines. When it comes to the point, Andronico is
unwilling to let Dina go, and more importantly Dina herself decides
that rural misery is too high a price to pay for fidelity. Bilora has a
monologue in which he fantasizes drunkenly about killing Andronico. There are quite a few laughs in this disjointed performance,
and the audience are no doubt prepared for the bravado to collapse
in the face of reality, as with most such displays by unconvincingly
bellicose characters. Astonishingly, when Andronico does emerge,
Bilora actually stabs him to death, and leaves him there with the

final words of the play – 'Didn't I tell you?' ('Te l'hegi dito?').
Comedy, for an upper-class audience, must surely be exploded at
this point, and it is hard to know what reaction Beolco expected –
unless (and this is not a very convincing theory) he felt licensed to
express this extreme degree of resentment from the Paduan mainland against the Venetian ruling class, and thought that even
Paduan noblemen would go along with it.

The relationship between the peasant and the city is explored
further in the five-act farce *La moscheta* ('The Posh-Talking
Comedy'), also dated to 1529. Ruzante and his wife Betía are living
in Padua, and have been followed there by their friend and *compare*[14]
Menato, who is desperately in lust with Betía. Betía, a woman with a
mind of her own, is also pursued by a neighbour, a Bergamask
soldier. Ruzante is persuaded by Menato to dress up as a city
student, and woo his own wife talking 'moscheto' – a word in *Pavano*
for any upper-class or literary speech ('Florentinish ... talking like
those Nealopitans from Urbino'). The aim is to test her fidelity in
the face of an upper-class seducer. Betía, as Menato hoped, is furious
with Ruzante; but she shows the fact by going next door to live with
Tonin the soldier, which is not what Menato intended. A number of
confrontations, tricks and arguments ensue before the situation is
resolved, including a night scene of great theatrical skill in which
Ruzante is groping about the stage entirely blind and cannot understand what is happening.

Commentators on the 1529 plays have found much to say in terms
of links between their content and real social history. Ruzante may
have been pandering, as all comedians must, to the prejudices and
favourite derisions of his audience; but at the very least he was
drawing laughs from the way in which peasants might really have
behaved, and from what they were undoubtedly having to cope
with, rather than from a preconceived set of caricature features
which would make the audience feel comfortably superior (as was
more the case with cruder peasant sketches, both from the Veneto
and from Siena). A modern sympathy with exploited classes is a
dangerous lens through which to view these plays – it is beyond
belief that they could have had any serious subversive programme
behind them. Nevertheless, Beolco has left in his texts, consciously or
unconsciously, a level of realism and insight which is impossible to
ignore. In some Ruzantian texts that sympathy even seems developed into some kind of philosophy of the 'natural' as against the

over-civilized: this too is a critical commonplace when writing about Beolco, and it is important to set it in its theatrical context and perceive its limitations. How far is the peasant figure credited with a paradoxical 'natural' wisdom which his alleged superiors do not share? How far does Ruzante take on the guise of the heroic Fool, licensed to preach to the wise?

In all the plays so far examined, the 'Ruzante' character regularly loses his woman to someone stronger or, at best, gets her back only by a charitable concession in order to create a happy ending. He is thus in plot terms an object of derision – a fool in the non-heroic sense, a coward, an inadequate, a loser. A character so thoroughly abject may express some miserable realistic truths, but cannot easily be used as a source of 'wisdom', however paradoxical. That is simply not the sort of relationship which 'Ruzante' builds with an audience, within his stage fictions. It was when he turned to address the audience directly, outside the *fabula*, that Ruzante (with or without the inverted commas) perhaps became something more complex. His philosophy of 'el snatural', and his claim to have something to communicate to the ruling class, is limited very firmly at this time to prologues, and to the separate compositions called *Orazioni* which have no fictional-dramatic dimension. That does not exclude them from consideration as theatre. On the contrary, they make us face more squarely a trend which we have already often had to mention: the ready acceptance by Italian audiences of a theatrical relationship with a single performer or haranguer, academic orator or *giullare* as he may have been.

Ruzante, in his two *Orazioni* as well as in his lengthy dialect prologues, shows himself able to be orator and *giullare* at the same time. The *Orazioni* which survive were composed in 1520 and 1528, both as formal addresses of welcome to visiting Cardinals associated with the Veneto region.[15] Ruzante adopts his peasant persona and *Pavano* dialect throughout – but there are a number of implicit admissions in the text that the author is really a man of considerable culture (sometimes in the form of parodic references and distorted names), and the reader is struck even at this distance by Beolco's fine diplomatic judgement, balancing outright flattery with whatever else he could get away with. We do not have here the incompetent humiliated 'Ruzante' of the dramatic fictions, but a more knowing balance between the stage mask and the actor/author's known personality and status. And this peasant, for all his surface clumsiness of language (which is exploited to the last ounce for its distorting comic effect), is in fact the most eloquent of speakers as he works through topics such as a lyrical exaltation of the Paduan countryside and its products, a teasing flattery of a Cardinal's prowess in the hunting field, a more sober evocation of the effects of severe famine (in the second *Orazione* of 1528), or the proposition of new laws for the countryside which mix paradoxical common sense with outrageous fantasy. A few brief snippets may dimly convey the mixture of frankness, carnival licence, and sheer verbal patter – though it has to be said that any attempt to translate Ruzante's dialect falls flat, because English has no register or variant which has the same status. The first of the following pieces is actually the opening words of the first Oration.

It's a right poxy trick to stick yourself where you shouldn't and where it's not proper – and so I, that is to say me, since I am, like the man said, an accompfished person, I watch what I'm doing, don't I? And theretofore, my Rebelend Lord Discardinal, there's no way I was going to come and do this disprologue in Padua. Why not? Well, because those poxy bigmouthed shithouses, those disliterary types, they wouldn't like it. Because, like the proverb says, 'You can't put Jews and Samaritans in the same room', which is the same as saying that married men and bachelors don't get along. Why is that? Well, because just as bachelors are always trying to cuckold the husbands, those town people are always making fun of us poor peasants from the country. And so we keep well out of their way, like sparrows dodging the hawk ... (*Prima Orazione*, 1–2)

I want to give Your Rebelence some advice, which those disliterary types from Padua wouldn't know how to give you: 'cos I've been with my boss and heard a lot of those public preaches they've made to you. You take it to heart now, 'cos it's important: 'It's better to live as a coward than to die as a brave man.' (*Prima Orazione*, 32)

(This is an oblique way of praising the Cardinal's bravery in the hunt, by making it clear that ordinary people are more cautious.)

there's a lot of poxy aggravation and bad blood between us peasants in the country and the townies in Padua, and it all gets under our skin and gives us a lot of hassle. And if we were the ones on top, like they are now ... well, bim bam thank you ma'am, they wouldn't last five minutes with us. Never mind. They call us peasants 'hicks' and 'snakes' and 'toads'; and we call them 'shithouses' and 'swine' and 'roosurers' and 'blood-suckers on poor decent folk'. So we'd like you – 'cos, like I said, we're the ones who are underneath – we'd like you to patch up our quarrels, and make us all the same. (*Prima Orazione*, 51)

(The scheme for 'making us all the same', proposed as number seven of a list of laws which the Cardinal is invited to promulgate, is to decree that all countrymen may take four wives and all country-women four husbands – this will make the town dwellers so envious that they will come and live in the country, and all the barriers will fall.)

Perhaps you're surprised to see me here. Well, it's true, I am here, but I'm here because I came here; and if I hadn't come here I wouldn't be here. (*Seconda Orazione*, 2)

We haven't got any law on our side, one that speaks for us, or which it was one of us that made it. All I ever hear about is 'Datus's law, Bartolus's law, the Digestive law', that sort of thing: I never hear anyone say 'Mènego's law, Nale's law, Duozo's law'. All the laws were made by townies.[16] (*Seconda Orazione*, 18)

I'm giving you this advice as a friend: I don't think you've got a better friend in the world than me, because if I needed a favour, I'd rather ask you for it than any other man I know. (*Seconda Orazione*, 24)

Some of the laws which Ruzante proposes, and the philosophy of 'natural' values which is pursued in the Prologues, have an over-simple attraction to modern readers who belong to a post-Romantic and secular culture. We are used to accepting that sometimes the common sense of the countryman (or proletarian) will defeat the sophistications of the over-educated; and we are not likely to be shocked by the suggestion that money-lending to peasants should be legalized at decent rates, instead of being technically banned by the Church and therefore clandestine and ruinously expensive. Nor will we be upset by the view that peasants should not be forced to fast, because of their heavy manual labour. It is important to stress, therefore, that in the context of the times all the proposals made are fascinating, but shocking, and none of them had any chance of being accepted. They are placed, after all, in the same context as the proposal about polygamy and polyandry, and the claim that priests should either be allowed to marry or else all be castrated. There is an echo of 'carnival' in all this, in Bakhtin's definition; but the text is proposed in the context of an entertainment by and for the ruling class, who are playing distantly with intriguing paradoxes rather than surrendering to them. Beolco may have seen further than they did, but must have been equally aware that his visions were unrea-listic.[17] The situation is summarized with rueful percipience in a dialogue between two peasants in his later play *La vaccaria* of around 1533 (Ruzante himself played the part of Truffo):

TRUFFO: A bit of 'natural' is worth a whole bag of logicals and philosorificals. ... That lot think that no one can do anything without running off to look at a book first.

VEZZO: If only the wheel turned, and the cards were re-shuffled, and we had all the loot and they were where we are now! We'd be the Harry Stottles then; and when we said something, everyone would shut up and listen like crazy. The way things are, people only listen to us for fun, to hear us talk all rough.

TRUFFO: They can say what they like, these rich bosses, but they can't do without us, 'cos if we weren't there to be the servants, they couldn't be the masters.

VEZZO: I wish they were all like *our* bosses: I'd swear myself into Hell for them. (*La vaccaria*, Act II, Scene 1)

In the end, Ruzante seems to acknowledge, his public only listen to him for the entertaining novelty of his inventive 'rough' talk, rather than because he makes sense to them; and after a carnival dig at the system of masters and servants, he has to put in an open tribute to his own 'master' Alvise Cornaro in the audience.[18] Linda Carroll (1983) has suggested that Ruzante, as an illegitimate son on the fringes of his social world, found an outlet for his concealed frustrations by impersonating the untouchable and giving expression to the unthinkable.

We should return, though, to the stage fictions themselves and the heritage which they left for Italian Renaissance dramaturgy. It is noteworthy how these texts have forced even Italian critics, generally reluctant to engage with the practicalities of theatre, to respond to them and analyse them in performance terms. Both their strengths and their weaknesses, as perceived on the page, relate to the real demands of staging and acting with a company of defined and limited talent. The recurrence of certain types of role and situation bears witness to the need to cast the same team of actors in roles where they have proved their competence, and to the equally strong need to give a regular audience another sight of material which they enjoyed the first time. Gags and catch-phrases resurface from one play to another, acquiring by sheer repetition an entertainment value which they do not inherently possess – expressions such as 'Co' disse questú' ('Like the man said'), or 'Con a' ve dego rivar de dire' ('As I was getting round to telling you'). In the earlier plays discussed so far, there are scenes for two or three interlocutors, each tending towards an autonomous structure which could be rehearsed on its own. But what emerges most of all is Ruzante's mastery in composing monologues, for himself and other performers, a skill also developed in the *Orazioni* and Prologues. Here his *giullare* talent is sometimes focussed in traditional fashion on an implicit dialogue with the audience, but at other times turned inward so that a character builds a comic conversation with himself and his own problems as dictated by the fiction. The performing rhythm, and the instinctive variety of tone and pace, are unmistakable, as indeed they are in the *Orazioni* themselves. Beolco shows a kind of 'professionalism', foreshadowing *commedia dell'arte* technique, in recycling and refashioning units of material, large and small, to fit new dramatic situations. What goes beyond mere exterior technique is the way in which the Ruzante mask itself grows by accumulation from one composition to the next. The best monologues pull together all their separate identifiable devices to express a cruel but still comic insight into the mentality of a congenital underdog or loser. With some trepidation, because of the huge translation problems from the dialect, we can look at the fifth scene of the *Dialogo facetissimo*. Mènego, the 'Ruzante' character, is in love with Gnua; but his stronger rival Nale has beaten him up and taken the woman away (as also in the *Parlamento*). Mènego's friend Duozo (probably played by Alvarotto) goes to find a priest-magician who he says can heal wounds, and takes Mènego's short sword (*storta*) to defend himself on the way. Mènego is left in the wood, injured and sorry for himself.

MENEGO: Oh hell, he'll never come back, the speed he travels. And a fat chance he's got of finding that whatsisname fellow, and God knows if he really exists anyway, and even if he does and he's at home he probably won't want to come.[19] And even if he comes, he's going to have a job making my hand better – it's been bashed out of shape. Even Dr Christian bloody Barnardo[20] couldn't get this hand straight. I'm crippled for life! I'll never prune a tree again! Who's going to hire me now? How am I going to earn my corn? All I'll ever cash in now is my poxy bleeding chips, I can't lift a finger, I'll have to go begging.

If I'd shown any guts at all, that bastard wouldn't have clobbered me like he did. It's always been the same: born a coward, christened a coward, now it looks as if I'm going to die in the faith. God, I was bound to die somehow this year – if it wasn't these bruises it would have been starvation, with the famine.

God help me, it would be better to get it over quickly, and kill myself now. Shall I do it, or shan't I? To be, or not to be?[21] Part of me says: 'Go on, Mènego, you're half dead already; and if you don't die of this, you'll starve afterwards.' And another part of me says: 'Don't do it, you'll get better.' And the first part says; 'You're going to starve in any case.' And the second part says: 'You'll be able to live by begging, now you're crippled.' And the first part says: 'You've lost your girl for ever: go ahead and do it.' So I don't know which poxy[22] part of me to pay attention to.

But I'm going to do it, to get my own back on that sneaky two-timing bastard who smashed me up like this – because if I die, they'll be after the swine for murder. That's it – I'll do it. That'll teach you, you poxy coward, you'll be run out of the country, I'll have done for you then! Who's going to believe I killed myself on purpose? They're going to look for the one that bashed me, mate, and *you* will be *it*!

Cor, that's it then, I'll kill myself. But what with? I haven't even got my sword – old Duozo took it. Oh poxing hell, comrade, trust you to make things difficult! Just when I really needed that sword, you go and take it away. I shouldn't have poxing well let you have it. Ah well, I'll just have to kill myself without it. Better still, I'll eat myself, all by myself, so at least I'll die with a full belly, even though there's a shortage. And nobody will ever guess, they'll think that bastard killed me and then the dogs came and ate me up – they'll still be after him for murder. You'll still be on the run, you bastard!

But what about old Duozo? I can't do it, after all, because of him. You know, you're getting to be a right drag, comrade! I can't do it after all, because if I kill myself then that sod will say it was you, comrade, because you've got my sword. And in that case *you'll* be on the run, comrade, for something you didn't do. I'm sorry, comrade, I'm still going to kill myself, whatever happens to you. You'll have to forgive me, and take what comes. You can keep the sword.

Hey, boots! You're going to be the only witnesses of a terrible mad violent death. Never before has it been known for a man to eat himself up on purpose. It's a great sin, though, God help me, for a man to die so young. Gnua! – you've seen the last of me. Oh Lord, forgive my sins, at least I shan't be able to commit any more. I confess that I've been a thief, but I did it in order to eat. Apart from that, I've done no harm. I'd better say a *paternoster* ...

No, I won't eat myself, it's too much of an effort, I'll choke myself instead. (*Dialogo facetissimo*, Scene 5)

And he is interrupted at this point, in the middle of whatever grotesque business Beolco had invented for himself, by Duozo's return.

The suicide monologue eventually became part of *commedia dell' arte* repertoire. Ruzante has a variant of this one in *La moscheta* (III, 6), shorter and adapted to the plot of that play: the idea of eating himself to death is used there too. In the example quoted, in a play written in the middle of a horrible famine, the joke about dying with a full belly has a defiant topicality which can never be reproduced again. There are gags and formats here which were very much part of his regular repertoire – the improvisation of a peasant paternoster, no doubt hilariously garbled; the dialogue with himself about what to do (the original versions refer untranslatably to 'Un cuore ... l'altro cuore – One heart ... the other heart'); and the direct address, aggressive or pathetic, to characters off stage and to inanimate objects. What is striking, though, is how these tried theatrical routines succeed in expressing plausible human reactions and moods, however comically exaggerated. It is this coincidence of technique and insight which puts Ruzante in a different category from any dramatist so far examined in these pages.

The accumulation of memorable texts in 1529 seems to show an intense burst of creativity, though the picture may be distorted by the accident of what has and has not survived. At all events, it was by no means the end of Ruzante's career. The year does mark a turning point, in that *La moscheta* adapts and expands its author's farcical skills both in prose and in the canonical five-act framework. Giorgio Padoan (1982, pp. 119–20) suggests that Beolco was coming out of a self-imposed anti-academic isolation, and allowing himself more influence from representatives of 'official' culture such as Ariosto and Pietro Bembo. Certainly the remainder of his production accepts, for good or ill, the need to integrate with *commedia erudita*, without surrendering his personal style and insights.

La Fiorina (*c.* 1531? – named after its heroine) is a rather lightweight, even hesitant attempt at turning the 'peasant betrothal' (*mariazo*) scenario of *La Betía* into a simple five-act piece in prose. But then Ruzante gained confidence, and perhaps became persuaded suddenly that there was enough in common between his aims and those of Plautus, each in relationship to his own time and society, to make of the Latin writer a model which would not be too cramping, not too 'disliterary' and academic. For *La Piovana* (1532) and *La vaccaria* (1533) he seems to have looked deep into the essential theatricality of Plautine texts (and it is significant that he shows less interest in Terence), and decided that here was a master from whom something could be learned – both plays are explicitly

based on identifiable Plautine models, using very much the same
process of updating and *contaminatio* as was to become standard
among Florentine dramatists. That Beolco was insisting on taking
Plautus as a theatrical model, rather than a literary one, emerges in
the first Prologue (the one in literary Italian) to *La vaccaria*: Plautus'
comedies, he says, 'were acted differently from how they are printed
nowadays; because lots of things work well on the page which on the
stage would work badly' ('molte cose stanno ben nella penna che
nella scena starebbon male').

La Piovana ('The girl from Piove') is a leisurely, expansive adaptation of *Rudens*. It uses the same unusual setting outside some
fishermen's huts on a beach (placed with careful accuracy near
Chioggia, at the south end of the Venetian lagoon); and the same
plot of an enslaved girl (from Piove di Sacco, inland) owned by a
pimp and pursued by a young lover. At a certain point the story is
complicated by extra elements from Plautus' *Mercator*, and echoes of
Pseudolus and even of Terence's *Heautontimorumenos*; and, as with later
Florentine comedies, the details are filled by a lot of local and
topical colour, even references to Lutheran heretics as objects of
popular wrath. It is linguistically monochrome, in that every character speaks Ruzante's *Pavano* – as though in this play he were trying
to insist on the validity of his dialect for every task that was needed
in 'regular' comedy, fighting a patriotic rearguard action on behalf
of local speech against colonization by an alien literary language.
The manipulation and stretching of what had been a crude and
limited linguistic instrument is a real *tour de force*, and the comedy is
highly regarded by Italian critics as much for this reason as for any
other. On stage, one would guess, it would contain many moments
to savour, endorsing the theatrical credentials of Ruzante and
Plautus in equal measure. It might also turn out, if performance
were now tried, that there is a little too much material in the play,
and a modern audience might find it fatiguing. However, this
judgement could well be influenced by the intractability, for a
reader whose mother tongue is different, of Ruzante's inventions in
a language which was localized in his own day and now effectively
does not exist at all. Modern Italian readers can be equally
inhibited.

La vaccaria ('The Cow Comedy') closely follows Plautus' *Asinaria*
('The Ass Comedy') for its first four acts, after which Ruzante adds
extra material to push the story closer to a conventional (in Renais-

sance terms) happy ending. Plautus ends his comedy with the old father Demaenetus (Placido, in Ruzante) humiliated and beaten home by his termagant wife Artemona, who caught him at a cheerful party with his son in a courtesan's house. Ruzante brings about a change of heart in his scolding matron Rospina, leaves us with an air of family reconciliation, and even points (though not clearly) towards a proper marriage for son and courtesan, as though she will be discovered to be of respectable birth like the heroine of Terence's *Andria*. (There are unresolved hints in Act v which, on one interpretation, might suggest an imperfect text or some non-textual resolution.) This can be seen as an accommodation with public taste and with developing theatrical formats. Equally significant for future theatre tradition is the linguistic policy adopted in this play, which reasserts and even over-asserts linguistic class and cultural differences. *Pavano* dialect is used by the servants Truffo (Ruzante himself), Vezzo, Betía and Piolo, and by the parasite Loron: all the other characters, even the bawd Célega and her prostituted daughter Fiorinetta, use literary Italian. (The action is set in Padua itself, and there is no place for Venetian dialect.) This is only half explicable in terms of social realism: the servants can plausibly be peasants moved into town (as in *La moscheta*), but the notion that citizens of all classes use the literary language is more convention than reality. Language is being used as a cultural or psychological badge for stage purposes: we could not be further, at a distance of just one year, from the defiant local patriotism of *La Piovana*. It is an early hint of what were to be the equally conventional linguistic stratifications of *commedia dell'arte*. One scene, deliberately contrasting refinement and vulgarity both of language and of thought, offers a remarkable likeness to formula scenes and scenarios of a hundred years later. The young man Flavio (Argyrippus in Plautus) is having a highly mannered dialogue of love with the courtesan Fiorinetta (equivalent of Philaenium), with the two dialect-speaking servants Vezzo and Truffo eavesdropping and commenting. The following is a typical extract of a rather long scene:

FLAVIO: No, you must live, light of my life, for you have reason to live; rather let me die, miserable and wretched, since deprived of you I shall be deprived of all the good and all the happiness that can be desired.

FIORINETTA: Do you wish me to live, when life without you will be worse than death? Tell me, what delight can delight me without my

Flavio? What joy can rejoice me, what pleasure can please me,
without you?

FLAVIO: Were it not that, if I died, there would also die with me all hope of
seeing you again, which is the greatest good that I possess, then know,
my love, that no man ever died more happily than I should, since I
would have the glory of dying for love of the most beautiful maiden
ever created by Nature.

FIORINETTA: If I ever remain living after you, Flavio, know that my life
will be so bitter and full of torment that death would be the greatest
delight the world had to offer. But since it would not be proper, after
losing you, to feel delight ever again, I shall force myself to live, so that
my tormented life lasts long enough to do penance for the death of
such a dear and fair lover as you.

VEZZO (*listening*): Cor, listen to those words, like honey poured on honey!
D'you hear what I hear? That really gets to me, that does – it's like
eating Spanish fly all fried up with honey on top. When I hear them
talk that way, I go all shivery inside.

TRUFFO: Yes, it's like dipping your arse in a bucket of hot milk.[23] (*La
vaccaria*, Act III, Scene 4)

The comments of the servants have a debunking effect which
reassure us that, on this occasion at least, the preposterous repetitive
rhetoric is meant to be laughed at. In dramas from later decades,
and in repertoire extracts from *commedia dell'arte*, it becomes increasingly hard for the modern reader to tell whether the high linguistic
register is being mocked or taken seriously. But whichever is true,
the theatrical formula involving two contrasting pairs of characters
remains identifiable and intact. It is noteworthy and curious that
this scene, Ruzante's first love scene outside the peasant register,
should show the same 'eavesdropping' structure as Act II, Scene 6 of
Gli ingannati, which we presented in the last chapter as having a
similar pioneering status: *La vaccaria* is currently dated just one year
later than the Sienese play. Was there some inhibition against
intimate love scenes in the new 'mimetic' mode, a taboo which was
diluted when such exchanges were shown as being overheard by
other characters in the fiction, as well as by the audience?

There is one more Ruzante text, *L'Anconitana* ('The Woman from
Ancona'), about whose date and place in the canon there has been
scholarly dispute. Many, including Ludovico Zorzi, prefer to place
it earlier, soon after *La moscheta*, more or less contemporary with *La
Fiorina*, and thus to make *La Piovana* and *La vaccaria* the last works of
the author's maturity. Others, including Giorgio Padoan, place it
last of all (*c.* 1534?), and argue that it represents the direction in

which Ruzante was moving *after* the two Plautine comedies. This seems to me to be the better critical interpretation, even if we must remain uncertain about chronology. Writers do not always produce things in the order which seems logical to their critics, and they may be working on more than one line of development at the same time. Speculations about Beolco's overall intentions are in any case cut short by the fact that he produced nothing more.[24] In the context of the current study, I would prefer to argue that *L'Anconitana* is indicative of later developments in Italian comedy generally, and thus that it should be treated last, if necessary in despite of chronology.

The 'Woman from Ancona' herself is the widow Ginevra, foot-loose in male disguise in the company of her maid Ghitta: she has come to Padua in pursuit of a youth, Gismondo, with whom she is infatuated. Gismondo is one of a trio of young men who have been slaves of the Turks, and are now ransomed, but regard it as a point of honour not to live as free men until they have raised the money to pay off their benefactor (whom we never see). But it transpires that Gismondo is really Isotta, Ginevra's long-lost sister: Ginevra mistook the call of family blood for the call of sexual love. When this is revealed, Isotta can unmask herself and marry her companion in adventure Tancredi, and her widowed sister can marry his brother Teodoro (whom she has never before met). In the meantime, the ransom money has been raised by the citizens of Padua, whose generosity is extolled across the footlights for the benefit of the Paduan audience. All this is acted out in the most composed, rhetorical and (by our standards) cold-blooded language, intended to maintain rigid standards of emotional and social propriety.

All this part of the play is, to a modern reader, mind-bendingly tedious, and leaves us wondering what appeal it could possibly have had. Some appeal there must have been, however: Ruzante was the last dramatist to force an audience to watch what they did not want to see, and in any case there are enough other plays with similar plot and style over the subsequent decades to confirm that this kind of dramatic writing must genuinely have stimulated the sentimental nerve of an Italian Renaissance public. What makes the play more significant, for present purposes, is that the plot so far outlined is interleaved with a much more scurrilous one. The false 'Gismondo' is purchased briefly by a married Venetian lady, whom we never see – we only hear at second hand of her disgust when the fancied youth turns out to be female after all. But the person who organizes and reports all this is the servant Ruzante, back on stage in his old persona; and Ruzante's master, husband of the lecherous wife, is an equally libidinous Venetian merchant, Sier Tomao. Sier Tomao is in pursuit of a courtesan, Doralice, whose maid Bessa is Ruzante's old flame from the village. All that happens is that Sier Tomao struggles with his avarice, but eventually agrees to stump up enough cash so that he and his servant can go off to the country with mistress and maid in a pleasure-seeking foursome. Around this very simple tale, Beolco strings some masterly scenes of mockery and chat, in which the miserly Sier Tomao (clearly a proto-Pantalone) makes a meal of deciding to go through with his amorous adventure, and Ruzante makes even more of a meal of delivering the simplest pieces of news, taking the chance to demonstrate his talents at song and dance in the process. The two long scenes between master and servant (each, of course, using his own native dialect) are glorious exercises in frustration, in which Ruzante narrates his childhood, tries out his singing prowess, expands with 'miser gags' to illustrate Tomao's unfortunate reputation (II, 4), then later pursues a long reminiscent anecdote about his life in the village, the only point of which is that he has met Bessa before (IV, 3). In all this, Ruzante the author demonstrates that his skill is not limited to monologues, and shows what an infallible theatrical device is that of comic delay. (The format is also very attractive for performers, in that the postponed dénouement of the scene is always waiting as a safety net and can be brought in as soon as memory or improvisation fail. This perception was crucial in the development of professional *arte* routines.)

In *L'Anconitana*, then, Ruzante the author brings back Ruzante the mask, subtly modified. The former desperate peasant, constantly cheated by his friends, has become a more self-sufficient town-dweller, able to persuade and organize a master more idiotic than he is. There has been a merger between Ruzante the victim of the *Parlamento* and *Moscheta* and Ruzante the more knowing author/performer of the *Orazioni*. The audience, after so many years of familiarity, now knows that its relationship exists with performer and character simultaneously; and no one can pretend any longer that the performer is not in control of the spectacle, so the character performed might as well also be controlling the intrigue. Perhaps the Ruzante mask has also absorbed some of the qualities of the scheming servant from Roman comedy, after Beolco's performances of such figures in the two Plautine plays. Certainly the Ruzante of *L'Anconitana*, while referring frequently to his peasant origins, has put down new roots not so much in a real city environment as in a 'Classical' urban stage set: his links with social reality are becoming attenuated, and he is settling into a conventional (albeit joyous and entertaining) function in a stereotyped theatrical plot – where, in this instance, he has obligatory musical numbers to perform as well as making a fool of Sier Tomao. At the end of the play, Venetian master and peasant servant scurry off for their dirty weekend, struggling with a burden of unnecessary luggage and bickering together in a kind of quarrelsome symbiosis[25] – with hindsight we are tempted to romanticize, and see the two *arte* masks walking away into the stage wings, from which they will keep reappearing in the same relationship for another two centuries. But in fact Ruzante and his *Pavano* dialect were to be lost, perhaps because nobody but Beolco could perform him so well; and his place would be taken by another migrant peasant, the equivalent of a stage Irishman in Venetian imaginative stereotype – exotic, half-bestial Zani from Bergamo.

In the canon of European writers, Ruzante is the great unapproachable. We sense his genius, but through a filter – because his favoured language can only be resurrected partially and with enormous effort; and because, like many great theatre practitioners, he threw all his effort and skill into formulating performance texts which were only partly verbal, and which were tailored carefully for particular actors, a particular audience, and a particular occasion. The bodies for which he did his tailoring have long gone, and we can only guess at the closeness and comfort of the fit. Our survey in these pages is inevitably inadequate to him, and must be supplemented by the expert labours of scholars who themselves are rooted in the Veneto, and can thus build on their native empathy with his dialect. It has been possible, though, to delineate in rough terms the individual contribution which he made to comic dramaturgy in Venice and in Italy. It is difficult to imagine that he would have been given his opportunity, at that time, in any other Italian centre. The Venetians continued, during the decades after he ceased production, to consolidate those aspects of his practice which could be generalized, and to pursue (by example more than by precept) an approach to theatre which gave relatively more weight to the performer and to the building of a recognizable repertoire.

MULTILINGUAL COMEDY

During the 1530s and 1540s there were a number of things happening simultaneously in Venetian theatre, and their chronology is hard to determine. Where texts were eventually printed, their printing date may come some time after they were performed; and on dates of performance a great deal of evidence is missing. The phenomenon identified by Giorgio Padoan as 'citizen comedy' survived only in one or two manuscripts of plays performed in strictly private circumstances. Two of these – *Ardelia* in prose, and *Crivello* in verse – still remain without modern editions. The more famous *La Veniexiana* has now been the object of much study and celebration, and is now dated firmly by Padoan to the year 1536.[26] Regretfully, in spite of its fascination, we have to omit *La Veniexiana* from this volume: it has little relationship in its structures and tone with either *commedia erudita* or *commedia dell'arte*.

There are three languages used in *La Veniexiana*. Bernardo the porter speaks his own Bergamask dialect; Iulio, the foreigner, speaks a near-literary lingua franca based on Tuscan; all the other characters speak Venetian, as Venetians of all classes naturally did and still do. In this case there seems to be no linguistic mockery involved, and no theatrical stylization such as was beginning to take shape even in the later texts of Ruzante – it is a simple matter of realism, of characters speaking as their equivalents would do in life. But in other contemporary Venetian theatre scripts, multilingualism was being developed as a device in its own right, in which simple realism was constantly giving way to linguistic experiment and sheer comic fantasy. It is this strand of theatre, represented by the surviving scripts of Andrea Calmo and Gigio Artemio Giancarli, which provides a more or less continuous bridge between Ruzante and the *commedia dell'arte*.[27]

If 1536 was the year of *La Veniexiana* (and of *Aridosia*, which began the continuous Florentine comic tradition), it was also the year in which Aristotle's *Poetics* was made widely available in Italy, and thus the moment when insistent, if pedestrian, discussions began about the 'rules' which governed theatrical composition in ancient Greece and Rome. The *Poetics* is of course about tragedy rather than comedy, but scholars and theoreticians could hardly ignore the fact that comedy in a Classical format was already established, and that it must logically be subject to the same kind of inquiry. In Venice as in Florence there would have been a drive during the late 1530s and 1540s to bring theatrical texts into the ambit of respectable literature; and in the eyes of obtuse or opportunistic writers this involved codifying rules and limiting formats so that new comedies should look more like old comedies. However, the context of performance and the tastes of the public were already markedly different in Venice. There was no central court theatre to impose its standards by sheer prestige, and no equivalent of the Accademia Fiorentina to dictate cultural policy – the Venetian government, if it got nervous, simply renewed bans against theatre performances in general, which we have noted as being ineffective. In the auditoria, attempts to standardize Classical comedy had to battle with an established public taste for buffoonery, for games with language and dialects, and for a level of comic aggression and crude farce which was something less than gentlemanly. And the audience which wanted such things could always find somebody – Compagnia della Calza, professional clown, or something in between – ready to offer them in private performances without asking permission of anybody.

The Venetian comedies which were published in the 1540s and 1550s all show signs of tension between on one hand the pressure to imitate literary models (which by now included the more successful Italian comedies,[28] as well as Plautus and Terence) and on the other hand a reluctance to ignore a growing theatrical repertoire which was in demand, and which was based on the discoveries and contributions of Ruzante and the local tradition. This is equally true, in my view, of the special 'multilingual' strain of comedy with overtones of professionalism, represented by Calmo and Giancarli, and of the more literary scripts of Aretino, Dolce and Parabosco – and there might be a case for treating Venetian comedy as a single genre, without further sub-categories. In the end, though, one has to recognize that the status of Calmo and Giancarli as actor-dramatists, and their insistence on using as many dialects as possible, call for separate treatment.

Andrea Calmo (1510–71) may not have been a fisherman's son, as is sometimes stated: the truth is that we know very little of his life, or of the context in which he usually performed his plays. It is safe to assume along with Giorgio Padoan (1982, pp. 155–60) that his origins were reasonably humble, perhaps in the lower bourgeoisie, and that his audiences also were socially a step or two down from those of Ruzante. More problematic is the question of whether he actually worked with Ruzante, or overlapped with him in respect of his surviving production. His six comedies have their first printing between 1549 and 1556, and there is no guarantee that their order of printing in any way reflects the order of composition or performance. Some performing dates can be proposed for *La Rhodiana* (1540, pub. 1553), *La Fiorina* (after 1542, pub. 1553), and *Travaglia* (1546, pub. 1556); but the dates for *La Rhodiana* and *Travaglia* need not necessarily be the first performance (and nor, indeed, need any of the texts have survived in the version first performed). For *La Spagnolas* (1549), *Saltuzza* (1551) and *La potione* (1552) we have only the date of first printing. In fact, along with Ireneo Sanesi, I am inclined to take at face value the suggestion in the Prologue to *Saltuzza* that this is one of his first plays;[29] and, more controversially, I think it is also worth proposing that the character of Saltuzza himself, a peasant speaking *Pavano*, is heavily based on Ruzante's mask as it appears in *L'Anconitana* and may even actually have been played by Beolco. This in turn would raise the question whether Calmo may have played the Venetian Sier Tomao in Beolco's last play. Such links between the two may not be supported by documentation, but the notion of a dramaturgical torch being passed on from Ruzante to Calmo is at least a useful concept in historical terms. Discussion of Calmo's work is thus based here on an unproven assumption that it began in the late 1530s, before Ruzante's death in 1542. (We should remember that the multilingual comedy *Ramnusia*, by Schioppi, was performed in Verona as early as 1531.)

Calmo has not yet benefited from the dedicated scholarly work which has so transformed our perception of Ruzante; and it is better to admit from the start that passages in his plays remain practically incomprehensible, from a combination of deliberate linguistic garbling and casual topical allusions – precisely the two features which no doubt helped to make his work hilarious to his contemporaries. Zorzi's and Padoan's editions of Ruzante suggest that much could be illuminated by a top-class scholar with a comprehensive knowledge of sixteenth-century Venice.

The most difficult one to read now is *La Spagnolas*, a confusing collection of gags, monologues and tricks which seems to have been printed in haste and with little thought, much in need both of scene divisions and of stage directions to help us know what is going on. Curiously, it is by far the most reprinted of Calmo's plays: Padoan quotes twelve editions between 1549 and 1600. One can only assume that readers found it fascinating for one of the qualities which make it hard for us, namely the dense, tortuous games it plays with language, using the excuse of diverse dialects and accents – Bergamask (with grotesque pseudo-Spanish additions, which seem to account for the play's title), Venetian, *Pavano*, German and *Greghesco* (Venetian spoken badly by a Greek, something regularly heard in a city with so many Greek colonies). Its episodic plot revolves round three pairs of male characters. In each case the socially senior of the two is in love with a woman who never appears, and the serving partner pretends to help but in fact lands his 'master' in one of a series of farcical humiliating messes. There are two marriages arranged at the end, neither particularly desired by the participants, and offered as a parody of the traditional happy ending.

Saltuzza, which I am also inclined to see as an early script, is a great deal more intelligible, but equally centred on mockery and sexual deceits, all organized by its eponymous protagonist. The pairing of Venetian master (Messer Melindo) and Paduan peasant valet (Saltuzza) seems to develop from Ruzante's *Anconitana*, but the 'partnership' here is one where the servant is simply a trickster and the master simply a victim. Messer Melindo wants to get into bed with a virtuous neighbour (never on stage) called Panfila, but finds himself coupling instead with Rosina, a remarkably characterized lame ugly maidservant – who, confusingly, speaks literary Italian. Meanwhile Panfila's brother Polidario (with whom Rosina is hopelessly in love) is helped successfully to seduce Melindo's wife Clinia.

These early examples are enough to show how much the vein of comedy which Calmo developed, or the taste to which he was pandering, depended on the creation and seizure of a comic victim, preferably one who was unsuitably in love. Calmo himself, as an actor, specialized in playing a mature Venetian merchant who loses his dignity completely in senile passion and gross stupidity – once more, as with Ruzante's Sier Tomao, we have to speak of a proto-Pantalone, a figure now developed more systematically as the mask adopted by an actor-dramatist, and thus becoming the star role: Messer Melindo in *Saltuzza*, Messer Zurloto in *La Spagnolas*. But there is little, in these two comedies or subsequent ones, of Ruzante's consistent and slightly anguished psychology; and less still of the rueful hidden agendas which we cannot quite resist attributing to Beolco. The stupidity of the proto-Pantalone goes way beyond normal plausibility, and most of his laughs are provoked by his language, through a comic clash between his high emotional pretensions and the distortions of a stylized Venetian dialect. The stupidity may be traceable to Machiavelli's Nicia, Bibbiena's Calandro and Boccaccio's Calandrino: the concentration on comic verbal invention is home-grown Venetian, springing from the tradition of local *buffoni*. Calmo in fact composed volumes of comic letters in his own version of stage Venetian – they were widely read, and used as commonplace books by subsequent generations of *arte* actors playing Pantalone.

In his other four published plays, Calmo responded to an apparent demand for more reference to a literary-dramatic tradition. Two of them are rewrites of other vernacular comedies – *La potione* ('The Potion') of Machiavelli's *Mandragola*, and *La Fiorina* of Ruzante's comedy of the same name. Both of them are reductions, rather than expansions, of their originals: *La potione* in particular, in four acts, is a very rudimentary version of Machiavelli's plot, with no equivalent of Fra Timoteo or of Sostrata (which means omitting the all-important persuasion scene in Machiavelli's Act III), leaving just four characters each speaking a different dialect. Calidonia, the equivalent of Machiavelli's Lucrezia, never appears on stage. Calmo's *Fiorina* is in three acts, as opposed to Ruzante's five; tells the story without giving special weight to the Ruzante character, who is now called Bonelo (suggesting that this time Calmo had no star actor to play the part); and alters the outcome, in terms of who marries whom, to what Padoan characterizes as 'an outright send-up of the customary happy ending'[30] – the heroine Fiore ends up being rejected by both her younger suitors and having to marry the old Venetian Cocolin. In both these plays Calmo seems to be acceding to a demand that his plays allude to, and thus belong to, a canon of established models, but he is trying nevertheless to bend those models to a faster, sharper, less demanding format which may well be characterized as 'popular' or 'farcical'. The reduction in the number of acts is significant: there was a public for whom a five-act show was simply too long, and three acts later became the norm for *commedia dell'arte* scenarios.

There was an alternative demand, it seems, for much longer five-act plays with multiple plots of great leisurely complexity, but still full of items from the *buffonesco* repertoire. *La Rhodiana* ('The Woman from Rhodes') and *Travaglia* ('Tribulation' – name of a principal character) both belong to this category, and thus on paper they seem to represent Calmo's most substantial dramatic achievement and give a greater idea of his range. They are also the clearest indication of an attempt to merge 'Classical' plot formats derived from culturally approved sources with items of individual theatrical bravura. Both, in particular, remain obstinately multilingual. Venetian, *Pavano*, Bergamask and *Greghesco* are offered more or less as standard dialects, and experiments are made with the speech of Slavonian, German and even Saracen immigrants to the Venetian linguistic scene. In the Prologue to *Travaglia*, Calmo makes it clear that his opposition to the pressure for a standard literary language is conscious and polemical – he insists that stage comedy must represent the real variety of people's speech, and that the high literary tongue belongs elsewhere, on the page. It is clear in practice, though, that he was also clinging, on behalf of himself and perhaps other acting colleagues, to a pride in comic linguistic virtuosity as a theatrical 'virtue' in its own right. In *La Rhodiana*, he gives to the Venetian merchant Cornelio (played by himself) a bravura scene of imitating different languages and dialects (Act IV, Scene 14). In the same play, there is a 'dream', or sleepwalking, scene of disconnected virtuoso nonsense for the German servant character Corado (v, 1);[31] and the Paduan servant Truffa, in II, 8, pretends to be possessed by spirits each of which expresses itself on conjuration in a different accent, so we get a taste of Neapolitan, French, Milanese, Ragusan, Spanish, Florentine and Albanian. Previously, in Act I, Scene 4, Truffa reveals that he is really a nobleman in disguise, speaking literary Italian instead of his usual *Pavano* in order to do so. This revelation is completely ignored for the remainder of the play – so either it is simply the chance for the actor to display one more accent; or else a relatively gentlemanly performer wished to salvage his dignity, before an audience of his peers, by establishing that his peasant accent was assumed and not natural. It is questions like this which make our lack of information about Calmo's performances extremely frustrating.

Both *La Rhodiana* and *Travaglia* are structured in an episodic manner, with a number of sub-plots and self-contained little stories which could easily be removed without affecting the main intrigue, but which from the audience's point of view may be the real point of the show. For instance *La Rhodiana* has a simple isolated *beffa* against a customs officer very reminiscent of similar games in Aretino,[32] and Scenes 6–10 of Act IV graft the story of *Decameron* VII, 4 on to the already complicated marital situation of the Venetian 'star' character Cornelio.[33] Both plays are full of separately rehearsable scenes and speeches (there is a high quotient of monologues and long set-piece speeches) which with hindsight could be seen as repertoire numbers for future *arte* masks – braggart Captains, food-obsessed servants, despairing lovers, even embryonic pedants or Dottori. The central plots of both, however, are of a stereotyped form reflecting both Roman and *novella* antecedents. Both plays contain rivalry between father and son for the hand of a girl, with the inevitable tendency to trick and humiliate the older suitor; and both involve long separations between parents, wives and children. In the case of *Travaglia* the two themes are merged, in that one of the rivals for the hand of Leonora turns out to be her lost brother Camillo, thus repeating a conflict from Piccolomini's *L'amor costante* of 1536. Indeed, the 'Classical' plot motifs which are implanted at this time into Venetian comedy are already mixed with the crucial 'romance' elements introduced by the Sienese. The eponymous 'Travaglia', in Calmo's comedy, is really the young girl Ersilia serving her beloved Camillo in male disguise, and trying to woo him away from Leonora, just like the seminal figure of Lelia in the Sienese *Ingannati*. There is, however, just as much derivation from Bibbiena and Boccaccio: as in so many other fields, the Venetians benefited from their late adoption of Renaissance models by being able to inherit all the work of other regions at once.

The lengthy, riotous multilayered intrigue of *La Rhodiana* and *Travaglia*, and their aggressively farcical tone, are all repeated in the two surviving plays of Gigio Artemio Giancarli. One would like to know just where, for whom, and with what resources it was possible to mount spectacles which were so long, had so many characters, and demanded such a high level of acting and production skill if they were not going to fall flat. Of Giancarli we know only that he was born in Rovigo, that he spent some time at the court of Ferrara, and that he died before 1561. In one of his prologues there is reference to two lost plays, *Il furbo* and *L'esorcismo*; but all we have now are *La capraria* ('The Goat Comedy') and *La zingana* ('The Gypsy Woman'), whose first editions are dated 1544 and 1545, dedicated from Venice respectively to the Cardinals of Ferrara and Mantua.[34] Performance dates are not known. The multilingual character of the plays is less insistent than in Calmo, but still significant. In *La capraria* we have just two heavily accented Greek characters and one Paduan peasant. In *La zingana* there is a Greek, a Bergamask, a Venetian bawd and another Paduan peasant – but most of all (and enough of a *tour de force* to give the comedy its title), the gypsy character whose language is said to contain Berber and Semitic vocabulary, but still awaits a detailed linguistic commentary. Giancarli, however, has even less reason than Calmo to claim that his use of dialects is based on realism, since most of his characters, including servants and low-life figures, speak standard Italian. His dedications to exalted patrons, and references to antique models, suggest that he was hoping for full recognition by the courtly cultural world – whereas in Calmo's case we detect a more ambiguous, even resentful, attitude to the pressures for humanist conformity.

Giancarli is nevertheless to be classed with Calmo as an artisan, not an aristocrat – he was a painter, possibly a musician of sorts, and he certainly acted in his own plays. His speciality did not involve a dialect: it seems certain from internal evidence[35] that in his two surviving plays he took the role of the central scheming servant who orchestrates most of the action – Ortica in *La capraria*, Spingarda in *La zingana*. The major comic assaults, as in the case of Calmo (and, as we shall see, Parabosco) are directed against the standard victim of the old man in love, who in Giancarli's plays is Greek rather than Venetian, and as babyish a figure of fun as can be imagined. One of the principal tricks played, which seems to have been a favourite with Venetian audiences, is that of advising the senile lover to get into his beloved's house either in disguise or in some kind of container – violent humiliation is then visited on the victim, which he has to bear without complaint for fear of revealing his true identity. This is of course the basic device used more than once against Falstaff, in *The Merry Wives of Windsor*; as we remarked when it appeared in the Sienese *Alessandro* (more or less contemporary, in 1544), it was also to become a regular plot motif in *commedia dell'arte* scenarios, with the victim usually being Pantalone. In *La capraria*, for instance, old Afrone is induced by long-winded and implausible arguments to dress up as a goatherd (in a fantasy costume which involves his actually wearing horns) and appear riding on one goat while he attempts to manage a number of others. If real animals were used, the result on stage could have been hilarious but uncontrollable, and Giancarli was either very brave or very foolish.

Like Ruzante and Calmo, Giancarli is fond of monologues, and gives various low-life characters the chance to build a direct relationship with the public. This tendency can be even more explicit than other examples mentioned so far. In *La zingana*, the bawd Agata constantly directs her confidences to the women spectators, treating them in the sly, affectionate tone which she also uses to young female characters whom she is trying to wheedle. In the same play, the boy servant Fioretto is an entirely pointless character, except in so far as he has an appealing or mischievous relationship with the audience. In Act IV, Scene 17, having been sent on a simple errand, he dawdles on stage playing with a ball, loses it among the spectators and asks for it back, and completely forgets his errand in the process. What comes through most of all, however, is the way in which the scheming servants Ortica and Spingarda, played by Giancarli, become overt masters of ceremonies in a self-confessed theatrical game, occasionally even allowing a glimpse of Giancarli's role as creator of the whole spectacle. There are plenty of models in Plautus of wily slaves gearing themselves up for combat, and confiding in the audience as they do so; and there are Roman antecedents also for the device whereby Ortica, in *La capraria*, actually bets his intended victim Famelico (a rather obviously Plautine pimp) that he will enter his house and steal some money. But the following soliloquy by Ortica lingers more firmly than ever before on the open admission that the whole story is a fictional contest played for fun:

ORTICA: It's a pity I've never read the comedies of the ancient Greeks and Romans, because I would have been able to memorize some of those tricks which slaves used on behalf of their masters. That's as may be: now I'm definitely going to collect up all the wicked wheezes I've ever heard about, or used myself, and combine them into one. Maybe it'll all work out. I was a bit too cocky, wasn't I? I let my tongue run away with me, with the pimp and with my master, telling one that he hasn't got a hope and giving too much hope to the other, with no idea of how to go about it. Hey, I've just thought now, would any of you lot feel up to getting into Famelico's house? Are any of you friends of his, by any chance? No? I've bitten off more than I can chew here, the more I think about it the less I know what to do. Listen, you're all sitting there with nothing to do – have a think for me, see if you can come up with something, talk it over among yourselves until I come back again, I won't be long. Please, now – don't forget. (*Exit*) (*La capraria*, Act I, Scene 5)

In Act II, Scene 3, he of course has to accept that the spectators are going to be no help at all, and just urges them not to tell Famelico what he's up to. There are a number of other references, in both of

Giancarli's plays, to the fact that a comedy is being played and to the Roman and Italian sources on which it is based.

The Classical models have a tendency to reduce the attention given to female characters, as was the case in Florentine comedy – unless those characters are lower-class servants, adulterous wives, or caricatured matrons. (Both Giancarli's plays have elderly wives in love with younger men, mocked and humiliated in parallel with the senile passions of their husbands.) There are however some occasional signs that this sexism was beginning to be resisted. Ruzante, with the excuse of dealing mainly with the lower classes, had created some forceful individual women in his scripts. Calmo is often dismissive of female characters, especially young ones; but his *Travaglia*, using the 'Sienese' device of a girl in male disguise, obviously allows itself some more freedom. The most interesting example, though, is Giancarli's *Zingana*. As well as the gypsy, the grotesque matron Barbarina, the bawd Agata, and the housekeeper Anetta (all of whom could comfortably be played by men), this play contains the younger figures of Stella and Angelica, both of whom appear rather more often on stage than some of their equivalents in previous Italian comedy.[36] Angelica connives in an elopement, in which her place at home is temporarily taken by a young man who looks remarkably like her. (The young man turns out to be Medoro, her twin brother, stolen as a baby and brought up by the gypsy woman of the title.) She shows a certain amount of spirit, and in Act IV, Scene 24 she appeals for sympathy in her lover's plight both to the God of Love and to the women in the audience – a speech which has the makings of a standard repertoire number. Stella is an unconventional figure who deserves some attention. She is the daughter of the bawd Agata, and lives with her mother and stepfather Lupo ('Wolf') who is also a petty criminal. She connives in various tricks against men who are pursuing her, but insists (in a monologue in II, 18) that she has maintained her sexual virtue and intends to continue doing so. Her other monologue, (III, 2) is a completely irrelevant conversation with the ladies in the audience, offering them her services as a needlewoman and going into technical details of the different kinds of work she can do. Both speeches are remarkable in that they seem to create a mood of female solidarity, as well as being entirely unnecessary to the story – it in fact makes little difference, in plot terms, whether Stella is strictly a virgin or not.

The reason why Stella may be significant is that in looking for the origins of *commedia dell'arte* we have also to look for the moment at which actresses were first tolerated on stage: the *arte* genre, once we find it established and documented, always uses female as well as male performers. There is no way in which we can prove that in *La zingana* we have an early example of a script which intended one of its roles for an actress. However, the rather careful way in which Stella's part is written, and the extra efforts made to get the ladies in the audience to feel approval for both character and performer, must at least entitle us to ask the question whether this might be so.

(The earliest documented example of actresses performing in *commedia erudita* is in fact a surprising one – it is a performance of Bibbiena's *Calandra* before King Henry II of France and his Queen Caterina de' Medici, by the Italian community in Lyons in 1548.[37])

ARETINO IN VENICE

After his arrival in Venice in 1527, Aretino settled down, in so far as that was possible for anyone of his temperament and precarious life style. He built a network of contacts with influential circles inside Venice and with patrons and potentates outside, but managed never again to be dependent on a single master. One might say that his cultural presence and his personal power base were indistinguishable. Having started by acting as a subversive threat to the establishment, he was prepared to move a little more with the tide in his later years, to the extent of composing a series of religious meditations in conformity with Counter-Reformation piety. However, his overbearing nature made it inevitable that he should still try to impose his will on fashion, and his verbal style in particular remained indelible. All this applies to his comedies as much as to any other aspect of his work; but they represent only a small part of his activity between 1527 and his death (recorded as resulting from 'apoplexy') in 1556. (He also wrote one stage tragedy, *Orazia*, printed in 1546 – a sign in itself of his urge to contribute to all the emerging models of 'official' literary culture.)

Aretino published two comedies – *Lo Ipocrito* and *La Talanta* – in 1542, and then *Il filosofo* in 1545. 1542 was the year in which *La Talanta* was performed, at a highly prestigious function mounted by a Compagnia della Calza (the 'Sempiterni', one of the last major associations of its type) with a stage design commissioned from Giorgio Vasari. The whole occasion is described as arousing enormous public interest,[38] though what sections of society this covered is not fully clear – in Venice, despite the aristocratic composition of the Compagnia itself, one cannot rule out a genuinely 'public' offering of the show to a wider range of social classes. The set was an elaborate representation of Rome, with models or backcloth paintings of most of its major momuments. Explicitly, on this occasion, the Compagnia dei Sempiterni were introducing Venetians to an example of the most up-to-date staging of 'regular' comedy, as was being mounted elsewhere by princely courts; implicitly, they and Aretino between them were forcing the city to take note of the current cultural prestige of 'regular' comedy itself.

The publication of *Lo Ipocrito* in the same year of 1542 may reinforce the notion that Aretino had a deliberate point to make to the Venetian public – or at least it suggests that both plays had already been fully drafted, and that it was convenient to issue them together. There is a reference in *Lo Ipocrito* to an event of 1540,[39] but Aretino's tendency to rewrite and update his texts makes this only marginally useful in dating the play's overall composition. No performance of this comedy is recorded. *La Talanta* is more likely to have been commissioned and composed especially for its first performance, and thus written in 1541 or 1542.

Lo Ipocrito, therefore, may rank more as a literary exercise than as a performing text. One notices in particular that the 'low-life' scenes involving servants are reduced to a minimum, and the play contains none of the gratuitous practical jokes or stage liveliness which are found in Aretino's other comedies. There is nothing unperformable about the script, however; and on another level it can be read alongside *La Talanta* (which was, obviously, both performable and performed) as a play which deploys a serious attack against a particular target in current social behaviour, thus continuing Aretino's previous tendency to overlay his dramatic action with a clear authorial voice. If they are both 'satirical' comedies, then *Lo Ipocrito* (as its title would suggest) attacks religious hypocrisy, which has ensured that the play is quoted as a source for Molière's *Tartuffe*, but in fact the resemblances are not very strong. *La Talanta* tilts at the corrupting influence of high-class prostitutes, represented by the character of Talanta herself. Both plays, however, contain a range of other material which may divert theatrical attention, for some of the time, from any preaching which they may contain.

Lo Ipocrito, as well as its targeted protagonist, contains some highly artificial (some would say 'baroque') moral and emotional problems, relating to two sisters and their four suitors, which are played out in carefully stylized rhetorical conversations. They are hard for the modern critic to assess. The play overall is so complicated that, knowing Aretino's sarcastic temperament, it is tempting to see the whole thing as a parody, intended to mock the sillier aspects of conventional stage plots. However, in 1542 such motifs had not had time to become 'conventional' on stage, despite a long literary ancestry – the only clear theatrical example is *L'amor costante* of Alessandro Piccolomini, a writer with whom Aretino was in friendly contact.[40] We may have to assume, as an alternative reading, that what we now see as a ludicrously formulaic approach to emotional and moral dilemmas was actually taken seriously by the audience of the time. A plausible case can be made, and in comedies written a little later it has to be made, for seeing such plots as an attempt to infuse proper aristocratic standards of rectitude into comic drama. Such standards, ultimately medieval in derivation, would revolve chiefly round spectacular acts of generosity or sacrifice, and rigorous adherence to one's given word. However, it remains difficult, here as in later decades, to assess the threshold beyond which an audience would start laughing rather than feeling sentimental approval.

With *La Talanta* there are fewer problems in detecting parody, if we so desire. The story which provides the happy ending is of a merchant called Blando who has three identical children of different sexes. Here there is plenty of dramatic arbitrariness, and it is easy to treat the story as a game played with a light touch, alluding to identity tangles already well established on stage by other dramatists. The plainly satirical element is expressed by the commanding presence of Talanta the courtesan, who has four suitors competing for her favours, all willing to beggar themselves to buy her. Extensive verbal attacks are made on the folly of all this, and the satire is entrusted mainly to such harangues delivered in effect from the author to the audience: Aretino, here as before, is happy to narrate at his own pace and to take plenty of time off for word-spinning of various sorts. Towards the end of Act II, the character Pizio actually asks his friend Orfinio to wait until he has finished what he wanted to say, and proceeds to talk at length (just to himself, as he claims) about the pleasures and advantages of loving a virtuous woman.[41]

However, as well as developing its verbal and conceptual content, and parodying literary-dramatic formats, *La Talanta* contains scenes which are pure 'performance', and draw on a repertoire which may be professional. Its mixture of styles need not surprise us, granted the long-standing tendency of Compagnie della Calza, such as the Sempiterni for whom it was written, to collaborate with professional actors and buffoons whenever they felt the need. And Aretino himself, before coming to Venice, had accepted influences from forms of ephemeral street theatre. Hence *La Talanta*, like the first two comedies, incorporates self-contained practical jokes played against victims who have no further role in the play. But it also offers some elements which must have been picked up from the specifically Venetian circuit of professional and semi-professional performers.

In one of the practical jokes (Act v, Scene 8), a group of servants gang up to trick the owner of a meat stall out of a basket of provisions. Fleeing with the loot, one of them (Fora) has to perform a lightning transformation. He slips round the corner, throws the food and his cloak to a colleague, and reappears in a flash – limping, with an eye-patch, his hat inside out, and his voice disguised. The sequence calls for extremely precise timing by all parties, and would need exhaustive rehearsal – to do it in an approximate way would be quite pointless. It thus has the hallmarks of a gag put together by professionals – and its gratuitous insertion into the play, simply because it is clever and will raise a laugh, would characterize it in the *commedia dell'arte* tradition as what came to be called a *lazzo*.[42]

In this context it becomes relevant that two of Talanta's suitors are Messer Vergolo the merchant from Venice, and the bombastic Capitan Tinca ('Tench'). The first is yet another proto-Pantalone, mocked among other things for his typically Venetian ignorance of how to ride a mule; the second is a braggart captain. Neither speaks in any form of dialect – in fact it appears that Aretino was irritated by a tendency of the actors, at the performance in 1542, to use non-standard language against his express wishes.[43] On this level he was clearly participating in the attempt to assimilate comic drama to a literary standard and thus a literary language (with his prejudices fuelled by being a Tuscan himself). But it is just as significant that the actors did in fact get out of his control, as professionals marketing their skills are likely to do. Aretino wrote parts which bore a relationship to fixed professional roles or masks, and the people who played the roles made them more linguistically stereotyped than he intended.

One scene in particular is especially significant in showing how a

literary dramatist could adapt his style for known performers. In Act
III, Scene 12, Capitan Tinca holds the stage, like so many of his *arte*
successors, in company with his parasite or feed man Branca
('Grab'). Some of the dialogue goes as follows:

TINCA: Tomorrow you must find me a poet who can put my exploits into
    music, and a musician who can set them to verse ... The immortali-
    zation of my deeds in figured chronicle should be the cause of two
    effects. On the one hand it will bring upon me the adoration of that
    Goddess [Talanta] of whom we have spoken, and of others besides: on
    the other hand it will instil panic not only in the present suitors of her,
    and of others, but in anyone who should dare in the future to fall in
    love with her, or with others.
BRANCA: By which you infer that you will be left master of the field.
TINCA: You have it.
BRANCA: Masterly tactics!
TINCA: We shall unsheath yet more robust devices in due course.
BRANCA: All the ponced-up young turkey-cocks will run for cover –
    dimples, downy cheeks, dingle-dangles, lacy doublets and all!
TINCA: Will it be so?
BRANCA: Inevitably.
TINCA: You think so?
BRANCA: Undoubtedly.
TINCA: Will it work?
BRANCA: Absolutely.
TINCA: As I desire?
BRANCA: No more, no less.
TINCA: According to my hopes?
BRANCA: Spot on.
TINCA: And I could help them on their way by skewering them with a
    thrust – thus!
BRANCA: Brilliant!
TINCA: Giving at the same time a terrifying leap – like so!
BRANCA: Incredible!
TINCA: And with a somersault – thiswise!
BRANCA: Bravo!
TINCA: And spitting in their cowardly faces – like that!
BRANCA: Elegant stuff!
TINCA: Assuming with my rapier – this menacing stance!
BRANCA: There are some talents one just has to be born with. (*La Talanta*,
    Act III, Scene 12)

The scene is much longer than quoted, and it is dense with
information for the theatre analyst. In the first place, the obvious
invitation for the actor playing Tinca to move into a grotesque

physical ballet, posturing and somersaulting and spitting, puts the role on a level of undignified clowning which could never have been accepted by a noble member of the Compagnia dei Sempiterni: it confirms once and for all that in a production of this sort the performers would be a mixture of amateurs and professionals.[44] The verbal structure of the dialogue is significant too. The concentrated, convoluted language of the longer speeches is pure Aretino, but the repetitive elements are of a kind which he does not normally use, and which do not appear elsewhere in the same play. On analysis, the dialogue splits down into identifiable units which resolve themselves into back-and-forth repetitions of the same concept – the most obvious example quoted is the sequence from 'Will it be so?' as far as 'Spot on.' Each unit is 'elastic', in the sense that once the idea is established it could go on for longer, or be cut short, without altering its content. The same can in fact be said of the more 'acrobatic' sequence quoted last: in a simple repetitive routine, Tinca has to do something silly, and Branca has to express admiration, and then the same again until they have run out of variants. If they forget one or two, or if they add one on the spur of the moment, it will make no difference. We shall be arguing that this structure of 'elastic' units, each easy to memorize in its own right, is one of the techniques which underlie the so-called 'improvisation' of *commedia dell'arte* professionals. Aretino, knowing the performers for whom he was writing this scene, has composed it in the style which comes naturally to them. It seems a little illogical for him then to complain that, on the verbal level too, they did things in their own way.

The scene between Tinca and Branca looks back as well as forward. Branca's function is to pretend to admire Tinca, but to wink at the audience at the same time and underline his idiocy. The same relationship was found back in 1513, in Bibbiena's *Calandra*, in the scenes between Calandro and Fessenio – the only difference was that the clever servant took a more active role. Scenes even more similar to those of Bibbiena are to be found in Calmo, Giancarli and Parabosco: a structure which from the start we characterized as potentially 'theatrical', rather than literary or rhetorical, was being recognized as such by Venetian professional performers in the 1530s and 1540s.

Aretino's last comedy to appear, *Il filosofo* ('The Philosopher') abandons the more elaborate sentimental plots which are used in *Lo Ipocrito* and *La Talanta*, and reverts to the dramatist's more natural predeliction for the aggressive practical joke. It had no known peformance, and we cannot tell whether it was a reversion to type, or whether it is a text composed much earlier and published in 1545 after some delay. Like *La cortigiana*, it picks two fictional victims and submits them to humiliation: an unworldly scholar (the 'Philosopher' himself) who pays more attention to his books than to his wife, and a young merchant who is just too gullible for his own good. The latter is given the name 'Boccaccio', and both stories are reminiscent of tales from the *Decameron*: the philosopher Plataristotile is like the impotent judge in Day II, Story 10, and 'Boccaccio' is undoubtedly Andreuccio da Perugia in II, 5. It is against 'Plato-Aristotle' that the play aims most of its aggressive satirical energy, both in the lunatic abstractions of that character's own speeches and in the comments of those who have to deal with him. Aretino's subversive relationship with humanist and neoplatonic culture comes out clearly, with a vigour (and perhaps a concealed fascination) which foreshadows Jonson's *Alchemist*. More unexpectedly, the comedy also contains a plea for wives in general to be better treated by their husbands. Characteristically, this theme emerges most in a long scene of verbal tirades from female characters (Monna Papa and Donna Druda, in I, 6), exploiting yet again a rhetorical relationship with an audience rather than using exemplary dramatic action.

Despite his diplomatic efforts to conform, Aretino's lingering image with the reading and theatregoing public was one associated with scandal and scurrility. In 1559, three years after his death, all his works were placed indiscriminately by the Church on the Index of prohibited books. Their underground survival is then attested by a unique phenomenon. At the turn of the seventeenth century all of them were reissued, attributed to different authors, with titles and characters' names altered.[45] It is clear that as texts they retained an energy, however tasteless and shocking, which was hard to ignore, which attracted readers, and which justified exploitation by a publisher. However, it is not known whether these disguised versions then had any renewed history on the stage. Ultimately, in his comedies as in the *Letters* which are his main bequest to posterity, Aretino's unique verbal energy as read straight off the page was a memorable enough experience in its own right.

DOLCE AND PARABOSCO

Throughout the 1540s and 1550s in Venice there seems to have been a struggle between different views of how to compose and perform a comic text. On the one hand there was an established local taste for what we should now describe as 'farce', for aggressive plots using standard formats, and especially for virtuoso performing numbers such as had been brought to a high level by Ruzante and Calmo. The public which demanded this, and perhaps especially the performers who were making it their livelihood, had become attached to games with language and to the use of dialects as a basis for comic speech – they were impatient with rules and constraints handed down from the Greeks and Romans, and with demands for the exclusive use of the 'Tuscan' literary language. But the pressure to conform to such rules was growing, as more and more 'regular' comedies were composed and published in other Italian centres, and as an increasing number of professional humanists pursued their own livelihood by setting themselves up as arbiters of cultural practice. From the 1540s onwards literary and linguistic theory became an industry – even a bandwagon for anyone who wanted to preach to, and in the process to join, the social and cultural élite. So increasingly, we must deduce, the argument over comic practice must have resolved itself into a class division, between popular and aristocratic, between the non-respectable and the respectable. It is curious to glimpse Aretino, in his irritation with performers using dialect in *La Talanta*, coming down on the 'respectable' side of the controversy – he had started in successive prologues to *La cortigiana* by being mockingly sarcastic about attempts to impose Classical rules on Milady Comedy ('Monna Comedia').

However, of the Venetian comedies which have come down to us from this period, those which on the whole reject the use of any non-literary language bear witness to an attempt, fraught with tension sometimes but an attempt none the less, to salvage something of both worlds. They try, that is, to offer some of the farcical formats and performing repertoire which a section of the Venetian public clearly loved, while at the same time acknowledging the Classical tradition, and avoiding those aspects – including dialect – which might be rejected as too plebeian. The apparently 'regular' comic writing of Dolce and Parabosco, on close analysis, shows signs of these competing influences and demands. The frustrating fact for the critic is that we have to deduce their dilemma almost entirely through the internal evidence of their texts, without any clear idea of their performing context and conditions. With these two dramatists, as indeed with Calmo and Giancarli, we lack the firm indications about occasion of performance, patronage, and composition of the audience, which in discussing comedy outside Venice has been the starting point for almost everything we have had to say. Who actually attended the comedies of Calmo and Giancarli, Dolce and Parabosco? What range – or what competing ranges – of taste, social prejudice and education were these dramatists trying to please?

Lodovico Dolce (1508–68) produced five comedies, published between 1541 and 1551, about which performing records are sparse. Three of them are openly derivative, in a way which we could now characterize as 'Florentine'. *Il capitano* ('The Captain', published and perhaps performed in 1545) is a more or less updated rewrite of Plautus' *Miles gloriosus*, written in verse. *Il marito* ('The Husband', also published in 1545 and also in verse) is a curious reworking of the same author's *Amphitruo*. Dolce's *Il roffiano* ('The Pimp'), which appeared later in 1551, is at first sight a rewrite of Plautus' *Rudens*, but the derivation is clearly mediated by a close knowledge of Ruzante's *La Piovana*, based on the same source.

Dolce's other two comedies, although some of their plot schemes still derive from Roman models, bear a more specifically Venetian stamp in the details of their composition.[46] His first play to be printed, in 1541, was *Il ragazzo* ('The Boy'). Here we have a simplified version of intrigues also to be found in Calmo and Giancarli. This framework is padded out with leisurely exchanges, confidential monologues and dialogue games, including an interesting tendency to concentrate on formats involving postponement and frustration. Act I, Scene 3, in which old Cesare slowly and reluctantly reveals to the parasite Ciacco that he is in love, has repetitive delaying sequences of dialogue very similar to those in an anonymous *arte* routine which we shall discuss in the next chapter. *Fabritia* ('Fabrizio's Play') was printed later than *Il capitano* and *Il marito* in 1549. Here there is a framework story of young Fabrizio trying to raise money to buy a slave girl from a pimp (which could be taken from a number of Plautine comedies), alongside a plot lifted straight from Terence's *Hecyra*. Again a relatively simple set of stories (by the standards of Calmo or Giancarli) is expanded and delayed by a relaxed writing style, involving repetitive monologues and conversations; and again Dolce shows a fondness for the purely theatrical game of comic delay, as when the boy servant Turchetto teases his master Pomponino:

TURCHETTO: Old Sir is over there – I'll pretend not to see him. Does anyone know where my master is?

POMPONINO: Can't you see me, time-waster?

TURCHETTO: Does anyone know? Does anyone know where my master is?

POMPONINO: Where are you looking, you bumpkin? Turn this way, and you'll see me.

TURCHETTO: My dear old master, my dear old master, has anyone seen him?

POMPONINO: This idiot must have gone blind and deaf, he can't see me or hear me.

TURCHETTO: Master! Sweet master, wise master, learned master, where are you?

POMPONINO: I'm here, you donkey, I'm here, you great baboon, I'm here, you little flirt.

TURCHETTO: Master! My head was so full of the story I had to tell you, that I couldn't see or hear a thing. (*Fabritia*, Act IV, Scene 3)

The punch line is weak, but the scene is easy for actors to exploit by playing with theatrical space – and it has the same 'elastic' quality, either prolongable or curtailable, which we identified in the dialogue from Aretino's *Talanta*.

This sort of material looks as if it was borrowed from an existing repertoire of gags; and *Fabritia* as a whole, in its length and leisurely structure, has a great deal in common with Giancarli. However, Dolce turns his back very firmly on dialect, and on the extremes of mockery and humiliation which tend to occur in dialect comedies. Characters who should realistically speak dialect in fact do not. What is more, although humiliating tricks are played on old men, they are relatively mild compared with the excesses found in Giancarli, and such characters are allowed to recover some dignity by the end of the play. One of the signs of 'aristocratic' comic drama, in these increasingly conservative and hierarchical times, was a greater reluctance to deploy farcical aggression against the patriarch, with whose authority key members of the audience might ultimately identify.

In the comedies of Girolamo Parabosco there is an interesting contrast, in that he does continue to use plots in which a proto-Pantalone figure is crudely humiliated, while trying to satisfy more refined or sensitive tastes in other ways. Parabosco (1524–57) was born in Piacenza, in central Lombardy, but made Venice his home from about 1541. By profession he was a musician, being the first person to hold the post of official organist in the Doge's chapel in San Marco, from 1551. He wrote eight comedies, published almost on an annual basis between 1546 and 1556: the regularity of their appearance suggests that he produced one every year for carnival and that they were printed soon after performance.[47] For whom he wrote them is not clear, though he composed music for a new Accademia dei Pellegrini ('Pilgrims' Academy') which may also have been interested in mounting plays. It emerges from his Prologues that the particular balance which he struck between respectable and non-respectable comedy provoked virulent criticism in some quarters, perhaps from adherents of a new Classical dogmatism. One feels a particular frustration at not being able to identify more precisely the participants in this controversy.

As a dramatist, Parabosco has been the object of little study and less sympathy from modern critics. Because of the repetitive nature of his plots, he has been dismissed as lacking in imagination[48] – and if one is seeking literary insight or originality, then perhaps this is fair comment. It is certainly true that he has no qualms about taking up intrigues from Calmo or Giancarli, nor even about repeating himself from play to play.

La notte (1546) and *Il Viluppo* (1547) quickly establish the preferences of Parabosco, or his audience, in terms of the constituent elements of a comic plot. An outline of one of his plays could be easily made indistinguishable from a scenario of *commedia dell'arte* – but a very run-of-the-mill scenario, with few special gimmicks or distinguishing features. There is always an old man in love, farcically credulous and stupid, and always a servant who leads him into disaster, usually by getting him to dress up in some unsuitable costume or hide himself in some place where he will be vulnerable. There is a particular fondness, traceable back at least to Giancarli's *La zingana*, for luring victims into graveyards[49] and scaring them with people dressed as ghosts or devils – another idea eventually to be taken up by Shakespeare in *The Merry Wives of Windsor*. The victim is usually involved in a rivalry for the favours of whatever young girl he has his eye on: such clashes are usually resolved by agnitions, in which one or more of the men concerned finds that he has been pursuing a girl who is really his sister or his daughter. Here, of course, we must remember that we are dealing with *topoi* which were just as common in 'regular' comedy outside Venice, formulae against which Grazzini railed ineffectually in Florence and to which he eventually succumbed along with all the rest. Reading Parabosco, one is increasingly reminded of twentieth-century British pantomime, where novelty in the story line is the last thing which audiences expect or want, and where the fixed framework leaves everyone free to concentrate on individual moments of theatre. Some of these can be inventive and suprising, but others are reruns of familiar jokes or sentimental formulae, and the public finds them none the less welcome for that.

However, the plays are not quite as relaxed as that description would suggest, nor is their relationship to the emerging *arte* repertoire quite so simple. Parabosco had also to avoid writing in too plebeian a manner, and had to include elements which would help the spectators to savour their own respectable social status and opinions. His plays contain moralistic insertions aimed at satisfying the prejudices of a gentlemanly audience. When happy endings are achieved, in the form of marriages between young lovers approved by their fathers, particular stress is laid on the fact that the partners have turned out to belong to the same respectable social class; and when there are liaisons which cross social barriers (as in *I contenti*[50]), Parabosco seems to have run into more criticism than usual.

It is also the case that compared with Calmo, Giancarli and the livelier plays of Dolce, Parabosco expends less energy on vivid caricature in his individual figures, and offers fewer overt 'gag' structures in his comic scenes. Instead of set-piece farce routines, we are more likely to note fixed rhetorical speeches, either in the moralistic insertions just alluded to or else in the parts given to young lovers. Love scenes are in fact developed in a way which we have not seen in any author so far discussed, and which merits examination.

Like so many other dramatists of the time, Parabosco shows nervousness about putting respectable young females on stage. He tends, however, to make a point of giving heroines at least one chance to lament their emotional difficulties in a monologue or set speech to a confidante, alongside his more frequent use of the same device in the case of young male lovers. Such speeches are heavily influenced by a turgid literary tradition – 'Petrarchan', but open also to other sources – in which a small number of very conventional feelings and conceits are woven into permutations using a standard vocabulary. The speeches, or large sections of them, become effectively interchangeable, and thus capable of becoming what they did eventually become in the hands of *commedia dell'arte* professionals: repertoire numbers, sentimental rather than comic, which could be stored, adapted and reused in any play which they would fit. There are hints of this tendency in earlier Venetian plays, particularly in Calmo; but it is in Parabosco that one senses the process whereby precisely those parts of a comedy which might seem most 'literary' are turning into 'theatergrams' (to adopt once again the very useful term coined by Louise George Clubb).

The trend is demonstrated very well by a remarkable structural similarity between the final scenes of Act I in *L'hermafrodito* and the exactly corresponding scenes of *I contenti* ('Everybody Happy'), both comedies being printed in 1549. In I, 7 in both plays, the young lover Zerbino (or Ottavio) persuades his beloved's nurse Nivetta (or Dorippa) to find a pretext for bringing the girl out on to the balcony, so she can listen to a wooing speech. Thus in I, 8 of both plays Furnia (or Angelica) appears, is annoyed with the nurse at having been tricked in this way, and responds with virtuous resistance to the young man's plea. (And in both plays the heroine subsequently relents and accepts her wooer, though she is simply reported as having done this off stage.) By 1549 there had still not been many instances in comedy from any part of Italy of wooing scenes between young lovers on stage. In these plays of Parabosco we see such encounters already settling into a formula. With hindsight, based on such information as we have about such scenes in *commedia dell'arte*, it is even possible to detect individual units of dialogue (and not just of set speech for a single person) which could enter a stock theatrical repertoire. In this extract from *L'hermafrodito*, I have intervened to break the dialogue into fragments, in a way which of course does not appear in the original: the translation is nevertheless continuous, without omissions.

(A)

ZERBINO: My lady, if men who are condemned to death for some grave and evil crime are entitled to be heard, how much more should you give ear to me, who have never done a single thing to cause you displeasure? Let it please you, before I die, which will be soon, to listen to the words which my love and my faith dictate to me in my last hour.

(B)

NIVETTA: Listen to him, silly. What harm can it do?
FURNIA: What is there to listen to?

(C)

You would do better to leave in peace a person who gives little
thought to you
ZERBINO: And you would do better to give some aid to a person who thinks
of little else but you.
FURNIA: Leave me alone, and do me a kindness.
ZERBINO: Give me some aid, and exercise justice.
FURNIA: You are too insistent, and too demanding.
ZERBINO: You are too cruel, and too beautiful:

(D)

but Heaven did not bestow this beauty on you simply to torture me
with the sight of you. Have pity on me, since I desire nothing and
think of nothing except to do what pleases you.
FURNIA: Tell me, do you think that I am content that you should suffer
such bitter pains as you say you do?
ZERBINO: I am certain of it.
FURNIA: Then if your desire is to give me pleasure, why do you not bear
those pains with patience and humility, since you see that that is what
pleases me? (*L'hermafrodito*, Act I, Scene 8)

Section (A), according to the above analysis, is a rhetorical
argument which could be memorized and used in its own right in a
number of different contexts. (B) is a brief linking insertion, to
establish the presence of the nurse and her part in the proceedings: it
appears with very similar wording at the same point in *I contenti*. (C)
is what in another context might be described as a 'dithyrambic'
sequence, divisible into three pairs of statements which are rhythmi-
cally similar but antithetical in content. This unit of dialogue is
'elastic' (in that there could just as well be four pairs of statements,
or two); and it contains the seed on one hand of more extended
sequences from known *arte* repertoire of the following century, and
on the other hand of a binary melodic structure suitable for opera
duets. Section (D), in which the lady rhetorically outwits the lover
by turning his own previous statements against him, is a more
complex sequence of conceits, but still capable of becoming part of a
repertoire. It is noteworthy that sections (A), (B) and (D), if taken
in isolation, could be reused (or memorized) principally in terms of
content, with different words being used to convey essentially the
same message; whereas (C) is more dependent on an exact verbal
echo, and would have to be reproduced more precisely.

In scenes of this sort, and in those repetitive comic dialogues which have been quoted from Aretino and Dolce, it emerges how single theatrical repertoire items could be built up not just in monologues, but also in exchanges between two and even three people. It is this sort of structure which is so much harder to detect in plays of this period from outside the Venetian area – we noted in particular that Florentine dramatists were actually reluctant to copy such set-piece theatrical games, when they occur, even from their approved Plautine sources. The plays of Calmo, Giancarli, Dolce and Parabosco, if subjected to an exhaustive analysis along these lines, would furnish a catalogue of such items which would presage, and merge into, the much larger catalogue which could be produced from our surviving information on *commedia dell'arte*.

It remains the case, though, that these writers did not fully belong to the *arte* genre, and that some of them even resisted the growing dominance and independence of the professionals or semi-professionals who performed their plays. Parabosco, like Aretino, expressed irritation at the liberties which some actors took with his texts.[51] In particular, the growing insistence that respectable writers in the humanist tradition should use a standard literary language made him, as well as Dolce, reject the adoption of spoken dialects (even the Venetian which could have been clung to for reasons of patriotism). On the other side of an emerging divide, professional actors, along with a large section of their public, loved the use of dialects as a caricature badge for stock characters and as an inexhaustible source of comic verbal distortion. In the end there was simply a split, in which the professional performers of farce and the gentlemanly composers of literary comedy went their separate ways.

CHAPTER 5

Improvised comedy

DEFINITIONS AND EVIDENCE

In 1567, the Duchy of Mantua was visited by two competing theatre companies, both including women: one was actually directed by an actress whose stage name was 'Flaminia', and the other run jointly by a 'Pantalone' (possibly Giulio Pasquati) and the actress Vincenza Armani. The artistic and commercial rivalry between the groups was made more interesting for the public by the fact that each leading lady was being courted by a different aristocratic patron – it is reported that the whole city was divided between fans of 'Flaminia' and supporters of Vincenza. As well as mounting improvised comic scenarios, each woman also starred in a more serious play, one based on the Virgilian story of Dido and the other taken from Ariosto's *Orlando furioso*.[1] By the 1560s, then, professional companies were an established fact of life in northern and central Italy. The first surviving notarial document regarding the constitution of such a group dates from 1545.[2]

It is not intended here to give a comprehensive presentation of *commedia dell'arte* – that is a task which has already been performed by various reliable scholars,[3] and readers who wish to acquire a full picture of the elements of the genre should turn to them. In this chapter we shall be pursuing only those aspects on which there may be something new to say, and which arise out of what has been presented so far: namely the links, in so far as they can be determined, between dramaturgical practice in scripted and in unscripted comedies. However, the very mention of 'dramaturgy' in relation to theatre which is 'unscripted' makes it clear that there will have to be some justification for what we are about to propose. This in turn creates a need for a selective factual outline. In describing a phenomenon which lasted over two hundred years, preference must be given in the present context to what seems to be true for the earliest period. Scholars now tend to identify a 'classic' (some even use the term 'heroic') phase which ends around 1625.[4]

The term *commedia dell'arte* as such is not found in print until it was used by the Venetian comic dramatist Carlo Goldoni in 1750[5] – the phrase may already have been current in speech. The word *arte* in this context refers simply to artisan skill, without the inflated pretensions now associated with 'art'; and in the sixteenth century itself it was also the term for a trade or professional organization, a guild. In theatre history we now use the expression *commedia dell'arte* to refer to a very particular phenomenon: a theatre based on the use of 'masks' (a term which we must then define rather carefully), and in which plays were improvised on the basis of an outline scenario, rather than being learned word for word from a script. With these two essential characteristics – 'masks' and improvisation – *commedia dell'arte* is eventually found in countries other than Italy, though its Italian origin is always recognized: within Italy itself, it has a third equally indispensable feature of identifying certain 'masks' by their language as well as by other traits, so that given figures in the plays always use the same stylized dialect or linguistic register. (Pantalone speaks Venetian; the Dottore is Bolognese; Zani, Arlecchino and the other servants tend to speak Bergamask or generic Lombard; the Lovers use high-flown literary 'Tuscan'. Only the braggart Capitano may vary between Spanish, Neapolitan, or the standard language. It is noteworthy that dialects which were popular in Venice but had too local a resonance, such as *Pavano* and *Greghesco*, disappear from a genre which was performed over a wider area.)

Cesare Molinari rightly points out (1985, pp. 9–13) that theatre of this kind cannot historically be restricted to professional performers, nor did the professionals confine themselves to performing *commedia dell'arte* (as is shown by the 1567 season in Mantua). Nevertheless there is an intimate link between the new breed of professional actor, who appeared in the mid-sixteenth century, and the improvisation of comic scenarios. The composition of most professional companies was dictated by the need to cover all the standard parts in a coventional comic plot, and stage names were almost always taken from *commedia dell'arte* masks. Most important of all, it is unlikely that improvisation method would have arisen at all in any context which was not professional and lower-class. On the one hand it is a technique which was probably forced into being by the illiteracy of some performers; on the other hand, as has been suggested by Roberto Tessari (1969), improvisation made it easy to multiply the number of different shows in the repertoire of a professional company. Scenarios could be composed more quickly than scripts, and could borrow material from a common stock in a less blatant way.

There has been much speculation on the origins of *commedia dell'arte* and of its individual masks. They have been related to various pre-existing figures of carnival and legend, sometimes going back to Roman times, and the performing structures have been traced by some to the Atellan farces of the pre-Christian era. For present purposes one point must be insisted on. All the 'comic' scenarios which have come down to us (and these are the vast majority, even though there are some which rank as 'pastoral' or 'tragicomic') base their plot schemes and characters on conventions established by *commedia erudita* between 1508 and the 1550s. The individual masks, whatever pre-existing images they may have drawn on, are chosen to fit the roles and functions normally demanded by such standard plots. A *commedia dell'arte* company categorized its members as *Vecchi* ('Old Men' – initially Pantalone and the Dottore), *Innamorati* ('Lovers') and *Zanni* ('Clowns' – low-life characters, usually in the role of servants): sometimes the women were listed separately, but it was clear that they in turn were either *Innamorate* ('Lovers', Heroines) or *Fantesche* ('Maidservants').[6] This obviously fits the kind of framework which we have seen becoming standard in the less inventive scripted comedies, both in Venice and in Florence. The *Innamorati* were to be obstacled by the *Vecchi*, who would be moved by motives of avarice, of obstinacy, or of senile lust; the *Zanni* would try to help the lovers and play tricks on the old men, but would also be the butts of comic violence and disaster when their conspiracies went wrong. The braggart Captain – and this also reflects scripted sources – might take the role either of 'lover' or of 'father', depending on the chosen story line and the resources of the company. Happy endings were procured, as in 'regular' comedy, by a combination of successful trickery and the discovery of lost family relationships.

Commedia dell'arte was thus an improvised form of theatre spinning off from a scripted form, an adaptation of a gentlemanly cultural pastime to a format which was more commercially viable. If its masks and clichés are also to be found in undisciplined carnival culture, it is likely that they were transferred *from* the professional stage *into* that culture, rather than vice versa. The single undisputed case of the genre picking up a popular legendary figure is that of Arlecchino or Harlequin. The other 'Zanni' masks derived from simple caricatures of a low social class, the Bergamask peasant immigrant labourer. (Zani, or Zane, was a Lombard dialect reduction of the common name Giovanni.) Harlequin, exceptionally, was imported from France,[7] where his name was that of a demonic elf, leader of the Wild Hunt, possibly the Erl-König of Germanic folklore. He was assimilated eventually, at least in his language, to the other Zani figures, but his patched costume and bestial black mask remained distinctive.[8]

Individual actors normally played the same 'mask' for their whole careers – this was a specialist trade, like that of other *Arti* or guilds. The use of the term 'mask' in this context is not always consistent from one scholar to another, so we had better define our terms. In one sense a mask is a facial disguise which needs no explanation, and facial masks were worn in *commedia dell'arte* by *Vecchi* and by *Zanni*, perhaps by some of the more grotesque *Capitani*. We can become familiar with them from the stock of contemporary visual material which is reproduced by major studies of the genre. In what we think of as the 'classic' form of the arte, young lovers, maidservants and some *Capitani* did not wear facial masks. It is better nevertheless to think of those roles as 'masks', rather than as 'stock characters' or some other term. All *arte* roles, whether facially masked or not, kept the same name, costume, language and other exterior characteristics from one play or scenario to the next. Leading ladies like Isabella Andreini were always 'Isabella' (or equivalent) on stage, always used the same language and delivery, always the same stage personality – they were fixed 'mask' roles in exactly the same way as Pantalone or Zani were. A familiar analogy would be the unchanging 'masks' adopted, without the use of a facial appendage, by actors in silent film comedy at the beginning of the twentieth century – Chaplin's 'tramp', Keaton's 'wooden-face', Harry Langdon's 'babyface' are fixed and instantly recognizable figures, whatever social or psychological traits they may have to adopt for a particular story. Those cinema roles lived and died with a single performer, as no doubt did Isabella Andreini's 'Isabella', or Flamminio Scala's 'Flavio'. The only difference with the facially masked roles was that the mask itself did not die, and so the role could be attempted by more than one performer. So there was a succession of Pantaloni, Zani, Dottori and Arlecchini over two centuries, with a constant dialogue and tension between the fixity of the mask and the personal genius of the actor.[9] By contrast, each young lover and each pert maidservant had to be created afresh – though still affected by conventional parameters – in relation to a new star personality.

The wealth of surviving visual evidence (of which equivalents are totally lacking in relation to *commedia erudita*) has left a vivid impression of all these strange personalities. Scholars and enthusiasts feel that they know them well, and the fact that they can be visualized has given us a tendency to concentrate on the non-verbal aspects of *arte* performance – mime, gesture, acrobatics, and the mysterious qualities bestowed by the facial masks themselves. All of these were undoubtedly crucial; but it would be a serious error to underplay the verbal element in this kind of comedy. We have seen in the previous chapter how the obsession with dialect and caricatured language was a central reason for the 'non-respectable' comedians to separate themselves from more literary practices. Much of the fun of *commedia dell'arte* came from its performers saying, as well as doing, things which made people laugh. Molinari points out (1985, pp. 21–4) that the Dottore and the Capitano were essentially verbal masks, in that the ridiculous things which they said took priority over any contribution they made to the action. Both characters, indeed, came to life via bravura set speeches, in which the Dottore's idiotic parody of learning, or the Capitano's fantastic boasting, held the stage in their own right. We might also add that the Lovers too, whether their role is to be seen as a parody or not, made their presence felt principally by rhetorical exchanges.[10] Pantalone and the myriad versions of Zani and Arlecchino may have injected more physical energy and clowning into the action, but they too, with their caricatured dialects and deliberate stupidities, used words as much as they used their bodies.

It is legitimate therefore to suppose that there must have been some interplay, if also some contrast, between the verbal content and style of *commedia dell'arte* and those of 'regular' Italian comedy. If improvised theatre grew out of a scripted genre, then it must have taken some of that genre's dramaturgy with it, on the small scale as well as the large. Later, when the *arte* was established and popular, writers of comic scripts could easily have been influenced, consciously or unconsciously, by what they saw and heard the professionals doing. The relationship between the two types of practice is bound to be complex, and it will involve (on both sides) rejecting as well as accepting influences; but some relationship has to exist, and sometimes it may still be detectable in the evidence which we possess.

It is the question of evidence, of course, which is the most debatable. From a purist point of view, there can be no *commedia dell'arte* text on which we can base any arguments. Since the actors improvised, whatever that may turn out to mean, from an outline scenario, they used no written script. Whenever we find a written script which looks as if it might be informative, then by definition it is no longer improvised and therefore no longer *commedia dell'arte*. This logical dilemma makes us rely, to a degree which is in theory dangerous, on personal judgement, even on hunch. In particular we have to decide empirically, not logically, what can rank in any dramatic script as 'evidence' of non-scripted performing practice; and that decision will depend largely on our having perceived features which we have decided, in advance, constitute the 'evidence' which we are seeking. The argument is circular, but unavoidable: we can comfort ourselves with the observation that most of the judgements we have to make in real life, as opposed to scholarship, are taken on the same unsatisfactory *a priori* basis.

In practice we have already taken some of the relevant decisions in the previous chapter, in quoting certain structures in written Venetian comedy as foreshadowing what was to develop into improvised theatre. It will be similarly necessary to use as evidence (relying heavily on the circular argument) later comic scripts which, in our judgement, show signs of being influenced by improvisation, and which therefore may inform us what detailed influence there might be. The need to get help wherever we can find it will force us to make use of material which falls well outside our usual chronological parameters, well into the seventeenth century. There are two bodies of plays in particular which have proven links with *commedia dell'arte*, and where it seems plausible to detect elements in the dramaturgy which come from improvisation. One is made up of the works of Molière, who is known to have had regular contact with Italian *arte* performers in France.[11] The second is a group of comedies now referred to by critics as 'Commedia Ridicolosa'.[12] These are fully scripted plays, written by amateurs for amateur performance in or near Rome, and published mostly between 1605 and 1630. The most popular authors (that is, the most often reprinted) are Giovanni Briccio (1579–1645) and Virgilio Verucci (dates unknown). The link between 'Commedia Ridicolosa' and *commedia dell'arte* comes on a secondary level from a proliferation in these scripts of regional dialects (one of Verucci's plays is actually entitled *Li diversi linguaggi*[13] – 'Various Languages', first published 1609); and on a primary level because the main characters in the plays are Pantalone, Zani, Arlecchino, Dottor Graziano, Franceschina, various Capitani and young lovers, plus other stereotypes of more ephemeral local interest. The accepted view of these plays is that their authors and performers wanted to reproduce something like *commedia dell'arte* in private performance, but lacked the ability to improvise with confidence and so needed the support of a full script. Therefore, we can argue, at least a part of their writing might reproduce the style and atmosphere of an improvised performance.

It is with reference to this wide and disparate range of evidence that we must propose a theory of what 'improvisation' meant in practice, and of what characteristics it may have tended to impose on the structure of a comic speech or scene.

IMPROVISATION AND MODULAR STRUCTURE

In his most recent study (1984), Roberto Tessari explores the tension which existed among *arte* actors, before and after 1600, between the more respectable and less respectable ends of the profession. The premise is that *commedia dell'arte* grew out of a socially unacceptable form of theatre, and that although by 1600 the actors were seeking and gaining a new status, they were still aware of, and nervous about, their historical origins.[14] The new status came from their having adopted the forms of respectable humanist comedy; however, the method which the professionals applied to this material, the method in particular of improvising rather than learning from a script, came from elsewhere. We can only conjecture that these practices already existed, and must have been adapted from such professional actors as were already performing: individual buffoons, and itinerant family companies who acted in the open and who had no cultural or social status at all.

It is likely that such performers were mostly illiterate, and that their approach to creating 'scripts' and memorizing them for performance would be different from the methods adopted by anyone who could read and write. In the first place, like comedians of all times and places, they would want to build up a mental store of single jokes, ranging from one-liners through question-and-answer routines to quite complex verbal and physical sequences. These would be created, learned and rehearsed piecemeal, and then used wherever they would fit, with the narrative line being adapted to the joke, if necessary, rather than vice versa. Such jokes would be the ancestors of what in *arte* jargon were eventually called *lazzi*. However, as well as a stock of autonomous gags, these actors would need a technique for creating and memorizing material which actually led somewhere, dialogue which was capable of building narrative and therefore of contributing to the plot. We are cut off, now in our society, from the mental processes of the creative intelligent illiterate – nevertheless, it is not impossible to hypothesize at least one of the mental techniques which could have been employed. Functional dialogues would be easier to memorize if they were built out of small manageable units, not so very different from the autonomous so-called *lazzi*. Each stage of a dialogued exchange would be identified in the mind by some label – the information it conveyed, or the joke it explored. In memorizing and performing the sequence, the stress would lie on conveying the information and/or getting the laugh, rather than on repeating the words identically every time.

This hypothesis relies heavily on the circular argument, because it was formed in response to the fact that certain relevant dramatic texts fall into a characteristic pattern – one whereby dialogue is built out of short units, many of which are interchangeable, or removable, or indeed recyclable into a different narrative context. Some examples have already been quoted in the previous chapter from Aretino, Dolce and Parabosco, and it would have been possible to add others from Calmo and Giancarli. Later, examples of the same structure are plentiful in 'Commedia Ridicolosa' and in Molière; but our starting point, and our basic illustration of the concept, is a single precious text from the period which concerns us.

Vito Pandolfi, in his indispensable six-volume collection of material published between 1957 and 1961, offers an anthology of surviving textual material relevant to the *arte*. Most of his examples are not dramatic texts as such, but spin-off material in the form of songs, verse dialogues, and pamphlet compositions often also in verse. This is hugely informative about the way in which Pantalone, Graziano and Zani made people laugh, but it tells us little about how they structured their jokes for improvisation on stage. But there is one exception: a dialogue in prose between the Venetian Magnifico and his servant Zani (*Dialogo de un Magnifico e Zani Bergamasco*),[15] which embodies the central master–servant confrontation, placed firmly in the Republic of Venice, which many scholars see as the core of *commedia dell'arte*. The text has an unusual ring of live performance about it, to the extent of making us wonder if it is a transcription of a scene actually staged, or a guide for new performers learning the trade. It could comfortably function as a scene – or as two scenes interrupted by other material – in a scripted play or in an improvised scenario.

The plot is simple and typical. The elderly lustful Venetian Magnifico wants to make contact with a courtesan. He sends his servant, country bumpkin Zani from Bergamo, into the lady's house with a message and a poem. After an interval, Zani comes out again, having had such a good time that he totally forgot to do what he was sent for. There are thus two distinct routines, both familiar from scripted comedy: one in which the old man reveals to his servant that he is in love, and is mocked for his pains; and a second in which the servant confesses his incompetence and is punished for it. The first 'scene' is further sub-divisible into shorter routines, of which the following are a sample:

(A)

MAGNIFICO: *[Introductory monologue, then . . .]* Zani!
ZANI: Yes sir. *[Probably at the window]*
MAGNIFICO: Come out a moment.
ZANI: What can I do for you, boss?
MAGNIFICO: Come out here a moment, my dear chap.
ZANI: Me?
MAGNIFICO: Thee.
ZANI: You want *me* to come to *thee*?
MAGNIFICO: Aye, *thee*, you donkey, get a move on.
ZANI: At your service, as you *see*. Shall I wear my hat?
MAGNIFICO: To hell with your hat, put your cap on.
ZANI: Yes si*ree*. Er . . . Pardon *me* . . .
MAGNIFICO: Now what?
ZANI: You want *me* to come out?
MAGNIFICO: Yes, you.

ZANI: Me myself in person?
MAGNIFICO: *YES*, for God's sake, come out!
ZANI: I'm coming, I've arrived, I'm here, what can I do for your honour?

(B)
MAGNIFICO: I want you to know that I am in love.
ZANI: In love?
MAGNIFICO: Yes, I am in love.
ZANI: You mean *you* are in love?
MAGNIFICO: Yes, idiot, don't you understand?
ZANI: You really mean it?
MAGNIFICO: Yes, I really mean it.
ZANI: *You* are in *love?*
MAGNIFICO: Yes, I am in *love.*
ZANI: *(Collapses with laughter)*
MAGNIFICO: What are you laughing at, you clodhopper?
ZANI: I thought you'd made a joke. You said you were in love.
MAGNIFICO: But I *am* in love. What's the matter, don't I look like a man
    with normal drives?
ZANI: Driving mules, more likely.

(C)
ZANI: And you're in love with *her?*
MAGNIFICO: She's the one.
ZANI: Then you've had it, boss, you're as good as dead.
MAGNIFICO: Dead?
ZANI: Dead, boss, you're dead.
MAGNIFICO: But I'm perfectly alive, you dolt, what's all this about?
ZANI: You're dead, boss.
MAGNIFICO: Why am I dead?
ZANI: Four brothers, real hotheads, they'd clobber you as soon as look at
    you.

The three 'sections' chosen above do not, of course, appear as
separate in the text. However, they are easy to isolate and consider
separately. (In fact, (B) follows almost immediately after (A),
whereas (C) comes after two or three intervening sections.) They are
autonomous units of dialogue, each reaching a simple conclusion
(which may also involve a joke), and each is potentially usable in
other situations. They can be seen as a series of beads threaded on a
string, or as a set of blocks which together will build a wall – in either
analogy, the structure of the scene which they compose can be
described as 'modular'.

In addition, the single units of the modular structure are in many cases 'elastic': they can be made longer or shorter, in improvisation, without losing their essential point. If the opening suspense about whether Zani is going to come on stage or not falls flat, then the actors can skip some of what is here written down and get on to the next unit: the same is true of the 'I am in love' sequence; while the section about the Magnifico being 'dead' could be lengthened with more repetitions, if the actors have struck the right rhythm and the audience is happy. What the units have in common is that their conclusion, or punch line, is never in doubt, so the actors cannot get lost – all they need to do is to identify each sequence by its climax and get them in the right order. For a smooth performance there has to be a previously agreed cue line or gesture, which brings the sequence to an end. So, in our section (A) above, when the Magnifico says 'YES, for God's sake . . .' with the agreed intonation or emphasis, the actor Zani accepts that he must come out of the house, and forget any further delaying variations. In the 'You're dead' sequence, it is perhaps Zani who is in control – he is the one who has to judge when to give the answer about the four brothers, and move on to the next unit. It was that kind of professional discipline, subordinating the single effect to the overall flow of the spectacle, which was later recognized as distinguishing a good company from a bad one. If either the Magnifico or Zani is selfish, and ignores the agreed signals to move forward (or exit, or enter), then the team-work is spoiled.

By the nature of things, 'elastic gags' or modular units are often suspense structures built up by sheer repetition (as we also saw in extracts from Aretino and Dolce). This is obviously the easiest shape to use, if the length is going to be varied. It is a relatively simple business for the actor to go on saying more or less the same thing until some signal tells him to stop. In fact any structure involving suspense and a postponed conclusion, repetitive or not, poses few problems. As long as the prearranged climax is waiting as a safety net, the actors can perform almost any verbal acrobatics without losing their balance. This process reaches its peak in the second scene of our dialogue, when Zani comes back from the courtesan's house and keeps his master poised on the edge of apoplexy waiting for his news:

ZANI: Good news, boss! I've been there.
MAGNIFICO: You've been where?
ZANI: To see your girlfriend. Good news!

MAGNIFICO: Really?

ZANI: Really, boss.

MAGNIFICO: My dear old chap, come on now, give me some consolation, give me some relief!

ZANI: Boss, I was in there talking to her for ages.

MAGNIFICO: Splendid! What did she say about me?

ZANI: She's so polite, so accommodating, so friendly.

MAGNIFICO: Yes indeed, she's got all the graces. What did she say about me?

ZANI: She gave me an enormous hunk of her cheese.

MAGNIFICO: Get to the point man, tell me what she thought of the sonnet, and what her answer was.

ZANI: She gave me some fresh, white bread.

MAGNIFICO: Do you want me to burst? You can tell me about all those things later – put me out of my misery, tell me about the sonnet.

ZANI: Yes boss, just a minute boss, good news! She wanted it, you know sir, she really wanted it.

MAGNIFICO: Wanted what?

ZANI: She wanted it from *me*.

MAGNIFICO: *WHAT*?

ZANI: She took hold of my hand, and she wanted me to touch her on her rosette.

MAGNIFICO: On her what? Her rosette?

ZANI: Oh yes, boss . . . And she wanted me to stick two buttons on it.

MAGNIFICO: What the hell is all this? What buttons, what rosette?

ZANI: Yes boss, you see, the rosette on the front of her bonnet, here . . . She wanted me to give her two of my buttons, to stick on her rosette. It was a great favour.

MAGNIFICO: God rot you, you great buffoon, will you stop this gibbering and tell me what she said about me?

ZANI: Oh boss, she was smiling, she was happy, she was so kind to me, she said if I go back again she'll give me some cake.

MAGNIFICO: I don't think I can stand this much longer – I'm going to die. *WHAT DID SHE SAY ABOUT MY MESSAGE?*

And finally he does get an answer – but it is that Zani forgot to give the message at all, and used the sonnet to wrap up some fried fish. The scene ends in tears, with a beating. There is no verbal repetition here (except for the irritating phrase 'Good news!' to be inserted at frequent intervals), but an inventive Zani, on the night, could no doubt think up some more dreamily suggestive double-entendres and spin out the comic delay for as long as the audience continued to laugh.

The whole sketch, then, appears as a flexible succession of 'elastic gags', or modular units of dialogue. Our proposal is that such modular components are a sign of improvisation technique, of a mode of performance in which an actor's existing repertoire of jokes, long and short, can be adapted and inserted into any plot with which they do not actually clash. Such techniques could have been developed first of all by illiterate performers, who needed them to help build their mental catalogue of material: they were then applied increasingly, especially in Venice, to the new 'erudite' material which was thus captured for professional use. When the acting profession ceased to be illiterate, as it did very rapidly around this time, then the mental memory bank was replaced by the personal *libri generici* (commonplace books), written collections of useful and transposable material which we know actors kept right down to the time of Goldoni.

If all this is true – and it is by no means a revolutionary suggestion, in the light of what is already known and documented – 'improvisation' did not mean that an *arte* performer invented his part from scratch every night, but rather that actors, singly and in teams, were constantly drawing on an accumulated stock of existing repertoire. The plots which they used were in any case stereotyped and repetitive, constantly offering similar situations. Creative ad-libbing could never have been ruled out – the genre would not have been such a phenomenal success without it – but when it happened it would be like a jazz musician playing variations on a known tune,[16] securely held by an existing framework and always moving towards a known conclusion or comic climax. And the structure of autonomous repertoire 'melodies' would not have been restricted to large-scale *lazzi*, monologues and long speeches, but would operate also in fast-moving dialogue, even in exchanges which advanced the plot rather than merely embroidering it.

Although we found some examples of modular structure in written comedy before 1555, it seems to be relatively rare; and this underlines a divergence of taste and aspirations as between 'literary' and 'theatrical' dramaturgy. Most of what we have quoted from the anonymous *Dialogo* is unexciting to read on the page. Writers with a literary training avoided circularity and repetition, which to them appeared as literary faults. (As we noted, when Florentine dramatists found such playful structures in Plautus,[17] they tended to exclude those scenes from their 'imitations'.) They wanted their comedies to perform well, but also to read well. The professional buffoon did not expect his material ever to be read, and by adopting improvisation even when he was literate he ensured that it would never be. He knew that repetitive and even silly material can work beautifully in the third dimension of live performance.

The tracking down of modular structures and 'elastic gags', in those written scripts which might be affected by the example of *arte* improvisation, is a task which has barely begun. Surveys of the appearance of such a structure in 'Commedia Ridicolosa' and in Molière are nevertheless encouraging. They even make it possible to point to particular types of scene, conventional and frequent in the 'regular' comic plot as developed between 1550 and 1600, in which the modular structure can be especially useful.

The anonymous *Dialogo* shows that one of the most obvious purposes of the modular game can be to cause delay and create suspense. The event which is delayed can be some major comic climax, like a beating or the delivery of unwelcome news; or the most banal thing imaginable, like the opening of a door. An unimportant action is made important simply because it is put off for so long: an event which is not funny in itself, when it happens, can be made hilarious because of a build-up of time during which it does not happen. (It is perceptions like these which a purely literary dramatist, with no performing experience, is slow to acquire.) In Act I, Scene 4 of Giovanni Briccio's *Pantalone imbertonao* ('Pantalone Besotted') of 1617, the delay in getting a servant to come out of a house is taken to greater lengths. Young master Tiburzio wants Zani to come down and let him in. But Zani is having a meal, and puts off moving for 'just one more mouthful . . . just one more glass of wine . . .', in a repetitive elastic sequence. Tiburzio naturally gets furious, and picks up a stick. But then Zani does not want to come out because he is afraid of being beaten, and there is a new elastic delaying sequence in which Zani says 'You'll hit me' and Tiburzio says 'No I won't.' When Zani finally does open the door, he does of course get beaten, as the audience anticipated all along. Much later, in Molière's *L'Ecole des femmes* ('School for Wives'), Act I, Scene 2, there are two servants, Alain and Georgette, to open the door to their master Arnolphe. To start with neither of them can be bothered, and there are elastic repetitions ('You go.' – 'No, you go') accompanied by fatuous excuses. Then Arnolphe threatens to starve them as a punishment, so they start falling over each other to open the door, and the contest between them to avoid blame causes more delays. The simple interposition of a door between characters seems to provide endless opportunities for such games.

A different opportunity is given by the reading of a document on stage. This can be done simply to invite repetitive comments from a listener, as in Act II, Scene I of Molière's *L'Avare* ('The miser'). In 'Commedia Ridicolosa', there are scenes in which a dowry is laboriously read through by the Dottore, acting as marriage-broker. This character's Bolognese dialect mixed with bad Latin produced complete gibberish: so, as he pieced his way painfully through reading the dowry contract, each impossible item of property had to be translated back into its proper sense by some other character on stage. So (to fudge up English equivalents, but with some Italian originals in mind), the meaningless phrase

One lousy farthing for an awkward haddock with pox

turns out to mean

One house and garden with an orchard, paddock and copse;

while

Nick wet the bed milking Persians for Mother Eileen

is really

Six sets of red silken curtains and another in green.

This sort of thing is harder to invent on the spot, and the distortions might have to be memorized; but if the 'real' meanings were written out on the document used on stage, the Dottore could exercise his judgement as to how many to use on a given night. Versions of this scene, in written form, appear in Briccio's *La dispettosa moglie* ('The Bad-Tempered Wife'), II, 3; and in *Pantalone imbertonao*, III, 4.

Another kind of dialogue which invites repetitive modular structure is one which works through a list of alternatives, as long or as short as necessary. In Briccio and Verucci there are leisurely reviews on subjects like what to do next (*Pantalone imbertonao*, IV, 4); the virtues which can be detected in a prospective bride (*La dispettosa moglie*, II, 4); and alternative places where Zani might go to hide (*Li diversi linguaggi*, V, 1). In Aretino's *Talanta*, in a scene probably written for professionals, we saw Tinca giving a list, in both words and gestures, of the ways in which he could frighten off his enemies, and such a structure could well be the basis for a large part of the repertoire of any braggart Capitano. But the most typical list of all is a list of people; especially a list of suitors for the hand of a son or daughter, where a parent is broaching the subject of marriage. In Briccio's *La dispettosa moglie* the same structure is used in two successive scenes (1, 2 and 3): the father works through a list of possible candidates, the son or daughter finds a reason for rejecting each in turn, until the suitor already favoured by the young person is mentioned and modestly accepted. Or, in a similar context, an argument can develop between parent and offspring over a marriage proposal, which can be reduced to the simplest repetitive structure of all – the one where one party is saying 'Yes' and the other is saying 'No', *ad nauseam*, until a third character breaks in to stop them. Act III, Scene 1 of Verucci's *Li diversi linguaggi* is an expanded form of such a confrontation, which I have analysed in detail elsewhere.[18] There are a number of successive 'units' in it, but all of them are elastic; and for good measure various of them recur, as the same routines but with different words, in separate scenes of Molière's *L'Avare*.

The confrontation between parent and child over a proposed marriage is a standard conflict in plots derived from *commedia erudita*, and a good example of the way in which professionals would want to milk a situation for its maximum number of laughs. In most Florentine and Venetian comedies where there is rivalry between father and son for the same girl, that situation is presented as antefact in an early expository scene, without much dramatic exploitation. In later comic tradition it is seen to provide an important opportunity for conflict on stage. In a scenario, it might be very simply summarized as 'Pantalone speaks to his son Flavio about marriage, and reveals that he wants to marry Isabella.' In practice, the modular structure of an improvised dialogue is going to delay the revelation as long as possible, and get some fun out of misunderstandings on the way. Father and son might spend some time discussing the desirability of marriage in general, appearing to be in full concord; they might then agree on the desirable qualities of Isabella in particular, with Flavio unable to believe his luck; only then would Pantalone drop the bombshell and reveal that he wants this girl for himself. That, at least, is the way it is done by Molière in Act I of *L'Avare*, where the father and son are Harpagon and Cléante. And since half the amusement of such a build-up comes from the audience's guessing in advance that Flavio is misunderstanding the situation, one can speculate that by Molière's time the routine was very familiar. We have not been explicitly told, at that point, that Harpagon wants to marry Marianne, but we will enjoy the scene more if, on the strength of many previous comedies, we can guess that this might be the case.

The appearance of elastic routines in Molière generally – and they are extremely numerous – should not be taken to indicate that his scripts are provisional, or that he intended his actors to ad-lib them in performance. Rather, he must have observed a particular rhythmic structure which was adopted by improvising actors, and seen that it had a theatrical validity in its own right which could be turned back into a written script. Some of his most penetrating comic scenes use the structure, such as the famous repetition of 'Le pauvre homme!' in *Tartuffe*; but his judgement is so perfect that any attempt to vary what he has written would spoil it completely. The most concentrated example of his using elastic gag structures is the whole first act of *Le Médecin malgré lui*, where performing experience shows that there is not a single word too many or too few.

Modular structure tends to accentuate the self-conscious game-playing element of comic theatre, as well as having the practical advantage of accumulating repertoire for the individual actor and making things easier for his hard-pressed memory. Having identified it as a technique, we must not allow ourselves to be mesmerized by it. The elastic gag cannot have been the only characteristic of the unwritten dramaturgy of improvised comedy. Nevertheless, when it is found in a written script, it is a useful sign of the presence or influence of professional *arte* practice; and in Italy it helps to high-light the grudging interplay between improvised *commedia dell'arte* and its parent, written *commedia erudita*.

LARGER UNITS OF IMPROVISATION

The earliest type of input into 'regular' scripted comedy from the performing routines of professional buffoons seems to have been in the form of the large-scale monologue. An essential part of the skill of a buffoon or *giullare* had always been that of holding the attention of an audience without help, often splitting himself into multiple characters or voices in order to do so. Ruzante, Calmo and Gian-carli all tended to isolate such moments in which they individually, as actor-dramatists, built a confidential relationship with their public. In their more lengthy compositions, they allowed some of their colleagues to do the same, thus contributing to a tendency inherent in all comic drama, whereby the spectacle fragments into individual bravura numbers and the audience savours them one by one.

Every mask in the canon would have been capable of taking the stage alone in this way; and there is still work to be done in tracing not only what verbal formats would be typical of each, but also the ways in which they may have influenced written comic scripts. In the years before the genre was fully established, the plays of Ruzante and Calmo contain some of this material in embryo, with Ruzante's monologues pointing in the direction of foolish one-man numbers for a Zani or an Arlecchino, and Calmo laying the foundations for monologues by Pantalone. There are also foreshadowings of the braggart Capitano mask in various plays, both Venetian and Sienese, which caricature the figure of the Spanish soldier; and Pedants in Aretino, in Belo and in *Gli ingannati* point – perhaps more tentatively – in the direction of the mask which will be Dottor Graziano. Capitano and Dottore in particular were identified by characteristic types of monologue or long set speech. In Pandolfi's anthology, jokes and themes which could also be used on stage are preserved in print in semi-dramatized songs, verses and pamphlets: most such compositions (though not all) tend to work in terms of longer 'speeches' rather than rapid dialogue. The so-called 'verbal masks' – Dottore, Capitano and Lovers – would have been especially prone to accumulating repertoires of long items, which may have needed memorizing more carefully because the verbal details were the essence of the effect sought.

The Capitano was a role much in demand during the 'classic' period of the genre, but had disappeared entirely by the eighteenth century. Pandolfi's material shows that his boasting could fall into two distinct categories, each no doubt preferred by different performers of this family of masks.[19] They are typified by two contrasting poems in *ottava rima*, each of which encapsulates for a reader the essence of one version of the theatrical role. The one by 'Captain Headsplitter and Arrowspitter', written (and performed?) by Antonio Pardi from Lucca,[20] goes for straightforward impossible hyperbole: 'I break, smash, shatter, fracture and dismember anyone who steps in my path . . . Many times have I broken the head of Cerberus, and routed the assembled ranks of Tartarus. Wherever I walk I can put Pluto and Satan to flight . . . And if my name is heard [in the heavens], then Hercules and Mars shit in their breeches.' Long rantings of this sort seem to have been remarkably popular, even the endless allusions to Classical mythology and abstract personified figures such as Death and Tumult, though one must always wonder whether the material was pushed culturally up market just for the printed page. This is very much the style of the famous Francesco Andreini (1548–1624), in his prose *Bravure* ('Boasts') of 1607,[21] which to judge by their introduction are acutely anxious about whether their material will be acceptable to literate society, and to ecclesiastical censors. An alternative Capitano, as exemplified by the 'Earthshaker' of Giulio Cesare Croce,[22] might go to the other extreme and describe the most banal or ridiculous exploits in inflated language, as though they were superhuman: 'I decimated a plateful of beans single-handed . . . And a Cricket once, who was singing unscathed in the forest, I assailed with such fierce and horrendous cries that he fled into his hole and I never saw him again.' This 'Seven [Flies] At A Blow' approach, as well as having roots in folk-tale, is closer to the one adopted by Pietro Aretino's Capitan Tinca, in *La Talanta* of 1542:

TINCA: Do you know that at the battle of Cerignola, which lasted until after dark with one man-at-arms dead and two wounded, I was the man who fetched the fire which lit the torch carried by the man who stepped between the combatants, quelled each side with a glance, and said: 'Gentlemen, you have done enough for today'? (*La Talanta*, Act III, Scene 12)

The fact that Tinca needs his parasite Branca as a 'feed' typifies the way in which a Capitano usually worked, with a companion always on stage to flatter him, provoke yet more boastings, and ironize for the audience: Andreini's published *Bravure* may differ considerably from what he did on stage, but they do retain the essential dialogue between 'Captain Terror' and his servant Trappola ('Trap'). The repertoire must have consisted of quite long complex sequences, largely memorized by the Capitano himself, but with practised interjections, following predictable patterns, from the servant or parasite.

The repertoire of the comic Doctor, on the other hand, mostly took the form of monologue – at least it could have been prepared and memorized as monologue, even if other characters were going to listen to it, because his speciality was to spin out any conversation to interminable lengths of verbiage, and over-ride all attempts to interrupt. So, at least, we gather from a late appearance of the figure in one of Molière's earliest surviving farces, *La Jalousie du Barbouillé* ('The Jealousy of Barbouillé'). The Doctor makes three appearances in this short piece, two of them lengthy and none of them in any way useful to the action or to the other characters – the whole basis of his comedy is that his endless drivel prevents everyone else from getting on with their business. In Scene 2, Barbouillé ('Doughface') makes the mistake of consulting this learned man about his marital problems, and has to listen to a tirade demonstrating that the Doctor is a doctor ten times over. The fact that Barbouillé keeps trying to interrupt turns what is basically a monologue into a modular delaying routine:

DOCTOR: Firstly: just as the unit is the basis, the foundation and the origin of all numbers, so I am the first among doctors, the Doctor of doctors. Secondly: since there are two faculties necessary to perfect knowledge of all things, namely sense and understanding; and since I am all sense and all understanding, thus I am a doctor twice over.
BARBOUILLE: Absolutely. The thing is . . .
DOCTOR: Thirdly: since the number three is the number of perfection, as Aristotle says; and since I and all my writings are perfect, so I am a doctor three times over.
BARBOUILLE: Yes. Well now, Doctor . . .
DOCTOR: Fourthly, since philosophy is divided into four parts . . . (*La Jalousie du Barbouillé*, Scene 2)

Barbouillé has no choice but to sit back and wait until number ten has been reached. Such ill-founded pretentiousness was always a characteristic of the Italian mask Dottor Graziano. Pedants in written comedy have the same characteristic, but it is not always expressed in the same repetitive games. However, one early example which does offer pre-echoes of Molière's Docteur is the pedant Aristarco in Bernardino Pino's otherwise untheatrical *Gli ingiusti sdegni* of 1553. What does not appear in scripted Italian comedy, and is lost both in Molière's French and in any conceivable English translation, is the barrage of twisted language which characterized the professional mask. The Dottore spoke Bolognese, a dialect which Italians from elsewhere tend to find amusing in its own right. To this accent he added streams of bad Latin (for the educated), or better still (for the uneducated, or for everybody) an endless flow of distortions and malapropisms which became a comic code in its own right, and was reputed in the mouths of the best performers to make audiences literally sick with laughter. A 'Gratianesque Dictionary'[23] compiled in manuscript for the help of aspiring performers gives a list of the distortions to which certain words should always be subject, most of them untranslatable in any literal sense. *Parer* ('opinion') should become *sparvier* ('sparrow-hawk'); *Capitano* becomes *Decapidan* (a non-word from *decapitare*, 'to behead'); *ordinar* ('to arrange') becomes, naturally, *orinar* ('to urinate'); *letto* ('bed') becomes *letame* ('manure'); and we know from earlier written texts including Ruzante that the academic discipline *Medicina* was regularly twisted to *Merdesina* (based on *merda*, 'shit'), and *Latino* to variants of *latrina*. Tastes were more robust and simple in those days, but one must not underestimate how laughter can come from accumulation – if every second or third word in a sentence was distorted in this way, the effect would have been entirely different from that of each piece of word-play on its own. Molinari (1985, p. 22) quotes a snatch of a letter in *Gratianesco* gibberish from an early Dottore, Ludovico de' Bianchi, to the Grand Duke of Tuscany: every single word is twisted into something else, and it takes considerable ingenuity to get any meaning out of it at all. No doubt audiences would build up an acquaintance with this code, and eventually congratulate themselves on seeing through it to the banalities which lay underneath.

How banal the content could be is shown by another spin-off composition in verse: the *One Hundred and Fifteen Conclusions of the Archperfect Doctor Gratiano*,[24] the first stanza of which might go like this in English:

1 A rose, when blooming, tends to smell all right;
2 And any man who's walking can't be dead;
3 A man who's always wrong is never right;
4 A ship at sea is far from home and bed;
5 If peace and quiet annoy you, start a fight;
6 And if you won't walk slow, walk fast instead;
7 A childless woman isn't often fecund;
8 You'll always miss the first place if you're second.

(Just eight 'conclusions' out of one hundred and fifteen.) But the core of the Dottore's role was a prepared repertoire of long implacable speeches, full of tongue-twisting virtuosity. The enforced pause in the dramatic action would make them almost into spoken arias, with the gibberish taking the place of melody. Any similar structure in a written comic script can probably be traced back to this mask.

The material which still leaves scholars feeling very hesitant is that used by the Lovers, a class of mask which included that brand new theatre phenomenon, the Leading Lady or (in every sense) *Prima Donna*. All the surviving evidence suggests that the repertoire and style used by the Lovers was unremittingly literary. In the previous chapter we quoted brief examples from Ruzante and from Parabosco of the kind of preciosity which their dialogue could involve, and those two examples highlight a major difficulty in modern interpretation. In Ruzante's *Vaccaria*, the tortuous verbal agonies of Flavio and Florinetta were brought down to earth by immediate contrast with the vulgar dialect of Vezzo and Truffo. In the passage quoted from Parabosco's *Hermafrodito*, on the other hand, there was no reason to suppose that Zerbino and Furnia were not to be taken seriously. Which of these two tendencies, or what balance between them, prevailed in *commedia dell'arte*? Was the verbosity laughed at, swooned over, appreciated as serious rhetoric, or made a sly cover for the sexuality contained in the plot? There is some evidence which points to each of these, and perhaps ultimately the answer is complex rather than simple.

Pandolfi in his anthology makes use of two principal sources, fragments put together in the early seventeenth century by the working actors Domenico Bruni of the Confidenti company,[25] and Isabella Andreini (1562–1604)[26] of the Gelosi, wife of Francesco ('Capitano Spavento'). The dialogues of Isabella, edited for publication by her widower, are more formal and literary, but both collections could relate to genuine items of repertoire. Bruni's unpublished dialogues are more prepared to admit an element of sexuality, even bawdry, into the relationship between hero and heroine, which corresponds better to the content of many surviving scenarios. Isabella's edited works are more decorous: this reflects the respectful adulation which she received in her lifetime, her admirers going to great lengths to stress her virtue and high moral tone. Both collections are good evidence for the view that actors learned and prepared material to cover stock situations, which would regularly recur in standard comic plots. Bruni's fifty-one items include the following titles:

A despised lover, in hatred of his rival.
The beginnings of love.
Whether beauty and grace are the same thing.
Lover's compliments at the window, on leaving his mistress.
A seducing bawd, on constancy in love.

Superiority of the soldier or the man of letters.
Parting.
Woman offended with her husband.
Man offended with his wife.
Isabella's twenty-seven items include:
Amorous debate on the dignity of lovers.
Debate on the passions of hatred and love.
Debate on those who have died for love.
Debate on the fever of love.
Debate on how to fall out of love.
On loving another more than oneself.
On jealousy.

That the role of the Lovers was not always approached seriously is plain from the situations in which scenarios often involve them – elopements, sexual escapades, pregnancies, and mad scenes for both heroes and heroines. One of Isabella's own dialogues, the 'Amorous debate on pretending to love one woman while loving another', between Valerio and Fedra, ends with an extended 'mad speech' for the hero Valerio, which is clearly meant to cause laughter with its nonsense and non sequiturs in the same way as was seen in 'drunk scenes' and 'sleep-walking scenes' in Calmo and Giancarli:

VALERIO: Now indeed night has fallen: now indeed the darkness of her cruelty invades and obscures my mind: now indeed I am blinded entirely! Ah! most cruel woman, you yourself said it, you yourself foretold it, that I should become all of a sudden the wisest man in the world, and should take over the lordship of the universe: and she spoke true! Hey, you, whoever you are! Bring me my royal robe, my sceptre and my crown; and get these rags off me, they are unworthy to clothe a King, an Emperor, a Monarch such as myself. *[Possibly he should remove or disarrange his clothes at this point?]* Come now, dress me quickly! There: now that I am royally dressed, bring in all my courtiers, summon my counsellors, because I wish them to advise me about my love, and about buttermilk curds. You, young gentleman, who gave you leave to carry that pistol loaded with Malmsey wine, in defiance of our edict? Take it away, and roast it, because I want to eat it stewed, casseroled and fried in the pan. Musicians! Play that dance tune which starts with the first of April and finishes with the end of May, because I wish to give a lunch for certain friends of mine who are fond of composing verses dressed in petticoats. Who would have thought that monkey knew so much about affairs of state? And yet it does; but if Aristotle hadn't drummed his *Politics* into its head, that great bell of justice would never stop ringing, and the sparrows would eat up all

the millet in Lodi. Calm down, madam, there'll be plenty left for you
. . .[27]

This continues for more than twice the amount quoted, with some of
the nonsense perhaps containing topical allusions, and it ends with a
demented snatch of disconnected folk-song worthy of Ophelia.
Isabella herself was famous for her own mad scene in the scenario *La
pazzia d'Isabella* ('Isabella's Madness'), of which we have an account
from 1589: whether she was as fey and 'comic' as this, or whether she
went for more dignity and pathos, we cannot tell. But on the
technical side, we have to conclude that most of this lengthy monologue would be learned by heart, perhaps split into independent
sections, certainly with room for variations to suit each performance.
In 1589, on an occasion to which we shall return, she was acting for
a Granducal wedding where the bride was a French princess: so in
her mad scene 'among other things she began to speak French, and
to sing various French ditties, which gave inexpressible pleasure to
the Most Serene bride'.[28]

The role in the Lovers' repertoire of solo numbers like this is not
difficult to imagine. The dialogues in Pandolfi are harder to fit
conceptually into the framework of 'improvisation', and Isabella's
examples all seem to demand that they be simply learned by heart.
They do not even have the embryonically 'modular' structure which
we claimed to identify in the exchange from Parabosco's *Hermafrodito* quoted in the previous chapter. Nevertheless, that scene from a
written play shows that even lovers' dialogues might be composed of
smaller interchangeable repertoire items. Many of these would be
what Elizabethan and Jacobean England called 'conceits', figures
half-way between the poetic image and the legal argument, with a
core of abstract content which could be divorced from a precise
verbal formulation. Other units, as the Parabosco scene suggested,
might have a more rhythmic character. Much later than our period,
in 1699, a compendium on the art of improvised performance by
Andrea Perucci contained a series of strange dialogues 'in parallel'
between lovers, in which the partners declaim their way through a
complex dispute and change of heart, each always expressing
exactly the same set of emotions, but never in the same words.

HE: Go! . . .
SHE: Disappear! . . .
HE: . . . from my eyes . . .

SHE: . . . from my sight . . .
HE: . . . Fury with the face of Heaven!
SHE: . . . demon with the mask of love!
HE: I curse . . .
SHE: I shudder . . .
HE: . . . the day that I set eyes on you.
SHE: . . . at the thought that I ever adored you.
HE: How can you dare . . .
SHE: Have you the insolence . . .
HE: . . . to look at me again?
SHE: . . . to remain in my presence?

This continues for fifty-three pairs of lines, during which the couple have second thoughts about each other and reach a reconciliation, ending as follows:

HE: Peace, dear eyes!
SHE: Peace, loving mouth!
HE: No more wars, apple of my eye!
SHE: No more scorning, o sweet glance!
HE: If thee alone I love . . .
SHE: If this my soul adores you . . .
HE: . . . Cupid comes back to life.
SHE: . . . this be the end of all our discords. (trans. Lovett F. Edwards)[29]

For any reader or listener, the rhythmic repetitions constitute the main point of the scene. They provide a kind of melody, and it is not for nothing that Pandolfi's anthology moves eventually in the direction of *opera buffa*. Standing back a little, one notices that neither lover is in any position to listen to what the other is saying, since their thoughts and emotions proceed independently, if in complete parallel. There could be a source of parodic fun here, even a psychological comment on the self-absorption of lovers. Here again, however, questions have to be asked in relation to 'improvisation', and we must suspect that the overwhelmingly literary origins and content of so much of the Lovers' dialogue must have meant more learning by rote, and less creative freedom on stage, than was the case with many of the other masks. Nevertheless, long passages of material were available for constant recycling, in just the same way as the more fluid jokes of a Zani or an Arlecchino. Verbal and rhetorical constructs, sometimes of considerable complexity, have taken on the status of theatrical currency, in a bank which also deals in songs, jokes and pratfalls.

The appeal of some of the more ornate and abstract constructions remains hard to evoke for the modern reader or scholar. Theatre history is sometimes the study of an alien culture, and we have to record what was there whether we can empathize or not. We should make the comparison, perhaps, with the films of the Marx Brothers in the 1930s and 1940s. In these comic 'texts', which seem in so many ways to parallel the spirit of *commedia dell'arte*, it was felt necessary – presumably by the public as well as by the makers of the films – to suspend the anarchic mayhem at intervals, and give way to ten minutes of sentimental exchanges and a song from Alan Jones (or equivalent) and his leading lady.[30] Fashions in sentiment change, and what seems vacuous to us must have appeared more substantial in the past. To revert to less distant comparisons, the conceit-laden exchanges to be found in Isabella Andreini are not so different in kind from those in *Love's Labours Lost* or other admired Shakespearean dialogues. The difference is that Shakespeare had a lighter touch, and pursued his conceits with reference to the design of a single scripted play, rather than storing them for modular use in a succession of different scenarios.

It has to be faced, however, that no modern audience can respond to the kind of material which *commedia dell'arte* lovers used with anything other than boredom or derision. This means that even the most meticulous modern revivals of the genre, such as the hilariously successful productions of TAG Teatro,[31] have to mock the verbal and emotional pretensions of the lovers and abandon any attempt at sentimentality. It is hard to say how far this choice is inherent in the material itself, and thus 'authentic', and how far on the contrary it responds to an irreversible change of taste in the theatregoing public.

Our survey of the repertoire used by 'verbal masks' is still provisional. We can nevertheless feel some confidence in proposing that actors who played these roles had to memorize a lot of fairly large-scale speeches and exchanges; and that their 'improvisation' consisted mainly in choosing and adapting what they had in their memories (and in their commonplace books) to fit the story being played. The longer the units of material are, the more we can perceive how literary sources, or at least written sources, contributed in significant measure to this unscripted, supremely theatrical medium. The links between *commedia dell'arte* and *commedia erudita* have, on this basis too, to be recognized as strong.

SCENARIOS

Pieces of repertoire and pieces of inspired invention, speeches, dialogues, songs, routines and slapstick numbers, everything had to be fitted on the night of a performance into the framework of a chosen story. The virtuosity of each performer must be allowed to flower, but the fictional patterns of the chosen *fabula* also had to be maintained. The story itself was based on a repertoire of stock units from 'regular' scripted comedy: family rivalries, love affairs, disguises, misunderstandings, tricks and discoveries. It was almost always divided into three acts, rather than five. At the same time it would seek to incorporate extra inventive elements, usually resolving themselves into single memorable comic scenes. An example would be *Il cavadente* ('The Dentist') from the Flamminio Scala collection. Here a large part of the first act is orchestrated to prepare for a scene just before the first interval, in which Arlecchino masquerades as a travelling dentist and unnecessarily extracts most of Pantalone's teeth. The remainder of the show goes on to explore different intrigues and gags, but the 'dentist scene' still gives the title to the show. The story to be told, the succession of scenes and conspiracies which gives shape to the evening's entertainment, is referred to now in English as the *scenario* – an Italian word which was not always the one most frequently used at the time, equally common terms being *canovaccio* and *soggetto*.

In practice, the scenario was a hand-written document which belonged (for the time being) to a given company of actors, and which would be available as aide-mémoire during rehearsals and performance. (That there were rehearsals is beyond doubt – company contracts mention the imposition of fines for missing them; and there would need to be a team consultation before each performance, to ensure that everyone was clear about the relationship of his/her mask to each of the others, the order of the scenes, and which pieces of concerted repertoire needed to be remembered and inserted.) There was no reason why this document should ever go to a printer: that would make material available to rivals in other companies, and perhaps reveal too many trade secrets to an audience whom one wanted to dazzle and mystify. Accordingly, nearly all the collections of scenarios which have survived from the seventeenth and eighteenth centuries are still in manuscript.[32] Just one set was published: that of Flamminio Scala, who acted as the lover

'Flavio' and was a director of various companies. He published a group of fifty scenarios entitled *Il teatro della favole rappresentative* ('The Theatre of Stories for Performance') in 1611.[33] This collection has inevitably attracted more attention than any other. It is the earliest one to have survived, it comes from a distinguished practitioner of the 'classic' period, and it is the only one available to the general reader. Nevertheless, comparison with the manuscript collections does not suggest enormous difference between Scala and the rest.

The whole point of a scenario is that it does not give away much detailed information as to what is going to happen in each scene. It outlines the story, says who is on stage at any given moment, but then leaves spaces for the material, new or old, of the individual performers, using phrases like 'they do their scene . . . he does his *lazzi* . . . they have their love scene . . .' and so forth. Important plot information which has to be conveyed to the audience is spelled out in detail, because the actors need to remember it too, but the entertainment for which the plot is a pretext can often hardly be glimpsed. Granted the particular emphases of our present study, which has tended to focus on the single theatrical moment rather than on larger-scale plot structure, scenarios are a subject over which we shall not be able to linger. What can be said at present on the analysis of the single scene has been said already, in the uniquely valuable monograph of Tim Fitzpatrick (1985), who establishes that improvisation scenes always seem to break into a binary pattern. Either only two characters are involved at a time, or larger groupings seem to be resolvable into two opposing parties, with at the most a third person acting as umpire in the contest. This observation coincides well with the kind of material which we have been able to choose for comment: there have rarely in our examples been more than two characters foregrounded at one moment.

A scenario was above all a practical document, a set of guidelines and instructions for performers. At the start there is a list of characters, but also a list of necessary properties ('Two boxes of sweets; a dentist's disguise; blacksmith's tools; a good armchair', in *Il cavadente*). The characters are always listed by households, whereas in 'regular' scripted comedy it was usually either in order of appearance or in order of importance. The following is the cast-list for *Il cavadente*:

PANTALONE

ORAZIO, his son

FLAMMINIA, his daughter
PEDROLINO, his servant.

FLAVIO
ISABELLA, his widowed sister
FRANCESCHINA, their serving maid
ARLECCHINO, their servant

DOCTOR, alone
CAPITANO SPAVENTO, alone

PASQUELLA, an old woman on her own

This layout is important for the actors, when they study it. In last night's performance, Pedrolino may have served the Doctor, and Isabella may have been his daughter; in a different story, the Capitano might have had a house on stage, rather than being 'alone' and always entering from the street. Here they can remind themselves at a glance of tonight's status, relationships and stage territory. The subsequent narrative is also usually disposed on the page in such a way that actors can spot immediately the next moment at which they will be needed. Continuing with *Il cavadente*, the first scenes go as follows:

PANTALONE tells Pedrolino of the love he bears to the widow Isabella, and how he fears that his son Orazio is his rival, so he has resolved to send him to university. Pedrolino disapproves, taking Orazio's part. They quarrel and come to blows: Pantalone attacks Pedrolino and bites him on the arm, making it seem a good hard bite. Pantalone leaves, threatening him, and telling him to talk to Franceschina on his behalf. He exits. Pedrolino: that he will get his own back for the bite he got from Pantalone. To him

FRANCESCHINA going to look for Orazio on her mistress's orders. She sees Pedrolino, and hears from him why his arm hurts. In revenge, they agree to pretend that Pantalone's breath stinks. Franceschina goes indoors, Pedrolino stays; to him

FLAVIO tells Pedrolino of his love, bumping into his arm. Pedrolino yells; then they agree to pretend Pantalone's breath smells. Exit Flavio, Pedrolino stays; to him

DOCTOR says he is owed 25 scudi by Pantalone . . . (*Il teatro delle favole rappresentative*, Day XII)

In fact there is a typographical error here, because Pedrolino should be highlighted for the first scene – following the conventions normally used in the same collection, it should read:

PANTALONE tells
PEDROLINO of the love he bears to the widow . . . etc.

Otherwise the text is careful in spelling out exits and entrances, and
also punctilious in using the phrase *in questo* or *in quello* – translated
as 'to him', 'to her', or 'to them' – indicating to a newly entering
character that he does not have to wait for an empty stage. By
contrast, other details are unexplained, because the actors know
what is intended: in the above opening scene there must be a
well-rehearsed sequence of slapstick comedy whereby a quarrel
between master and servant leads to a bite on the arm. The decision
to pretend that Pantalone's breath stinks seems quite arbitrary, and
has to be handled by the actors as they see fit. Its rationale is in fact
that it prepares for a lengthy sequence at the end of the act,
involving a large number of the cast in quick succession – a good
example of a scenario which calls for thought and team discipline,
and where the structure is not entirely fragmentary:

> . . . Pantalone hears how Pedrolino has talked to Franceschina; then
> hears Pedrolino say 'Hey, boss, your breath stinks something awful.'
> Pantalone laughs it off; to them
> FRANCESCHINA does the same, saying that if his breath didn't smell, then
> Isabella would love him, and goes indoors again. Pantalone surprised;
> to them
> DOCTOR arrives; Pedrolino signals to him about the breath; the Doctor
> does the same routine, and exits. Pantalone: he wants to ask his
> daughter if it's true about the smell. He calls her.
> FLAMMINIA admits to Pantalone that his breath does smell awful, and goes
> in. They remain; to them
> ORAZIO from his house, confirms the same, then goes back in. Pantalone
> decides the tooth which is causing the stench must be pulled out. He
> orders Pedrolino to bring him a dentist . . . (*ibid.*)

And this leads to the gruesome climax of comic sadism with the
disguised Arlecchino, which is the set-piece finale of Act I:

> . . . Arlecchino gets his tools out, all blacksmith's tools, giving them all
> silly names. He makes Pantalone sit down, and with a pincers pulls out
> four good teeth. Pantalone, in his pain, grabs the dentist's beard,
> which is false and comes off in his hand. Arlecchino runs away,
> Pantalone throws the chair after him and, moaning at the pain in his
> jaw, goes indoors,
>   and this ends the first act. (*ibid.*)

The rapid succession of characters all feeding the same story to
Pantalone is a good example of laughter built up by accumulation.

It also shows, in its repetitive variations on a theme, a version of our 'modular' structure on a slightly larger scale. One can imagine Orazio and Flamminia listening in the wings, picking up ideas and phrases from Franceschina and Flavio, and deciding whether to follow on by simply echoing what has gone before, by introducing a variant, or by doing something which is a total contrast. Once again the analogy with jazz is an attractive one: each soloist takes his or her turn and improvises round the established 'melody' in the light of what has just gone before. Ideally, they should also make up an ensemble.

THE COMEDY OF *COMMEDIA DELL'ARTE*

The climax to Act I of *Il cavadente* would hardly rank as 'high' or sophisticated comedy. A great deal of *commedia dell'arte* laughter, to judge both by scenarios and by visual material, was based on the infliction of pain and humiliation by one character on another: it seems proper that in the English tradition it should have led to the beatings, hangings and infanticide of the Punch and Judy show. Punch and Judy are wooden puppets which always bounce back unharmed, and their place has been taken in the late twentieth century by filmed cartoon characters which can be shredded full of holes and then in the next frame return to their full anatomy. The violence inflicted on them can therefore be seen as harmless, thera-peutic, the purging of aggressive instincts without doing any real damage. The puppets, or Tom and Jerry, belong to a world apart and they are immortal: the spectator has understood the rules of the game, and knows that the same figures will be seen in new and equally disastrous adventures tomorrow.

Although sensibilities may not have been so delicate in the six-teenth and seventeenth centuries, and people may have recoiled rather less from laughing at real pain, the fixity of the *commedia dell'arte* mask must have given the experience something in common with Punch and Judy and with cartoon film. Pantalone and Zani inhabit a clear-cut world of performed fiction, which may contain some distorted references to the real world of the spectator, but feeds even more off its own formats and expectations – it is primarily theatre about theatre, and only to a lesser degree theatre about life. Here too the masks, like the cartoon characters, will be there unharmed if we come back tomorrow, ready to go through a fresh set of jokes and intrigues and beatings for our amusement. Some masks will even survive the death of their performers: Pantalone and Dottor Graziano and Arlecchino will be incarnated successfully over two centuries, altering slowly but still recognizable, just as Tom and Jerry were drawn by more than one artist. The *arte* professional had discovered, by accident or design, a mode of theatre which seized the imagination, entertained without making demands, and had a remarkable autonomy and capacity for survival.

We are proposing that professional comedians broke away from the learned tradition, and its attempts to censor them, in order to permit themselves greater vulgarity, more comic subversion, and the continued use of dialects. This might imply that there was one public which wanted such things, and another which was not so sure. More gentlemanly audiences had been persuaded to insist that proper dramatic compositions, even comic ones, had to stick to the freshly canonical literary language, and to observe Classical rules of composition which were increasingly being formulated in print. They may also have begun to object to plots and scenes in which too much violence and humiliation was visited on a figure of authority. If, as seems likely, the 'Vaccaro' engravings[34] in the Recueil Fossard represent the earliest and most basic use of the masks, then they show how much gleeful use was made of situations in which masters were humiliated by servants, and became grotesquely indistinguishable from them. There is a level of aggression here which an audience of masters and rulers could have found hard to take.

However, *commedia dell'arte* companies are soon found performing for courtly audiences too. Indeed, the thesis of Roberto Tessari (1984) is that they were eventually bought up and controlled by princely patrons. In Florence, the Teatro alla Baldracca[35] was a hall thrown open for theatre performances to a plebeian public; but it was owned and controlled by the Medici Grand Dukes, who had a private corridor to a window from which they could watch the shows unseen. By the 1580s, if not earlier, professional actors were hired to perform both scripted plays (comedies, tragedies and pastorals) and improvised scenarios, sometimes on successive nights of a single festivity. The vogue for *commedia dell'arte* did not remain for very long exclusive to the lower classes. The actors must have rapidly become more flexible in adjusting the tone of their humour to the type of audience before them; though it is also possible that the aristocrats may have learned to distinguish between genres, and accepted things in improvised comedy which would not have been tolerated in scripts with cultural pretensions. (We should remember how many English sophisticates enjoyed visiting the music-hall, in the late nineteenth and early twentieth centuries.) Such anarchic comedy, which ignored rules of decorum (in both senses of the word, which will be examined in the next chapter), was acceptable provided that it was identified as belonging to a class of its own. Improvisation and dialects may in the end have provided the necessary demarcation, and given the courtiers their excuse to enjoy à more subversive spectacle.

Visual evidence makes it clear that the level of vulgarity could be extreme, and the scenarios give an impression of repeated comic situations which we would now expect to amuse children more than adults. There is a recurrence of anally oriented humour: swords, syringes, stomach pumps and bellows applied to the rear quarters of both men and animals.[36] In the Recueil Fossard engravings, dated to 1577, Harlequin puts his hand up Franceschina's skirt.[37] Implausibility is added to vulgarity when Pantalone is persuaded to wear horns,[38] or dress up as a mule with reins, saddle and bridle;[39] or (as we have seen) when Pantalone bites Pedrolino's arm, or in numerous scenes which allow servants to give masters a beating. In scenarios (and in Giancarli and Parabosco), we often find people in terror of fake 'spirits' or devils: one remembers how, in an English pantomime, the one episode which is sure to make children go wild with delight is the 'Look behind you' scene, with characters being stalked by a ghost or a skeleton. How much of this was toned down for more sophisticated audiences there is no way of telling. To avoid becoming too superior, we should remember that a kick on a policeman's behind, or a custard pie in the face, are neither sophisticated nor original as gags, but that timing and style can still make them remarkably funny when the performer is a Chaplin or a Keaton.

As with Chaplin and his policemen, the attraction of the masks themselves was largely founded on mockery against figures of authority, or against types who could be felt as a threat. Pantalone, the Dottore and the Capitano all fit into that category, all have their pretensions to dignity undermined and ridiculed, and are usually victims of tricks played by a servant on behalf of a lover. The fixed and increasingly stylized costumes, and the facial masks themselves, had the effect of dehumanizing characters to some degree,[40] so the violences visited upon them became all the more tolerable and enjoyable. All such dehumanizing is the logical conclusion of the search for a comic victim: even in more realistic narrative or drama, the reader or spectator has to find an excuse for not minding that such awful things are being done to a human figure. We are back in the area of aggressive and punitive laughter discussed in Chapter 1.

The servant masks were subject to the same distancing and grotesque stylization, but in the end the reactions which they aroused were more complicated. Again the analogy with early film comedy, with recurrent figures such as Chaplin, Keaton, Laurel and Hardy, is useful. The myriad versions of Zani the peasant were first conceived – certainly in their scripted ancestors, such as the stage figure of Ruzante – as objects of derision, appealing to the contempt felt by the town-dweller for the rustic, or by the self-sufficient for the inadequate. Throughout their history – multiplying into Arlecchini and Truffaldini and Pedrolini and Mezzettini, being joined from southern Italy by the more mysterious and ungraspable figure of Pulcinella – they entertained their audience by doing stupid and ridiculous things. They misunderstood their betters, they became lost in comic fantasy, they forgot messages, they pursued hopeless love affairs and were humiliated, they got distracted by food and drink, they caught flies and ate them with salt and pepper, they tried to kill themselves in impossible ways, always pursued by their masters and by the furious beating which they would receive sooner or later. In theatre as well as in folklore there was an insatiable appetite for stories of true idiocy, to which absolutely everyone could feel superior, and in this sense they were targeted by the audience just as much as Pantalone and the other victims. And yet, in a way which 'regular' written comedy could never quite accept, Zani and Arlecchino and Pedrolino also paradoxically became the heroes of their stories and of their genre, joined eventually by the pert serving-maid, Franceschina or Colombina, as partner and heroine. A number of features could contribute to this: the tendency in plots derived from Plautus for slaves to orchestrate the intrigue, a carnival atmosphere, a greater amount of sympathy from a public made up more of employees than employers; perhaps most of all the very indestructibility of the stage mask, which ensured that these figures would always come up looking for more adventures and could never really be defeated. At all events, the *commedia dell'arte* produced eventually, in masks such as Harlequin, the figure which superior educated dramatists in Italy could not bring themselves to create: the Fool as Hero, the person whose very idiocies could somehow be felt as a kind of victory. It was a status probably sought, and occasionally achieved, by Ruzante: 'I'll eat myself to death, then at least I'll die with a full belly.' Fantasy triumphs for a moment over logic, and the Fool has won.[41] It is a moment of release which we all secretly need, but which elaborately formal societies have great difficulty in acknowledging. When the *arte* was sufficiently established to be used for a regular parody of official culture, it was Harlequin or Pulcinella who figured in apotheoses and triumphal processions, it was the underdog servant figure who dominated carnival as unofficial Lord of Misrule. In the rest of Italian Renaissance culture, in spite of the fame of the Erasmian *Praise of Folly*, the Fool as Hero is banned, or at best refined into a sophisticated ironic commentator, who deploys words with eloquence and no loss of dignity.[42] The marvellous authorial irony of Ariosto, in both the *Orlando furioso* and the *Satire*, shows a unique self-confidence in being able to make the author himself the object of rueful mockery. Ariosto admits to participating in various less dignified aspects of the human condition, and he turns the scatterbrained knight Astolfo into a hero and a saviour; but the superior verbal elegance and wit, with which he undermines his own status, paradoxically restores that status to him and prevents him from being a full-blown Fool. He may present himself as not being in control of his life, but he is patently in control of his poetry: his teasing attacks on rationality are themselves too obviously rational for him to end up as an exile from his class. The Italian Renaissance is on the whole somewhat poorer without the uncomfortable vulgarity, the abandonment of all status, the shocking or illuminating irrationality, which a proper Fool can provide. *Commedia dell'arte*, carefully fenced off from approved culture but then enjoyed by all none the less, provided in its Zani and Arlecchino the only permissible safety valve for both rulers and ruled.

Even such a stylized outlet was not in fact seen as permissible by some sections of society, increasingly inhibited by rules and prohibitions of a theoretical, social, political or religious nature. It is constraints of this sort which we must discuss in the next chapter.

CHAPTER 6

Obstacles to comedy

Most studies of an aspect of Italian Renaissance culture take it for granted that weight must be given to the theory which supported and explained such practice. There may be an element of perversity, or of devil's advocacy, in our decision both to postpone the discussion of theory until this point, and then to treat it as a factor which, if not exactly marginal, is at least intrusive.

On the question of chronology, at least, there is a serious point to be made. It is axiomatic to this study that 'regular' comedy was produced in imitation of the dramaturgical practices of Plautus and Terence: such a programme had a theoretical drive behind it, and theoretical discussions are bound to have taken place among those who were involved. The commentaries of 'Donatus' must have been a prominent source of as yet unwritten precepts, and there may also have been some practical use made of Horace's *Ars poetica* and Aristotle's *Poetics*.[1] The existence of argument and polemic is very occasionally apparent from the dramatic texts themselves. In Machiavelli's *Mandragola*, the remark of Fra Timoteo (IV, 10) that the action of the play is not going to be 'interrupted' between evening and morning implies that spectators might notice a breach of what later became known as the unity of time. Aretino's prologues to successive versions of *La cortigiana* also refer to rules imposed on comedy by scholars, which at that time he clearly found pedantic: he derides restrictions on the number of times characters may appear on stage, and the prohibition on speaking direct to the audience.[2] However, during the whole formative phase of 'regular'

comedy such detailed theoretical arguments were restricted to practitioners and interested parties, and never achieved the status of
print: even Prologues to comedies rarely go beyond alluding to the
general legitimacy (which therefore must have been contested by
some) of writing original comedies rather than just translating the
ancients, or of deviating even in minor ways from Plautine and
Terentian practice. (Typical Prologues of this type are those to *La
cassaria*, *Calandra*, *Clizia*, *Aridosia*, and Ruzante's Italian prologue to
La vaccaria from which we quoted on p. 138.)

A new printed edition of Aristotle's *Poetics* appeared in 1536, in a
convenient-sized volume with the Greek text faced by the Latin
translation of Alessandro de' Pazzi:[3] it is from this moment that
theoretical argument on literature seems to have become a widespread pastime in Italy. 1536 was the year of *L'amor costante* in Siena,
of *Aridosia* in Florence, and of *La Veniexiana* in Venice. From before
that date, Bernard Weinberg's massive anthology of treatises on
literary theory[4] contains only six items: there are then twenty-one
up to 1560, and another thirty-two to 1600. The relevance of all
these to comedy in particular varies greatly, of course; but the
statistics make it apparent how the vogue for literary and poetic
theory belongs firmly to the second two-thirds of the sixteenth
century. Playwrights who composed comic texts before 1540 were
not perhaps free from all theoretical constraints, but they were not
yet hemmed in by systematic attempts to dictate literary practice, in
print and in the public domain. It was from the 1540s onwards that
this became the context in which all writers, of texts both dramatic
and literary, had to operate.

By this time, as we have argued in relation to Venice, writers for
the theatre were faced with demands and expectations from their
audiences, as well as from the academic sector. (For pioneers such as
Ariosto and Machiavelli there can have been no expectations, since
they were inventing a new mode of theatre from scratch.) Depending on who the audiences were, such demands might or might not
take account of the increasing volume of polemic relating to the
function of art and literature, and to the Classically-derived rules
which could govern dramatic composition. The fact that some
sections of the public cared nothing for such matters, that they
resented anything which interfered with spontaneously developing
taste, is implicit in the arguments and uncertainty to which Venetian texts bear witness, and implicit (or so we would argue) in the

rise of *commedia dell'arte*. It is equally clear that other kinds of audience did care about Classical theory, and certain Prologues give the impression of a dramatist looking over his shoulder with some apprehension at the pedantic objections either anticipated or already received from some spectators.

Even for those who took them seriously, many Classical rules and precepts were of a kind which would concern an educated reader, but make little impact on an audience. As an example, one might cite the case of the comedy *I gelosi* by Vincenzo Gabiani, produced for an aristocratic audience in Brescia in 1548 and published in 1551. Noemi Messora has argued convincingly that this play carefully obeys structural precepts derived from Terentian comedies, as interpreted in particular by a critical school from north of the Alps.[5] This fact is much clearer to someone reading the printed text at leisure than it would be to an audience on the night of performance. Factors such as the carefully balanced stages of a plot, spread across five acts according to a particular interpretation of written rules, are not always fully perceivable in the moment-to-moment experience of live theatre, especially in the chaotic conditions of a one-off amateur performance. This is not to say that Gabiani did not have such considerations in mind, but in practice his obedience to particular canons would be more appreciated by readers than by spectators. His dramaturgy shows again how many humanist playwrights were torn between two visions of their product: as a text for performance, and as a work of literature for an educated readership.

Other aspects of Classical precept were more communicable to the average audience, as much through habit and thus through expectation as through knowledge of a set of written rules. The so-called unities of time and place would be a case in point. Once spectators have become unconsciously accustomed to all comedies being staged in a fixed open street surrounded by buildings, and to a story which seems to take place over a limited time within about twenty-four hours, they are at least going to notice if either of those conventions is broken. To such an audience, though not to one raised on quite different conventions, an enormous time-lapse between episodes in a story is going to seem odd (whether or not it is marked by a Chorus speech from Father Time), as is a change of scene, in medieval style, from Jerusalem to Saragossa (or from England to France, or from Sicily to the coast of Bohemia). We have already argued that the inability to stage action indoors, as opposed to outdoors and in public, was a serious constraint on the development of more intimate scenes and of female characters: one only has to look forward to Molière to see how the exploration of family tensions, which seems central to specifically 'classical' comedy, is enhanced by the regular use of a domestic interior setting. In this area, then, the observance of a strict rule had become an accepted convention for audiences as well as for theorists; but it was at the same time blocking what now seems to be theatrical logic, and restricting the development of the comic genre.

On the other hand, Aristotelian recommendations for unity of action, as applied to tragedy in the *Poetics*, were felt by audiences to be so inappropriate in comedy that it became accepted in theory, as well as in practice, that sub-plots and decorative intrigues were a proper part of comic dramaturgy. When Machiavelli's *Mandragola* was reissued in Ruscelli's canonical collection of 1554 (see p. 65), its single-minded plot was regarded if anything as a weakness which the play's other qualities managed to compensate. The Prologues of Calmo and Giancarli, introducing their long involved multi-lingual farces, suggest that the 'real' plot of the play is the love intrigue resolved by agnitions and the reuniting of a family, but add that it is none the less legitimate to pad out the story with extraneous pieces of anarchic fun. This pays lip-service to an 'official' view of the comic text, while offering a quite different one in practice – in that the love story is dramatically undeveloped, the family reunion is merely a mechanical way of bringing the story to an end, and the scenes of fantastic aggressive trickery are the theatrical high points which the audience has really come to see.

There were some areas, therefore, where the application or neglect of theoretical rules would be overlooked by the average audience of comedy; and other areas where the rules might have to capitulate, explicitly or implicitly, in the face of spectator demand and the dynamics of comic performance. In the first category we would be inclined to place any detailed recommendations about the large-scale structure of the intrigue (with concepts like prologue, protasis, epistasis and catastrophe); in the second, unity of action and – at least in earlier periods – the prohibition against direct address to the audience. Other aspects of theory had a more inescapable practical effect on dramaturgy and on taste. This was all the more true in so far as aesthetic considerations were constantly being mingled, even confused, with moral issues and inhibitions which really mattered to the society of the time, and could be ignored by nobody. The most important topics to single out are theories and attitudes relevant to laughter itself – an area where Renaissance theory was particularly inadequate – and the thorny but all-pervading concept of *decorum*.[6]

THEORY OF LAUGHTER

Humanist rhetoricians, scouring the ancients for an authority who would tell them what they were allowed to laugh at, had very few texts to help them. However, the two sources which they commonly used did at least seem to be saying roughly the same thing. Aristotle in the *Poetics* had said that comedy represented the worst types of men, and that 'the ridiculous is a species of ugliness or badness' (the Greek word used was *aiskhròs*):

For the ridiculous consists in some form of error or ugliness that is not painful or injurious; the comic mask, for example, is distorted and ugly, but causes no pain. (Aristotle, *Poetics*, Chapter 5, trans. Dorsch)

Cicero, in Book II of *De Oratore* (Chapter LVIII, 236), had also characterized the essence of the *ridiculum* as lying in *turpitudo* and *deformitas*: in the 'unpleasing', but indicated and treated in a pleasing manner ('non turpiter'). (The Latin word *turpis* ('vile') thus comes to be the equivalent of the Greek *aiskhròs*, which itself has the original meaning of 'shameful'.) In both cases, to return to categories which we explored in Chapter 1, the accent is very much on derision, rather than on carnival release. The object of laughter is someone or something which, as Vincenzo Maggi interpreted it in his treatise of 1550,[7] 'falls short of' ('recedit ab . . .') a standard which can reasonably be expected. By laughing, we are either attacking that object or at least enjoying our own distance from it.

It was on the *De Oratore* that Baldassare Castiglione chiefly based his discussion of jokes and humour in the *Book of the Courtier* (Book II, Chapters 45–94); and one has to note how often the word *mordere* ('to bite') is used to describe the function of a witty remark, and how both verbal and practical jokes have a victim who is in some way 'bitten' or 'stung'. There seems to be little conception of wit without some element of aggression. The earliest full-scale study of laughter in relation to comic literature and drama comes in the Fifth Division of Gian Giorgio Trissino's *Poetica* (composed *c.* 1549, but not published until 1561).[8] Trissino makes full use of both Aristotle and Cicero, and takes their joint position to a logical conclusion whereby we never laugh at anything which attracts our approval: *ammirazione* (usually 'wonder', but here closer to the English 'admiration') is quite distinct from *riso* ('laughter').[9] Laughter involves pleasure, to be sure, but the pleasure is inspired by an object 'mixed with some ugliness' ('mescolato di alcuna bruttezza'). Man's nature, says Trissino, is 'envious and malicious ('invido e maligno'): we never take pleasure in the good fortune of others (unless we see some chance of sharing in it), but only in 'that evil [misfortune?] which is not found in ourselves' ('quel mal che non si truova in noi'). There is a point, he admits, where the spectacle of another person's suffering or handicap goes beyond laughter; but this is seen not as a threshold between laughter and pity, but between laughter and fear. We stop laughing when we start fearing that the same misfortunes might happen to us or our loved ones.[10]

We have shown sufficiently in these pages how current practice in Italian comic theatre did correspond to a great extent with this one-sided theory. There are in both scripts and scenarios plenty of examples of laughter being derived from the shortcomings, and the resulting misfortunes, of characters marked by some kind of defect, inadequacy or misjudgement. Foolishness, cuckoldry, avarice, hypocrisy, blinkered obsession, ignorance, arrogance, and the inability to talk in an approved manner – all these 'admixtures of ugliness' have been staple ingredients of the comic texts we have discussed. Even so, the rather extreme theory of Trissino is not adequate to cover everything in these texts and performances. It does not cater for approving laughter, which in drama may be evoked by a virtuous trickster preying on a comic victim (like Sofronia in Machiavelli's *Clizia*), by the ingenuity of a piece of intrigue, or by any verbal wit and paradox which is a piece of deliberate skill rather than the result of error.[11] Nor does Trissino's formulation make any reference to the carnival spirit whereby a fool, rogue, bawd or lecher can temporarily get the audience on his or her side, winning collusive approval for precisely those elements of 'ugliness' which in normal life would be disapproved and avoided. There is no explanation here, in other words, for all those occasions when a villainous character strikes up a confidential relationship with spectators, giving them a safely monitored holiday from the rules which normally constrain their lives. If we had only Trissino to rely on, a large part of the comedy of Bibbiena, Aretino, Ruzante and the Venetians would remain a mystery.

Such carnival instincts, involving deliberate titillating play with the scurrilous, were firmly present in both life and texts of the Italian Renaissance, but the comic theory of the time was quite unable to face them. This was because all aesthetic theory, whether inherited from Classical sources or from medieval theologians, was inextricably bound up with ethical and moral theory; and it had to obey a verbal logic which we might not now find appropriate or useful. A moral justification for comedy (as for all fiction, all culture) had been implicit in the commentaries of 'Donatus', and explicit in Aristotle, Cicero and Horace. The need to reiterate it in the later sixteenth century was accentuated by a new moralistic climate, prompted by the anxieties of the Counter-Reformation. As the century moved on, there were increasing demands that art should support social and religious orthodoxy and even political hierarchy. Otherwise, it was both implied and said, there was little justification for its existence. (And this not only in Italy – Sir Philip Sidney, after all, felt moved to write an *Apology* for, or *Defence* of, Poetry.) The surprising thing about Trissino's robust formulation of comic theory is that he does not make the obvious logical link between the notion of aggressive laughter and the moral purpose of comedy in making vice unattractive. The link was there none the less, and it was taken up by subsequent writers such as Vincenzo Maggi in 1550,[12] and Antonio Riccoboni in 1579.[13]

If one was willing to admit that the portrayal or enactment of vice could actually be fun, this tended to upset the image of moral seriousness and respectability with which the humanists now needed to invest artistic fiction. It was safer and more logical to maintain that laughter is always derisive. A caricature of the argument, with Socratic overtones, might run as follows: 'Man's true happiness lies in virtue, does it not? Therefore the spectacle of virtue must attract us, and the spectacle of vice must repel us. If we laugh at things which are immoral or unrespectable, then our laughter must be based on condemnation and rejection: the effect of comedy is thus to expose those defects, and make us wish to be dissociated from them.' It was that conclusion which needed to be reached, somehow or other; and it was much easier to reach it, in syllogistic terms, if one insisted that laughter was based on rejection. Vice was depicted in comedy in order to expose and condemn it: the essence of the risible was fully defined in Aristotle's *aiskhròs* and Cicero's *turpitudo*. But the more complex forms of carnival laughter went on existing, despite the theory, and simple experience must have begun to undermine the logical certainties. What could be made of the empirical obser-vation that some audiences actually enjoyed watching vice and subversion triumphant on stage? How was it that some (or all) spectators were actually applauding the appalling Zani and Arlec-chino in their assaults on authority, logic and decency? Nobody at that time had access to post-Freudian notions of repression and sublimation: it was verbally and intellectually inadmissible that the enjoyment of something immoral or undignified could be a harmless or even necessary piece of therapy. So any rhetorician forced by observation to admit that scurrilous comic spectacle could be attrac-tive and arouse collusion, rather than being repellent and provoking derision, was seized by a kind of panic and forced back into extreme positions.

The most profitable example to address is that of Bernardino Pino (birth date unknown, d. 1601) from Cagli in the Romagna, a cleric and scholar like the Sienese Alessandro Piccolomini – and not only a theoretician but a comic dramatist, author of six influential plays.[14] His *Brief Consideration on the Composition of Comedy in Our Times* was written in 1572 and published in 1578.[15]

Pino's position in this treatise is defensive from the very start. Comedy is having its whole legitimacy questioned, accused of being a degrading and dangerous activity. Professional comedians are especially suspect, and they are producing 'works . . . full of ugli-ness, obscenity, stupidity, impropriety and ignorance'. It becomes necessary to spell out what may be included in comedies and what may not; and most of Bernardino's treatise is devoted to reducing the range of 'turpitude' which is legitimate on stage. Aristotle is still taken as the starting point, but Bernardino restricts the scope of his definition: 'The ridiculous springs from the ugly, that is from the misformed, but not from the vicious, that is from the wicked and harmful.' It is accepted as a fact by Pino, however unwelcome it may be in theory, that the spectacle of vice on stage is enjoyable to some. He fears, in fact, that it is potentially corrupting, that it can put vicious ideas into innocent minds, and that it can even offer some instruction in how to get away with immoral actions. The argument that man is always repelled by immorality is false, because 'that perverse judgement which comes from our ill-regulated desires does not regard as a vice anything which might satisfy those desires'. (A Socratic view of man's natural taste for virtue is replaced by a Christian concept of original sin.) In that case, 'embellished adulteries, fornication, rape and other similar indecencies' must be eliminated from the stage, and laughter must be provoked only by absurd and ignorant behaviour with which we could not possibly wish to be associated – 'we', effectively, being the educated ruling class for whom any treatise on literary theory was written in the first place. Bernardino's most notable attempt to apply this theory was in his second comedy, *Gli ingiusti sdegni* ('Unjustified Rages') of 1553. The determination to avoid making any character even remotely reprehensible results in a puzzling plot where the contests between characters seem forced and artificial: there is an old miser and a ridiculous pedant, and the servants tend to be rather stupid, but the lack of conflict produces an equal lack of vigour. None the less, the play had achieved nineteen editions by 1626: its performing appeal must surely have been weak, but it no doubt attracted the approval of theorists and moralists as a model text for reading. It exemplifies on stage a set of rules about how noble-minded people should behave.

It is noticeable, in fact, how the inhibitions deployed in Pino's treatise are not only moral but also political and social. Bernardino bans any hint of criticism against the laws, customs and government of any state: in this area only complimentary references are acceptable, even in relation to foreign rulers. Comedy is thus not to be used for political propaganda, except for the eulogizing kind. Moreover, one notes how often he approves the turning of ridicule against servants, and other 'employee' figures such as the ignorant pedant and the braggart soldier, rather than against respectable fathers of families. One of the standard comic types, the old man foolishly enamoured of a young woman, is ruled out on grounds of the character's social position and patriarchal status. (In *Gli ingiusti sdegni* there is an old man in love, but he controls his passion with the utmost propriety.) It does not matter so much what the servants get up to, because a gentleman is not going to identify with them and be led astray. The assumption seems to be that the lower classes are bound to have lower standards of behaviour, even that it is proper for them to be vulgar, gluttonous and immoral. The criteria applied throughout are those of social as well as moral discrimination, and in Pino's treatise the comedies of Terence are held up as the supreme model because they are 'fine and worthy of a nobleman' ('belle e da gentiluomo').

We thus see Bernardino Pino taking the classic theory of the ridiculous and making it more prescriptive than descriptive. He accepts that laughter arises from the 'ugly', from 'turpitude', but observes that some of the laughter aroused may be of the wrong kind: he therefore selects those types of turpitude which conform with his moral and social purposes, and outlaws the rest from comic drama. A more extreme view was expressed in 1574 by the Florentine Giulio Del Bene, in a debating speech given to the Accademia degli Alterati: his brief was 'That the story of a comedy should be decent, and not contain any bad behaviour'.[16] Giulio argues that laughter is essentially pleasurable, and it is illogical to suppose that pleasure can arise from indecency ('disonestà'), which is unpleasant. It follows that if comedies are to give pleasure, they must contain no representation at all of anything immoral. In this way he comes within a hair's breadth of saying that comic things are not 'ugly' after all, and thus of contradicting Aristotle, to whose authority he pays lip-service at the start.

It is unfair to dwell on Giulio Del Bene's inconsistencies, because he was taking part in a formal debating exercise and had been given an impossible case to argue. But that he should have had to do it at all is symptomatic of the moral anxieties which Counter-Reformation critics and Academies felt about comedy as such. To redress the balance, it should be noted that other theorists were able to accept that laughter had a function of solace and relaxation, and were more prepared to treat the subject in a benign manner, without inquiring so much into the strict morality of the object of laughter. However, even in these more generous passages, there is a desire to make social dinstinctions between what amuses a gentleman and what entertains the general public. Lionardo Salviati, in a draft commentary on Aristotle's *Poetics* which had been written by 1586, offers the following observation on popular forms of comedy, with specific reference to *commedia dell'arte* – he is tolerant, but still distinguishes between different levels of taste and sophistication:

since pleasure is sufficient for men, they care about nothing else, nor are they bothered by the obscenities, or the lack of verisimilitude, or the other errors of the art, or the improprieties and the impertinences of which these plots [in the *commedie di Zanni*] are everywhere full, so long as the laughter and the pleasure last continuously. Grave men of substance [*i severi uomini grandi*] also find extreme pleasure in them, because of their admirable imitation; but on the other hand, they feel greater annoyance at the absurdities and other defects than if this were not so. From the striving for pleasure nothing but praise can come to these plots, because pleasure must be said without any doubt to be the end of comedy. (trans. Weinberg, 1961, p. 618)

Sperone Speroni, in his *Apologia dei dialogi* dated around 1574–5, says that it is one thing for a gentleman to relax and laugh, but quite another thing for him to waste time composing comic material for others:

If I once said that in the laughter of comedy the wearied mind is rested and that such repose is useful to it, I say it now again; and I say again that it is one thing to laugh in the theatre for an hour or two, another to write in order to make people laugh on purpose; the former gives repose and is necessary, the latter is an indecorous labour and an antisocial activity [*fatica indecorosa ed incivile operazione*]. (trans. Weinberg, 1961, p. 543)

There were others, as also much later in European history,[17] who were doubtful as to whether a truly well-bred person ought ever to laugh at all – the act of laughing seemed to involve a physical indignity and surrender of control which made it unsuitable for an aristocrat. Battista Guarini, arguing the case for tragicomedy as opposed to outright comedy, felt that a more mixed genre 'does not make us so dissolute in laughter that we sin against modesty and against the decorum of a well-behaved man'.[18] (The Italian word *decoro* was actually used here, and it is relevant to our next section.)

Renaissance theorists were very short of concepts with which to analyse laughter. Their biggest handicap was the insistence of all Classical authorities on the notion – firmly contested in modern criticism – that all art is essentially an 'imitation' of things in nature. This premise made it impossible to accept any distinction between responses to fiction and responses to reality. Renaissance theorists were unable to accept a relatively simple principle – that the fictional status of a piece of behaviour, or of a human character, can entitle us to have an entirely different reaction to it, as compared with what we should have to feel if we encountered the same behaviour, or person, in real life. And yet a large part of the comic drama of the period is effectively founded on such a principle. We are invited to collude with the adultery of Fulvia in Bibbiena's

Calandra or of Callimaco in the *Mandragola*, with the theft of money from a miserly father in comedies derived from the *Aulularia*, with the total humiliation by a Zani of his master Pantalone, precisely because they are happening in the magic territory of the stage where normal rules are suspended – where, to use the fruitful concept of Nicholas Greene in his book of 1980, a 'comic contract' is drawn up which can choose to ignore everyday sensibilities and normal morality. Comic playwrights and performers, together with their audiences, demonstrated constantly in practice that they understood this on an instinctive level; but the straitjacket of ancient precepts about the nature of art made it impossible for them to formulate it in theory.

The attitudes expressed by Bernardino Pino provide a blueprint for a more refined form of comic drama, which was actually being written in the second half of the sixteenth century, in a period when many critics would argue that the term 'Renaissance' can no longer usefully be used. It is a comedy in which the central characters, all of good family, display nothing but the noblest sentiments and scruples, and the scrapes which they get into are almost always the result of honest misunderstanding. The servant class, in this dramaturgical formula, has very little active part in the main story, but may be allowed extensive scenes of sub-plot and comic relief for the audience's superior amusement: they will be joined by contemptible upstarts like cowardly Capitani and foolish Dottori. It becomes the essence of the lower classes, on stage, to be turpitudinously laughable, whereas the upper classes are never worse than well-meaningly misinformed. A good example, which we shall be examining shortly, is Bargagli's *La pellegrina*, composed in the mid-1560s.

We must not exaggerate – comic theatre in Italy was not all reduced to a single potentially sterile formula. This was because theories rarely manage to dictate practice as efficiently as they wish, because human societies have always preached one thing and done another, and because laughter in particular is difficult to control with formal rules. There was also a less controllable type of comic theatre, the *commedia dell'arte*, where professional actors and their public were hardly aware of the existence of cultural theorists (though they had to take more notice of the disapproval of the Church). Nevertheless, the rigidity of some of the ideas proposed is itself a sign that real tastes and ideology were changing. The witty freewheeling scurrilities of Machiavelli, Aretino and Bibbiena, the cross-cultural subversions of Ruzante, were not going to be repeated – at least not by writers of the class for which 'regular' comedy had been pioneered. That sort of performance material had descended to the market-place, becoming coarsened in the process, and gentlemen had to distance themselves and show that they were not trading on that level. Their apparent renunciation of the rougher kinds of fun was made all the easier by the fact that the common professionals would go on providing it anyway; and educated aristocrats could go and sample the commodity when they chose, even purchase it to contribute to their own festivities, and yet remain untainted by having to produce it themselves. The class which at the beginning of the century had felt confident enough to laugh at almost anything – at least in private, where performances had mostly taken place – was now looking more nervously over its shoulder and worrying more about its 'decorum'. This term itself had both social and artistic meanings, and it needs to be examined in its own right.

THEORY OF DECORUM

The word *decorum* was taken by medieval and Renaissance scholars from Horace's `Ars poetica*, and used extensively in discussions of literary theory. It translates into English as 'appropriateness' or 'suitability'; and it has all the potential ambiguity associated with those words, in that there are a number of quite different grounds on which we might judge whether something is 'suitable'. It would be 'unsuitable' in a Renaissance comedy to make a peasant preach a sermon in Latin, because no peasant would realistically be capable of such a thing; but it was also 'unsuitable' for Ruzante to make Betía show her backside in Venice in 1525, because the audience found it too shocking. The second example offends against 'decorum' in the English sense of dignified and acceptable behaviour (and against Italian *decoro* in Guarini's sense, quoted in the previous section). The difficulty in the Renaissance was that the Latin concept of *decorum* would be breached by the first example as well. The distinction between *decorum* as verisimilitude and *decorum* as moral and social orthodoxy was never very clear, and was constantly being blurred.

One also has to identify a third meaning of the term which related to demarcations between different genres and styles. It was Classical *decorum* of genre which decreed that tragedy should depict princes and rulers, while comedy should deal with the middle range of society. As we have seen, the creation of 'regular' comedy at the start of the sixteenth century depended on an acceptance of this principle, departing consciously from medieval practice in which different social classes, and different tones, could mingle in the same play. Having chosen the correct content for his genre, a writer was also required to choose appropriate language – and this in practice caused rather more problems. In medieval as well as ancient literary precept, one of the most important demands of decorum was that style and diction should be matched to the subject matter of a work – if the content was lofty then the style had to be 'high' and ornate, if the content was trivial then the linguistic register should be 'low', and so forth. In a narrative or dramatic work, where characters were made to use direct speech, this requirement could clash with *decorum* in its sense of verisimilitude. If a lower-class person appeared in a serious or 'tragic' composition, should that person be made to speak in the register suitable to the artistic genre, or in the register appropriate on grounds of realism? This is a problem less liable to arise in comic drama, if the choice available is merely stylistic. In sixteenth-century Italy, however, the choice was linguistic as well; and dramatists were torn between literary standard Italian, which was respectable, and spoken dialects, which were realistic. Even though the genre of comedy was a 'low' one, it was increasingly being regarded as 'literature' (or 'poetry', to use a more contemporary term). The drive to unify Italian literary culture by means of its language led to a demand that grammatical Tuscan speech, in despite of realism, should be used by all characters in all plays. This linguistic issue, which we have seen to be thorny, was essentially one of *decorum*. In the case of stage comedy it was partly solved by two schools of practice electing to go their separate ways: gentlemen playwrights accepted the rules, and used standard Italian for all comic characters, while *commedia dell'arte* performers retained dialects (although not perhaps entirely in the cause of realism), choosing to ignore *decorum* and other theoretical concepts. The possible controversy over writing comedies in verse or prose was another aspect of the same debate: should the fact that all Roman comedies were in verse be seen as prescriptive? Here it was the cause of verisimilitude which triumphed: the partisans of verse were always in a minority, and the argument seems to have interested Florence much more than it did other centres in the peninsula.[19]

It was the concept of *decorum* as applied to character which had the potential for imposing real inhibitions on the writing of comedy. There were ways of interpreting it which led to exactly the same moralistic problems as were produced by the theories of laughter which we have just described. Originally *decorum* of character was a simple concept, by our standards even banal. Having established the parameters of a fictional person (in terms of factors such as age, social class, temperament, situation and current predicament), the writer should not make that person do or say anything in the fiction which was implausible. Old men should speak and act less impetuously than young ones; lovers should reveal their obsessions through their speech; servants should be less educated and more vulgar than their masters; young girls should be timid (because in real society they were trained to be so); a person of an irascible nature should not suddenly behave in a conciliatory manner; a soldier should use military metaphors, and a pedant make lengthy display of his learning. Such investigations into the external behaviour of typical characters is one of the main stimuli for the aborted project of Alessandro Piccolomini, to which we referred on pp. 105–7.

However, there was a steady tendency (in the Classical sources as well as in Renaissance interpretations) to confuse two different aims; on the one hand the need to portray characters as they usually are, and on the other hand the wish to portray them as they ought to be. In order to show this briefly, we can look at a résumé by Bernard Weinberg, including some direct quotations, of the views expressed by one particular treatise. The work referred to is an influential commentary on Aristotle's *Poetics* by Bartolomeo Lombardi and Vincenzo Maggi (1550) – 'a work . . . for which, in its final form, Maggi was undoubtedly largely responsible' (Weinberg, 1961, p. 406).

if the audience is to derive from the poem the proper utility in the form of moral instruction, it must be willing to accept as 'true' the characters presented, and it will do so if these correspond to recognizable, traditional types. The people presented in poems are exemplars of good behavior: 'Since they [the poets] imitate the best people, when they present their behavior they must make exemplars of it, that is, they must express the highest probity of character in those persons whom they undertake to imitate.' Maggi relates the *parádeigma* of his text at this point to Platonic Ideas of character, 'Nature considered in itself, and not as manifested in this or that particular object' . . . These Ideas, however, rapidly become the collections of traits habitually associated with certain types: a servant will be gluttonous and will think only of food; his master will think only of honor and glory; a king must do and say those things proper to a king . . . 'The meaning is that the poet deals with the universal. For if he introduces a king as saying or doing a given thing, what he says or does must belong to those things which are usually or necessarily attributed to kings.' In a still more general way, a man must not have feminine attributes (Ulysses should not be presented as weeping), and a woman should not show virility of soul . . . (Weinberg, 1961, pp. 414–15)

There is an inextricable tangle here between what we should now see as quite different aims and considerations. On the one hand, in a mimetic art which considers itself based on imitation of nature, a writer should not portray behaviour which is unlikely in a given category of person, and which thus contradicts the 'universal' or typical. This is *decorum* as verisimilitude. The reason given for it, however, puts realism as secondary to moral purpose: we wish to persuade our reader or audience that our story contains an ethical message, and they are more likely to accept the message if they can believe in the characters. The message itself is to be conveyed by example, therefore the characters must be 'exemplary': the 'universal', instead of merely identifying general tendencies, moves towards reflecting the way in which we *want* categories of people to behave. 'A man *must not* have feminine characteristics . . . a woman *should not* show virility of soul.' Who is saying 'must not . . .', and to whom? The prohibitions are ambiguous: they could be imposed on the artist, in the name of verisimilitude, or on the fictional character, in the name of morality. In practice they are imposed on both, indiscriminately, because behaviour which a particular society regards as correct is assumed also to be typical and even natural. Societies fail to distinguish not only between two types of 'suitability' but between two types of 'normality'.

As soon as *decorum* of character is conceived as imparting lessons by the use of 'exemplars', the concept leads in the same direction as does a moralistic theory of laughter. Characters who behave badly are not necessarily ruled out, since they can be made unattractive and come to a bad end. But in a comedy written mainly for the upper classes, there was a tendency to make gentlemanly characters decent at heart, models of correct intentions even if sometimes flawed in their behaviour. If the dramatist wished to characterize a miser or a villain or a layabout or a coward, he would certainly call on *decorum* of verisimilitude in depicting such a person, but would also want to ensure that his audience felt no sympathy – and the surest way to distance the character was to present him as not belonging to the audience's class, and therefore impossible to take as a model. The result was what we have already described: an intrigue of thwarted good intentions on the part of heroes and heroines, with vulgar comic relief from servants and other more plebeian characters.

In one area in particular, *decorum* of orthodoxy took entire precedence over *decorum* of verisimilitude in the second half of the sixteenth century. From Boccaccio onwards, there had been a tradition in Italian comic literature of portraying the misbehaviour, alleged or real, of clerical figures such as monks, nuns, friars and parish priests. Such narrative formats appear as early as 1518 on the 'regular' comic stage, starting with Machiavelli's Fra Timoteo in *La mandragola*. Because of the derivation from the prestigious *Decameron*, the corrupt friar became a recurrent figure, for a while, in imitative Florentine comedy in particular. However, this spurious literary respectability could not resist attacks from the ecclesiastical authorities, who had no doubt at all as to which sort of *decorum* they regarded as important. It was indecorous, in the modern English sense, for any clerical figure to be shown misbehaving. No real authority in society, least of all Church authority, could accept its ministers being depicted in a bad light. It is significant, of course, to note the source from which these prohibitions were emanating – a source which had to be taken more seriously than a clique of literary theorists. Self-regulation by intellectuals was not enough for this period: all cultural production was subject in the end to the scrutiny of real power structures, including a Church and an Inquisition whose sanctions could in the last resort be horrendous. When they chose, both religious and political censors could constitute the biggest potential 'obstacle to comedy' of all.

SUPPRESSION AND CENSORSHIP

The latter part of the sixteenth century is recognized as a period of increasing cultural, political and religious rigidity, during which the atmosphere now associated with the concept of 'Renaissance' was replaced by something else. The sympathies and ideologies of historians and critics will result in different emphases, and different names, being given to the leading tendencies of the period – but whether we speak of 'Mannerism' followed by 'Baroque', or of 'Reformation' or of 'Counter-Reformation' or of 'Catholic Reform', and however many merits or defects we may choose to detect in the new culture, there is no escaping the fact that Church and state combined during this time to exercise more control over artistic and cultural activity than had been attempted in previous periods. This is true in many parts of Europe, Protestant as well as Catholic. In Italy it is a phenomenon associated with certain clear trends – with the more efficient structures of a reformed Catholic Church; with the tendency for new Italian political régimes to identify their hierarchical position with that of the Church; and with the fact that a number of these régimes either involved direct foreign rule (as in Milan and Naples) or a new autocratic system installed and backed by a foreign power (as in Florence or Parma). Older systems, such as those of Venice and the Papal State itself, had to find a new relationship with an international Catholic hegemony which felt itself to be embattled (against both Protestants and Turks), and which in consequence became repressive and self-righteous.

Such changes involve concrete political measures on the one hand, and a genuinely altered climate of opinion on the other – it is a mistake, when dealing with this period, always to assume a model of repression exercised against an unwilling populace. A number of Italians, whether themselves powerful or not, were open to the anxieties which afflicted those in authority, and they were often ready to accept new constraints in the name of stability. (Alessandro Piccolomini, in Siena, seems carefully to have absented himself from his city's last-ditch stand against the Medici and their Spanish backers, and then to have accepted its absorption into the Grand Duchy of Tuscany. His desire may have been partly for peace, and for an end to sterile political faction; but it was also for a guarantee that his own patrician class would maintain its former status in a changing world.[20])

On the level of concrete enactment, however, the most significant event was the vast enterprise of the Council of Trent, during which the Catholic Church put its house in order in respect of ideology and organization. It took place at intervals between 1545 and 1563. In the area of art and culture, it produced some precise measures for supervision and control (such as the reorganization of the already existing indexes of prohibited books), and some more general attitudes and guidelines which perhaps were even more influential. A number of its pronouncements, in all fields, involved an attempt to return to first principles, to the views of the earliest Church Fathers. In turn, one effect of this trend was to call into question the new respectability which the Renaissance had restored to theatrical performance. It was not merely a question of objecting to some plays, or to some types of theatre, or of trying to restrain particular examples of blasphemy, subversion or dissent. There were texts in the older traditions of the Christian Church which made no fine distinctions at all, but simply stated that theatre as such was an evil activity. This is a view with which Christian Europe had to contend for a long period, particularly during the late sixteenth century and the whole of the seventeenth.

For Italy in the 'Baroque' period, the story has been studied most of all by Ferdinando Taviani,[21] who summarizes the position as follows:

The campaign against performed spectacle which follows on from the Catholic Counter-Reformation operates on two parallel fronts: on the one hand it concerns the city, the moral and religious reorganization of community life; on the other hand it addresses the individual, scrutinizes the corrupting effect of theatre performances, condemns comedy as a fomentor of passions, and sees the pleasure offered by the actor's art as the sign of a diabolic presence. (Barbieri/Taviani, 1971, p. xvii)

We have said enough already in this chapter to show some of the worries which were felt about the corrupting moral influence on individuals of specifically comic theatre. The theological justification for objecting to theatre as such was based on a number of considerations – they included the essential 'falsity' of the acting process, the ability of theatre to exercise a fascination which distracted people's minds towards 'vanities' and away from spiritual life, and the more pragmatic observation (whether true or false) that theatre crowds were a breeding ground for vice and crime. On the corporate side, Taviani has shown the desire of Church leaders to ensure that at least during religious festivals there were no distractions: diocesan authorities made constant efforts, sometimes supported by secular government and sometimes not, to ban actors and entertainers from performing at those times in particular. The attention of historians has often been focussed on the career and views of Carlo Borromeo (now canonized and therefore San Carlo), who was Archbishop of Milan from 1564 to 1584. San Carlo had objections to all forms of carnival, equating them with the Chaos which is the antithesis of divine Order.[22] His reluctance to accept comedy of any kind can be imagined; but it is noteworthy, in passing, that many of his efforts were devoted more to banning traditional plays on sacred subjects, enacted by secular companies, which he saw as competing illicitly with those liturgical rituals which were both sanctioned and performed by the Church itself.[23] He was thus a leading figure in the process, somewhat ironical in modern eyes, by which the Church brought about the decline of the *sacra rappresentazione*. Where comedy is concerned, the story is repeatedly told of how he inspected and eventually licensed some *commedia dell'arte* scenarios submitted for perusal by the Gelosi company in 1583. There has been much debate on how to interpret this episode, and on whether or not it shows him as more moderate in his views than would otherwise appear: Taviani tends to see his actions as part of a complex political negotiation with the Governor of Milan.[24]

In the end, of course, ecclesiastical opposition never succeeded in banning theatre, or even in banning comedy. The humanists had been too successful in persuading the aristocracy that theatre was not only an enjoyable pastime, but one which bore the stamp of high culture and was inseparable from the image of the newly educated ruling class. The aristocracy had taken drama to its heart, and attached it firmly to the whole system of display which was an essential part of princely politics. Those clerics who took a different view had to recognize that the Church's alliance with the political system demanded a compromise, on this front as on others. In any case, ecclesiastical opinion was never unanimous on the subject: the aristocracy itself continued, as it had done in the High Renaissance, to feed into the Church hierarchy a body of well-educated prelates, who might want to influence or control humanist culture but certainly had no intention of abolishing it. The generation of Alessandro Piccolomini was followed by that of Bernardino Pino.

Nevertheless, in Italy as elsewhere in Europe, the actor's profession remained controversial, harried and threatened by the hostility of individual churchmen and local ecclesiastical administrations. A century after the time with which we are dealing, in the age of Molière, actors might become star celebrities and be patronized by royalty, but they still were barred from burial in consecrated ground. In Italy, from the 1560s onwards, sermons were regularly preached against the alleged sinfulness of either practising or attending theatre. What stuck most of all in the ecclesiastical throat was the emergence on a regular basis of actresses alongside actors. This indeed was fertile ground for the hostile sermonizer. At all levels of the patriarchal society, a centuries-old prejudice assumed that any woman who 'exhibited herself' must by definition be a whore; and it was easy to turn this assumption into an automatic link between theatre and sexual immorality. The accusation was levelled principally at the players, but the audience was guilty by association. This may have made theatregoing more exciting – it certainly never seems to have stopped people doing it – but it also left an uneasiness on the subject which could produce anti-theatre feeling at times of moral crisis. By the seventeenth century, professional actors were having to work systematically to counter the propaganda regularly levelled against them. Nicolò Barbieri produced his *Supplica* explicitly to refute well-known accusations. The extraordinary eulogies written for the actress Isabella Andreini (1562–1604) seem in part to express some relief that in her, at least, there was a real example of theatrical talent combined with impeccable family virtue and cultural sophistication. The chronicles suggest, in all honesty, that a number of her rivals were in fact more sexually freewheeling, and thus open to the sort of charges which hostile clerics gleefully deployed. In the Papal State, where the Church and the secular authority were more or less identical, actresses were banned from the public stage for much longer than elsewhere – as, indeed, was the inclusion of any clerical character, even a virtuous one, in a dramatic fiction.

This last prohibition relates to that criterion for censorship, among all those considered during the Counter-Reformation period, which was pursued with the most conviction: the elimination of the smallest vestige of satire against the clergy. Arguments could take place about how to handle the representation of vice in art and fiction, and indeed about whether to handle it at all – but opinions varied on this, and to some extent common sense had to prevail. Where it did not prevail was in the absolute ban on any suggestion that priests, monks, nuns and friars (let alone bishops and popes) could ever behave with other than the utmost virtue. When Boccaccio's *Decameron* was censored, the events and words in the more scurrilous tales were sometimes censored, sometimes left untouched; but whenever the participants were clerics their status was altered, so that friars and corrupt priests became anonymous lay ruffians. The same applied to comic drama. In most cases the climate of opinion worked satisfactorily on its own without the need for actual censorship, and dramatists spontaneously refrained from tackling any potentially offensive subject. That texts could actually be tampered with, and anti-clerical material could be cut out, is demonstrated in documents by the case of one well-known comedy, which deserves a more extended analysis as demonstrating the practical outcome of all these theoretical restrictions.

LA PELLEGRINA

The play concerned happens to be one of the most important comedies written after 1560, both in terms of its quality and because of the historical occasion of its first performance. The discovery of the discrepancies between manuscript and printed versions was made by Nino Borsellino.[25] It is called *La pellegrina* ('The Pilgrim Woman') and is formally attributed to the Sienese Girolamo Bargagli (1537–86). It comes in fact from the collective pens of the Accademia degli Intronati in Siena: a letter from Alessandro Piccolomini says that Bargagli created the plot and the detailed scripting was in the hands of Fausto Sozzini, while Piccolomini himself may have acted as consultant.[26] Borsellino placed the composition of the play in 1564: recent studies, especially by Bruno Ferraro,[27] have left the matter less precise, but it was clearly written in the mid-1560s. It was offered to Ferdinando de' Medici, at that time a cardinal and brother of the Grand Duke of Tuscany – Ferdinando accepted it, but left it in manuscript form. The play was then 'rediscovered' and first performed in 1589, for one of the best-documented celebrations of the whole Italian sixteenth century: the wedding of that same Ferdinando, now no longer a cardinal but the new Grand Duke, to Christine ('Cristina') of Lorraine.[28]

There are few other known examples, if any, of a script being performed and published at such a long interval after its original composition. Some minor alterations were to be expected, especially the change whereby the heroine of the comedy, Drusilla, is made to originate from France rather than Spain, in deference to the new Florentine–French alliance symbolized by the wedding. But the cuts and changes are more substantial than that. In one strand of the plot, young Lepida who is feigning madness in order to avoid an unwanted wedding (shades of Ariosto's *Negromante*, among other possible sources) is taken by her father to be examined and possibly exorcised by a monk. In the original version, the nurse Giglietta is made to question the wisdom of exposing any young girl to any community of monks. Later, the scurrilous servant Targhetta gives an account of how Lepida was pestered by the so-called celibates; and how he himself explored some of the cells in the monastery, finding them laden with luxury and signs of a lifestyle very far from austere. All these passages are removed from the version of the play performed and printed in 1589; and a number of other minor cuts are made to lines which continue to hint at misbehaviour among the clergy, or which treat prayers and other religious matters with sarcasm or humour. We can only speculate as to whether Cardinal Ferdinando intended to revise the play even in the 1560s, when he first received it, or whether at that time the satirical passages were still seen as fair comment. Scholars have noted the fact that Fausto Sozzini, who is recorded as responsible for the detailed writing of the script, ended his life as a Protestant exile in northern Europe. The corruption of Catholic religious institutions was a favourite topic for reformers, whether they tried to operate inside or outside the Church. It is interesting that Alessandro Piccolomini, himself a cleric, does not seem to have regarded the original version of the play as an inappropriate offering to a cardinal. But however one interprets the details, there is an undeniable trend whereby what was acceptable, at least to some, in the 1560s became unacceptable later on. Whether we see comedy being obstacled or merely altered, there is no doubt that in the second half of the sixteenth century *commedia erudita* was entering a new and more sensitive world.

CHAPTER 7

Scripts and scenarios

LA PELLEGRINA AS 'SERIOUS' COMEDY

La pellegrina as a whole, even with its cuts restored, is a well-crafted example of the kind of comedy which was required by new moralistic theory and altered taste. It has one major plot strand, the one involving Lepida, which comes straight from Ariosto's *Suppositi* of 1509. The heroine is seduced by, and needs to be married to, a young gentleman in disguise who has taken service in her house – this time he is a false Pedant, acting as tutor to her young brother. This involves traditional amorous schemings and misunderstandings, including a rivalry with another suitor, the potential crisis being solved by a family agnition. The comedy also offers some vulgar skirmishings among the servants, which can fairly be described as 'comic relief', in that they do not impinge in any real sense on either of the two major plots.

However the principal story, alluded to in the title, is not an intrigue in the strict sense at all, but a massive and very simple misunderstanding between hero and heroine. It produces refined emotional suffering, and a final almost orgasmic relief of tension when the false assumptions are removed. Lucrezio was secretly married in Valencia (or, in the revised version, in Lyon) to a virtuous young woman named Drusilla; but he had to return home to Pisa before the marriage was either made public or consummated. Subsequently he learned, on seemingly impeccable evidence, that Drusilla had died, and so never went back for her. But Drusilla is not dead: she now arrives in Pisa as 'the pilgrim woman', looking for her faithless husband – and finds him betrothed, though reluctantly, to that Lepida who is in her turn really attached to her fake Pedant. Drusilla even speaks to Lucrezio, without revealing her identity, and to begin with the distance between them increases because each one has a different view of the facts. Lucrezio is faithful in his heart to a woman he believes to be lost for ever, while Drusilla is increasingly bitter and desperate at what seems to be his wilful infidelity. The truth transpires, laboriously, in time for a happy ending.

The play thus concentrates, in three scenes in particular, on the close exploration of emotions with which the audience are to sympathize, rather than on intrigue or subversion; and in those scenes there is no intention at all of arousing laughter. The comedy thus tends towards a category which has been given labels such as 'serious comedy', 'romantic comedy', or even – perhaps stretching terminology – 'tragicomedy'. In Italy such categories tend to indicate a truly 'Baroque' style of drama which has difficulty in arousing any interest among readers and theatre practitioners of the twentieth century. However, in *La pellegrina* the emotions are portrayed in dramatic dialogue of some delicacy, rather than in the over-laden rhetoric which can be found in some other attempts. In particular, the characters and their feelings have a certain psychological coherence; and it is not impossible to imagine the play being performed with reasonable conviction by a modern cast, even though the ideology which it expresses could then grate on a present-day audience. The following extract from the first encounter between the two characters might show how some emotional truth is drawn out of a basically implausible situation. Lucrezio, in search of expert medical opinion on his fiancée, has decided to consult the anonymous stranger who has the reputation of a wise woman. She knows him, but he does not recognize her. Drusilla's faithful retainer Ricciardo hovers in distant and uneasy attendance.

LUCREZIO: You must know, then, that a few days ago I was betrothed, but before I even visited the girl there appeared in her certain deranged humours, so that from time to time she says and does demented things.

PILGRIM [Drusilla]: A pitiful case indeed, especially since you must have loved the young lady to begin with.

LUCREZIO: Well, no: in fact I was moved to take her only by the persuasions of my family.

PILGRIM: At least you must have come to love her, after having accepted her?

LUCREZIO: Not even that, since I have only seen her twice.

PILGRIM: Have you formally exchanged rings?

LUCREZIO: Not yet, and this is some comfort, for otherwise I should be truly desperate. But since I am not yet bound to her, I want to understand fully the nature of her illness.

PILGRIM: If her malady were beyond cure, do you have it in mind to break off the match?

LUCREZIO: The nobility apparent in your bearing encourages me to speak freely. Madam, however things stand, my true inclination is to avoid this marriage.

PILGRIM: If that is your desire, why do you wish me to examine her?

LUCREZIO: I should like to establish the truth, with the aid of a qualified person, so that if the matter is as I suspect, I shall have a more reasonable excuse to offer her father.

PILGRIM: That is the recourse of a prudent man, and I think you have good reason not to pursue the marriage; because humours of this kind can never be fully cured, and there is the danger that children born from such women may suffer from the same infirmity. And as well as the hardship of having such a wife in the household, there is some element of public shame.

LUCREZIO: You confirm me in my resolve. But I should like to take this step without offending her father, or those around me who almost forced me into the match.

PILGRIM: Forced you? How so? Was the young woman not suitable to your rank?

LUCREZIO: Quite suitable, as far as that is concerned. But marriage affairs are not quite like other transactions, where if a man cannot have what he would like he must like what he can have. In this case, if he cannot have the woman he wants, he may prefer to have none.

PILGRIM: I marvel that a man like you, clearly among the most nobly born, should be refused any woman in the city. What obstacle did you encounter?

LUCREZIO: Madam, my affairs cannot interest you, and to me it brings great pain to reconsider them, here or elsewhere. Suffice it to say that my hopes were shattered, and there is no more remedy.

PILGRIM [*aside, or to Ricciardo*]: So – he left me cruelly to my fate.

LUCREZIO: I beg your pardon, madam?

PILGRIM: I said you have felt the cruelty of fate.

LUCREZIO: In all its force! And now, still not satisfied, Fortune faces me with this new trouble.

PILGRIM: You are not alone in suffering the cruelties of Fortune: I can still feel my share of them. I had scarcely taken the husband of my heart's choice, when my evil luck snatched him away from me. That is why I have embarked on this long pilgrimage, and I had stopped here to repossess a jewel of mine, of great worth and very dear to me. But from what I now hear, I have journeyed in vain.

LUCREZIO: Please consider whether I can be of any help to you in your search, for I desire nothing more fervently than to employ myself in your service.

PILGRIM: You could have done a great deal, once, but now I find that the affair is hopeless. There is no more to do.

LUCREZIO: I am truly sorry for this, because I should have liked to give you proof of my feelings.

PILGRIM: I think I now understand your intentions, without further proof.

RICCIARDO: I'm on tenterhooks: either he will recognize her, or she'll betray herself. Madam, if it please you to hasten matters, your waiting woman has been taken unwell. (*La pellegrina*, Act II, Scene 7)

The confrontation (conceived by Bargagli?) has dramatic irony laid on with a trowel, in almost every speech of Drusilla in particular – but the detailed dialogue (by Sozzini?) has a surprisingly light touch. It even dares to make sentimental use of a routine comic device – the revealing aside hastily converted into something innocuous, which is more often used by subversive servants mocking their masters. It is not impossible to imagine the scene both moving an audience and remaining compatible with the overall 'comic' mood. Most significantly, it is a dialogue which offers an attractive part for an actress, full of emotional light and shade, hard to entrust to an amateur boy actor. These academic dramatists, surely, must have been accepting in the 1560s that a real female presence was indispensable for sentimental comedy – and in this way they were maintaining the Sienese sympathy for female characters[1] which had been pioneered with *Gli ingannati* in 1532.

As well as its sentimental conflict and its more traditional amorous intrigue, *La pellegrina* is full of verbal discussions on themes likely to interest an aristocratic audience of the 1560s or 1580s. Relatively light-hearted libels, as from one male to another, on the behaviour of different types of women are found in exchanges between the German Messer Federigo and the servants Targhetta and Cavicchia (III, 5 and 6), while the low-life female characters Giglietta and Violante put the subversive female point of view (III, 7 – mainly on the merits and demerits of students as lovers). A more serious contrast emerges between the different attitudes to love and sex expressed by the gentry and by the plebs. Giglietta the nurse clearly foreshadows her equivalent in *Romeo and Juliet*,[1] in trying to urge a pragmatic but immoral course of action first of all on the young hero Messer Terenzio (I, 2) and then on her own charge, the heroine Lepida (II, 6): the latter gives an epigrammatic summary of the whole ethos of love and fidelity which should apply to the upper classes:

LEPIDA: Women who do that cannot have noble minds. A generous heart must think long and hard before yielding and giving its soul to another; but once it has attached itself to a worthy object, then no matter what may happen, it must remain constant until death. (*La pellegrina*, Act II, Scene 6)

The assumption that the 'noble minds' of stage heroes and heroines behave in this way, whereas the lower orders are likely to be more relaxed in their sexual relations, is one which was to underpin European comedy for another two centuries. It was challenged in the end by Beaumarchais' Figaro and Susanna.

A similar contrast emerges in III, 6 between the servant Cavicchia and the German gentleman Messer Federigo. The latter is, for most of the play, an unattractive character, bent on winning Lepida by fair means or foul, and vindictively outraged when she is discovered in bed with her true lover Messer Terenzio, who has been serving in her house in the menial capacity of hired tutor. His change of mood when he discovers that Terenzio is his long-lost brother, and the ritual by which the two of them beg Lepida's hand formally from her dishonoured father (V, 4), make up a fascinating piece of sociology on stage, and an insight into the increasingly rigid stratification of Italian society at this time.

The problem of masters and servants is approached from below in III, 4, in an emblematic exchange between the 'bad' opportunistic plotter Targhetta, and the 'good' conscientious servant Carletto, who believes that 'good servants always share and take part in the misfortunes of their masters'. Even here there is a brief evocation of noble and non-noble behaviour in affairs of the heart.

TARGHETTA: You really do have some daft opinions sometimes! Like when it comes to love affairs, and you will insist on sticking to just one woman, instead of going with lots at once, like I do, for the good of the human race.
CARLETTO: Yes, that's what I think is right. How does the good of the human race come into it?
TARGHETTA: Well it does; because there are lots of different ways for people to die, but there's only one way they can get born. So we need to keep at it as hard as we can, to make sure there aren't more people going out of the world than coming in.
CARLETTO: What an idiotic argument!

TARGHETTA: You're the idiot, for worrying more about other people than about yourself. Don't you see that since people only go into service because they have to, they should serve with the body but not with the will?

CARLETTO: Targhetta, true service is more in the mind than in the body. Otherwise horses and mules would be as good servants as we are.

TARGHETTA: We get treated like horses and mules, don't we? So why shouldn't we give the bosses a kick or two?

CARLETTO: Then we really would be behaving like animals; because the worst animal in the world is a servant with no patience and no loyalty.

TARGHETTA: Loyalty? That's the word the bosses are always using to make us serve them better. (*La pellegrina*, Act III, Scene 4)

Targhetta is even prepared to be a sixteenth-century trade unionist: 'If all us servants got together, then they'd have to treat us properly.' This takes up a comment (quoted in Chapter 4) from Ruzante's *Vaccaria*, and may also have become a 'theatergram'. It is easy to see where the overt sympathies of an upper-class audience ought to lie, but the scene is not as ideologically simple as it might be. Targhetta is the one who raises the laughs, with paradoxical arguments, and thus gets some subversive comic sympathy. And in a later part of the scene, it is apparent that he is shifting towards a discussion of ungrateful princely masters and badly-treated courtiers, rather than gentlemanly masters and plebeian servants. A number of courtiers in the audience would recognize some of his arguments, both from their own experience and from a tradition of literary complaint about the miseries of court life. In the 1560s the radical Fausto Sozzini was not prepared to take a simplistic view of the theme of 'service', and in 1589 the Medici Grand Duke and ex-Cardinal was content to leave this particular scene uncensored.

Despite this moment of mild subversion, *La pellegrina* is to its bones a play written for aristocrats, and one which takes as its central theme an exploration of how the upper class should think and behave. By the very sophistication and confidence with which it explores and narrates that theme, it shows how the restrictions placed on comedy by academics and by clerics were not entirely imposed – they were also influenced by the taste of a new theatregoing generation, for whom *Calandra*, *Mandragola*, *Cortigiana* and *Moscheta* had become too crude and perhaps too unrealistic. If this new generation was wary of too much subversive comedy, at least in drama which had cultural pretensions, this was because its age was bent on building and defending a new order of social and political stability, and on constructing its very identity in fictional images which were either sentimental or heroic. However, a full account of the occasion on which *La pellegrina* was finally performed shows what a wide range of different theatrical experience had become admissible, by 1589, into a celebration which became legendary for its use of culture to proclaim and attract political prestige. The 'lower-class' professional scenario took its place in the same festivities alongside the 'upper-class' academic script, with the two cultural products clearly labelled and demarked.

THE FLORENTINE FESTIVITIES OF 1589

As has already been said, *La pellegrina* was taken out of its limbo to contribute to a princely wedding celebration – that of Ferdinando de' Medici, new Grand Duke of Tuscany, to Christine of Lorraine. Like a number of other Medici propaganda occasions, this one was meticulously documented in chronicle form,[2] so a considerable amount is known about what took place. Moreover, the survival of extensive evidence about both the visual and musical aspects of what was staged[3] has helped this event to be regarded by historians of music, scenography, theatre and even opera as a cultural landmark.

The set of *La pellegrina*, designed by Bernardo Buontalenti, reproduced all the famous landmarks of Pisa while setting the action on the bank of the river Arno. But this is practically all we know about the staging of the comedy itself – even for this decade we have little idea about casting, costumes or acting styles in amateur *commedia erudita*. In any case, in Florence it continued to be true that the play as such was considered as a side-dish to the main menu. The 'Florentine Intermedi', remembered under that name, are a culminating example of the tendency for the interlude or *intermezzo* to swamp the dramatic production which it was ostensibly framing. The six Interludes which surrounded the five acts of *La pellegrina* (and, as we shall see, indiscriminately also of other productions) were of unparalleled splendour and costliness, and in effect became a dramatic event in their own right.[4] They made full use of elaborate stage mechanisms – by now the Italians had learned to manage moving scenery and spectacular transformations, all much more interesting than the fixed street setting prescribed by the rules of 'regular' comedy. The Pisan townscape of *La pellegrina* alternated with a series of fantastic backgrounds, including Heaven, Hell and a sea with a ship on it. The interludes were organized as a series of learned mythological pageants, revolving round a neo-Platonic theme of Harmony on earth and in heaven, all pointing dutifully towards the personal and political harmony inherent in the dynastic marriage. The use of the most intricate up-to-date music, both for solo singers and ensembles, combined with the story-line of the pageants to produce what scholars now see as a first step towards opera: two of the composers, Jacopo Peri and Giulio Caccini, both claimed later to have invented the musical form now known as recitative. The historical implications of this whole spectacular creation tend to take us a long way from questions of comic drama-turgy. Nevertheless, comic drama was an important component of the Florentine wedding spectacle – and it appeared in more than one form, and in more productions than just *La pellegrina*.

This comedy itself had its Sienese origins acknowledged in the fact that it was performed by a team of noblemen from the Intronati Academy. The Academy, influenced in this as in other matters by Alessandro Piccolomini, had been reconstituted after making obei-sance to the Medici régime, which by 1589 had in any case been operative in Siena for over thirty years. The aristocratic amateur presence of the Intronati, in the performance of this supremely aristocratic play, set the seal not only on a unified Tuscan state, but also – apparently – on the cultural victory of a particular brand of comedy: sophisticated, 'literary', high-minded, conforming to the rules both of academic theory and of upper-class taste. The first performance on 2 May 1589 seems to have been followed by a second one, mounted on 15 May which was the last day of the festivities, for the benefit of those who had previously missed the comedy and – more importantly – the Interludes.

But alongside the aristocratic Intronati, the city was graced with the presence of the Compagnia dei Gelosi, one of the best pro-fessional troupes of the time, temporarily furnished with two leading ladies – Vittoria Piissimi and Isabella Andreini. The Grand Duke was anxious to make use of their talents, as well as those of the Intronati. This was partly in the cause of increased variety: the fortnight's celebrations had already included a football match, animal baiting, tilting, a naumachy, and a major religious proces-sion. But the Grand Duke wanted the Gelosi to appear in the same prestige location as *La pellegrina* and the Interludes – the Uffizi theatre, a purpose-built hall in a Granducal palace, inaugurated only three years before. The two genres of comedy, academic and professional, were effectively given equal status.

The invitation, says the chronicler Giuseppe Pavoni, caused some predictable problems in a company with two leading actresses:

it was the Grand Duke's pleasure that as an entertainment they should perform a Comedy of their choice. This meant that the two said ladies very nearly started a quarrel; because Vittoria wanted them to perform *The Gipsy*, and the other lady wanted them to put on her *Madness*, since Vittoria's favourite role is the Gipsy, and the mad role is the favourite of Isabella. However, they eventually agreed that the first play to be performed would be *The Gipsy* [on 6 May], and that the Madness would be done on a second occasion [on 13 May].[5]

The Gipsy could well be Giancarli's *La zingana*, or a scenario based on that text: Vittoria must have cultivated the extremely odd dialect of the eponymous role. *La pazzia d'Isabella* ('The Madness of Isabella') is the title of one of Flamminio Scala's scenarios, published in 1611: however, Pavoni (who seems to have been a fan of Isabella Andreini) gives a very detailed résumé which shows that the 1589 version had little in common with the printed one. A brief extract will give some essential points:

And so, the Grand Duke having conveyed his wishes to the Gelosi company, at about five in the evening, on the same stage where *La pellegrina* was performed they also did the Madness, with those same Interludes as have been described elsewhere ...

Isabella, overcome thus [in the stage plot] by her passion and giving full rein to her rage and fury, went out of her mind, and ran through the city like a mad woman, stopping first one person and then another, and speaking first in Spanish, then in Greek, then in Italian and many other languages, but always nonsensically: and among other things she began to speak French and sing various French ditties, which gave inexpressible pleasure to the Most Serene bride. She then turned to imitating the speech of all her colleagues in the company, such as Pantalone, Dottor Graziano, Zanni, Pedrolino, Francatrippe, Burattino, Capitan Cardona, and Franceschina – all with such natural conviction, and with such senseless utterances, that no tongue can utter the power and talent of this lady.

One of the leading men, 'Fileno', also had to go mad in this story, but it is Isabella who gets the write-up. The performance sounds gloriously over the top, and shows how professional actresses could now be accepted on the level of virtuoso *prime donne*, with Isabella's 'number' (and Vittoria's speeches in dialect, in the other performance) taking the place of an aria with plentiful high Cs. Clearly the presence of the Gelosi lent splendour to the occasion, just as much as the activities of the Intronati; but equally clearly the two forms of drama were being treated as quite separate activities, each with its own distinct merits and attractions. (We hear nothing, for example, about the person who played Drusilla for the Intronati, even though the role must have attracted some sympathy.) Moreover, both the academics and the professionals had to accept being framed in, and potentially obliterated by, the sumptuous Interludes. The Medici had been doing this sort of thing since they were still in exile, since the production of Plautus on the Roman Capitol in 1513.[6] Vittoria and Isabella may have had second billing in this show, but the real star was the Prince himself. This fact was established both by the level of expense, which constantly imposed the presence of the patron on the minds of all the spectators, and by a seating arrangement which made the Granducal dais a kind of second competing stage in the centre of the auditorium – as much a focus for the gathering as was the primary stage with the performers and materials for which the Duke had paid.[7]

There had been a divorce between academic and professional comic theatre: they had adopted different dramaturgical principles and different moral tones, they had diverged entirely in terms of the social status of their respective practitioners. But the professionals had not in the end cut themselves off from noble and princely audiences. Professional companies may have made their name most of all by the 'Italian' method of improvisation in comedy, but they were perfectly able to play scripted plays as well, including pastorals, tragedies and tragicomedies. They were not cast into a social wilderness. The first known Arlecchino, Tristano Martinelli, could claim the patronage of the King of France, who had stood godfather to his child: this simply meant that he was one of the most successful at gaining the protection which all his colleagues sought. If anything, as Roberto Tessari argues,[8] the limitations of *commedia dell'arte* came partly from an excessive attachment to safe but sterilizing courtly patronage.

However, the example of the 1589 celebrations also offers a complementary argument on the other side. Professional theatre had not been rejected in favour of academic scripted comedy, but it had not supplanted it either. The Intronati Academy survived alongside the Gelosi, and was pursuing its own cultural and literary goals, also with full patronage. By the nature of things, printed academic texts survived and unwritten scenarios did not; but at this time, and well into the seventeenth century, both genres must have been equally visible. That there was constant interchange between them is beyond dispute. The more educated professionals continually hankered after literary respectability, wrote scripted comedies to demonstrate their competence, and (probably) upgraded some of their stage material to standards which they thought suitable for print. On the other side, amateur comic dramatists, whatever their moral or literary prejudices in theory, found it impossible to ignore the methods and entertainment value of *commedia dell'arte*, and were continually making private decisions about how much of it they could incorporate into their own work without losing their treasured amateur status. The interplay between the two genres is something of which everyone is aware, though its details and ramifications on the level of dramaturgy remain, even now, largely to be explored.

PLAYS AND AUTHORS AFTER 1550

We cannot now attempt in this volume a full account of Italian comic drama in the second half of the sixteenth century. The leap forward which we have already made, to a play composed in the 1560s and performed in 1589, leads us for now towards résumé and synthesis, with the Florentine Interludes standing as a useful model of the complex theatrical interchanges which eventually developed. Some brief indications of major landmarks are all we can now include, before the torch is passed on to other scholars (such as Louise George Clubb, in English) who have dealt with what Italians see as the post-Renaissance period.

From 1508 to the 1540s, the main task of reviving ancient modes of drama and creating a more modern concept of theatre as culture had fallen to the comic genre in particular. From the 1540s onwards, tragedy was also offered to court audiences, and pastoral drama and other mixed genres followed on.[9] The mixed genres were particularly productive of theoretical debate. If the ancient world had seemed to separate comedy and tragedy so sharply, was it now legitimate to write tragicomedy, or tragedy with a happy ending, or comedy with a serious moral and emotional component? And where did pastoral fit in? It dealt with a fantasy world, picked up from purely literary sources, transformed into drama, and somehow open to a greater range of emotional nuances than any of the more rigid formats. It could absorb elements, *topoi*, characters, even masks, from other types of drama. It could switch illicitly from comedy to pathos and back again. All its moods were distanced through the patina of an escapist rural Arcadia – very far from any realistic view of the countryside, as Ruzante had made plain by satirical contrast in his own *Pastoral* back in 1521. But court audiences seem to have found relief in projecting their own more sensitive emotions on to these detached, idealized rustic figures. It was as though, by recourse to what was almost a form of symbolism, they avoided any compromise of their emotional dignity. The rarified atmosphere encouraged an expressive style which was also half symbolic – it was certainly poetic, rather than mimetic – and led to a tendency whereby pastoral could invite music as an accompaniment to, or even component of, its dramaturgy. When musical drama, or opera, finally developed at the very end of the century, its earliest subjects (Apollo and Daphne, Orpheus and Eurydice) involved a rustic or pastoral setting.[10]

The fact that theatre was becoming pluralistic is one of the contexts in which later comedy itself has to be seen. Comic characters and scenes, even *commedia dell'arte* masks and formats, penetrated regularly into pastoral frameworks, as has long been known from the studies of Kathleen Lea.[11] On the other hand, some of the changes in comic plots after the 1550s can be attributed to the influence of tragedy. The possible 'corruption' of comedy by tragic elements was made a polemical issue for a while. It was raised most famously by the Perugian comic dramatist Sforza Oddi (1540–1611),[12] when in his prologue to *La prigione d'amore* ('Love's Prison') of 1589 he mounted an argument between Tragedy and Comedy personified, aimed at defending his own practices in the preceding comedies *Erofilomachia* (1572) and *I morti vivi* ('The Living Dead', 1576). He made the figure personifying Tragedy express criticisms which had already become current, so that the figure of Comedy could refute them on the author's behalf. Oddi insisted that it was legitimate and even desirable to include moments of edifying pathos, based on serious moral conflict, alongside the more cheerful elements of comic drama.

If we had to select half a dozen scripted plays as landmarks during the period 1550–1600, then *Erofilomachia* (or 'The Struggle of Love and Friendship') would probably be the second in chronological order. The first has to be *Gli ingiusti sdegni* of Bernardino Pino, appearing as early as 1553 and already described in Chapter 6. In identifying these two as important, we are judging largely by the number of times they were printed, before publishers' interest in sixteenth-century comedies lapsed altogether around 1630. *Gli ingiusti sdegni* reached nineteen editions, a total surpassed only by *Calandra* and *Gli ingannati*, both of which had decades more of attention. The play offers few attractions to anyone approaching it with a view to performance: one can only conclude that it was popular as a text for reading among academics and theoreticians – people who wanted to study and promote a moralistic anodyne view of what was permissible on stage.

Oddi's *Erofilomachia* appeared in 1572, and achieved ten editions in the dwindling time available. It has a great deal more stage viability than the Pino comedy, and offers a workable model for a large number of successful later plays including those of Giovan Battista Della Porta. Its central plot has all the gentlemanly high-mindedness of *La pellegrina*; but it is interleaved with more aggressive intrigues against a braggart Capitano Rinoceronte and a foolish medical man named Ippocrasso, thus introducing 'comic relief' with unmistakable robust *commedia dell'arte* overtones, of a type from which the authors of *La pellegrina* preferred to abstain. The more serious story does not get properly explored until the last two acts, though its central dilemma is plain from the beginning. Two young gentlemen are in love with the same girl, Flamminia, in Florence. One is a courtier named Amico ('Friend') who can bid for her openly: the other is Leandro, a Genoese gentleman serving incognito as a servant in her house (and calling himself 'Fabio' like the disguised Lelia in *Gli ingannati*). There are two moral complications to the story. In the first place, Flamminia's family are also Genoese in exile, trying to avoid a bitter family feud with Leandro's parents – so the affair has shades of *Romeo and Juliet*. But the main 'Struggle of Love and Friendship' comes from the fact that the false 'Fabio' is deeply bound to Amico by ties of comradeship and obligation, because Amico ransomed him from captivity in a Turkish galley and has since kept the confidence of his real Genoese identity. Both young men are sufficiently possessed by their ideal of friendship to renounce the girl to one another in a contest of generosity – but the sacrifice of 'Fabio' is all the greater in that he was more or less betrothed to Flamminia in secret when they were both still living in Genoa. In medieval stories of this type, the woman often takes on the status of an inert gift to be bestowed on one or other of the heroes. In *Erofilomachia*, Flamminia's preference for 'Fabio' no doubt tips the balance in his favour, from an audience's point of view. Flamminia herself is given just one long scene on stage in which to assert her feelings; but one suspects that the real issue is *his* formal commitment, rather than *her* emotions, and there is still a strong tendency to recoil from giving a respectable virgin too much stage time. (It was a prohibition which had been justified in print by the tragicomic dramatist Giraldi Cinthio, in his *Discourses* on general poetics published in 1553, the year of *Gli ingiusti sdegni*.)

The combination of this material with japes against the Capitano and Doctor Ippocrasso is on one level a little cynical, in terms of making sure that the comedy does contain some laughs and that an audience will remain entertained. The plot is not exactly integrated, in terms acceptable to a literary purist. However, the scenes themselves, and indeed the comedy as a whole, probably worked well enough in performance, granted that audiences were showing interest in the sentimental side as well as in the clowning. Dramatists for the remainder of the century tended to play their own minor variations on the same formula: a serious plot at the core, with some rudimentary moral issues, combined with comic sub-plots which showed undoubted influence from *commedia dell'arte*, presented with whatever literary modifications were felt necessary. Of all the fully 'comic' stereotypes which at this time were shared both by scripted and improvised comedy, the braggart Capitano is the one which seems to have been most in demand: both aristocratic and popular audiences, perhaps for different reasons, wanted to vent their derision against the windbag who claims to live by violence, but is never actually prepared to fight.

One of the most successful practitioners of the formula, and subject of a detailed study by Louise George Clubb (1965), was the Neapolitan nobleman Giovan Battista Della Porta (1535–1615), who finally established the competence in 'regular' comic dramaturgy of Italians from south of Rome. He also figures in encyclopedias for a range of eccentric contributions to the history of science, magic and astrology, which brought him into a couple of brushes with the Inquisition. Della Porta began composing comedies in the

1550s: he tended to try them out in private performances for friends, and then offer them to the Spanish viceregal court of Naples which accepted some of them for lavish staging suitable to the patron's status. Della Porta's primary interest in performance values rather than publication is attested by the fact that the comedies tended to get printed rather late – the fourteen surviving ones appeared between 1589 and 1616. If we were writing a full study of comedy in this period, then Della Porta's methods and achievements would loom large. He would be competing and contrasting with other names such as Gian Battista Cini, Girolamo Razzi, Cornelio Lanci and Raffaello Borghini, all from Florence; Gian Francesco Loredan from Venice; Niccolo Secchi (or Secco) from Milan; and Luigi Groto, the 'blind man of Adria', who also wrote tragedies. Giovan Maria Cecchi (see Chapter 3) continued his output of plays both religious and secular, and had a number of comedies published or reissued in the year 1585.

The main parameters for this phase of Italian scripted comedy have been effectively identified even by our brief surveys of *La pellegrina* and *Erofilomachia*. If we compare their aims and dramatic methods with the Classically derived one which we hypothesized in Chapter 1, we find significant differences in some fields, and perhaps not enough differences in others. The area where academic dramatists could have used the time available to them for reflection, and introduced essential innovations earlier than they did in fact appear, was one which we have mentioned before: the imprisonment of comic action in the setting of the public street. By 1589, as we have seen, stage technology was quite capable of dealing not merely with an alternative to the perspective townscape, but even with changes of scene during performance: there was no practical reason why in 1590 they should not have done what Goldoni naturally did in 1750, and move scenes between the street and the salon as the plot demanded. But here the models of Plautus and Terence seem to have held sway for too long. By the time of the so-called *commedia ridicolosa* scripts of the 1620s and 1630s, there is occasional ambiguity as to whether scenes are taking place indoors or outside – but it is hard to say whether this step, if there is such a step, had been taken by the *arte* companies whom these amateurs were imitating, or by the amateurs themselves. It thus remained the case, even in the comedies of Della Porta, that young female characters often found themselves in plots which shut them off from proper dramatic development, unless they could be put into male disguise. Meanwhile *commedia dell'arte* continued to give full rein to the talents of its leading actresses: its more stylized farcical mode enabled it to take less account of social verisimilitude, and if 'domestic' scenes had to be played in the street, then that is where they were played. The 'regularity' of *commedia erudita*, which had been revolutionary at the start of the century, was a conservative restraint on scripted comedy by the century's end.

The area where there was development, or at least change, was in the style of language used by dramatic characters. It is no longer possible to see later Italian comedy as even paying lip-service to a 'mimetic' mode where language is concerned. Machiavelli, in his *Discourse or Dialogue on the Subject of our Language*, had been able around 1520 to argue about whether Ariosto's comic style, for example, was sufficiently colloquial to be realistic and effective.[13] By the 1560s, such arguments were irrelevant to scripted comedy: not only had it abandoned dialect, for the most part, but there was a level of Baroque stylistic elaboration which, starting with languishing lovers, spread also to braggart captains and even to pert servants. As in Elizabethan theatre, linguistic inventiveness took the place of attempts at accurate mimicry – but the result was not so much poetry as rhetorical formula. We have argued throughout this book that rhetorical confrontation, and therefore also rhetorical style, was an integral part of the Renaissance conception of theatre. The language to be found in long speeches by Oddi and Della Porta had been foreshadowed as early as Bibbiena and Grasso in 1513, and established even more firmly by Aretino. However, by now these flourishing antitheses and carefully structured conceits had acquired a specifically theatrical patina, easier to deliver and more predictable than those of John Lyly (who perhaps springs to mind in the first instance, as a parallel from a contemporary culture). Theatrical rhetoric was becoming separately identifiable, with set patterns of its own. It may even be that the example of *commedia dell'arte*, which naturally used pre-established formulae as part of its technique, helped to impose stereotype rather than true invention on the language of scripted comedy. 'Literary' dramatists may not have wanted to sound like improvising professionals; but they could have been influenced by an unconscious consensus as to what stage language should sound like, and that consensus might be traceable to the *arte* troupes as much as to the theorizing Academies.

Our catalogue of landmarks of comic drama would not be complete, at least in the eyes of most Italian critics, without a mention of *Il candelaio* by Giordano Bruno (1548–1600). The author is known as an unorthodox cabalistic philosopher whose battle with the Catholic Church started when he left his monastic order, and ended when he was burned for heresy in Rome, his execution acting as a prelude to the carnival celebrations of 1600. His lone comedy was printed just once (in Paris) in 1582, and is most unlikely to have been performed. The weird energy of the text on the page has, nevertheless, fascinated readers ever since. It seems inspired principally by the more aggressive comedies of Aretino – *La cortigiana, Il marescalco* and *Il filosofo*.

The 'candlestick' of the title, the recipient into which one sticks candles, is a crude slang term for the character Bonifacio, who has been homosexual for most of his life, then married late, and then fallen in love with a courtesan in text-book literary style. He is one of three characters, all defined in the Prologue as 'sordid, insipid and inept', whom the comedy sets up as victims to be mocked, tricked and brutalized at some length: the other two are Bartolomeo, obsessed with the alchemistic fantasy of making gold and thus open to the tricks of any charlatan, and Manfurio, an apotheosis of the caricature stage Pedant. Their tormentors are a variety of jokers, servants and outright criminals, in whom Bruno includes clear allusions to the contemporary low life of Naples. The three stories interweave, as in Aretino's *Cortigiana* and *Filosofo*, and culminate in various brands of humiliation for the victims. Aretino is also the model for extensive, leisurely, satirical monologues and exchanges, in which Bruno deploys his own intense, quick-witted, allusive language and even references to his eccentric personal philosophy.

Bruno was too much of an outcast to find a patron or an amateur group to perform *Il candelaio*, but it is probable that by the 1580s nobody would have wanted to perform it anyway. Its unveiled aggression was no longer in fashion; much of its language would have been fatiguing to audiences wanting straight entertainment; and the play is much too long. This last fact, together with a rather large cast, would be an obstacle to a modern revival as well: Bruno constantly writes scenes which have theatrical potential, but he has no feeling as to when to stop. The comedy would not be impossible to produce, but it would be a major and daunting enterprise not to be tackled lightly – perhaps rather like Jonson's *Bartholomew Fair*, but without that play's humanity or variety. Italian critics tend to see *Il candelaio* as closing the genre of Renaissance comedy, and this is true in the sense that when it appeared it was incurably out of date.

CONCLUSIONS

Scholars both inside Italy and outside refer freely to the 'birth of modern theatre', when dealing with Italian drama in the first half of the sixteenth century.[14] It is accepted that, by recycling models from nearly two millennia before their time, the Italian Humanists played an indispensable role in recreating a theatre with its own autonomy as entertainment and as 'culture' – using both the major senses in which that last word is currently understood. Such a theatre may have been destined to appear in Europe by one means or another; but in point of fact, as is proved by sheer chronology, it was the Italians who launched it. Chronology also shows that 'regular' comedy, rather than tragedy or some other genre, carried the main burden of this innovation. It seems paradoxical in these circumstances that individual comedies from the period now hardly figure at all in any active theatre repertoire: even in Italy perform-ances are rare and limited to half a dozen texts, which are approached by performers and audiences with dutiful resignation and with little real trust. It may be unfashionable now in criticism to pursue value-judgements, and to arrange texts in a hierarchy of artistic quality; but in the theatre the survival or otherwise of a play in the performing canon is an objective fact, with critical as well as historical signficance. How is it that the Italian sixteenth century, a lively and seminal period of theatre, has produced no texts now revived and enjoyed as 'classics'?

From some points of view, the very question could be challenged as being unfair. The vast majority of successful theatrical 'texts' – whether or not they are preserved in written form – work because they construct a rapport with a particular audience at a particular time. The elements which contribute to their success can often, almost by definition, militate against the same text's ability to appeal to subsequent generations. As an example, we could look at European theatre in most of the nineteenth century. English Victor-ian melodrama, one of the most vibrantly successful theatrical genres ever, with one of the largest audiences, has rapidly dis-appeared from our stages and become, no less than *commedia erudita* itself, the province of academic specialists. Moving up a social class, 'boulevard' or 'West End' theatre flourished in Paris and London during the same century, and yet few of its texts have survived: we are reaching the point where we venerate and replay the scripts of Ibsen and Chekhov (and to a lesser extent of Pirandello and Shaw), but have an increasingly hazy notion of what they were reacting against. Probably ninety-nine per cent of successful drama – let alone that which was seen as bad in its own time – necessarily disappears into historical limbo, along with the irrecoverable talents of the great actors who performed it. The fact that any theatre scripts at all should ever breach the generation barrier, and become 'classics', should perhaps be a cause for amazement. By the same token, we ought not to demote a whole theatrical culture, or even be surprised at it, because it failed to produce similar freaks.

Such arguments can provide a sense of proportion: however, to pursue them to their limit can seem disingenuous. If Italian Renaissance comedy is seen as 'the birth of modern comedy', it is because it produced as descendants some plays which are still performed and enjoyed, and thus do have 'classic' status. Shakespeare may not have stuck with the format represented by *The Comedy of Errors* and *Two Gentlemen of Verona*, but he did at least start with it. Spanish dramatists of the 'Golden Age' also absorbed numerous Classical influences, taken in practice from Italian models, into their own lively explorative tradition. Respected eighteenth-century comedies, and comic operas, are in the direct line of descent. Most particularly there is the example of Molière, who for all his qualities, whether they are Gallic or peculiar to himself, would not have had a comic genre in which to deploy his art if the Italians had not largely created it for him. It is Molière most of all who, by contrast, makes readers feel that the Italian scripts lack something, since he is the dramatist who seems most of all to be working within the same parameters.

Why, in nearly 150 years before him, was there no Italian dramatist approaching Molière in long-term appeal? Italian 'regular' comedy would seem to have developed most of the constituent elements in the tradition on which he and his contemporaries drew. As we have been trying to show, it built the necessary stock of 'theatergrams' both verbal and scenic; it established the audience expectations which Molière either exploited or deliberately upset; it set rational and aesthetic standards for the structure of a comic plot (something which in the present study there has not been space to investigate); and it established the principle of using comedy to display and comment upon social behaviour and values. If we take a single famous example like *L'Avare*, and try to follow up its sources, they will all turn out to be Italian when they do not come directly from Plautus. The folly of avarice, as a central theme for comedy and caricature, is not just a learned copying from the *Aulularia*, but a censorious stage tradition started by the Florentines in the 1540s – they too were using the *Aulularia*, but they gave the theme its stage impetus by sheer repetition. A contest between parent and children over love and marriage, and its resolution with the help of an agnition or family reunion, is also a format established by *commedia erudita* – and when Monsieur Anselme appears in Act v to tell the long story of how he lost his children, he is repeating not only an Italian plot device but an Italian tendency to alternate stage action with verbal narrative.

Close analysis of *L'Avare*, however, provides some clue to what the Frenchman did and the Italians, in the end, could not do. Many of the roles in this comedy – frantic young lovers, servants either cunning or disorganized, scheming parasites like Frosine, caricature judges brought on towards the end – derive indiscriminately from scripted *commedia erudita* and from improvised *commedia dell'arte*. Of identifiable sources, some of the closest to Molière's own time are to be found in *commedia ridicolosa* plays which attempt to write down for amateurs what the professionals did without a script. Whole scenes – or, more importantly, the underlying routines on which scenes are based – can be traced back to plays by Briccio and Verucci, which in turn provide part of our evidence for 'modular' improvised structure in comic dialogue.[15] (Not that Molière necessarily knew either Briccio or Verucci – their scripts are surviving representatives of a vast undocumented common stock of devices available to every theatre practitioner of the seventeenth century.)

The point here is that Molière inherited, pillaged and revitalized the achievements of both scripted and non-scripted Italian comedy – the two genres which in Italy itself, whatever covert interchange there was between them, were pursued separately between 1550 and 1650, and not allowed to merge. Each of these parallel strands of stage comedy was making major contributions to European theatre; each of them, within Italy, was stunted by being deprived of qualities monopolized by the other. *Commedia dell'arte* possessed all the verve, the subversion and the energetic scenic technique which could appeal to most classes of theatregoer; but its formulaic character, and the pressures of pure commercialism, never gave it the chance to apply those qualities to an effective dramatic investigation of character and behaviour. Written academic comedy showed an increasing desire to comment on issues and to investigate subtleties of character; but its upper-class inhibitions kept such subject-matter rigorously separate from such knockabout farce as it allowed into its scripts. The professionals were trapped by their very virtuosity into giving the public more and more of the same thing: the amateurs were equally trapped by the need to demonstrate that in the last resort they lived by the same dignified standards as their peers in the audience. Both genres, perhaps, suffered like the rest of Italian culture in this period from the post-Renaissance exhaustion, declining economy and subjection to foreign hegemony which were leading the separate Italian states to seem increasingly provincial alongside the centralized national cultures of England, France and Spain. But dramatists could not even turn and satirize this decline, because intelligent perception and theatrical energy were kept in two separate channels – perhaps partly, as Roberto Tessari tends to argue,[16] because that is where nervous, mean-minded autocratic rulers preferred to keep them.

Molière, by this view, realized the potential of his Italian heritage by bringing together those elements which had been kept apart south of the Alps. His dialogue makes full use of the formulaic and rhythmic discoveries of 'modular' improvisation, but then puts it down in a script and gets it definitively right, so that no ad libbing can improve on it. He takes all the techniques of gross caricature, all the pure theatrical games, and manages to apply them so that they make devastating revelations about real human behaviour – such formulae do not actually *represent* such behaviour, but rather reveal its essence through hilariously artificial stage ritual. Orgon in *Tartuffe* expresses his obsession with his parasite and his indifference to his wife, with reiterations of 'Le pauvre homme!'; Alceste in *Le Misanthrope* tries to wriggle out of condemning a sonnet with constant recourse to 'Je ne dis pas cela ...' In both cases we have Molière making his own use of the repetitious 'elastic gag' – but as well as being gloriously silly, he is anatomizing the characters concerned so that they are left exposed, recognizable and unforgettable. In Italy, the *arte* professionals would have taken the technique for granted, but failed to apply it with such insight: the academic amateurs would have appreciated the insight, but felt that the technique was beneath them. Scripts and scenarios were drifting steadily apart, when ideally they needed to come together again. But each of them, in their way, had left an indelible mark on modern theatre.

Notes

I PRECEDENTS

1 I have no precise references for these letters. The views summarized should nevertheless be familiar enough to readers, as attitudes which are frequently expressed.

2 My authority here is my own memory – I was one of a group of students in the Collegio Borromeo, Pavia, who had intended to watch the television play.

3 Bergson, 1900; Meredith, 1877; both in Sypher (ed.), 1956.

4 I am particularly indebted for what now follows to Thomas, 1977, an important article which deserves to be made more available.

5 In Rome, public executions were sometimes postponed until carnival time, in order to form part of the entertainment as well as warning the populace against excess. Clementi, 1938–9 (Vol. I, pp. 302, 310, 344) cites three examples from 1581, 1594 and 1600, the victim on the third occasion being the illustrious philosopher (and author of one comedy) Giordano Bruno. I am grateful, for this reference, to an unpublished thesis on Roman carnival by Denis Mooney (University of Glasgow, 1989).

6 P. Mortimer in an article in the *New Statesman*, 30 March 1979.

7 For a full discussion of this matter, see Barański, 1991.

8 An obvious example would be Jonson's *Volpone*; but one thinks also of strategies used in earlier morality plays and Interludes, relating to the figure of the Vice.

9 Curtius, 1948, pp. 417–35.

10 Welsford, 1935, p. 204 (1968 edition).

11 Thomas, 1977, p. 77.

12 Thomas Hardy: *The Mayor of Casterbridge*, Chapter 36.

13 I have read this formulation in Thomas, 1977 and elsewhere. The true text is worth quoting, from *Leviathan* (first published 1651), chapter 6:

> *Sudden Glory*, is the passion which maketh those *Grimaces* called LAUGHTER; and is caused either by some sudden act of their own, that pleaseth them; or by the apprehension of some deformed thing in another, by comparison whereof they suddenly applaud themselves. And it is incident most to them, that are conscious of the fewest abilities in themselves; who are forced to keep themselves in their own favour, by observing the imperfections of other men. And therefore

much Laughter at the defects of others, is a sign of Pusillanimity. For of great minds, one of the proper workes is, to help and free others from scorn; and compare themselves onely with the most able. (T. Hobbes: *English Works*, Vol. III, ed. Molesworth (John Bohn, London, 1839), p. 46.)

I am grateful, for time saved in tracking down the text, to my colleague George MacDonald Ross.)

14 For this and similar episodes, see Luzio and Renier, 1891, p. 637; and also Bertoni, 1903.

15 Welsford, 1935 pp. 199–203; Chambers, 1903, Vol. I, pp. 274–371.

16 A document from the Chapter of Sens, 1444, quoted in Welsford, 1935, p. 201.

17 Appendix to works of Peter of Blois (Petrus Blesensis) in Migne: *Patrologia Latina*, Vol. CCVII, col. 1171: 'Nonne utres et dolia vini saepius rumperentur, si spiraculum ipsorum interdum non laxaretur? Nos quidem utres veteres sumus et dolia semirupta, quare sapientiae vinum nimis fervens, quod per totum annum in Dei servitio nos comprimentes vi retineremus, efflueret inaniter, si non interdum ludis et fatuitatibus vacaremus.' The author ('a Doctor of Auxerre', according to Welsford, 1935, p. 203) is in fact quoting defensive arguments of which he disapproves, and which he then tries to demolish.

18 For example, in Hastings, 1975 and 1989. My own view of the *Decameron*, as summarized in these pages, does not entirely coincide with his; but the issues and contrasting views are cogently summarized and explored in the 1989 article.

19 Bakhtin, 1947, p. 10.

20 *Ibid.*, pp. 11–12.

21 Described in Zorzi, 1977, p. 10, with relative bibliography in footnote 20 on p. 39.

22 A humiliating public race for Jews, the *giudiata*, was for centuries a feature of carnival events in Rome. See the thesis by Denis Mooney quoted in note 5 to this chapter; and Clementi, 1938–9.

23 Ariosto/Segre, 1974, pp. 545–7: this Prologue was discovered separately from the final (1529) version of the play.

24 Jacopone/Mancini, 1974, pp. 201–6. Jacopone lived from *c.* 1236 to 1306.

25 Faccioli, 1975, tomo I, pp. XIV–XV. The text of the poem is on pp. 28–34 of the same volume.

26 These commentaries are available in Donatus/Wessner, 1902–8.

27 The five-act structure was adopted by a number of early verse dramas, around 1500–10, which do not in other respects fit into the patterns which the present book has chosen to study.

28 *La rappresentazione di Santa Uliva*, in Faccioli, 1975, tomo I, pp. 193–270.

29 Poliziano's *Favola di Orfeo*, in Poliziano/Carrai, 1988. This celebrated play (of disputed date, around 1480) is a landmark in many senses, imbued with humanist spirit in its text and preoccupations; but it is

little influenced by the theatrical structure or performance modes of Greek and Roman theatre.

30 In some earlier comedies, including Machiavelli's *Mandragola*, this 'unity' was still fairly loose – a play would be set firmly in a particular city or neighbourhood, but individual houses or buildings in the set might be regarded as present and visible only for some of the time.

31 Donatus/Wessner, 1902–8, Vol. I, p. 20: 'nihil ad populum facit actorem velut extra comoediam loqui, quod vitium Plauti frequentissimum' (passage assigned by the editor to Evanthius: *De Fabula*).

32 *Ibid.*, Vol. I, p. 22: 'comoediam esse Cicero ait imitationem vitae, speculum consuetudinis, imaginem veritatis' (passage assigned by the editor to Evanthius: *De Comoedia*).

33 It is striking that even in the earliest dramas of 'mixed' form, preceding *commedia erudita* proper, the figure of the parasite was often seized on as being one which the spectators would understand and relate to: he is frequently given the role of *giullare*, mediating with monologues between action and audience. Jacopo Nardi has 'Saturio parasito' in his *Due felici rivali* (performed 1513?), and 'Ergasilo parasito' in *Comedia de Amicitia* (published 1518?). There is a 'Ligurio buffone di corte' in the anonymous Florentine *Comedia d'Adulatione* (dated before 1520) – significant because of the reappearance of the name 'Ligurio' for parasite characters in Machiavelli's *Mandragola* (*c.* 1518) and in Francesco Serleone's unpublished '*Il geloso*' (transcribed in 1520). In 'regular' comedy, as well as in the *Mandragola*, the type appears in the *Formicone* of 1503 ('Licopino'); in Ariosto's second comedy, *I suppositi* of 1509 ('Pasifilo'); in Lorenzo Strozzi's early '*Commedia in versi*' ('Saturio' again), and *La nutrice* ('Pachierotto'); in Grasso's *Eutychia* of 1513 ('Gastrinio'); and in the anonymous *Aristippia* published 1523 ('Antratio').

34 I am thinking here particularly of Martines, 1983; but the point is one which is made increasingly often in studies of the Renaissance.

2 THE FIRST 'REGULAR' COMEDIES

1 The standard source for information on this phenomenon is Stäuble, 1968.

2 No modern edition is available.

3 Edited and dated by Giorgio Padoan, (Antenore, Padua, 1974).

4 For a full account of this occasion, see Cruciani, 1968.

5 Statistics can be found in Stäuble, 1968, pp. 200–1.

6 For a further account, with examples, see Sanesi, 1954, Vol. I, pp. 189–92; also Stefani, 1979.

7 Isabella's letters are pieces of standard reference in theatre histories of the period. At present they are most conveniently consulted in Davico Bonino, 1977, tomo I, pp. 412–13; or in fuller versions in Sanesi, 1954, Vol. I, p. 188.

8 In particular Zorzi, 1977, Chapter 1; and Povoledo, 1969, pp. 364–7 (pp. 305–7 in the Eales translation).

9 One letter of the time reports that ladies were trapped standing in this theatre 'pit', with no access to toilet facilities, for an excessive length of time – eventually leaving the floor in a very unsavoury state.

10 For example, in Ariosto's first prologue to *La Lena* in 1528.

11 Now edited by L. Stefani (Bovolenta, Ferrara 1980).

12 I have pursued these speculations in more detail in Andrews, 1991a.

13 See Stefani, 1979.

14 For all Ariosto's comedies, see Ariosto/Segre, 1974.

15 Italian text in, among other places, Davico Bonino, 1977, tomo 1, pp. 413–14.

16 This interpretation seems infinitely preferable to the hypothesis of Ireneo Sanesi (1954, Vol. 1, pp. 222–5), who was prepared to argue that Ariosto wrote an early verse version of *La Cassaria* for the 1508 performance, then put it into the prose form first printed around 1510, and then back into hendecasyllables for the version performed in 1531 and published in 1546. The best single reason for rejecting this story is Ariosto's well-documented irritation at the prose version being printed at all.

17 This very sensible suggestion is made by Angela Casella in the 'team' edition of Ariosto's comedies: Ariosto/Segre, 1974, p. XVIII. It has not always been taken up by subsequent commentators, e.g. Guidotti, 1983.

18 For a succinct but very revealing comparison of the two plays, see Salingar, 1974, pp. 222–5; there are earlier comments on *I suppositi* alone on pp. 203–8.

19 It was familiar in reality, as well as in fiction. Guido Ruggiero (1985) documents how seduction and even rape received mild, or suspended, punishments from Venetian law courts if the situation was capable of being regularized by marriage.

20 Jeffery, 1969, pp. 21, 191, 193.

21 Rennert, 1909, p. 21; Shergold, 1967, p. 236.

22 He expressed irritation on more than one later occasion, and in a letter to the Duke of Urbino (17 December 1532) blamed members of his cast (*li recitatori*) for the pirated editions.

23 Edited by Luigina Stefani (D'Anna, Messina-Florence, 1978). Few details are known about the life and background of Nicola Grasso.

24 Edited by Giorgio Padoan (Antenore, Padua, 1985), but also in many other editions and anthologies. It is Padoan who has pointed out that the orginal form of the title was *Calandra*, not *Calandria*.

25 The closest rewrites were Angelo Firenzuola: *I Lucidi* (perf. *c.* 1542, pub. 1549); and Gian Giorgio Trissino: *I simillimi* (pub. 1548).

26 In an interesting article, Anna Fontes-Baratto (1974) has argued for close parallels between Fessenio's double loyalties in the play and Bibbiena's own complex role in contemporary politics.

27 On *Calandra* see also Salingar, 1974, pp. 208–11 (where the play is still referred to as *Calandria*).

28 As well as the dramaturgical programme which I suggest, there may have been a linguistic point being made. One of the Urbino courtiers (from 1506 to 1512) had been Pietro Bembo, known already to be offering Boccaccio and fourteenth-century Florentine as a canonical model for literary Italian prose. Bibbiena, as an adoptive Florentine and adherent of the Medici, may have been more enthusiastic about this programme than were either Castiglione or Machiavelli. For a general discussion of the relationship to Boccaccio, see Padoan's edition of the play, pp. 19–34.

29 Exemplified in a recent anthology: Stefani (ed.), 1986.

30 Texts and discussion on dating in Strozzi/Gareffi, 1980.

31 Numerous texts, singly and in anthologies, and several translations into English (the most recent in Penman (ed.), 1978). The most convenient Italian edition, along with *Clizia*, is Machiavelli/Raimondi, 1984.

32 Though Ridolfi thinks that the performance had some connection with the marriage of Lorenzo de' Medici (the younger) in 1518, and puts the first printing of the play in that year.

33 When *La mandragola* was collected in the anthology *Delle commedie elette* of 1554, the editor Girolamo Ruscelli aknowledged its failure to observe what had become the 'rules' in respect of structure: the plot was too simple, and did not build up a sufficiently complicated climax in the fourth and fifth acts.

34 This has been established very thoroughly by Perocco, 1973.

35 The translation is important in its confirmation of how seriously Machiavelli took Terence, rather than Plautus, as a source for the genre: a support for my remarks on dramaturgy in the next section of this chapter. Both *Mandragola* and *Clizia* contain some precise verbal borrowings from the *Andria* translation.

36 Text also available in Machiavelli/Raimondi, 1984.

37 Biblioteca Nazionale Marciana, Venice, cod. It. ix, 364 (7167), cc. 209r–244r. For attribution and title, see Cioranescu, 1991. The transcription is clearly dated at 1520. The author's name is read by Padoan (1982, p. 81) as 'Leoni'; and I myself had considered reading 'Colleoni'.

38 Raimondi notes similarities between this prologue and the unpublished prologue to Lorenzo Strozzi's *Commedia in versi*, especially in the standard references (from 'Cicero' via 'Donatus') to mirroring life, and to instruction through entertainment. The ideas could well have been known collectively to Machiavelli's literary circle, long before they attained the canonical status of printed theory.

39 Borsellino (ed.), 1962, tomo ii, p. 10.

40 Published in 1539; no modern Italian edition. English translation in Minor and Mitchell, 1968.

41 Sumberg, 1961, attributes symbolic meaning to the speech, and makes this a basis for finding political allegory in *La mandragola*. It seems

simpler to propose that Callimaco's exaggerations are there to make people laugh.

42 Grasso was presumably aware that the name 'Eutychia' is derived from the Greek for 'good fortune'. He seems to have favoured meaningful or 'transparent' names for his characters.

3 THE SECOND QUARTER-CENTURY, OUTSIDE VENICE

1 *Formicone*; *Cassaria* and *Suppositi* in prose; *Eutychia* and *Calandra*; *Mandragola* and *Clizia*; *Floriana*; *Aristippia*; the first version of Ariosto's *Negromante*.

2 Strozzi's *Commedia in versi* and *La nutrice/La Pisana* (accepting the dates offered by Gareffi); the *'Geloso'* of Francesco Serleone; and Aretino's 1525 version of *La cortigiana*. Ruzante's earlier compositions, which will be discussed in Chapter 4, are not 'regular' enough to be included, and nor is Degli Pennacchi's *La Perugina*.

3 Again, taking account only of plays in five acts: another fifteen or so could be added by relaxing this criterion. Thirteen comedies first published after 1600 were written by authors who began their careers in the previous century.

4 *La Piovana* had been published in 1548.

5 Ariosto: *Commedie . . . ricorrette per Thomaso Porcacchi* (Giolito, Venice, 1562). Ruzante: *Tutte le opere* (Greco, Vicenza, 1585); *Tutte le opere* (Perin, Vicenza, 1598); *Tutte le opere* (Amadio, Vicenza, 1617).

6 See Bradbrook, 1955, especially the section on 'The Oral Tradition' (pp. 21–6), for the much looser relationship between playtexts and 'literature' in Elizabethan England.

7 A fact perpetuated by his listing in the British Library catalogue under 'Pietro' rather than 'Aretino'.

8 The biography in English by Edward Hutton (1922) is coy and prejudiced at times, but based on good Italian sources.

9 For fuller studies of Aretino's comedies, including those to be discussed in Chapter 4, see Baratto, 1964; Larivaille, 1980 (a thesis first published in French in 1972); Ferroni, 1977; and the editions by Innamorati (1970) and Petrocchi (1971).

10 Biblioteca Nazionale Centrale, Magliabechiano Cl. vii, 84. Although the existence of this text has been known to scholars since 1888, it was not edited until 1970, by Giulio Innamorati. It now also appears in the complete Petrocchi edition of Aretino's plays (1971).

11 To the extent of making reference in the Prologue to a rather obscure convention, of dubious definition and origin, about the number of times each character is permitted to appear on stage: 'And if Messer Maco or someone else should appear on stage more than six times, don't get cross about it, because Rome is a free city, and even the chains that keep a mill on the river couldn't pin down these crazy Lesbians . . . er, that is, Thespians.' The background to this comment is examined in exhaustive

detail by Paul Larivaille, in his 1972 thesis, in an Appendix which is only briefly summarized in his Italian book of 1980, pp. 455–6.

12 This central gag is itself based on a purely verbal confusion. Maco is encouraged to make himself a courtier *'per le forme* – according to the forms', as it were 'by the book' (and there may be another mocking reference to Castiglione's work). But 'le forme' can also be taken as the 'moulds' in which substances were steamed or melted into a different shape – perhaps the image most obviously in mind was the steaming of felt or heavy cloth into the shape of a hat. So Maco is taken to the steam baths and actually put into a cauldron of hot water.

13 Giulio Innamorati, in his edition of 1970 (p. 17), suggests influences from 'farcical shows of Neapolitan origin', and from the so-called 'pre-Rozzi' drama of Siena. The Sienese dramatist 'Strascino' (Niccolò Campani) is actually named in Act II, Scene 19.

14 I have explored this point in full detail in Andrews, 1988.

15 For a very full examination of the relationship between passages of this sort and Aretino's biography, see Cairns, 1985.

16 Larivaille, 1980, pp. 123–37 and relevant footnotes.

17 In the Petrocchi edition (1971), 121 pages as against 100.

18 Full documentation on this can be found in Andrews, 1988. I would propose that the expression used in the 1525 Prologue – 'abbiate pazienza se alcun parla fuor di commedia / be patient if someone speaks "out of the comedy"' – refers to this phenomenon, and not (as most Italian critics take it) to whether or not a scene is relevant to one of the main plots.

19 Translated into English under this title by George Bull, in Penman (ed.), 1978. Because of this accessibility, treatment of the play here will be briefer, and include few quotations.

20 Zuan Polo was a well known Venetian buffoon (praised elsewhere by Aretino himself), who was attached also on occasion to the courts of Ferrara and Mantua. He is known to have died in 1540. His identity is not fully appreciated in the George Bull translation (p. 133), though the fact that there must be some extensive stage business at that point is recognized.

21 There is a possibly unresolvable dispute here about chronological priority. The other contender for the first stage pedant is the protagonist of a rather nasty comedy, actually called *El pedante*, by the Roman Francesco Belo. There is no record of performance: the play appears in some modern Italian anthologies. It is traditional to date the first printing of *El pedante* to 1529, on hearsay evidence; but the first surviving edition is from 1538, and for reasons internal to the text it might be worth reconsidering whether the hearsay is to be relied on.

22 Christopher Cairns (1985, Chapter 3) proposes a complex set of references to Erasmus and Erasmian models of learning, which may have been apparent to a restricted audience or readership.

23 The fact that they must show some tolerance, if mixed with scorn, for

his homosexual preferences raises thorny questions. The penalty for sodomy in most Italian states was no less than being burnt alive; and Guido Ruggiero (1985) shows that, in Venice at least, that penalty could be applied in practice even to the upper classes. On the other hand remarks in Ariosto's prologues, as well as *Il marescalco*, seem to show that the 'crime' was prevalent and presumably unpunished in court circles.

24 See also Bertinetto, 1976.

25 The exchange of letters between Ariosto and Federico Gonzaga is reproduced, among other places, in Davico Bonino (ed.), 1977, tomo I, pp. 425–6.

26 His competence in this respect is recognized in a letter of 1532 from Angelo Beolco ('Ruzante'), whose standards, for the time, were probably high. See Davico Bonino (ed.), 1977, p. 417.

27 For fuller studies of Ariosto's plays than these pages allow, see Grabher, 1946; Ferroni, 1980 (pp. 99–162).

28 Giulio Ferroni (1980) shares this approach, though we have slightly different emphases.

29 Ferroni, 1980, p. 118. Other scholars put it a little later, but all agree that in its original conception it is not the last comedy which its author began drafting.

30 Ludovico's younger brother Gabriele produced *La scolastica*, which was published in 1547: although Gabriele represents his labours, in the Prologue, as being encouraged by the Duke of Ferrara who wanted to perform the play, no performance date is known. The version by Ludovico's son Virginio, under the title *L'imperfetta*, was probably performed in 1556 for the Duchess of Parma, but has been preserved only in a single manuscript in the National Library in Florence. Full texts and details are in Ariosto/Segre, 1974.

31 Although this cuts across some theatrical stereotypes, it is not without precedent: the character of the mischievous old gentleman does occur in Plautus, and it plays its part in the central polemical argument of Terence's *Adelphi* ('The Brothers'), where the issue is the attitude of the older generation to the vagaries of the young.

32 Canto XXIII, stanza 121, where Love is depicted as the executioner who gives Orlando the coup de grace. The parallel is pointed out in Ariosto/Segre, 1974, p. 1131.

33 Unlike Aretino's rewrite of *La cortigiana*, the second version of *Il negromante* does contain considerable stretches of unaltered text. But as well as detailed variants and expansions, there is a substantial reordering of scenes and speeches, and the addition of three new scenes at the end.

34 Ferroni, 1980, p. 132, questioning the long-standing proposals in Catalano's biography of Ariosto (1931), and indeed showing up Catalano's inconsistency.

35 The Giolito edition of 1551 carries two prologues, explained as belong-

ing to 'before' and 'after' the play was 'extended by two scenes at the end' ('ampliata di due scene nel fine').

36 I do not know of any systematic study on this, but there would seem to be a need for one. The 1551 printing has what amounts to an extra scene in Act IV, which Gabriella Ronchi in the Segre edition (wrongly, in my view) chooses to leave out of the definitive text and print as an appendix (p. 963). Other features tend to be overlooked by editors. Some lines are left not properly distributed between various Sbirri (IV, 7) and Staffieri (V, 1); and the movements of Lena and Pacifico between one house and another (V, 5–10) are not signposted by dialogue, leaving a certain amount of potential confusion for a director. Published discussion of the textual history of the play centres on Ronchi's edition, which questions some of the hypotheses of Michele Catalano (1930–1, and edition of the comedies 1940).

37 This part of the plot is needlessly more complicated in the first draft of the play, with a fake marriage between Lavinia and an older man. Ariosto realized that this was contributing nothing, and slimmed the situation down.

38 These crucial closing scenes had not been written in 1520, and are not in the earlier version of the play, where the magician – unsatisfactorily – does not appear after Act III.

39 In the first version, he was sent away to read it by himself indoors – a criminal waste of theatrical opportunity.

40 In Act I, Scene 3 of that version, the encounter with Massimo, which Ariosto then moved to Act III, Scene 4.

41 Eavesdropping as such is common enough in Ariosto's Roman sources; but he seems to develop the double-focus technique in ways of his own.

42 This may have been a late decision – Gabriella Ronchi, in the Segre edition, 1974, pp. 1078–9, points out some topographical inconsistencies.

43 In the latter part of the play, Pacifico begins to attract laughs as a comic coward.

44 In fairness, it should be acknowledged that some other critics, such as Achille Mango (1966), do not share this low opinion. The play was anthologized by Sanesi (ed., 1912), and the original edition (Vitale, Venice, 1533) has been reprinted anastatically (Forni, Bologna, 1981).

45 For both Rozzi and Pre-Rozzi, see Mazzi, 1882 and Alonge, 1967.

46 The play was printed in 1520, though copies are rare; it has been rediscovered by Robert Black and Louise Clubb, who have been generous enough to let me see a photocopy, and an edition will be appearing shortly.

47 A good introduction to the subject is the article of Nerida Newbegin (1980); though her political analysis of *Gli ingannati* may raise as many questions as it answers.

48 There are many uncertainties of date and other detail surrounding the

foundation of the Intronati. The best single source of information remains L. Petracchi Costantini (1928).

49　Two other comedies, both anonymous and unpublished, may be dated earlier than 1532 – *I prigioni*, and *Aurelia* (see Newbegin, 1980). It seems, though, that attempts to perform them fell through, and they were unlikely to have been influential outside Siena itself.

50　This confusion explains the use of the date 1531 in many earlier studies and histories.

51　They actually had a state subsidy for the performance, underlining their central position in the governmental and caste system – see Newbegin, 1980, p. 124.

52　The most coherent, but not yet decisive, theory is that of Giovanni Aquilecchia (1977), who proposes a collaboration between Francesco Maria Molza (who would have been responsible for the setting of the play in his home town of Modena) and the Sienese Claudio Tolomei. There remain unsolved problems about the possible clash between the political bias of these authors and that of the Intronati themselves.

53　For references and sources, see Leo Salingar, 1974, pp. 188–9; and for his perceptive account of the comedy, pp. 211–18. For an expanded version of my own analysis, see Andrews, 1982.

54　I have been involved in two stagings of this comedy in English – in Leeds in 1987, and in Siena in 1991.

55　For more detailed evidence and discussion, see Andrews, 1982.

56　For a full background to this statement, see the crucial study by Daniele Seragnoli (1980); especially Part II, pp. 91–197.

57　For the link between concepts of the 'comic' and artistic representation of the everyday, see Chapter x ('Dal "comico" al "genere"') in Battisti, 1962.

58　For Piccolomini, see Cerreta, 1960; Celse, 1973; and Seragnoli, 1980, especially pp. 91–197.

59　See Seragnoli, 1980, pp. 167–8 and the discussion to p. 180. We shall be examining *La pellegrina* in detail in Chapters 6–7 of the present study.

60　But the audience already knows the real situation, and can laugh indulgently at the character's mistake. We must stress once again how Classical comedy tends to work on the spectators' superior knowledge, rather than springing surprises on them.

61　See Seragnoli, 1980, pp. 142–5, with discussion of the relative demands of realism and of art.

62　Clubb, 1989, especially pp. 1–26.

63　Translated from Alessandro Piccolomini: *La sfera del mondo* (Varisco, Venice, 1561), dedicatory letter – text as in Seragnoli, 1980, p. 99.

64　Clubb, 1989, pp. 1–89.

65　Cesare Molinari (1985, p. 73) records that in 1542 some Sienese noblewomen were punished for acting in a private show – he gives no source for this story. It is undoubtedly true that an actress named Lucrezia from Siena is the first woman to appear in any surviving document as a full partner in a professional company of actors (in 1564: the document is reproduced in Taviani and Schino, 1982, pp. 183–4).

66 Using the dates given by Bruno Ferraro (1981), Cecchi's plays are: *La dote* (1544), *La moglie* (1545), *Il corredo* (1545–6), *La stiava* (1546), *Gli incantesimi* (1547), *L'assiuolo* (1549), *Lo spirito* (1549), *I dissimili* (1550), *Il donzello* (1550), *La maiana* (1550–1), *L'ammalata* (1555), *Il servigiale* (1555–6); and the three-act *La pittura* (*c.* 1547). The first anthology of Cecchi's comedies appeared in 1550. All scholars accept that some dates of first performance are approximate.

The other plays are: Lorenzino de' Medici's *Aridosia* (1536); Giannotti's *Milesia* (1530s?) and *Il vecchio amoroso* (1536); Landi's *Il commodo* (1539); Grazzini's *Il frate* (3 acts, 1540) and *La gelosia* (1550); Firenzuola's *I Lucidi* and *La trinutia* (both *c.*1542); Gelli's *La sporta* (1543) and *Lo errore* (1555); D'Ambra's *Il furto* (*c.* 1544) and *I Bernardi* (1547); Varchi's *La suocera* (1546); Giovanni Da Pistoia's *La gioia* (1550); Mercati's *Il sensale* (1551); and Alamanni's *La Flora* in attempted Classical metre (1555). Further plays (to a total of eight) by Anton Francesco Grazzini may have been composed before 1555: but except for *La spiritata* (performed 1560, published 1561), they were unperformed, and printed in anthology in 1582. Grazzini's work thus presents a chronological dilemma for the present study.

67 For some details, see Povoledo, 1969: an important part in the story of early stage mechanisms was played by Leonardo da Vinci.

68 The occasion is remembered in the 'Quarto Ragionamento' of *I Marmi*, a set of conversations by Anton Francesco Doni published in 1552. The first performance of *L'assiuolo* was in 1549, and could indeed have been the one now referred to.

69 For details, see the chronological information on performances at the beginning of Mamone, 1981; and also the entry on 'Firenze' in *EDS*.

70 For a fuller résumé of the occasion, with references, see the edition of *Aridosia* by Emilio Faccioli (Einaudi, Turin, 1974).

71 Lorenzino justified his act in an *Apologia* (discovered and published in 1818), with reference to famous approved tyrannicides from ancient history. More recent historians point to a vein of psychological instability in him, throwing doubt on the political purity of his motives: see the Faccioli introduction mentioned in the previous footnote.

72 The theme is foregrounded in *Aridosia*, in Gelli's *La sporta* (1543), and in Cecchi's *La dote* (1544), *La moglie* (1545) and to some extent in *Il corredo* (1546). In some other comedies, miserliness is a secondary characteristic of an old man foolishly in love; and the problem of inflated dowries is discussed as a topical issue in Landi's *Il commodo* (1539).

73 The parentheses denoting an aside to the audience are used in the original text.

74 Including *La serpe, ovvero la mala nuora*, which has a didactic element but does not venture outside the secular in its content.

75 Bruno Ferraro's catalogue of 1981 is an indispensable résumé, both chronological and bibliographical. Ferraro has also edited two of Cecchi's late plays for the first time ever: *I contrasegni* in 1986 and *L'andazzo* in 1989.

76 See the inaugural lecture by Peter Brown (1973).

77 Out of around 280 'regular' comedies produced by writers who began their career before 1600, only 59 are in verse. Of these, 36 are by Florentine authors; of these in turn, 23 are by Cecchi.

4 THE SECOND QUARTER-CENTURY, VENICE AND PADUA

1 This whole chapter is indebted to the indispensable volume by Giorgio Padoan (*La commedia rinascimentale veneta*, 1982), to which reference must be made for fuller treatment and documentation. Confident in the knowledge that the ground has been covered, we can here concentrate more on aspects of the material which relate to the themes of this book.

2 There were also, of course, Venetian possessions overseas open to cultural colonization. Eventually dramatic scripts in *commedia erudita* format emerged from Dubrovnik/Ragusa, on the Dalmatian coast (written in Croatian); and from Crete (written in Greek).

3 Messora, 1978 and 1989.

4 The best single source for study of Compagnie della Calza is still Lionello Venturi, 1909, who gives thorough documentation and leads the inquirer to some fascinating visual and archive material in the Biblioteca Correr, Venice. The constraints of space and relevance prevent us from lingering further on the subject in these pages.

5 The earliest clear reference to a ticket price in the diaries of Marin Sanudo relates to February 1517, but the practice is not made to sound like an innovation. A touring actor nicknamed 'Cherea' is said by Sanudo to have been 'earning' from his production of *I Menaechmi* in 1508: see Molinari, 1985, p. 66.

6 The studies of Guido Ruggiero (1980 and 1985), relating to criminal prosecution, leave the impression that Venetian legal practice was not tied very firmly to the exact wording of legal statute. Formulated law seems to have had more of an enabling function, leaving courts to adopt a discretion which was based as much on political as on legal criteria.

7 Cornaro's treatise on the 'Sober Life', the first version of which was published in 1558, acquired a reputation lasting centuries – as can be seen from his entry (as *Luigi* Cornaro) in the catalogue of the British Library. A late spin-off from his work was an English edition of 1951 entitled *How to Live a Hundred Years, by One Who Has Done It*. See Andrews, 1986.

8 The nickname is attested in documents as attached to real people in the peasant community. In dialect it seems to mean 'Growler', or 'Grumble-Gut'. Later on, in the comedy *L'Anconitana*, it is linked with the Tuscan word *ruzzare*, meaning 'to play', 'to have fun'; but the

consensus now is to spell the name with one 'z' only and emphasize its Paduan origin. The spelling 'Ruzzante' is found in many studies written before the 1960s.

9 *La pastoral* was first published in 1951 by Emilio Lovarini, and then re-edited in the Zorzi anthology of Ruzante's *Teatro* (1967), which also contains the first printing of the earlier and longer version of *La Betía*. A cut version of the latter, from a different manuscript, had appeared in 1894 edited by Lovarini.

10 Main sources for Ruzante are Padoan, 1982, Chapter 3; Padoan's edition of the *Dialoghi* and *Orazioni*, 1981; and the complete *Teatro* by Ludovico Zorzi, 1967. On questions of dating, I have preferred Padoan to other scholars; but Zorzi's edition is indispensable for its massive accumulation of detailed notes on language, history and society. See also Mortier, 1925; Grabher, 1953; Baratto, 1964; Carroll, 1981 and 1983; Calendoli, 1985.

11 The pastoral had not yet established itself as a regular *theatrical* form, as it was to do later in the sixteenth century; but it had emerged in some Italian literary experiments, notably Jacopo Sannazaro's *Arcadia* published in 1504. The mode can be traced back at least as far as Boccaccio. See Pieri, 1983, especially pp. 85–109.

12 See Ruzante/Zorzi, 1967, footnote on pp. 1311–12, quoting from the diary of Marin Sanudo. Padoan (1982, p. 88) quotes the same document, but seems more cautious about linking the occasion specifically to *La Betía*.

13 I have examined the *Dialogo facetissimo* in some detail, though in quite a different methodological context, in Andrews, 1986.

14 The terms *compare* and *comare* have no equivalent in modern English, but were important in medieval and Renaissance Italy. They refer to a formal relationship of intimacy and (allegedly) trust, established either by A having been a witness at the wedding of B and C, or by A having stood godfather to B's and C's child. A married woman was in theory 'safe', sexually, in the company of her *compare*, as with a blood relation – there are lots of scurrilous stories in which the relationship is abused.

15 The earlier visitor was Cardinal Marco Cornaro, who then died in 1524; the second was his younger brother Cardinal Francesco Cornaro. Both were related to Caterina Cornaro, the deposed 'Queeen of Cyprus' who set up a kind of court in exile in Asolo. They were not related to Ruzante's patron Alvise Cornaro, much though he might have wished they were. Ruzante's *Orazioni* seem to have been delivered in the minor villa of Barco d'Asolo.

16 Mènego, Nale and Duozo are all typical peasant names used in Ruzante's comedies. The other names are distortions of Roman and medieval legal sources: Donatus [?], Bartolo di Sassoferrato, and the Digest of Justinian. The perception that 'all laws are made by townies' has persisted in Italian peasant culture down to the twentieth century.

17 For possible links between these texts and the 'utopias' of More and Erasmus, see Carroll, 1989.

18 This seems an inevitable interpretation, and it is shared by Zorzi in his 1967 edition, p. 1533, footnote 90.

19 To underline for non-Italianists the difference between Ruzante's *Pavano* dialect and standard Italian, I append here the text of these first two sentences, first in the original and then in an Italian translation by Zorzi:

> *Original text:* Mei sí, st'omo no vegnerà mé pí, elo, sí èlo longo! E po l'ha bel'e catò quelú che 'l dise, e po Dio sa se l'è vero, e po, se ben el foesse a ca' e che'l lo catasse, fuossi no voràlo vegnire.

> *Italian translation:* Ma sí, quest'uomo non tornerà mai piú, tanto è lento! E poi chissà se troverà quel tale che lui dice; e poi Dio sa se è vero; e poi, se anche fosse in casa e lo trovasse, forse quello non vorrà venire.

20 In the original, 'Stòtene', a distortion of 'Aristotele'.

21 This Shakespearian insertion expresses the spirit, rather than the letter, of the text.

22 The all-purpose swear word of the time, attested in other texts than Ruzante, was *cancaro* in dialect (*canchero* in Tuscan), used especially in the expression 'cancaro te magne! (canchero ti mangi!) – may the cancer eat you'. One still has some inhibitions about translating it with the equivalent all-purpose word in modern English, which of course comes from a different semantic area.

23 This highly surprising comparison appears elsewhere in Ruzante – it is either a successful coinage of his own, or a genuine piece of peasant vernacular.

24 He died in 1542, so there may have been a period as long as eight years in which he composed nothing which has survived. No evidence is available to explain this.

25 Ruzante uses more than once what may be a proverbial image of friendship and mutual dependence: two people are pulling at opposite ends of a rope, and if one stops pulling the other one will fall down. It remains true that the 'friends' have to pull in contrary directions, which makes it an excellent image of a theatrical double act.

26 *La Veniexiana* and *Ardelia* are in cod. Marciano It. IX 288 (6072); *Crivello* is in Marciano It. XI 90 (6774). The tenuous nature of their survival is emphasized by the fact that *La Veniexiana* is now totally illegible without infra-red equipment, after some inept chemical treatment by its first modern editor.

27 The fact that the phenomenon was more widespread than the work of just two authors is demonstrated by the way it appeared also on Venetian mainland territory. G. A. Schioppi's *Ramnusia* (performed in Verona in 1531 – see Messora, 1989), and the Brescian *Il Sergio* by Ludovico Fenarolo (performed 1558 – see Messora, 1978), are both multidialect plays in Venetian style.

28 At this stage these were *Calandra, Mandragola, Ingannati,* and the available plays of Ariosto and Aretino.

29 Sanesi, 1954, I, pp. 486–7: the Prologue excuses the inexperience of both author and performers. Giorgio Padoan (1982, pp. 174–5) thinks that the comedies with fewer characters, *Saltuzza* and *Spagnolas,* come later in the canon, and that they bear witness to Calmo's having to operate with a smaller company. It is not clear, though, why contraction should be more likely than expansion.

30 Padoan, 1982, p. 180.

31 Audiences at this time seem to have been enchanted by a character speaking total nonsense, on whatever pretext. The phenomenon emerges in set-piece 'drunk scenes' in Giancarli and Parabosco, and settles finally into the format of a 'mad scene' for a demented hero or heroine, examples of which are prominent in *commedia dell'arte* repertoire – see Chapter 5, pp. 191–2.

32 It is in fact the ancient gag of asking the victim to hold one end of a piece of string, going off allegedly to deal with the other end, and never coming back.

33 The same story is reused more than a century later in the early farce by Molière, *La Jalousie du Barbouillé.*

34 In subsequent editions, of which there were three to 1610, *La zingana* is falsely Tuscanized to *La cingana* – in fact a hypercorrection, not a true Tuscan form. *La capraria* was only printed once more, in 1553.

35 The point is passed over by both Sanesi and Padoan. It is supported by the fact that the two servants concerned speak the *plaudite* at the end of their respective plays; by the implication that they are also involved in the Prologues, speaking apologies on behalf of 'Gigio' the author; and by a speech of Spingarda in *La zingana,* V, 2, which seems to be 'out of character' and to take full responsibility for the play.

36 In addition to the line-up of all the characters in the dénouement, we see Angelica in seven scenes, (including a monologue), and Stella in no fewer than thirteen (including two monologues).

37 Describing these festivities, Pierre de Bourdeille, Seigneur de Brantôme, alludes on what sounds like reliable hearsay to the presence of both 'comédiens et comédientes': the latter 'estoient très-belles, parloient très-bien et de fort bonne grâce' (*Œuvres complètes de Brantôme,* ed. L. Lalanne, Vol. III (Renouard, Paris, 1867), pp. 256–8). I am indebted for this reference to Judith Bryce, of Hull University: for an account of the whole occasion, see her 1988 article.

38 For reference sources on this festivity, see the bibliography in Padoan, 1982, pp. 187–9.

39 Act III, Scene 15, an allusion to the downfall of Thomas Cromwell at the hands of Henry VIII of England. It should perhaps be said here that I am unable to take seriously the statements of Aretino and numerous other dramatists of the period (e.g. in particular Giancarli) that they

had dashed off a comedy from start to finish in a few days or weeks. In some cases the sheer labour of writing it out by hand would take longer. Claims of this sort are a stylized rhetorical ploy, pretending to play down the importance of the composition and at the same time excusing its faults.

40 Such plots were much more firmly established in non-dramatic fiction. It may be necessary to consider the constant overlaps between written and performed fictional *topoi*.

41 For more on this episode, see Andrews, 1988.

42 The word, which is sometimes over-used by scholars of *commedia dell'arte*, refers to any identifiable repertoire joke or sequence, long or short. As a piece of vocabulary it does not appear until the late seventeenth century: as a concept it was from the start one of the basic building blocks of *arte* improvisation method.

43 Padoan (1982, p. 205) quotes a letter implying this from Aretino to Galeazzo Gonzaga, 22 February 1542: the date fits in with a recent performance during carnival.

44 That there were limits beyond which a gentleman could not go, in entertaining his peers, is confirmed and spelt out by Castiglione's *Book of the Courtier* (Book II, Chapter 50).

45 The details need recording, for reference. *Il marescalco* became '*Il cavallerizzo*, by Luigi Tansillo' (1601, 1606 (twice), 1608). *La cortigiana* became '*Lo sciocco*, by G. Caporali' (1604 and 1628). *Lo Ipocrito* became '*Il finto*, by Tansillo' (1601 and 1610). *La Talanta* became '*La Ninnetta*, by Caporali' (1603/4). *Il filosofo* became '*Il sofista*, by Tansillo' (1601 and 1610). Both were real authors, whose names were borrowed. There has been no close study of these disguised versions and the extent to which they have been altered from the originals.

46 I have to disagree here with the judgement of Giorgio Padoan (1982, pp. 190–1); 'looking at *Il ragazzo* in the abstract, there is nothing to indicate Venice, rather then Milan or Rome, as its city of origin.' He seems here to be responding to the over-familiar plot schemes, rather than to the more detailed dramaturgy.

47 The full list of his comedies, with their date of publication, is as follows: *La notte* (1546); *Il Viluppo* (1547); *L'hermafrodito* (1549); *I contenti* (1549); *Il marinaio* (1550); *Il pellegrino* (1552, in verse); *Il ladro* (1555); *La fantesca* (1556).

48 This is the judgement of Sanesi, 1954, taken up uncritically by *EDS*. Giorgio Padoan (1982, pp. 198–209) independently reaches a similar view.

49 The fixed set of such plays seems to include a tomb or vault as one of its features, presumably attached to a church.

50 The dissatisfied wife Leonora is in love with the courtier Periandro, but finally accepts a liaison with a servant, Ruspa, who happens to be Periandro's physical double. There are no eventual revelations of any

family relationship, which might restore Ruspa to respectability. Criticisms of the play are mentioned in Parabosco's dedicatory letter to Cardinal Niccolò Doria.

51 In a letter to Count Alessandro Lambertino: see Padoan, 1982, p. 204.

5 IMPROVISED COMEDY

1 The 1567 'season' is narrated by Cesare Molinari (1985, p. 74).

2 The text is reproduced in Taviani and Schino, 1982, pp. 185–6; and translated in Richards and Richards, 1990, pp. 44–6. No woman is included among the partners of this early company. The first company contract to include an actress dates from 1564: see Taviani and Schino, pp. 183–4.

3 Major informative accounts have been produced by Pierre Louis Duchartre (English trans. 1929, repr. 1966), Kathleen Lea (1934), Allardyce Nicoll (1963), and Cesare Molinari (1985, so far only available in Italian). The translated documents of Richards and Richards (1990) are now indispensable for English readers. Duchartre and Molinari have a good selection of essential visual material; Lea and Molinari make the best critical use of available written sources, with Molinari obviously more up to date. Other important critical studies in Italian are those of Taviani and Tessari, listed in the general biography.

4 This means setting aside a number of apparent commonplaces about the genre, which date from eighteenth-century accounts, and especially from the version given by Luigi Riccoboni. Lea and Molinari show awareness of this problem, and distinguish between earlier and later periods: Duchartre and Nicoll are sometimes less discriminating.

5 In a comedy, *Il teatro comico*, which is a play functioning as a manifesto.

6 For a typical catalogue of a company, divided up in this way, see Molinari, 1985, p. 76.

7 It is tempting to think that the 'classic' series of engravings of the Recueil Fossard, reproduced by Duchartre and by Molinari, might actually record the entry of a stage Harlequin figure into a *commedia dell'arte* ensemble. The engravings have captions in French, and are believed to relate to a visit to Paris by the Gelosi company in 1577.

8 The story of Arlecchino and Brighella originating in the upper and lower towns of Bergamo is an eighteenth-century legend of relatively late fabrication.

9 Some 'masked masks', such as the 'Beltrame' created by Niccolò Barbieri, were nevertheless so individual as to die along with their impersonators.

10 Molinari is less disposed than I am to use the word 'mask' in relation to the *Innamorati* – it is a difference of semantic choice rather than of perception.

11 For a closer look at *arte* influences in Molière, see Andrews, 1989.

12 There is a study of the genre, plus texts of five comedies, by Luciano

Mariti (1978). Kathleen Lea, with her usual acumen, identified the body of material independently, and lists many of the texts in her book of 1934, but she was not aware of the 'Ridicolosa' label.

13 Reproduced in full in Mariti, 1978.

14 Molinari (1985, pp. 77–82) shows how status was defined by whether a company performed in the open air (less respectable) or in a hired room or hall (more respectable).

15 Pandolfi, 1957, Vol. I, pp. 174–7; taken from Biblioteca Nazionale, Florence, D.4.6.23, no. 10 (Rari incunaboli palatini, Striscia 959). My own translated version of most of the dialogue appears in Andrews, 1991b.

16 The analogy with jazz is proposed independently by Molinari (1985, p. 40). It could well be a fruitful notion for critics to pursue: jazz, like *commedia dell'arte*, is in practice subject to severe stylistic restrictions, within which its creative improvisations flourish.

17 There is room for an enquiry into the frequency of modular scenes, and even of 'elastic gags', in Plautus: there is no reason why they should not have appealed quite independently to the professional actors for whom he wrote in the 3rd–2nd century BC.

18 Andrews, 1989, with the whole scene translated in an appendix.

19 One uses the term 'family of masks' in the sense that every Capitano was substantially different from every other – they had different names, no facial masks, and varied in stage personality as much as individual Lovers.

20 Antonio Pardi, *Stupende Forze e Bravure del Capitano Spezzacapo e Sputa-saette* (Heredi di Giovanni Rossi, Padua, 1606), reproduced in Pandolfi, 1957, Vol. I, pp. 343–8.

21 Francesco Andreini, *Le bravure del Capitano Spavento* (Somasco, Venice 1607).

22 Giulio Cesare Croce, *Vanto ridicoloso di Trematerra* (Bartolomeo Cochi, Bologna, 1619), reproduced in Pandolfi, 1957, Vol. I, pp. 353–9.

23 Anon, *Vocabulario Gratianesco*; Biblioteca Nazionale, Roma, cod. Sessoriana no. 587. Reproduced in Pandolfi, 1957, Vol. II, p. 32.

24 Anon, *Le cento e quindici Conclusioni in Ottava Rima del Plusquamperfetto Dottor Gratiano . . .* (s.l. 1587); reproduced in Pandolfi, 1957, Vol. II, pp. 11–19.

25 A manuscript entitled *Dialoghi scenici di Domenico Bruni detto Fulvio, comico Confidente . . .*, Biblioteca Burcardo, Rome, cod. 3–37–5–35. Bruni also published *Fatiche comiche* (Paris, 1623) and *Prologhi* (Turin, 1621).

26 Isabella Andreini: *Fragmenti di alcune scritture . . .* (Tarino, Turin, 1621).

27 Quoted in Pandolfi, 1957, Vol. II, pp. 58–9.

28 Translated from the *Diario* of Giuseppe Pavoni (Rossi, Bologna, 1589).

29 Oreglia 1968, pp. 119–22.

30 This refers not only to *A Night at the Opera*, but also to *A Day at the Races, At the Circus*, and *The Big Store*.

31 At the time of writing, this company under the direction of Carlo Boso

has probably got closer than any other to reproducing the *commedia dell'arte* experience on a regular basis, with the full approval and enjoyment of modern audiences. It is based in Mestre near Venice, but has toured in other European countries.

32 The most important collections are listed by Lea, 1934 (Vol. II, pp. 506–9) and Molinari, 1985 (pp. 42–3). Lea has a list of known scenario titles on pp. 509–54; perhaps not exhaustive, but very useful.

33 A modern edition is available: Scala/Marotti, 1976. Regrettably, the English translation by Salerno (*Scenarios of the commedia dell'arte . . .*) is so full of material errors as to be practically useless.

34 Reproduced in Molinari, 1985, pp. 84–9.

35 The word *baldracca* could refer to a canopy or curtain, like the more familiar *baldacchino*; but it was increasingly used as a term for 'whore'. See Zorzi, 1977, pp. 124–6; and Anderson, 1991, p. 16.

36 See the Vaccaro engravings (Duchartre, 1929, pp. 292, 335–8; Molinari, 1985, p. 86); a number of engravings by Callot (Duchartre, facing p. 176, and between pp. 229–9); and the Amsterdam engravings of 1710 on 'Harlequin as a mother' (Duchartre, between pp. 56–7; Molinari, p. 168). For mules or donkeys propelled by syringes or bellows, the Trausnitz frescoes (Molinari, p. 60); and paintings based on Callot (Molinari, pp. 130, 132).

37 Duchartre, 1929, p. 320; Molinari, 1985, p. 103.

38 Duchartre, 1929, p. 339; Molinari, 1985, pp. 134 and 135.

39 In the Recueil Fossard (Duchartre, 1929, p. 327).

40 There is no intention of proposing here that *all* facial masks are dehumanizing: there are a number of other theatre traditions, as well as modern experiments, where the effect is quite different. But illustrations from the period, and modern revivals such as those of the Piccolo Teatro di Milano and TAG Teatro in Venice, all point to the conclusion that in *commedia dell'arte* masks, specifically, there is a tendency towards the bestial.

41 It is paralleled by the moment in Chaplin's *Shoulder Arms*, set in the trenches of the First World War, when Charlie marches in a cluster of German prisoners at bayonet point, and explains: 'I surrounded them.'

42 I am grateful to Roberta Mullini, who has written penetratingly in Italian about the Fool in Elizabethan English culture, for confirming that the phenomenon has no equivalent in Italy during the same period.

6 OBSTACLES TO COMEDY

1 For texts of the *Poetics* available before 1536, see Weinberg, 1961, pp. 349–71.

2 See note 11 to Chapter 3, pp. 254–5 above.

3 See Weinberg, 1961, pp. 367–73, where it is clear that prior to the 1536 edition very limited use was made of the *Poetics*.

4 Weinberg, 1970–4; henceforth referred to in footnotes simply as *Trattati*.

5 Messora, 1978, pp. 107–50: the volume also contains the full text of the play.

6 The survey which follows has been greatly helped by my being able to view a draft thesis for Cambridge University, writen by Anastasia Markomihelaki.

7 V. Maggi: *De ridiculis* (1550); reproduced in *Trattati*, Vol. II, pp. 91–125; discussed in Weinberg, 1961, pp. 417–18.

8 G. G. Trissino: *La quinta e la sesta division della Poetica*, in *Trattati*, Vol. II, pp. 7–90; discussed in Weinberg, 1961, principally on pp. 750–5.

9 This view is contested on stage by the Pedant in Pino's *Gli ingiusti sdegni* (1553), to deflect the implications of the fact that he is being laughed at.

10 *Trattati*, Vol. II, pp. 69–71.

11 When Trissino does refer to verbal wit, he concentrates on the way that it can mock or expose someone else, as when a person 'feigning ignorance in himself reveals defects (*bruttezza*) in others'. The emphasis is not on admiration of the speaker, but (as in Castiglione) on the damage done to a victim. The closest thing to any reference to approving laughter is in the mention of 'moving laughter by a sharp response to some proverb that is spoken'. See *Trattati*, Vol. II, p. 74.

12 See note 7 above.

13 A. Riccoboni: *De re comica ex Aristotelis doctrina* (1579) in *Trattati*, Vol. III, pp. 257–76; discussed in Weinberg, 1961, principally on pp. 586–8.

14 Titles are: *Lo Sbratta* (perf. 1551, pub. 1552); *Gli ingiusti sdegni* (perf. and pub. 1553); *Gli affetti* (perf. 1556?, pub. 1559); *L'Eunia* (pub. 1582); *L'Evagria* (pub. 1584); *I falsi sospetti* (pub. 1588). Not all of these count as 'regular comedies', *Gli affetti* and *L'Eunia* ranking more as dialogued debates in a pastoral setting.

15 B. Pino da Cagli: *Breve considerazione intorno al componimento de la comedia de' nostri tempi* (1578) in *Trattati*, Vol. II, pp. 631–49; discussed in Weinberg, 1961, pp. 203–4 and 581–2.

16 Giulio Del Bene: *Che la favola della Comedia vuole esser onesta, e non contenere mal costumi* (from manuscript), in *Trattati*, Vol. III, pp. 177–90; discussed in Weinberg, 1961, pp. 533–8.

17 It was a point of view expressed sometimes in seventeenth-century France, and also in Lord Chesterfield's letters to his son in the English eighteenth century.

18 In his *Verato secondo . . . in difesa del Pastor Fido* (1593): text and translation of the passage quoted are in Weinberg, 1961, p. 1087.

19 See P. M. Brown, 1973.

20 See the study of Mireille Celse, 1973.

21 Taviani, 1969; and a significant part of his conclusions summarized in the Introduction to Barbieri/Taviani, 1971. See also Pandolfi, 1957,

Vol. III, pp. 325–469; and Chapter 9 of Richards and Richards, 1990 (pp. 235–55).

22 See a summary, with references for further reading, in Barbieri/ Taviani, 1971, p. xxix.

23 As well as studies by Taviani already referred to, see D'Ancona, 1891, Vol. II, pp. 162–97.

24 The story first appears in *La supplica*, by the actor Nicolò Barbieri, in 1634; and it was repeated in the eighteenth-century histories and memoirs of Luigi Riccoboni. See Barbieri/Taviani, 1971, p. xxx.

25 See the chapter 'Il manoscritto della *Pellegrina*' in Borsellino, 1974, pp. 107–19. In Borsellino's own anthology (1962), the play appears in its censored form as published in 1589; there is now a full edition in Bargagli/Cerreta, 1971, and a full English translation ('The Female Pilgrim') in Bargagli/Ferraro, 1988.

26 Borsellino, 1974, p. 109; see also Seragnoli, 1980, pp. 167–80.

27 Bargagli/Ferraro, 1988, pp. 11–16, with accompanying bibliography.

28 Ferdinando had succeeded his brother Francesco, after the latter's unexpected death in Ferdinando's own house in 1587. So this may be a second case (after *Aridosia*) of a comedy existing in close proximity to a Medici dynastic murder.

7   SCRIPTS AND SCENARIOS

1 For the later history of this whole 'theatergram', see the Preface to Clubb, 1989, and the subsequent chapter on 'Woman as Wonder'

2 The 'official' account, prepared beforehand and sometimes overtaken by events, was that of Bernardo de' Rossi, secretary of the Accademia Della Crusca which took overall responsibility for all the performances. His account is both reinforced and corrected by a number of others: for the full list of sources, and for a résumé of the whole event, see Nagler, 1964, Chapter 6, pp. 70–92.

3 Many of the set and costume designs of Bernardo Buontalenti are still extant, as are the scores of most of the musical numbers used. They are supplemented by the rehearsal diary of Girolamo Serjacopi, and by court account books.

4 Five of the six Interludes have now been reconstructed using the most advanced camera technology in the television programme *Una Stravaganza dei Medici*, produced by Thames Television/Taverner/Framestore for Channel 4, and first broadcast in December 1990. The accompanying booklet (Kenyon and Keyte, 1990) is a good introduction to the Interludes as a whole, and contains a full libretto of the five which were broadcast.

5 *Diario descritto da Giuseppe Pavoni delle feste celebrate nelle solennissime Nozze* . . . (Rossi, Bologna 1589).

6 See Chapter 2, p. 32.

7 For more information on the layout, together with an analysis of the social and political semiology involved, see Zorzi, 1977.

8 This is one of the main proposals of Tessari, 1984.

9 The court of Ferrara played a pioneering role yet again in the establishment of stage tragedy and pastoral. A key figure for both genres was Giovambattista Giraldi Cinthio, who wrote the first performed tragedies, and hosted one of the first pastoral dramas (*Egle*, 1545) in his own house.

10 For the whole progress of stage music towards opera in Renaissance Italy, see Pirrotta, 1969. The earliest operas were *Dafne* and *Euridice* (Florence 1597 and 1600: both libretti by Rinuccini, music by Peri and Caccini). In 1607, in Mantua, there followed Monteverdi's *Favola d'Orfeo* (libretto by Alessandro Striggio).

11 See the summarized and translated scenarios in Lea, 1934, Vol. II.

12 Or Sforza d'Oddo, or Sforza dell'Oddo: his name appears in a variety of forms in catalogues and title pages. He earned his living as a professor of law.

13 Machiavelli/Trovato, 1982, pp. 62–4. The date of the work is uncertain – Trovato puts it before 1524 – and Professor Cecil Grayson has even argued that it should not be attributed to Machiavelli at all.

14 E.g. the titles of Radcliff-Umstead, 1969, and Pieri, 1989.

15 I have investigated these links in more detail in Andrews, 1989 and 1991b.

16 I am expanding, perhaps, on Tessari, 1984; but his description of how princely patrons effectively took possession of the professional theatre companies seems at least to provide one half of my thesis.

Chronological bibliography of comedies, 1500–1560

in order of appearance, as ascertainable, with
modern editions and English translations

Criteria for inclusion: a comedy (preferably designated as such) in five
acts, with urban setting and entirely secular content, with 'mimetic'
rather than 'symbolic' presentation. Some non-qualifying works by
relevant authors are included.

Author: inverted commas denote a pseudonym or stage name.

Title: inverted commas denote a title supplied by later scholars; '*I*, *II*'
refer to first and second versions of the same play.

Number of editions is to 1630 – plays only printed in modern times thus
have 'o editions'; 'ms.' denotes a play never printed.

Remarks in small capitals draw attention to non-'regular' features,
including a play being written in verse rather than prose.

References to modern editions are in some cases selective. Short references are to items also in the general bibliography, especially anthologies.

1503
'Publio Philippo Mantovano': *Formicone* (perf. 1503; pub. 1524; 5 editions);
ed. L. Stefani (Bovolenta, Ferrara, 1980)

1506
L. Strozzi: '*Commedia in versi*' [untitled] (perf. 1506?; o editions); VERSE; in
Strozzi/Gareffi, 1980

1508
L. Ariosto: *La cassaria* (*I*, prose) (perf. 1508; pub. 1510?; 9 editions); in
Ariosto/Segre, 1984; ENGLISH: *The Coffer*, in Beame and Sbrocchi,
1975

1509
L. Ariosto: *I suppositi* (*I*, prose) (perf. 1509; pub. 1510?; 12 editions); in
Ariosto/Segre, 1984; ENGLISH: *The Pretenders*, in Beame and Sbrocchi,
1975

1513
B. Dovizi da Bibbiena: *Calandra* (perf. 1513; pub. 1521; 22 editions); ed.

G. Padoan (Antenore, Padua, 1985); also in many other editions and anthologies; ENGLISH: in Bentley (ed.), 1964

N. Grasso: *Eutychia* (perf. 1513; pub. 1524; 5 editions); ed. L. Stefani (D'Anna, Messina-Florence, 1978)

1518

Anon: *Floriana* (pub. 1518; 3 editions); VERSE; no modern edition

N. Machiavelli: *La mandragola* (perf. 1518?; pub. 1521; 15 editions); ed. E. Raimondi (Mursia, Milan, 1984); also in numerous other Italian editions and anthologies; ENGLISH: in Bentley (ed.), 1958; Machaivelli/Hale, 1961; Penman (ed.) 1978

L. Strozzi: '*La Pisana/La nutrice*' [untitled] (perf. 1518?; 0 editions); VERSE; in Strozzi/Gareffi, 1980

1520

L. Ariosto: *Il negromante* (*I*) (comp. 1520; pub. 1535; 9 editions); VERSE; in Ariosto/Segre, 1984

F. Serleone: '*Il geloso*' [untitled] (ms transcribed 1520; 0 editions); VERSE; no modern edition

1521

'Ruzante': *La pastoral* (perf. 1521; 0 editions); VERSE, RUSTIC; in Ruzante/Zorzi, 1967

1523

Anon: *Aristippia* (pub. 1523; 4 editions); no modern edition

'Ruzante': *La Betía* (*I*) (perf. 1523; 0 editions); VERSE, RUSTIC; in Ruzante/Zorzi, 1967

1525

P. Aretino: *La cortigiana* (*I*) (perf. 1525; 0 editions); ed. G. *Innamorati* (Einaudi, Turin, 1970); in Aretino/Petrocchi, 1971

N. Machiavelli: *Clizia* (perf. 1525; pub. 1537; 5 editions)

ed. E. Raimondi (Mursia, Milan 1984); also in numerous other Italian editions and anthologies; ENGLISH: in Machiavelli/Hale, 1961

'Ruzante': *La Betía* (*II*) (perf. 1525; 0 editions); VERSE, RUSTIC; in Lovarini (ed.), 1894 (repr. 1969)

1526

A. Degli Pennacchi: *La Perugina* (pub. 1526; 1 edition); NO UNITY OF PLACE; no modern edition

SACK OF ROME, 1527

1527

P. Aretino: *Il marescalco* (perf. 1527; pub. 1533; 18 editions); in Aretino/

Petrocchi, 1971; ENGLISH: *The Stablemaster*, trans. G. Bull in Penman (ed.), 1978

1528
L. Ariosto: *La Lena* (*I*) (perf. 1528; o editions) – VERSE; first version lost
L. Ariosto: *Il negromante* (*II*) (perf. 1528; pub. 1551; 5 editions) – VERSE; in Ariosto/Segre, 1974; ENGLISH: *The Necromancer*, in Beame and Sbrocchi, 1975
'Ruzante': *Primo dialogo: El parlamento de Ruzante* ... (perf. 1528; pub. 1551; 8 editions); I ACT, PROSE; in Ruzante/Zorzi, 1967; in Ruzante/Padoan, 1981; ENGLISH: *Ruzzante Returns from the Wars*, in Bentley (ed.), 1958
'Ruzante': *Secondo dialogo: Bilora* (perf. 1528; pub. 1551; 8 editions); I ACT, PROSE; in Ruzante/Zorzi, 1967; in Ruzante/Padoan, 1981; ENGLISH: *Bilora*, in Clark (ed.), 1956

1529
L. Ariosto: *La Lena* (*II*) (perf. 1529; pub. 1535; 13 editions); VERSE; in Ariosto/Segre, 1974; ENGLISH: *Lena*, in Beame and Sbrocchi, 1975; trans G. Williams in Penman (ed.), 1978
F. Belo: *El pedante* (pub. 1529?; 4 editions); in Borsellino (ed.), 1967; in Davico Bonino (ed.), 1977; (Forni, Bologna, 1979 – anastatic reprint)
V. Gambaro: *Manfrino* (pub. 1529; 1 edition); no modern edition
'Ruzante': *Dialogo facetissimo* (perf. 1529; pub. 1551; 8 editions); ONE ACT, RUSTIC; in Ruzante/Zorzi, 1967; in Ruzante/Padoan, 1981
'Ruzante': *La moscheta* (perf. 1529; pub. 1551; 9 editions); in Ruzante/Zorzi, 1967

1530
Anon: *I Prigioni* (comp. 1530?; o editions); no modern edition
M. Podiani: *I megliacci* (pub. 1530; 1 edition); no modern edition
A. Ricchi: *I tre tiranni* (perf. 1530; pub. 1533; 1 edition); VERSE; ed. M. Calore (Forni, Bologna, 1981 – anastatic reprint)
L. Strozzi: *Violante* (comp. 1530; o editions); in Strozzi/Gareffi, 1980

1531
L. Ariosto: *La cassaria* (*II*, verse) (perf. 1531; pub. 1546; 5 editions); VERSE; in Ariosto/Segre, 1974; ENGLISH: *The Coffer*, in Beame and Sbrocchi, 1975
'Ruzante': *La Fiorina* (comp. 1531?; pub. 1552; 10 editions); in Ruzante/Zorzi, 1967
G. A. Schioppi: *Ramnusia* (perf. 1531; pub. 1550; 1 edition); no modern edition

1532
Anon: *Gli ingannati* (perf. 1532; pub. 1537; 20 editions); ed. N. Newbegin (Forni, Bologna, 1984 – anastatic reprint); also in many Italian anthologies; ENGLISH: trans. B. Penman in Penman (ed.), 1978

L. Ariosto: *I suppositi* (*II*, verse) (comp. 1532; pub. 1551; 6 editions); VERSE; in Ariosto/Segre, 1974

'Ruzante': *La Piovana* (perf. 1532; pub. 1548; 9 editions); in Ruzante/Zorzi, 1967

1533
P. Aretino: *La cortigiana* (*II*) (pub. 1533; perf. 1538; 16 editions); in Aretino/ Petrocchi, 1971

'Ruzante': *La vaccaria* (perf. 1533; pub. 1551; 8 editions); in Ruzante/Zorzi, 1967

1534
'Ruzante': *L'Anconitana* (comp. 1534?; pub. 1551; 8 editions); in Ruzante/ Zorzi, 1967

[1530–40]
Anon: *Ardelia* (perf. 1530–40?; 0 editions); no modern edition
Anon: *Crivello* (perf. 1530–40? 0 editions); no modern edition
G. Cenci: *Gli errori* (pub. 1535?; 3 editions); no modern edition
P. Foglietta: *Il barro* (comp. 1535?; 0 editions); ed. M. Rosi (Genoa, 1894)
D. Giannotti: *Milesia* (comp. 1530–40?; 0 editions); in Giannotti/Polidori, 1850

1536
Anon [A. Vignali?]: *Aurelia* (comp. 1536?; 0 editions); ed. M. Celse-Blanc (Sorbonne Nouvelle, Paris, 1981)
Anon: *La Veniexiana* (perf. 1536; 0 editions); NO UNITY OF PLACE; ed. G. Padoan (Antenore, Padua, 1974); also in many Italian anthologies
L. de' Medici: *Aridosia* (perf. 1536; pub. 1548; 10 editions); ed. E. Faccioli (Einaudi, Turin, 1974); also in earlier Italian anthologies
D. Giannotti: *Il vecchio amoroso* (perf. 1536; 0 editions); in Borsellino (ed.), 1962–7
A. Piccolomini [with collaborators?]: *L'amor costante* (comp. 1536; pub. 1540; 15 editions); in Borsellino (ed.), 1962–7, and other Italian anthologies; ed. N. Newbegin (Forni, Bologna, 1990 – anastatic reprint)

1537
L. Contile: *La trinottia* (comp. 1537; pub. 1544; 2 editions); no modern edition
L. Contile: *La pescara* (comp. 1537; pub. 1550; 1 edition); no modern edition

1538
F. Belo: *El Beco* (pub. 1538; perf. 1540; 1 edition); ed. M. Calore (Forni, Bologna, 1979 – anastatic reprint)

1539

F. Landi: *Il commodo* (perf. and pub. 1539; 2 editions); no modern Italian edition; ENGLISH: in Minor and Mitchell, 1968

1540

'Arsiccio Intronato' (A. Vignali): *Floria* (comp. 1540?; pub. 1560; 2 editions); 3 ACTS, PROSE; no modern edition

A. Calmo: *La Rhodiana* (perf. 1540; pub. 1553; 6 editions); ATTRIB. RUZANTE IN EARLY EDITIONS; no modern edition

L. Dolce: *Il ragazzo* (comp. 1540?; pub. 1541; 7 editions); no modern edition

A. Grazzini: *Il frate* (perf. 1540; 0 editions); 3 ACTS, PROSE; in Grazzini/ Grazzini, 1953

L. Raineri: *L'Altilia* (comp. 1540; pub. 1550; 1 edition); no modern edition

1541

A. Firenzuola: *I Lucidi* (perf. 1541–3; pub. 1549; 9 editions); in Barini (ed.), 1858

A. Firenzuola: *La trinuzia* (perf. 1541–3; pub. 1549; 6 editions); ed. D. Maestri (Einaudi, Turin, 1970)

1542

P. Aretino: *Lo Ipocrito* (pub. 1542; 10 editions); in Aretino/Petrocchi, 1971

P. Aretino: *La Talanta* (perf. and pub. 1542; 6 editions); in Aretino/ Petrocchi, 1971

A. Calmo: *La Fiorina* (perf. after 1542; pub. 1553; 5 editions); no modern edition

F. D'Ambra: *Il furto* (perf. 1542–4; pub. 1560; 6 editions); in Borlenghi (ed.), 1959

1543

G. B. Gelli: *La sporta* (perf. and pub. 1543; 11 editions); in Borlenghi (ed.), 1959

1544

P. Aretino: *Il filosofo* (comp. 1544?; pub. 1545; 4 editions); in Aretino/ Petrocchi, 1971

E. Bentivoglio: *I fantasmi* (pub. 1544; 3 editions); no modern edition

E. Bentivoglio: *Il geloso* (pub. 1544; perf. 1549; 5 editions); no modern edition

A. Caro: *Gli straccioni* (comp. 1544; pub. 1582; 3 editions); in Davico Bonino (ed.), 1977–8; and numerous other Italian anthologies; ENGLISH: *The Scruffy Scoundrels*, trans, M. Ciavolella and D. Beecher (Waterloo, Ontario, 1980)

G. M. Cecchi: *La dote* (1, prose) (perf. 1544; pub. 1550; 5 editions); no modern edition

G. A. Giancarli: *La capraria* (pub. 1544; 2 editions); no modern edition
A. Piccolomini [with collaborators?]: *Alessandro* (perf. 1544; pub. 1545; 16 editions); (Daelli, Milan, 1864)

1545
G. M. Cecchi: *La moglie* (*1*, prose) (perf. 1545; pub. 1550; 4 editions); no modern edition
L. Dolce: *Il capitano* (perf. and pub. 1545; 6 editions); no modern edition
L. Dolce: *Il marito* (pub. 1545; 5 editions); no modern edition
G. A. Giancarli: *La zingana* (pub. 1545; 4 editions); in Cibotto (ed.), 1960

1546
A. Calmo: *Travaglia* (perf. 1546; pub. 1556; 5 editions); no modern edition
G. M. Cecchi: *Il corredo* (perf. 1546; pub. 1585; 1 edition); VERSE; no modern edition
G. M. Cecchi: *La stiava* (*1*, prose) (perf. 1546; pub. 1550; 1 edition); no modern edition
G. Parabosco: *La notte* (pub. 1546; perf. 1548; 3 editions); (Forni, Bologna, 1977 – anastatic reprint)
B. Varchi: *La suocera* (comp. 1546; pub. 1569; 1 edition); in Barini (ed.), 1858

1547
L. Ariosto (and G. Ariosto): *La scolastica [I studenti]* (pub. 1547; 6 editions); VERSE; in Ariosto/Segre, 1974; ENGLISH: *The Students/The Scholastics*, in Beame and Sbrocchi, 1975
G. Baroncini: *La fante* (pub. 1547; 1 edition); no modern edition
G. M. Cecchi: *Gl'incantesimi* (*1*, prose) (perf. 1547; pub. 1550; 2 editions); no modern edition
G. M. Cecchi: *La pittura* II (comp. 1547?; 0 editions); 3 ACTS, VERSE; in Scotti-Bertinelli, 1906
F. D'Ambra: *I Bernardi* (perf. 1547–8; pub. 1564; 2 editions); VERSE; in Barini (ed.), 1858 and Sanesi (ed.), 1912
A. Mariconda: *La Philenia* (perf. 1547; pub. 1548; 1 edition); no modern edition
G. Parabosco: *Il Viluppo* (pub. 1547; 6 editions); (Forni, Bologna, 1977 – anastatic reprint)

1548
L. Contile: *La Cesarea Gonzaga* (perf. 1548; pub. 1550; 1 edition); no modern edition
V. Gabiani: *I gelosi* (perf. 1548; pub. 1551; 3 editions); in Messora, 1978
G. G. Trissino: *I simillimi* (pub. 1548; 1 edition); (Daelli, Milan 1864)

1549
A. Calmo: *Las spagnolas* (pub. 1549; 13 editions); no modern edition

G. M. Cecchi: *L'assiuolo* (perf. 1549; pub. 1550; 2 editions); in Borsellino (ed.), 1962, and earlier Italian anthologies; ENGLISH: *The Horned Owl*, trans. K Eisenbichler (Waterloo, Ontario, 1981)

G. M. Cecchi: *Lo spirito* (perf. 1549; pub. 1585; 1 edition); VERSE; no modern edition

L. Dolce: *Fabritia* (pub. 1549; 3 editions); no modern edition

L. Fenice: *Primavera* (pub. 1549; 2 editions); no modern edition

G. Parabosco: *I contenti* (pub. 1549; 7 editions); (Forni, Bologna, 1977 – anastatic reprint)

G. Parabosco: *L'hermafrodito* (pub. 1549; 3 editions); (Forni, Bologna, 1977 – anastatic reprint)

N. Secchi: *Gli inganni* (perf. 1549; pub. 1562; 9 editions); ed. L. Quartermaine (Exeter University Press, 1980)

1550

G. G. Brusonio: *Comedia di mandata Sophia* (pub. 1550; 1 edition); no modern edition

G. M. Cecchi: *I dissimili* (pub. 1550; perf. 1556; 2 editions); no modern edition

G. M. Cecchi: *Il donzello* (perf. 1550; pub. 1585; 1 edition); VERSE; no modern edition

G. M. Cecchi: *Commedie* (pub. 1550; 1 edition); ANTHOLOGY

G. Da Pistoia: *La gioia* (perf. 1550; pub. 1586; 1 edition); no modern edition

A. Grazzini: *La gelosia* (perf. 1550; pub. 1551; 6 editions); in Grazzini/Grazzini, 1953

G. Leggiadri Galanni: *La Portia* (pub. 1550; 2 editions); no modern edition

G. Parabosco: *Il marinaio* (comp. and pub. 1550; 5 editions); (Forni, Bologna, 1977 – anastatic reprint)

G. Parabosco: *Il pellegrino* (comp. 1550; pub. 1552; 5 editions); (Forni, Bologna, 1977 – anastatic reprint)

S. Tarentino: *Il capitan bizzarro* (pub. 1550; 2 editions); no modern edition

C. Turco: *L'Agnella* (perf. 1550; pub. 1558; 2 editions); in Messora, 1978

1551

P. Caggio: *Flamminia prudente* (pub. 1551; 1 edition); no modern edition

A. Calmo: *Saltuzza* (pub. 1551; 3 editions); in Borlenghi (ed.), 1959

G.M. Cecchi: *La maiana* (perf. 1551; 0 editions); ed. G. Tortoli (Florence 1855)

L. Dolce: *Il roffiano* (pub. 1551; 5 editions); no modern edition

F. Mercati: *Il sensale* (perf. 1551; pub. 1561; 1 edition); no modern edition

B. Pino: *Lo Sbratta* (perf. 1551; pub. 1562; 6 editions); no modern edition

1552

A. Calmo: *La potione* (comp. and pub. 1552; 4 editions); 4 ACTS, PROSE; no modern edition

H. Salviano: *La ruffiana* (perf. 1552; pub. 1554; 6 editions); no modern edition

1553
B. Pino: *Gli ingiusti sdegni* (perf. and pub. 1553; 19[?] editions); no modern edition

1554
L. Comparini: *Il ladro* (pub. 1554; 2 editions); no modern edition
L. Comparini: *Il pellegrino* (pub. 1554; 1 edition); no modern edition
G. Ruscelli (ed.): *Delle commedie elette*, Vol. 1 (pub. 1554; 1 edition); ANTHOLOGY
C. Scalini: *Erithia* (pub. 1554; 1 edition); no modern edition
P. M. Scardova: *Il cornacchione* (pub. 1554; 2 editions); no modern edition
P. M. Scardova: *La nave* (pub. 1554; 2 editions); no modern edition

1555
L. Alamanni: *La Flora* (perf. 1555; pub. 1556; 3 editions); QUANTITATIVE VERSE; in Poggiani (ed.) 1808–12
G. M. Cecchi: *L'ammalata* (perf. 1555; 0 editions); VERSE; ed. G. Tortoli (Florence, 1855)
G. M. Cecchi: *Il servigiale* (perf. 1555; pub. 1561; 1 edition); VERSE; no modern edition
G. B. Gelli: *Lo errore* (perf. 1555; pub. 1556; 3 editions); no modern edition
G. Parabosco: *Il ladro* (comp. and pub. 1555; 1 edition); no modern edition

1556
Anon [G. B. Gelli?]: *Polifila* (pub. 1556; 1 edition); no modern edition
G. M. Cecchi: *I rivali* (perf. 1556; 0 editions); VERSE; ed. G. Tortoli (Florence, 1855)
G. Parabosco: *La fantesca* (pub. 1556; 3 editions); no modern edition
G. M. Pico Sforza: *Insoliti amori* (pub. 1556; 1 edition); no modern edition

1557
G. M. Cecchi: *Il medico/Il diamante* (perf. 1557; 0 editions); VERSE; ed. G. Tortoli (Forence, 1855)

1558
G. M. Cecchi: *Gli sciamiti/I forzieri* (perf. 1558; 0 editions); VERSE; ed. G. Milanesi (Florence, 1856)
F. Contrini: *Lite amorosa* (pub. 1558; 1 edition); no modern edition
L. Fenarolo: *Il Sergio* (perf. 1558; pub. 1562; 5 editions); in Messora, 1978
G. B. Pescatore: *Nina* (pub. 1558; 1 edition); no modern edition

1559
N. Carbone: *Gli amorosi inganni* (pub. 1559; 1 edition); no modern edition
A. F. Doni: *Lo stufaiolo* (perf. 1559; 0 editions); ed. C. Teoli (Daelli, Milan, 1861)

1560

A. Grazzini: *La spiritata* (perf. 1560; pub. 1561; 8 editions); in Grazzini/ Grazzini, 1953

G. Razzi: *La balia* (pub. 1560; 3 editions); no modern edition

Post-1560 comedies mentioned in the text

1562

L. Ariosto: *Comedie* (pub. 1562; 1 edition); VERSE ANTHOLOGY

1564–7

G. Bargagli [with collaborators]: *La pellegrina* (comp. 1564–7; perf. and pub. 1589; 4 editions); in Borsellino (ed.) 1967; ENGLISH: *The Female Pilgrim*, trans. B. Ferraro (Dovehouse Editions, Canada, 1988)

1566

A. F. Grazzini: *L'arzigogolo* (comp. 1566?; pub. 1750; 0 editions); in Grazzini/Grazzini, 1953

1572

Sforza Oddi: *L'Erofilomachia* (comp. 1572; pub. 1572; 10 editions); in Borlenghi (ed.), 1959

1576

Sforza Oddi: *I morti vivi* (pub. 1576; 12 editions); no modern edition

1582

G. Bruno: *Il candelaio* (pub. 1582; 1 edition); ed. G Barberi Squarotti (Einaudi, Turin, 1973), and in other Italian editions

A. F. Grazzini: *Comedie* (pub. 1582; 1 edition) [includes first appearance of *I parentadi*; *La pinzochera*; *La Sibilla* (1 further edition); *La strega* (1 further edition); all also issued separately in the same year]; all in Grazzini/Grazzini, 1953

1584

Ruzante: *Tutte le opere* (pub. 1584; 3 editions); ANTHOLOGY

1585

G. M. Cecchi: *Comedie* (pub. 1585; 1 edition); VERSE ANTHOLOGY

1589

Sforza Oddi: *Prigione d'amore* (perf. 1590; pub. 1589; 10 editions); no modern edition

General bibliography

Altieri Biagi, Maria Luisa. 1970 'Appunti sulla lingua della commedia del Cinquecento', in *Il teatro classico italiano nel '500* (Accademia Nazionale dei Lincei, Rome)

Alonge, Roberto. 1967 *Il teatro dei Rozzi di Siena* (Olschki, Florence)

Anderson, Michael. 1991 'The Changing Scene. Plays and Playhouses in the Italian Renaissance' in Mulryne and Shewring (eds.), 1991, pp. 3–20

Andrews, Richard. 1982 '*Gli Ingannati* as a Text for Performance', in *Italian Studies* 37: 26–48

   1986 'Observing Italian Theatre', in *University of Leeds Review*, 29: 7–25

   1988 'Rhetoric and Drama: Monologues and Set Speeches in Aretino's Comedies', in Hainsworth, Lucchesi, Roaf, Robey and Woodhouse (eds.), *The Languages of Literature in Renaissance Italy* (Clarendon Press, Oxford), pp. 152–68

   1989 '*Arte* dialogue structures in the comedies of Molière', in Cairns (ed.), 1989, pp. 141–76

   1991a 'Printed Texts and Performance Texts of Italian Renaissance Comedy', in Dashwood and Everson (ed.), 1991, pp. 75–94

   1991b 'Scripted Theatre and the *Commedia dell'Arte*', in Mulryne and Shewring (eds.), 1991, pp. 21–54

Appollonio, Mario. 1930 *Storia della commedia dell'arte* (Augustea, Rome)

Aquilecchia, Giovanni. 1977 'Per l'attribuzione della commedia *Gli Ingannati*' in *Giornale Storico della Letteratura Italiana*, vol. CLIV – 487: 368–79

Aretino/Innamorati. 1970 Pietro Aretino: *La cortigiana* [first version, 1525], ed. G. Innamorati (Einaudi, Turin)

Aretino/Petrocchi. 1971 Pietro Aretino, *Opere, Vol. II: Teatro*, ed. G. Petrocchi (Mondadori, Milan)

Ariosto *see also* Beame and Sbrocchi

Ariosto/Catalano. 1940 Ludovico Ariosto: *Commedie*, ed. M. Catalano (Bologna)

Ariosto/Segre. 1974 Ludovico Ariosto: *Tutte le Opere, Vol. IV: Commedie*, ed. Cesare Segre (with A. Casella, G. Ronchi, E. Varasi) (Mondadori, Milan)

Attolini, Giovanni. 1988   *Teatro e spettacolo nel Rinascimento* (Laterza, Bari)

Aurelia/Celse-Blanc. 1981   *'Aurelia', comédie anonyme du XVIe siècle*, ed. M. Celse-Blanc (Université de la Sorbonne Nouvelle, Paris)

Bakhtin, Mikhail. 1947   *Rabelais and his World* (presented as a thesis 1947, published in Russian 1965), trans. H. Iswolsky (Indiana University Press, Bloomington, 1984)

Barański, Zygmunt G. 1991   ' "Primo tra cotanto senno": Dante and the Latin Comic Tradition', in *Italian Studies*, 46: 1–36

Baratto, Mario. 1964   *Tre studi sul teatro: Ruzante, Aretino, Goldoni* (Neri Pozza, Venice)

   1975   *La commedia del Cinquecento: aspetti e problemi* (Neri Pozza, Vicenza)

Barbieri/Taviani. 1971   Nicolò Barbieri: *La Supplica* ... (1634), ed. F. Taviani (Il Polifilo, Milan)

Bargagli/Cerreta. 1971   Girolamo Bargagli: *La pellegrina*, ed. Florindo Cerreta (Olschki, Florence)

Bargagli/Ferraro. 1988   G. Bargagli: *The Female Pilgrim* (*La pellegrina*) translated and introduced by Bruno Ferraro (Carleton Renaissance Plays in Translation, Dovehouse Editions, Canada)

Barini, G. (ed.) 1858   *Biblioteca classica italiana, no. 7: Teatro classico* (Lloyd Austriaco, Trieste) [Anthology]

Battisti, Eugenio. 1962   *L'antirinascimento* (Feltrinelli, Milan)

Beame and Sbrocchi. 1975   L. Ariosto: *Comedies*, trans. Beame and Sbrocchi (Chicago University Press)

Bentley, Eric (ed.). 1958   *The Classic Theatre, Vol. 1: Six Italian Plays* (Doubleday, New York) [Anthology]

   1964   *The Genius of the Italian Theatre* (Mentor, New York) [Anthology]

Beolco, Angelo   *see* Ruzante

Bergson, Henri. 1900   *Le Rire*. Collected in Sypher (ed.), 1956

Bertinetto, Pier Marco. 1976   'Il ritmo della prosa e del verso nelle commedie dell'Ariosto', in Segre (ed.), 1976, pp. 347–77

Bertoni, Giulio. 1903   'Buffoni alla corte di Ferrara', in *Rivista d'Italia*, Anno 6 fasc. 3–4, March–April

Bibbiena/Padoan. 1985   Bibbiena: *La Calandra*, ed. G. Padoan (Antenore, Padua)

Borlenghi, Aldo (ed.) 1959   *Commedie del Cinquecento*, 2 vols. (Rizzoli, Milan) [Anthology]

Borsellino, Nino. 1974   *Rozzi e Intronati: esperienze e forme di teatro dal 'Decameron' al 'Candelaio'* (Bulzoni, Rome)

   1962, 1967   *Commedie del Cinquecento*, 2 vols. (Feltrinelli, Milan) [Anthology]

Bradbrook, Muriel C. 1955   *The Growth and Structure of Elizabethan Comedy* (Chatto & Windus, London 1955): references are to the paperback edition by Cambridge University Press, Cambridge, 1979

Bragaglia, A. G. (ed.) 1946–7   *Commedie giocose del Cinquecento* (Colombo, Rome) [Anthology]

Brand, Peter. 1988 'Disguise, Deception and Concealment of Identity in Ariosto's Theatre', in Millar (ed.), 1988, pp. 129–43

Brown, Peter M. 1973 *Prose or Verse in the Comedy: A Florentine Treatment of a Sixteenth-Century Controversy* (University of Hull inaugural lecture)

Bryce, Judith. 1988 '"Palla ch'io amo": The Theatrical Activities of Palla di Lorenzo Strozzi', in Millar (ed.), 1988, pp. 192–209

Cairns, Christopher. 1985 *Pietro Aretino and the Republic of Venice* (Olschki, Firenze)

(ed.). 1989 *The* Commedia dell'Arte *from the Renaissance to Dario Fo* (Edwin Mellen Press, Lampeter and Newiston, New York)

Calendoli, G. 1985 *Ruzante* (Corbo e Fiore, Venice)

and Vellucci, G. (eds.) 1987 *Convegno internazionale di studi sul Ruzante* (Corbo e Fiore, Venice)

Carnazzi, G. 1965 'Posizione storica del Ruzzante e i suoi rapporti con Alvise Cornaro e gli influssi della satira rusticale', in *Ateneo Veneto* 5: 45–67

Carroll, Linda L. 1981 *Language and dialect in Ruzante and Goldoni* (Longo, Ravenna)

1983 'Linguistic Variation and Social Protest in the Plays of Ruzante' in *Allegorica* 8: 201–17

1989 'Ruzante's Early Adaptations from More and Erasmus', in *Italica* 1, pp. 29–34

Catalano, Michele. 1930–1 *Vita di Ludovico Ariosto*, 2 vols. (Olschki, Geneva)

Cecchi/Ferraro. 1986 G. M. Cecchi: *I Contrasegni*, ed. Bruno Ferraro (Commissione per i Testi di Lingua, Bologna)

1989 G. M. Cecchi: *L'andazzo*, ed. Bruno Ferraro (Salerno Editrice, Roma)

Celse, Mireille. 1969 'Un Problème de structure théâtrale: "Beffa" et comédie dans le théâtre des Intronati de Sienne', in *Revue des Etudes Italiennes* 15: 243–57

1973 'Alessandro Piccolomini, homme du ralliement', in Rochon (ed.), 1973 (première série), pp. 7–76

Cerreta, Florindo. 1960 *Alessandro Piccolomini, letterato e filosofo senese del Cinquecento* (Accademia Senese degli Intronati, Siena)

Chambers, E. K. 1903 *The Medieval Stage*, 2 vols. (Clarendon, Oxford)

Cibotto, G. A. (ed.) 1960 *Teatro veneto* (Guanda, Parma) [Anthology]

Cioranescu, Alexandre. 1991 '*Il geloso*, comédie inédite de Francesco Serleone (1520)', in Plaisance (ed.), 1991, pp. 9–23

Clark, B. H. (ed.). 1956 *World Drama* (Dover, New York) [Anthology]

Clementi, F. 1938–9 *Il Carnevale romano nelle cronache contemporanee* (Città di Castello)

Cliness Boughner, Daniel. 1954 *The Braggart in Renaissance Comedy* (Da Capo Reprints, New York)

Clubb, Louise George. 1965 *Giambattista Della Porta, Dramatist* (Princeton University Press)

1989   *Italian Drama in Shakespeare's Time* (Yale University Press)
Cruciani, Fabrizio. 1968   *Il teatro del Campidoglio e le feste romane del 1513* (Il Polifilo, Milan)
Curtius, Ernst. 1948   *European Literature and the Latin Middle Ages*, trans. W. R. Trask (Routledge, London, 1953)
D'Amico, Silvio (ed.). 1955–6   *Teatro italiano*, 3 vols. (Nuova Accademia, Milan) [Anthology]
D'Ancona, Alessandro. 1891   *Origini del teatro italiano* (Loescher, Turin)
Dashwood, J. R. and Everson, J. E. (eds.). 1991   *Writers and Performers in Italian Drama from the Time of Dante to Pirandello. Essays in Honour of G. H. McWilliam* (Edwin Mellen Press, Lampeter and Newiston, New York)
Davico Bonino, Guido. (ed.). 1977, 1978   *Il teatro italiano, Vol. II: La commedia del Cinquecento, 3 tomi* (Einaudi, Torino 1977 (1 and 2), 1978 (3)) [Plays and documents]
de Panizza Lorch, Maristella (ed.) 1980   *Il teatro italiano del Rinascimento* (Edizioni di Comunità, Milan)
Donatus/Wessner. 1902–8   *Aeli Donati quod fertur commentum Terenti ...* Recensuit Paulus Wessner, 3 vols. (Leipzig, Teubner)
Dovizi, Bernardo   *see* Bibbiena
Duchartre, Pierre Louis. 1929   *The Italian Comedy*, trans. R. T. Weaver (Harrap; reprinted Dover, New York, 1966)
EDS. Enciclopedia dello Spettacolo (Le Maschere, Roma 1954–62; supplements 1966, 1968)
Faccioli, Emilio. 1975.   *Il teatro italiano, Vol. I: Le origini e il Quattrocento, 2 tomi* (Einaudi, Torino) [Plays and documents]
Falavolti, L. (ed.). 1982   *Commedie dei Comici dell'Arte* (UTET, Torino) [Anthology]
Ferraro, Bruno. 1981   'Catalogo delle opere di G.M. Cecchi', in *Studi e Problemi di Critica Testuale* 23: 39–75
1985   'Form, Reform and Counter-Reformation in G. M. Cecchi's *commedie osservate*' in *Bibliothèque d'Humanisme et Renaissance* 47 no. 2: 321–41
Ferrone, Siro. 1976   'Sulle commedie in prosa dell'Ariosto', in Segre (ed.), 1976, pp. 391–425
(ed.) 1985–6   *Commedie dell'Arte*, 2 vols. (Mursia, Milan) [Anthology]
Ferroni, Giulio. 1977   *Le voci dell'istrione. Pietro Aretino e la dissoluzione del teatro* (Liguori, Naples)
1980   *Il testo e la scena. Saggi sul teatro del Cinquecento* (Bulzoni, Roma)
Fiocco, G. 1965   *Alvise Cornaro, il suo tempo e le sue opere* (Neri Pozza, Vicenza)
Fiorani, L. *et al.* 1970.   *Riti, cerimonie, feste, e vita di popolo nella Roma dei Papi* (Cappelli, Bologna)
Fitzpatrick, Tim. 1985   *Commedia dell'arte and Performance: The Scenarios of Flaminio Scala*, Renaissance Drama Newsletter Supplement 5 (University of Warwick)

Fontes-Baratto, Anna. 1974 'Les Fêtes à Urbin en 1513 et la *Calandria* de Bernardo Dovizi da Bibbiena', in Rochon (ed.), 1974, pp. 45–79

Grabher, Carlo. 1946 *Sul teatro dell'Ariosto* (Edizioni italiane, Rome)
    1953 *Ruzzante* (Milan-Messina)

Grasso/Stefani. 1978 Nicola Grasso: *Eutichia*, ed. L. Stefani (D'Anna, Messina-Florence)

Grazzini/Grazzini. 1953 Anton Francesco Grazzini: *Teatro*, ed. G. Grazzini (Laterza, Bari)

Greene, Nicholas. 1980 *Shakespeare, Jonson, Molière: The Comic Contract* (London, Macmillan)

Guidotti, Angela. 1983 *Il modello e la trasgressione: commedie del primo '500* (Bulzoni, Rome)

Hastings, Robert. 1975 *Nature and Reason in the 'Decameron'* (Manchester University Press)
    1989 'To Teach or Not to Teach? The Moral Dimension of the *Decameron*', in *Italian Studies* 44: 19–40

Herrick, Marvin T. 1950 *Comic Theory in the Sixteenth Century* (University of Illinois Press, Urbana)
    1960 *Italian Comedy in the Renaissance* (University of Illinois Press, Urbana)

Howarth, W. D. 1978 *Comic Drama: The European Heritage* (Methuen, London)

Hutton, Edward. 1922 *Pietro Aretino, the Scourge of Princes* (Constable, London-Bombay-Sydney)

Ingannati/Cerreta. 1980 Anon: *Gli ingannati*, ed. Florindo Cerreta (Olschki, Florence)

Ingannati/Newbegin. 1984 *Il Sacrificio degli Intronati* and *Gli ingannati*, ed. Nerida Newbegin (Forni, Bologna – anastatic reprint of an edition of 1537)

Jacopone/Mancini. 1974 Jacopone da Todi: *Laude*, ed. F. Mancini (Bari, Laterza)

Jacquot, Jean (ed.). 1964 *Le Lieu théâtral à la Renaissance* (Centre National de la Recherche Scientifique, Paris)
    and Konigson, E. (eds.). 1975 *Les Fêtes de la Renaissance* (Centre National de la Recherche Scientifique, Paris)

Jeffery, Brian. 1969 *French Renaissance Comedy* (Clarendon, Oxford)

Kenyon, Nicholas and Keyte, Hugh. 1990 *Una Stravaganza dei Medici. The Florentine Intermedi of 1589* (Channel 4 Television) [Booklet to accompany broadcast performance]

Larivaille, Paul. 1980 *Pietro Aretino fra Rinascimento e Manierismo* (Bulzoni, Rome)

Lawrenson, T. E. and Purkis, H. 1964 'Les Editions illustrées de Térence dans l'histoire du Théâtre', in Jacquot (ed.), 1964, pp. 1–23, plus illustrations

Lea, Kathleen M. 1934 *Italian Popular Comedy*, 2 vols. (Clarendon, Oxford)

Lorch, Maristella de Panizza *see* de Panizza

Lovarini, Emilio (ed.). 1894 *Antichi testi di letteratura pavana* (Romagnoli, Bologna – anastatic reprint by Commissione per i Testi di Lingua, Bologna 1969)

  1965 *Studi sul Ruzante e la letteratura pavana*, ed. G. Folena (Padua)

Luzio and Renier. 1891 'Buffoni, nani e schiavi dei Gonzaga', in *Nuova Antologia di Scienze, Lettere ed Arti* third series 34 (pp. 619–50) and 35 (pp. 112–46)

Machiavelli/Hale. 1961 *Literary Works of Machivelli*, translated and edited J. R. Hale (Oxford University Press)

Machiavelli/Raimondi. 1984 N. Machiavelli: *Mandragola* and *Clizia*, ed. E. Raimondi (Mursia, Milan)

Mamone, Sara. 1981 *Il teatro nella Firenze medicea* (Mursia, Milan)

Mango, Achille. 1966 *La commedia in lingua nel Cinquecento* (Lerici, Milan)

Mariani, V. 1930 *Storia della scenografia italiana* (Rinascimento del Libro, Florence)

Mariti, Luciano. 1978 *Commedia Ridicolosa . . . Storia e Testi* (Bulzoni, Roma)

Martines, Lauro. 1983 *Power and Imagination: City States in Renaissance Italy* (Harmondsworth, Penguin Books)

Mazzi, C. 1882 *La Congrega dei Rozzi di Siena nel secolo xvi* (Le Monnier, Florence)

McKendrick, Melveena. 1989 *Theatre in Spain, 1490–1700* (Cambridge University Press)

Menegazzo, E. 1976 'Alvise Cornaro: un veneziano del Cinquecento nella terraferma padovana', in *Storia della cultura veneta* 3/ii, pp. 513–38 (Neri Pozza, Vicenza)

  and Sambin, P. 1964 and 1966 'Nuove esplorazioni archivistiche per Angelo Beolco e Alvise Cornaro', in *Italia Medioevale e Umanistica*, 7 (1964): 133–247 and 9 (1966): 229–385

Meredith, George. 1877 *The Idea of Comedy and the Uses of the Comic Spirit.* Collected in Sypher (ed.), 1956

Messora, Noemi. 1978 *Commedie bresciane del Cinquecento* (Monumenta Longobardica, Bergamo)

  1989 'Il teatro sotto la Repubblica di Venezia. L'enigma del teatro a Verona (1480–1548)' in *Quaderni Veneti* 2: 75–131

Millar, Eileen A. (ed.). 1988 *Renaissance and Other Studies: Essays Presented to Peter M. Brown* (University of Glasgow)

Minor, Andrew and Mitchell, Bonner. 1968 *A Renaissance Entertainment. Festivities for the Marriage of Cosimo I, Duke of Florence, in 1539* (Missouri University Press) [Translated documents and play text]

Mitchell, Bonner. 1971 'Circumstance and Setting in the Earliest Italian Productions of Comedy' in *Renaissance Drama* n.s. 4: 185–97

Molinari, Cesare. 1985 *La commedia dell'arte* (Mondadori, Milan)

Mortier, Alfred. 1925 *Ruzzante* (Peyronnet, Paris)

Mulryne, J. R. and Shewring, M. (eds.). 1991 *Theatre of the English and Italian Renaissance* (Macmillan, London)

Nagler, A. M. 1964 *Theatre Festivals of the Medici, 1539–1637* (Yale University Press)

Newbegin, Nerida. 1978 'Una commedia degli Intronati: *I prigioni*' in *Rivista Italiana di Drammaturgia* 7: 1–15

1980 'Politics and Comedy in the Early Years of the Accademia degli Intronati of Siena', in de Panizza Lorch (ed.), 1980, pp. 123–34

Nicoll, Allardyce. 1963 *The World of Harlequin* (Cambridge University Press)

Oreglia, Giacomo. 1968 *The Commedia Dell'arte*, trans. F. Lovett Edwards (Methuen, London)

Padoan, Giorgio. 1982. *La commedia rinascimentale veneta (1433–1565)* (Neri Pozza, Vicenza)

Pandolfi, Vito. 1957 *La commedia dell'arte, storia e testo*, 6 vols. (Sansoni, Florence) [Anthology]

and Artese, Erminia (eds.). 1965 *Teatro goliardico dell'Umanesimo* (Lerici, Milan) [Anthology]

Panizza Lorch, Maristella de *see* de Panizza

Penman, Bruce (ed.) 1978 *Five Italian Renaissance Comedies* (Penguin Books, Harmondsworth) [Anthology in translation]

Perocco, Daniela. 1973 'Il rito finale della *Mandragola*', in *Lettere Italiane* 25/4: pp. 531–6

Petracchi Costantini, L. 1928 *L'Accademia degli Intronati e una sua Commedia* ('La Diana', Siena)

Piccolomini/Newbegin. 1990 *Alessandro Piccolomini: L'amor costante*, ed. Nerida Newbegin (Forni, Bologna – anastatic reprint of Farri, Venice, 1540–1)

Pieri, Marzia. 1983 *La scene boschereccia nel Rinascimento italiano* (Liviano, Padua)

1989 *La nascita del teatro moderno in Italia tra XV e XVI secolo* (Bollati Boringhieri, Turin)

Pirrotta, Nino. 1969. *Li due Orfei* (ERI, Torino) translated by Karen Eales as *Music and Theatre from Poliziano to Monteverdi* (Cambridge University Press, 1982)

Plaisance, Michel (ed.) 1991 *Théâtre en Toscane: La comédie (XVIe, XVIIe et XVIIIe siècles)* (Presses Universitaires de Vincennes)

Poggiani, G. D. (ed.) 1808–12 *Teatro italiano antico* (Società Tipografica de' Classici Italiani, Milan) [Anthology]

Poliziano/Carrai. 1988 *Angelo Poliziano: Stanze; Fabula di Orfeo*, ed. S. Carrai (Milan, Mursia)

Povoledo, Elena. 1969 *Origini e aspetti della scenografia italiana*, pp. 337–460 of Pirrotta, *Li due Orfei* (and pp. 281–373 of the Eales translation)

Radcliff-Umstead, Douglas. 1969 *The Birth of Modern Comedy in Renaissance Italy* (University of Chicago)

1986   *Carnival Comedy and Sacred Play: The Renaissance Dramas of Giovan Maria Cecchi* (University of Missouri Press)

Raimondi, Ezio. 1972   *Politica e commedia* (Il Mulino, Bologna)

Rennert, H. A. 1909   *The Spanish Stage in the Time of Lope de Vega* (Hispanic Society of America, New York; also reprinted Dover, New York, 1963)

Richards, Kenneth and Richards, Laura. 1990   *The Commedia Dell'Arte*: A Documentary History (Blackwell, Oxford)

Rochon, André (ed.) 1973–4   *Les Ecrivains et le pouvoir en Italie à l'époque de la Renaissance* (Centre National de la Recherche Scientifique, Paris)

Ruggiero, Guido. 1985   *The Boundaries of Eros: Sex, Crime and Sexuality in Renaissance Venice* (Oxford University Press)

Ruzante/Mortier. 1926   Ruzante: *Œuvres en français*, trans. A. Mortier (Peyronnet, Paris)

Ruzante/Padoan. 1981   Ruzante: *I Dialoghi, etc.*, ed. Giorgio Padoan (Antenore, Padua)

Ruzante/Zorzi. 1967   Ruzante: *Teatro*, ed. Ludovico Zorzi (Einaudi, Turin)

Salingar, Leo. 1974   *Shakespeare and the Traditions of Comedy* (Cambridge University Press)

Sanesi, Ireneo. 1954   *Storia dei generi letterari italiani: La Commedia*, 2 vols. (Vallardi, Milan, 2nd edition; 1st edition 1911)

(ed.). 1912   *Commedie del Cinquecento*, 2 vols. (Laterza, Bari) [Anthology]

Scala/Marotti. 1976   Flaminio Scala: *Il teatro delle favole rappresentative* (1611), ed. Ferruccio Marotti (Il Polifilo, Milan) [Anthology of scenarios]

Scotti-Bertinelli, Ugo. 1906   *Studio sullo stile delle commedie in prosa di G.M. Cecchi* (Lapi, Città di Castello)

Segre, Cesare (ed.) 1976   *Ludovico Ariosto: lingua, stile e tradizione (Atti del Congresso organizzato dai Comuni di Reggio Emilia e Ferrara, 12–16 ottobre 1974)* (Felitrinelli, Milan)

Seragnoli, Daniele. 1980   *Il teatro a Siena nel Cinquecento* (Bulzoni, Rome)

Shergold, N. D. 1967   *A History of the Spanish Stage from Medieval Times until the End of the Seventeenth Century* (Oxford University Press)

Stäuble, Antonio. 1968   *La commedia umanistica del Quattrocento* (Istituto Nazionale di Studi sul Rinascimento, Florence)

Stefani, Luigina. 1979   'Sui volgarizzamenti plautini a Ferrara e a Mantova nel tardo Quattrocento' in *Paragone/Letteratura*, 30 no. 358: 61–75

(ed.). 1986   *Tre commedie fiorentine del primo Cinquecento* (Corbo, Ferrara) [Anthology]

Strozzi/Gareffi. 1980   Lorenzo Strozzi: *Commedie*, ed. A. Gareffi (Longo, Ravenna)

Sumberg, T. A. 1961   'La Mandragola: An Interpretation', in *Journal of Politics*, 23 no.2: 320–40

Sypher, Wylie (ed.). 1956 *Comedy* [essays by Henri Bergson and George Meredith] (Doubleday, New York 1956)

Taviani, Ferdinando. 1970 *La commedia dell'arte e la società barocca. La fascinazione del teatro* (Bulzoni, Rome)

and Schino, Mirella. 1982 *Il segreto della commedia dell'arte* (Usher, Florence)

Teatro classico. 1970 *Il teatro classico italiano nel '500*, Atti del Convegno 9–12 febbraio 1969 (Accademia Nazionale dei Lincei, Rome)

Tessari, Roberto. 1969 *La commedia dell'arte nel Seicento. Industria e arte giocosa nella società barocca* (Olschki, Florence)

1984 *Commedia dell'arte: la maschera e l'ombra* (Mursia, Milan)

Thomas, Keith. 1977 'The Place of Laughter in Tudor and Stuart England', in *Times Literary Supplement*, 21 January 1977: 77–81

Toschi, Paolo. 1976 *Le origini del teatro italiano* (Einaudi, Turin)

Veniexiana/Padoan. 1974 '*La Veniexiana*', *commedia di anonimo veneziano del Cinquecento*, ed. G. Padoan (Antenore, Padua)

Venturi, Lionello. 1909 'Le Compagnie della Calza (sec. xv–xvi)' in *Nuovo Archivio Veneto* n.s. anno viii, tomo xvi Parte ii: 161–221; and n.s. anno ix. tomo xvii Parte i: 140–233

Weinberg, Bernard. 1961 *A History of Literary Criticism in the Italian Renaissance* (University of Chicago Press)

(ed.). 1970–4 *Trattati di poetica e retorica del Cinquecento* (Laterza, Bari) [Anthology of treatises]

Welsford, Enid. 1935 *The Fool: His Social and Literary History* (Faber, London, 1935, repr. 1968)

Zorzi, Ludovico. 1977 *Il teatro e la città. Saggi sulla scena italiana* (Einaudi, Turin, 2nd edition)

Index

(Names and titles which appear exclusively in the bibliographies are not indexed here.)